HALIFAX II
XX motors)

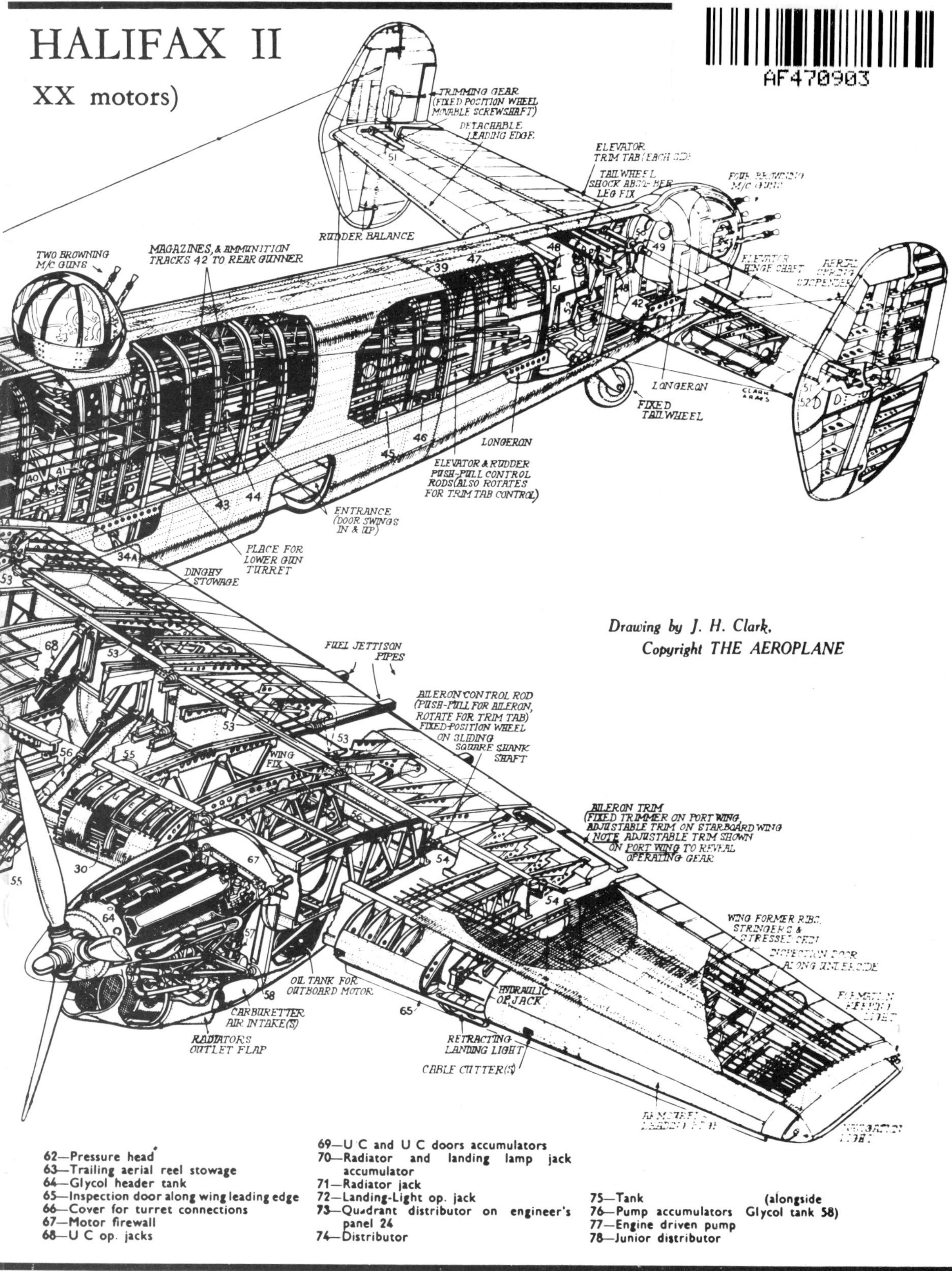

62—Pressure head
63—Trailing aerial reel stowage
64—Glycol header tank
65—Inspection door along wing leading edge
66—Cover for turret connections
67—Motor firewall
68—U C op. jacks
69—U C and U C doors accumulators
70—Radiator and landing lamp jack accumulator
71—Radiator jack
72—Landing-Light op. jack
73—Quadrant distributor on engineer's panel 24
74—Distributor
75—Tank (alongside Glycol tank 58)
76—Pump accumulators
77—Engine driven pump
78—Junior distributor

HALIFAX

An Illustrated History of a Classic World War II Bomber

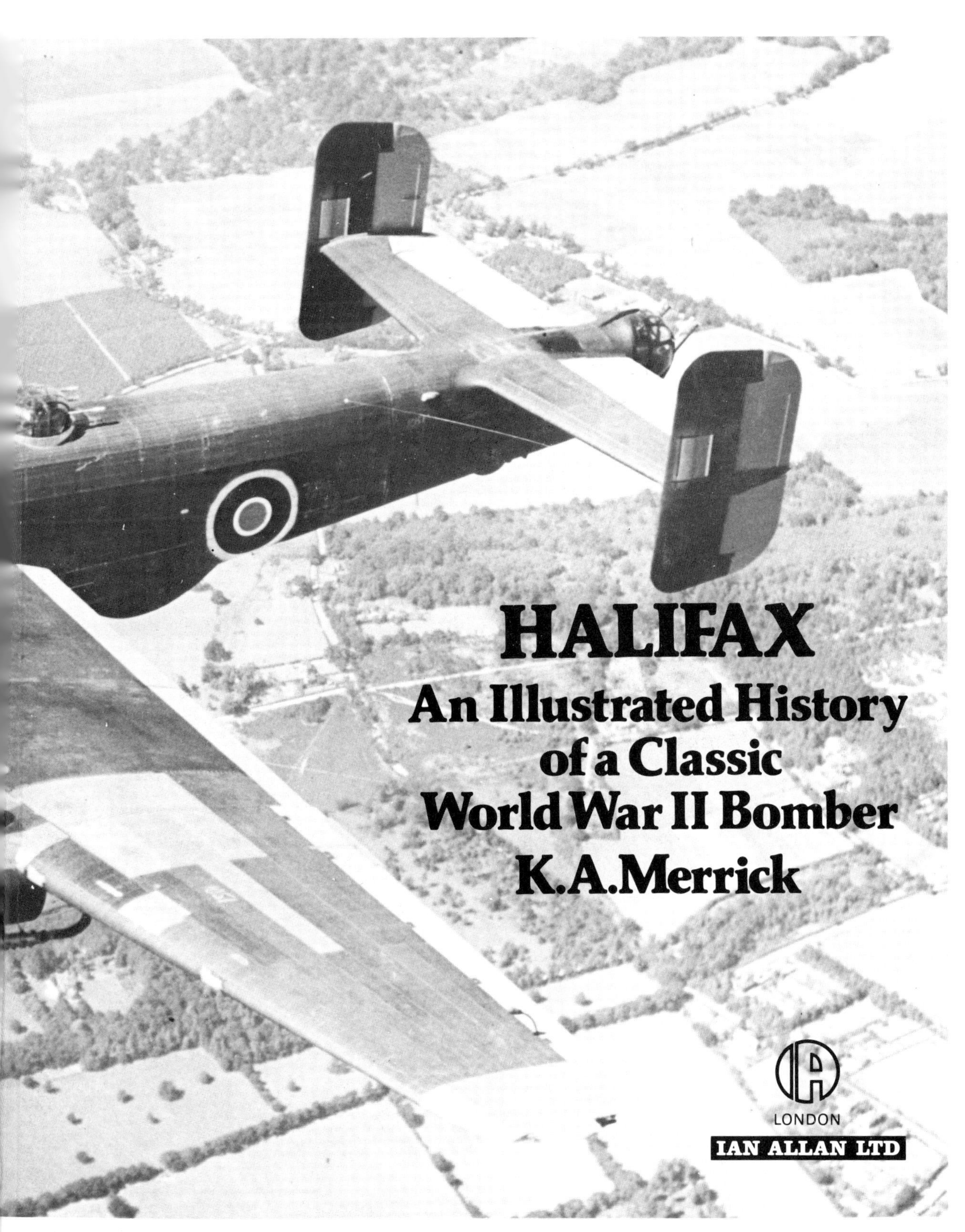

HALIFAX
An Illustrated History of a Classic World War II Bomber
K.A.Merrick

LONDON

IAN ALLAN LTD

First published 1980

ISBN 0 7110 0767 5

Published by Ian Allan Ltd, Shepperton, Surrey;
and printed by Ian Allan Printing Ltd at their works
at Coombelands in Runnymede, England

Contents

Glossary

ABC Airborne Cigar transmitter was used to jam German VHF night fighter control frequencies. It entered service October 1943.

ASV Air to surface vessel search radar.

Boozer Passive radar-type receiver covering the frequencies of Lichtenstein night fighter radar and Würzburg gun laying radar. It activated a visual signal in the cockpit. It entered service in June 1943.

Gee Radio navigational aid using a grid system and three ground stations.

H2S Centimetric radar blind bombing and navigational aid. It entered service January 1943.

Mandrel Electronic jammer to block signals from Freya early warning radar. It entered service December 1942.

Metox German passive radar tuned to ASV frequencies.

Monica Rearward searching radar to give warning of aircraft approaching. It activated an audible device connected to the intercom. It entered service in June 1943 but was withdrawn summer 1944.

Oboe High precision radar blind bombing aid controlled by two ground stations. It entered service December 1942.

Window Strips of metal foil dropped to jam Würzburg radar by causing a cloud effect to mask the real target echo. It entered service 24 July 1943.

Introduction

Halifax, a name overshadowed by its contemporary the Lancaster. The reasons are well known to most who have a general knowledge of the war-torn years of the 1940s; they are less well understood by those who have probed a little more discriminatingly. Hopefully, what follows in the pages of this book will redress the balance of the historical record in more objective terms.

Like the Lancaster, the Halifax was born a mutation of its original concept. Unlike the Lancaster it suffered an initial defect that was accepted as a justifiable risk in those desperate days when the whole future of Bomber Command hung in the political balance. The almost daily need to add extra equipment, bomb loads and tasks upon the whole of Bomber Command's meagre force of 'heavies' combined with that initial fault to cause losses that might otherwise not have occurred; at least not in the same proportion.

The result was an initially bad reputation that lingered long after it had ceased to be in any way true. In more peaceful times the fault would have been rectified before the Halifax entered service and the historical record may well have been less prejudiced. Whatever its reputation the record stands; a most distinguished one for all who built the Halifax, maintained it and flew in it. To all concerned this work is respectfully dedicated.

When the research for this work began there was no yardstick for guidance: very little information was available so what was discovered came about through a rather laborious process. It might have proved daunting had I not received the whole hearted co-operation of so many people who gave more than generously of their time, knowledge and patience. The numbers are prodigious and it is near impractical to acknowledge each and every one individually. The list that follows, therefore, names those who made extensive contributions but all are thanked equally.

Mr L. A. Jackets, at the time head of Air Historical Branch, granted me access and the facilities for the examination of the Squadron and Group records and other official documents upon which this work is mainly based. Mr E. H. Turner of his staff never tired in pursuing my every enquiry, no matter how obscure. Mr H. F. Vessey, Air Technical Information and Library Services, made the crucial Boscombe Down and Farnborough technical reports available to me. Miss A. N. Marks and Mr F. S. White of the Ministry of Defence Library were also instrumental in securing primary documents. Mr E. C. H. Hine of the Imperial War Museum guided me in my search for photographs. Where the official records were missing I had to seek those who were present at the time of the events and I am endebted to Sqn Ldr J. A. Stewart-Crump whose diary, log book and memory enabled the gaps in the 38 Wing/Group record to be filled. Wg Cdr W. Russel was equally valuable in setting straight the record of the Middle East operations. Bruce Robertson, with patience and gentle guidance, has maintained an interest in the work that is appreciated beyond measure of thanks. The bulk of appendix three exists because of his generosity.

So often the provision of information and photographs became a simultaneous process and I wish to record my thanks to the following individuals, companies and associations. D. Weir, M. Savage and A. G. Knivett of Handley Page Ltd; E. W. Barlow, W. A. Moody and M. B. Schroeder of English Electric Co Ltd; D. O. Thurgood and B. H. McCoy of Fairey Aviation Co Ltd; E. M. Lea-Major of Rootes Motors Ltd; J. R. Hitchcock of Boulton Paul Aircraft Ltd; C. C. Morris of Dowty (Boulton Paul Aircraft Ltd); M. H. Evans and R. H. Butcher of Rolls-Royce Ltd; A. H. Attwood and R. D. Caesar of Bristol Siddeley Engines Ltd; R. J. Glover of de Havilland Aircraft Co Ltd; F. D. Storrs and R. Shaw of Short Brothers and Harland Ltd; Sqn Ldr A. P. Heathcote and Flt Lt F. J. Hatch of the Department of National Defence, RCAF; Australian War Memorial; Department of Air: RAAF; Mr F. Purser of the West Australian Air Force Association; Grp Cpt E. W. Deacon, Wg Cdr A. Warton, Wg Cdr A. Hollings, Sqn Ldr G. V. Smith, Sqn Ldr W. E. Eagleton, Flt Lt T. Ling, WO H. Burns; N. Gray, G. Carver, J. H. Stanley, M. Carlyle, V. P. Annells, K. G. Beetson, G. Warnes, W. Diamond, S. Good, E. C. Darby, P. J. R. Moyes, R. Riding, A. J. Jackson, C. Bowyer, F. Smith, M. C. Bradley, S. Martin, R. Hayward, T. Sennan, W. Witts, D. Carpenter, D. Vincent, P. Cornish and S. Usher.

Finally, to my family my sincere thanks for their patience during my long absence, and my neglect during the compilation of this work, in order that history might be preserved.

K. A. Merrick

Highbury,
South Australia

Below: The 9ft deep forward fuselage of the Halifax. The wireless operator is in his compartment immediately below the pilot and the flight engineer is standing on the steps leading down into the nose section. Just above the engineer's left shoulder can be seen the armoured glass screen, locked in the up position, in the astro dome. /*AVM*

1 Design and Testing

At the close of World War I the Royal Air Force held a distinguished position as the most powerful force of its kind in the world. A unique feature of this air force was the fact that it alone had designed and organised a strategic bombing force independent of the control of the other two Services. However, within a few short years it had dwindled to a mere shadow of its former strength. The reasons were not hard to find and many were inevitable. The extreme youth of the RAF as a separate and independent entity did nothing to assist its struggle for survival and expansion alongside the older established Services. Not until 1923 was the issue of its independence finally and favourably settled as a result of the findings of the Salisbury Committee. The struggle for expansion had still to be fought.

The ensuing years bore witness to a constant series of debates and committees to decide the exact composition of the RAF with regard to the ratio of day and night bombers and fighters. A distinct lack of any urgency did little to assist matters. The continuing efforts of the League of Nations disarmament commission, which had begun in 1925 and dragged on unsuccessfully until 1933, had its own deleterious effect on the expansion for while no positive agreement was reached, one of the sub-proposals made and accepted in 1931 stipulated that there should be no increase in armaments during the term of the conference.

When, in 1934, the British Government found itself faced with the problem of reconstructing an air force which could compete with that of other European countries, the immediate prospects were found to be far from ideal. Not only was the quality and quantity of existing aircraft below international standards but several vital technical aspects were also found to have been sadly neglected. Long distance navigation, particularly at night, was virtually unpractised and any form of aids other than those which had been used in World War I were unknown. Lack of funds for research was a major factor in this case and the bombing results of the first three years of World War II were to bear sad testimony to this neglect.

The immediate result of this alarming state of affairs was a five year period of rapid expansion during which large numbers of, what were to prove, in some cases, tactically unsuitable aircraft were produced. This came about not by design but rather by necessity, since more advanced types were not ready for production. Indeed some were still little more than rough ideas on the drawing board.

The evolution of the faster, more heavily armed fighter types reflected a direct need for improving the performance of bomber types in the face of such opposition. Of equal necessity was the requirement for increased range, a factor which had been brought home during the Abyssinian crisis. The British forces in Egypt had been forced to place their aircraft dangerously close to the frontier in order to make it possible to attack the Italian bases in Libya if so required. All these factors combined to prove the inadequacy of the light and even medium bomber as a long range offensive weapon.

Specification B3/34, which produced the Armstrong Whitworth Whitley, was less than 12 months old when specification B1/35 was issued by a now far sighted Air Ministry who were now looking for an eventual Whitley replacement. Handley Page, along with several other companies, submitted a twin-engined design bearing the company designation HP55. This was to be powered by two Bristol Hercules HE1SM air cooled radial engines but as a safeguard alternative layouts were studied using either Rolls-Royce Merlin or Vulture engines, a decision which was to prove useful. The successful tenderer was Vickers whose design eventually evolved as the Warwick.

Such was the radical trend of the times that the following year, 1936, the Air Ministry was thinking in terms of a heavy four-engined bomber. This emerged from specification B12/36 as the Short Stirling and was intended to have an approximate all up weight of 55,000lb. A second, medium heavy, twin-engined class with an all up weight of approximately 45,000lb was called for in specification P13/36. This was to be an all metal, mid-wing cantilever monoplane powered by two Rolls-Royce Vulture engines.

Development contracts were issued to several firms including Handley Page whose design team, headed by Mr G. R. Volkert, undertook a redesign of their HP55 project. The new design, the HP56, was successful and the company was awarded a further development contract in April 1937, the serial numbers L7244 and L7245 being allocated for the two prototypes ordered. Design work began immediately and progressed rapidly including the construction of a mock-up. However, before the design was completed Rolls-Royce experienced some serious teething troubles with their Vulture engine. Under the circumstances the Air Ministry had no alternative but to revise the Handley Page specification and instructed the company, very much against their wishes, to rework the HP56 design to take four Rolls-Royce Merlin engines. The use of four

Above and below: The second prototype, L7245. An astro dome has been fitted to the flight engineers compartment and teardrop blisters to the navigator's side windows. Twin radio masts became standard for production aircraft. A1 type roundels have replaced the A type; the standard fin flash dates the photograph as not earlier than December 1940, a point verified by some of the modifications mentioned. The characteristic cutaway of the fuselage, forward of the cockpit, can be seen. The A type underwing roundels were still retained and the serial number was repeated, in black, beneath each wing.
/ Rolls-Royce; Handley Page Ltd

engines was dictated by the fact that no other engine of comparable power to the Vulture was available.

The redesign, although extensive, produced only minor variations to the main contours of the wing and fuselage despite the increase in size of these units, the estimated all up weight rising from 26,300lb to 40,000lb. With these alterations came a change in the company type number to HP57. In order to cover construction of the two prototypes the original contract was cancelled and a revised one, 32/37, was issued in its place.

Construction of the first prototype, L7244, was begun at Handley Page's Cricklewood plant in January 1938 and completed in the autumn of the following year. The original design had called for an integral fuel cell system in the wings but this idea was abandoned during construction and four separate fuel tanks were fitted in each wing. The aircraft was transported in sections to RAF Bicester where it was assembled and, on 25 October 1939, underwent its first test flight with Maj J. L. Cordes at the controls. No armament was fitted and the front and rear turret positions were faired over with metal panels. The flight was satisfactory but a defect developed in the hydraulic system. This defect was to prove troublesome and continued to plague the aircraft during its early service career. After further testing the aircraft was flown to the Experimental Establishment at Boscombe Down, arriving on 25 November for completion of the test programme.

The second prototype, L7245, flew for the first time on 17 August 1940 , and was transferred to Boscombe Down on 11 September where it joined L7244 on an extensive series of tests. This aircraft was more representative of the production series being fitted with mock-ups of the nose and tail power-operated gun turrets and two floor guns situated in the fuselage well position aft of the bomb bay. It was intended to supplement this armament, at a future date, with either beam guns or a power-operated dorsal turret. The fuselage and wing bomb cells had a total capacity of 11,000lb and held alternative loads of either 15 250lb or 500lb bombs or four 2,000lb bombs in the fuselage and six 500lb bombs in the wing cells. Provision was also made for the carriage of two 1,500lb mines plus either 12 500lb or 12 250lb bombs.

The main series of performance tests were concentrated on an all up weight of 50,000lb. The aircraft had been designed to include leading edge slats but tests showed that the flight characteristics were quite satisfactory with these locked shut. At an all up weight of 50,000lb and using 40° of flap L7244 recorded a mean take-off run of 505yd, 880yd to clear a 50ft screen and an unstick speed of 84mph. Comparative figures for L7245 with the slats locked and sealed were 570yd, 1,000yd and 80mph. The minor discrepancies between the figures being due almost entirely to errors in measurement and take-off technique. The aircraft was found to have a medium tendency to swing to port as the throttles were advanced but this could be easily countered by applying full rudder plus, if necessary, a slight touch of brake. The control column load was high during the initial stages and it was almost impossible to get it fully forward. However, once the airflow built up over the elevators the tail could be raised easily and take-off was then straightforward, the aircraft needing no assistance to become airborne. Raising the undercarriage and flaps required very little change of trim. However, at the overload weight of 55,000lb a marked difference occurred and the aircraft had to be pulled off the ground.

The first production Halifax, as the type was now designated, joined the test programme in October, L9485 having flown for the first time on the 11th of that month. Externally similar to L7245 in most respects it was distinguishable by its beam gun hatches. Not so obvious was the change from de Havilland three bladed metal propellers to Rotol constant speed units with compressed wood blades. The ailerons fitted to the first two prototypes had been considered effective but the response was sluggish over initial small angles of attack at all speeds. At speeds in excess of 250mph they became increasingly heavy and in order to overcome these deficiencies the ailerons on L9485 were given a slight reflex which proved satisfactory in most respects but they still remained a little sluggish. The wooden aileron trim tabs also proved a source of trouble, becoming rapidly waterlogged and warping badly. These were replaced by plywood-covered tabs but a recommendation was put forward at the same time to replace them with metal tabs. For some obscure reason this proposal took nearly a year to effect. The new metal tabs were eventually tested on L7245 on 16 August 1941 and proved entirely satisfactory.

By far the most significant fact to emerge from the trials was a report concerning rudder response. At speeds below 120mph the rudders gave little response but were effective at high speed. While it was thought at this point that they would probably have sufficient power to cope with asymmetric power loads the matter was to be made the subject of a special series of tests with one and two engines cut. At speeds below 150mph there was a tendency for the rudders to overbalance with application of rudder trim. This was particularly noticeable when one engine was throttled back and rudder applied to overcome the resultant yaw. In the meantime a modified trim tab was fitted in an attempt to overcome the problem.

For its unprecedented size the Halifax's stall characteristics were remarkably mild. The stall was straightforward with no tendency to drop a wing and control could be quickly regained. Dive tests were carried out up to a limiting speed of 320mph. The aircraft remained steady and required little stick force up to 280mph after which it became progressively tail heavy. It was during these tests that airframe vibration was first encountered. Subsequent investigation isolated the trouble as being caused by the nose turret when it was offset by more than 5° from dead ahead. Some rotation difficulties were also experienced with the turret due to the high slipstream forces but this was remedied by fitting balance flaps. These were operated by cams attached to the turret such that either flap opened as the turret rotated away from it.

No difficulties were experienced with the landing technique and the aircraft could be put down smoothly in a three point attitude. Full brakes could be applied at any time during the landing run without any tendency to swing. The tailwheel retraction jack rod was found to be slightly

bent on several occasions and had to be replaced. This was thought to be caused by play in the knuckle joint which, in turn, caused the tailwheel shimmy that was experienced from time to time. This shimmy and tailwheel failure was to recur throughout the Halifax's early service career and with the exception of L9485 production aircraft had their tailwheel fixed down.

The interior layout of the crew positions and equipment

Left: This view shows the Halifax's clean sturdy lines. The four small masts on the wings, between the engines, are fuel tank vent pipes. The underslung aileron mass balances can also be seen. The only break in the fuselage upper surface is a glazed escape hatch forward of the wing roots. / *B. Robertson*

Centre left: Photographed in May 1941, L7244 shows minor variations to its original form. Type A roundels are carried on the fuselage but fin flashes are still missing. The interim radio mast seen here proved unsatisfactory. Spinners and propellers are bare metal, the rear face of each blade being painted black. / *B. Robertson*

Below left: Here the length of the leading edge slats can be clearly seen. Engine serial numbers are 120758, '59, '66 and 120825. Following a minor crash in January 1942, L7244 was repaired at Airspeed's depot and passed to the AFEE on 15 March 1942 before finally going to No 4 School of Technical Training as instructional airframe 3299M. / *B. Robertson*

Below: Routine maintenance for L7245. It too was damaged in an accident, on 24 October 1941 and returned to Handley Page as Category B for repairs on 5 November. It then passed to No 28 Halifax Conversion Flight on 7 December, finally being struck off charge on 24 February 1942. Permission was given on 24 December 1942 for conversion to an instructional airframe, 3474M, and subsequently it was used as a synthetic trainer. / *Real Photographs*

was considered to be satisfactory although subject to some minor criticisms. Communication between the navigator's compartment and the astrodome position involved crawling underneath the second pilot's controls, a task which would have proved extremely difficult in full flying kit. The ammunition drums and plastic ducts for the rear turret had proved unsatisfactory under test and were to be replaced on the production series aircraft by ammunition boxes and chromium plated steel ducts instead. The size and position of the drums had necessitated an extensive platform for the port beam gun position in order to allow the gunner to carry out depression shooting. The beam gun windows were easily removed and the guns could be locked on their pillar mountings quickly. Although the draught was bad, firing trials on L9485 proved that the guns could be operated at all normal speeds ie up to 260mph. Above this speed a certain amount of effort was required to move the guns against the airflow but steady aiming could still be carried out. The ventral position, also armed with two Vickers K guns, proved satisfactory despite the strong draught. However, it was proposed to replace this manually operated position with a Boulton Paul K Mk I turret, armed with two .303in Browning machine guns with 1,000 rounds per gun, and sighted by means of a periscope. The main communication set, a T1083-R1082, was also recommended for change over to a T1154-R1155 set, this being incorporated from the 13th production aircraft onwards.

Since it had been proved that the performance was virtually unaltered with the leading edge slats locked shut a recommendation was passed for the deletion of these items; barrage balloon cutters and ramps being installed in their place. This came into effect from the 61st aircraft, the first 60 having the slats fitted but locked shut and sealed. With the completion of these modifications the Halifax was ready to enter service.

2 The Halifax Enters Service

On 5 November 1940, No 35 Squadron was resurrected as a unit in Bomber Command and attached to the A&AEE at Boscombe Down for formation as the first Halifax squadron and placed under the control of Wg Cdr R. W. P. Collings. The task was not an easy one from several aspects not the least of which was the fact that no one had any previous experience with four engined heavy bombers and the crews were left with no alternative other than to learn as they went. The task was, however, alleviated to some degree by the fact that all the initial crews were led by experienced operational pilots each of whom wore the ribbon of either the DFC or the DFM.

Progress was rather retarded at first by the lack of aircraft coupled with a series of moves. Flg Off M. T. G. Henry, DFC, and crew collected the squadron's first aircraft, L9486, and ferried it back to Boscombe Down on 13 November. An attempt was made to begin some form of organised instruction with this aircraft but this was hampered by the squadron's move to Leeming on 20 November, where it came under the jurisdiction of No 4 Group, Bomber Command. Here an effort was made to ease the training situation by allotting the first prototype, L7244, on temporary loan from the Ministry of Aircraft Production for dual instruction, Wg Cdr Collings ferrying it in on 23 November.

Within 12 days the squadron had moved once more, this time to Linton-on-Ouse on 5 December and the only progress that could be reported for the remainder of the month was the arrival of four pilots and one observer. However, the new year brought with it the promise of better things and the slow trickle of production aircraft commenced once more with the arrival from 24 MU of L9487 on 4 January. Limited though they were by the shortage of aircraft the squadron commenced a serious training programme at last with six crews under instruction. This consisted of fuel consumption flights, one hour flights at operational heights, handling at 50,000lb all up weight, use of the Standard Blind Approach equipment, W/T procedures and auto-pilot tests. On 12 January L9489 arrived to swell the squadron's meagre supply of aircraft to four but within 24 hours the number had been reduced to three, Flg Off Henry and his crew being killed when L9487 crashed in flames at Homefield Farm.

The training programme continued unhindered for the next few days but further trouble in the form of continuous bad weather reduced the squadron effort to a low ebb for the next five weeks. There were other more serious delays during this period, all the aircraft being grounded in mid-January due to persistent trouble with the hydraulic system, a similar situation reoccurring during early February. At the same time the supply of aircraft continued at a frustratingly slow pace only a further five, L9493:G, L9496:N, L9488:M, L9490:L and L9498:T being received. The bad weather continued to hamper the training during the remainder of February but a steady increase in the number of aircraft finally managed to offset this and by early March 15 crews were under training, six of whom were ready for operations.

On 10 March a signal was received ordering the squadron out on its first operation since reforming. Seven aircraft, including L9486, '88, '89, '90, '93 and '96, were detailed to attack the docks and shipping canal at Le Havre with the alternate target of shipping at Boulogne. During the briefing for the raid a signal was appreciatively received from the AOC-in-C Bomber Command. It read: 'Good wishes to No 35 Squadron and the heavyweights on the opening of their Halifax operations tonight. I hope the full weight of the squadron blows will soon be felt further afield.'

Weather conditions over England were perfect at the time of take-off, Wg Cdr Collings being the first to depart in L9486:B at 1900hrs and the other five aircraft followed at approximately five minute intervals with the last, L9488:M, leaving at 1920hrs. The seventh aircraft, which was to have been piloted by Plt Off J. W. Murray, DFM, was unable to proceed due to the Halifax's old enigma — hydraulic failure. The primary target was successfully attacked by four of the Halifaxes but one, L9493:G flown by Flg Off R. V. Warren, DFC, was damaged by shrapnel from a near miss which also wounded the navigator. The radiator of the port inner engine was punctured causing it to overheat badly and Warren was forced to cut the engine. To complicate matters an hydraulic failure allowed the port undercarriage to come down but despite these difficulties the aircraft was brought safely back to base. Of the other two aircraft, L9496:N was unable to locate the primary or secondary target due to cloud and bombed Dieppe while L9488:M, after continued attempts to locate the primary through thickening cloud, was forced to return to base through fuel shortage, the bombs being jettisoned safe in the Channel. The overall success of the operation was marred by a tragic accident when Sqn Ldr Gilchrist's Halifax, L9489:F, was mistaken for an enemy aircraft and shot down by a British night fighter over Surrey at 2240hrs.

Above: L9490, seen here, was ferried to No 35 Squadron with L9488 on 16 February 1941 by Plt Offs J. W. Murray, DFC, and G. A. L. Elliot, DFC, respectively. Both aircraft took part in the first Halifax operation, L9490:L departing at 1915hrs and L9488:M five minutes later. Camouflage style is characteristic of early B Mk I Series I aircraft which were also distinguishable by the depth of the window just aft of the nose turret and underslung aileron mass balances. / B. Robertson

Below: L9503:P, veteran of No 35 Squadron's early operations including the first daylight attack on Kiel by Halifaxes. It was also used by Leonard Cheshire for several operations. It is seen here at Northolt on 21 July 1941 with Plt Off E. R. P. S. Cooper and crew during a visit by Winston Churchill in company with Russian and Polish ministers. It was lost on a mission on 15/16 September. / IWM

Above: **A production B Mk I Series III aircraft undergoing a test flight. Camouflage style had altered slightly with a straight division line along the engine nacelles.** / *Real Photographs*

Below: **The 77 production Halifax, L9601. A Series III aircraft it has Merlin XX engines with englarged oil coolers requiring a revised nacelle shape with the** distinctive central bulge to the lower edge. The revised shape of the nose window, now covered by a perspex blister, cable cutters and ramps along the leading edge of the wings and repositioned aileron mass balances were features introduced on to Series II aircraft. Posted to No 76 Squadron it became F-Freddie and took part in most of the unit's early operations, including the daylight attack on the *Tirpitz*. / Flight International

Only Sqn Ldr Gilchrist and the flight engineer Sgt Aedy were able to bail out in time, the rest of the crew perishing with the aircraft. Such was the price of security.

The following night three aircraft were despatched to attack the Blohm und Voss works at Hamburg, two being successful while the third was forced to return with both gun turrets unserviceable. The same target received the attention of two more of the squadron's aircraft the next night but despite the lack of immediate results both crews reported a large fire burning in the centre of Hamburg, visible from 80 miles away during the return trip. This was to be the squadron's last operation for a month but they were far from inactive as is shown by the total of 204 hours spent on flying training during March alone.

Plt Off E. G. Franklin proceeded to Duxford on 23 March with L9486 for the AFDU Tactical Trials but was forced to return on the 31st due to hydraulic failure of the undercarriage, making in the words of the squadron diarist '. . . . a sad but beautiful landing on the belly of the aircraft, causing the minimum amount of damage.' These hydraulic failures were to be a source of much frustration for some time to come.

On 12 April orders were received to prepare for the formation of another Halifax squadron, No 76, to be commanded by Wg Cdr S. O. Bufton, DFC. The crews, posted in from No 10 Squadron, were to be trained within No 35 Squadron and upon achieving operational standard were to be formed initially into a third flight for operational experience. Three days later 40 airmen arrived on posting from No 10 Squadron for No 76 Squadron and were duly attached to existing crews in flights for experience.

The same night the squadron operated again, despatching five aircraft to Kiel. Whilst in the target area the starboard undercarriage leg of Sgt Lashbrooks' aircraft, L9493, came down and he was forced to fly back to base in this configuration, but was prevented from landing by the presence of an enemy aircraft in the area. Whilst circling the field both port engines failed in rapid succession and correction of the resultant downward swing ended in a forced landing near Tollerton village, the aircraft hitting a tree in the process. Fortunately, only the navigator and the tail gunner were slightly injured, the rest of the crew escaping unharmed.

The squadron now once more entered a period of operational inactivity, due mainly to the aircraft being grounded at the beginning of May through persistent undercarriage hydraulic failure. All second pilots were temporarily attached to No 58 Squadron, who shared the base with No 35 Squadron, for experience on Whitleys.

The Halifaxes may have been temporarily inactive but the enemy was not. At 0145hrs on the 12th the station was subjected to a bombing attack which lasted for approximately half an hour. The initial stick of incendiaries hit No 35 Squadron's hangars starting multiple fires and only the prompt action of the aircraft guards and other airmen brought the blaze rapidly under control. Damage was fortunately light, being limited to some holes in the hangar roofs, a lightly burnt mainplane on one Halifax and the front fuselage of another burnt out. The loss of life was however, not so light, No 35 Squadron losing three airmen with seven badly injured. The Station Commander, Grp

Capt F. F. Garraway, also lost his life conducting fire fighting operations.

During this period of operational inactivity the squadron carried out several 'social' engagements including demonstration flights for the American Mission at Hatfield, the War Weapons Week appeal, local fund raising appeals, an inspection by the Prime Minister at West Raynham and an inspection by their Majesties and the Princesses at Abingdon. The squadron was represented on the latter occasion by Plt Off J. W. Murray, DFM and crew with L9495:B.

Perhaps of slightly less 'social' nature but undoubtedly of prime importance in the light of the squadrons' first operational loss was a joint exercise held on the east coast where, along with other new types of aircraft, L9491 was demonstrated to the Observer Corps by Plt Off Owen.

Operations were renewed on 11 June with the largest effort to date, nine Halifaxes being despatched to Duisburg, which was attacked with moderate success despite 10/10ths cloud at the planned bombing height.

No 76 Squadron, having completed its training satisfactorily, had moved to Middleton St George from where it began operations with an attack on the Hulls Rubber Factory on 12 June. Both squadrons continued to operate with increasing numbers of aircraft, No 35 Squadron despatching 10 on the night of 15 June to attack Hanover. This operation was hampered by heavy cloud extending from the coast to the target area and while most of the force delivered their attack from between 8,000 to 14,000ft one Halifax went down to 2,000ft, to be sure.

There had been many discussions at Bomber Command HQ as to the practicability of daylight bomber operations. The Command had some very vivid and bitter memories of such operations during the opening phases of the war and there were strong arguments against such operations. However, the introduction of the new generation of heavy bombers with greatly increased defensive armament brought about a serious reconsideration of this type of operation. The answer to its feasibility lay in a practical test.

During the latter half of June Kiel was the recipient of a series of attacks by Halifaxes at night and on the 30th it received a further attack, this time, however, in daylight. Two flights of three, in 'V' formation, set out from No 35 Squadron's base in conditions of excellent weather and visibility which were to continue right throughout the operation. Both flights delivered successful attacks from 17,000 and 18,000ft respectively, all bombs being seen to burst in the target area hitting the docks and starting several fires. Both formations encountered heavy and accurate flak over the target and on completing the bombing run the second came under heavy attack from a flight of Bf110 fighters. One of these was seen to fall to the guns of the formation leader, Flt Lt Robinson's aircraft L9499:Q, before it succumbed itself and went down in a shallow dive. Flg Off Owen's Halifax, L9501:Y, was then subjected to five successive attacks by three Bf110s which inflicted extensive damage, the starboard outer engine being put out of action along with the wireless set while the wings and fuselage were badly holed. One of the beam gunners, Sgt Simpson, was seriously wounded during the attacks and although every possible aid was rendered by the crew he died during the return journey. One of their attackers was believed to have been shot down.

A signal was received that same day from the Chief of Air Staff congratulating the squadron on its outstanding success. It read, 'I was delighted to hear of your most successful daylight attack on Kiel today. This is a great new development which will have far reaching results. Heartiest congratulations and best wishes for successs in future operations of the same kind.' The final seal of success was received the next day with the notification of the immediate ward of the DSO to Sqn Ldr K. B. Tait who had lead the raid and the DFC to Flg Off Owen. Results appeared to vindicate the view that daylight bombing was a practical proposition from all aspects.

For the next three weeks both squadrons continued to operate at night with a series of attacks against Hanover, Frankfurt, Leuna, Magdeburg, Bremen and Mannheim. It is worthy of note at this juncture that losses by both squadrons had been very light since commencing operations. However, the effects of German flak were none the less pertinent when applied to the human anatomy. Handley Page's field representative, Mr A. G. Knivett, had the task of ensuring that any problem which rose over the Halifax was quickly and efficiently overcome. He was presented with one such problem by a certain pilot who complained that the Halifaxes lacked sufficient armour plate, a piece of shrapnel having penetrated the underside of his seat and caused him considerable discomfort. Knivett, ever willing to oblige, obtained some armour plate that had been left over when some Hampden fuel tanks had been modified. This duly arrived and was transported to a small workshop in Leeds where it was cut into small pieces.

News spread rapidly and soon many crew members had their own personal piece of security. Unfortunately, one evening the commanding officer happened to see one of the navigators literally staggering under the weight of his green canvas navigation bag and questioned him about the contents. The result was a discreet word to Knivett to let him know that the practice had been brought to a halt, because pretty soon '... the bloody aircraft would be so heavy that they would never get airborne!'

During these three weeks Bomber Command had been assessing the results and merits of daylight bombing operations and it was resolved that the deciding factor in such operations was primarily one of defence. British fighter aircraft had, until recently, lacked the range for other than shallow penetration escort operations which seriously limited the choice of targets for the bombers. However, the introduction of long range tanks during July, in sufficient quantities to equip five Spitfire squadrons, alleviated this situation to a limited extent.

It was planned to launch a surprise attack on 24 July against the *Scharnhorst* and *Gneisenau* in Brest harbour using a mixed force of approximately 150 medium and heavy bombers. Three of the Spitfire squadrons were to escort the second wave of the attacking force, the other two squadrons following later to deal with enemy fighters that managed to refuel and rejoin the battle. At the last minute the *Scharnhorst* moved to La Rochelle, some 200 miles south and the heavy bomber element was withdrawn from

the main force and detailed to attack this target—unescorted! For some unknown reason the already meagre size of this force was further diminished by the withdrawal of the Stirlings. For an even more obscure reason these six Stirlings were sent to attack the *Scharnhorst* on the evening of the 23rd losing one of their number in the ensuing action and putting the German defences on the alert.

The following day while the main force set out to attack Brest 15 Halifaxes, nine from No 35 Squadron and six from No 76 Squadron, formed up their vics of three into two large 'V' formations over Stanton Harcourt. The Halifaxes had been attached temporarily to this southern station to reduce the distance to the target and thus allow an increase in the bomb load. The formation went out via Lizard Point then across to a position 50 miles west of Ushant maintaining a height of 1,000ft or less to avoid detection by the German radar screen. From there they flew direct to the target intending to bomb from 19,000ft, although, as events turned out, the attack was actually delivered from 15,000ft.

Weather conditions were excellent with brilliant sunshine, no cloud and perfect visibility. Unfortunately, a little too perfect. An enemy destroyer was passed in the vicinity of the Isle d' Yeu and believing itself about to be attacked began evasive action and opened fire. However, as soon as it was realised that it was not being attacked it radioed the course and size of the formation to the shore facilities, thus destroying the element of surprise. The Halifaxes were greeted by a very heavy concentration of flak and a force of approximately 18 Bf109 fighters from the four aerodromes around La Rochelle. The attack was continued in echelon formation as planned but the intense flak barrage soon began to take its toll. Several aircraft were hit and one, Flt Sgt Godwin's L9527:M, went down in a slow spiral with smoke coming from one or two of its engines. Only two parachutes were seen to emerge.

Attempts at evasive action, necessary due to the heavy flak, caused further disruption of the formation. Some of the enemy fighters, paying little heed to their own flak, pressed home attacks during the bombing run. However, a concentrated attack was carried out as the Halifaxes were

Above right: **A Series II aircraft coming in to land after an attack on an Italian target. Either a No 35 or No 76 Squadron machine since both operated this mark of Halifax and both carried out raids against Italy in August/September 1941.** / *IWM*

Right: **L9608, the last production B Mk I and subject of the official naming ceremony by Lady Halifax at Radlett on 12 September 1941. A Series III aircraft it carried all the features previously mentioned. Like L9601 it shows a further revision to the camouflage style on the engine nacelles. Delivered to No 76 Squadron it became H-Harry and eventually passed to No 1652 HCU, recipient of many of the surviving B Mk Is. Retaining its code letter H it was part of the HCU's force used in the third 1,000-bomber raid. After completing 218 hours of flying it was written off due to a crash.** / *Flight International*

HALIFAX

Above: The size of Bomber Command's new heavy bombers can be gauged from this shot of L9530:MP-L, a B Mk I Series II of No 76 Squadron. The personal mount of Plt Off Christopher Cheshire, it had completed four missions when photographed. It was shot down by flak during an attack on Berlin on 12/13 August 1941. Except for the front and rear gunners all the crew escaped by parachute. / IWM

withdrawing, the fighters only breaking off the engagement long after the target area had been left. Those Halifaxes which had managed to stay in formation faired somewhat better than the stragglers who received most of the attention of the fighters, one aircraft sustaining 20 separate attacks.

When the reports from the survivors had been assembled the results of the operation were highly debatable. Five Halifaxes, two from No 35 Squadron and three from No 76 Squadron, had been lost. Five more were damaged to the extent that they required approximately three weeks to repair while two others were damaged to a lesser degree. The remainder suffered only superficial damage. Against this had to be weighed the damage inflicted to the *Scharnhorst*. All crews except one, whose bombs had hung up, had succeeded in delivering an attack but only one claimed a direct hit. In actual fact five direct hits had been scored and the *Scharnhorst* sailed for Brest, and the security of its smoke screens and fighters, that same evening with 3,000 tons of water in her. These facts would undoubtedly have provided a more cheerful note for the Halifax survivors had they only known. Despite the losses, morale remained high and the gunners had displayed the highest standards of coolness and skill throughout the long fighter attack claiming five destroyed, three probables and several damaged.

The two squadrons once more returned to their nocturnal operations while Bomber Command assessed the merits of the daylight operation. The results were not considered to be conclusive and it was felt in some quarters that improved defensive armament might yet make such operations practical. The chance to prove or disprove these theories was close at hand for in October the first of the improved B Mk II Halifaxes began to reach the squadrons.

3 Development of the B Mk II series and B Mk V

The Halifax had already undergone a series of minor improvements during its brief operational service. The first of these had involved some strengthening of the airframe to allow an increase of the all up weight by 5,000lb to 60,000lb. Designated B Mk I Series II, these aircraft were introduced into service soon after the initial production batch. Externally they had little to distinguish them from the earlier model; the most significant changes, although not directly related to the strengthening, were the repositioning of the aileron mass balance above the wing and a reduction in the size of the fuselage window immediately behind the front turret.

Some of the additional weight lifting capacity was sacrificed for increased range. The total fuel capacity was raised by 88gal, through replacing the Hampden fuel tanks, normally fitted in the fuselage rest bay, with an additional permanent tank in each mid-wing section. Total capacity was thus raised from 2,242 to 2,330gal. Engine overheating had also been experienced and to overcome this problem larger diameter oil coolers were introduced. These modifications to the fuel system and engines produced a further variant disignated to B Mk I Series III.

While these modifications were being introduced to improve the performance of the existing basic model, Handley Page's design team were already looking further ahead and the 31st production machine, L9515, had been set aside for development trials. Again the emphasis was on two major points, increased range and improved performance. The first of these was met by the installation of an additional 123gal tank in the outboard wing section, this No 6 tank, as it was designated, being connected to the No 5 tank to effect a 245gal unit. This increased the standard fuel capacity from 1,640 to 1,886gal and the maximum fuel capacity to 2,576gal. The optimum range was thus raised from 1,700 to 2,000 miles.

The second point was achieved by installing Rolls-Royce Merlin XX engines in place of the existing Merlin Xs. By a very ingenious piece of engineering Rolls-Royce had managed to produce an engine of almost identical external dimensions, delivering 1,280bhp at 3,000rpm for take-off as compared with the 1,075bhp of the Merlin X, for the relatively small increase of $8\frac{1}{2}$% in the dry weight. The new engine had a considerably improved performance over its predecessor both with regard to maximum power available and the altitude at which it maintained this figure. At 3,000rpm the Merlin X produced 1,010bhp at 17,750ft while the appropriate Merlin XX figures were 1,175bhp at 21,000ft. Perhaps the most significant feature of all was the fact that both engines were fully interchangeable which meant that the new engine could be introduced on to the production lines without any delay.

Fitted with these engines, L9519 began a series of six tests carried out between 18 and 31 August 1941. These were made at an all up weight of 60,000lb and, apart from the lack of beam guns and the additional tankage, the aircraft was representative of the standard B Mk I Series III model. The improvement in performance was sufficient to warrant a series of bomb door tests at 23,000ft on 4 September. Speed tests had already been made at heights up to 26,000ft and the aircraft had been operated continuously at 23,000ft for a period of 65 minutes.

Handley Page's original contract for 200 B Mk I Halifaxes was amended and from L9609 onwards they were produced as B Mk II Series I Halifaxes. Similar revisions were made with the other contractors and Handley Page were thus the only ones to build the B Mk I version, their last machine, L9608, being made the subject of the official naming ceremony carried out at Radlett by Lord and Lady Halifax on 12 September.

Externally there was little to distinguish L9515 from a standard B Mk I apart from the revised engine cowlings. The radiator bath had been reduced in frontal area as much as possible resulting in two semi-circular apertures with a dividing, central lower lip. Less conspicuous was the change to 12ft 6in diameter Rotal, three bladed RXF 5/1, propellers. The first few production B Mk II aircraft followed this pattern until the introduction of the Boulton Paul C Mk II mid-upper turret. This bulky item clearly established the identity of the B Mk II Halifax. The first production Halifax, L9485, had been retained for armament trials and fitted simultaneously with the C Mk II turret and a Boulton Paul K Mk I turret in the ventral position. The latter had been designed specifically for the Halifax. Mounted on two vertical guide rails it could be retracted until almost flush with the fuselage belly. Fully equipped it weighed 642lb and like all Boulton Paul turrets it was electro-hydraulically driven and operated, azimuth being continuous while the guns could be depressed from a minimum angle of 30° down to 90°. It was not adopted for service use, although a Mk II version was tested on an Albemarle, but L9485 was still flying with it as late as mid-1942.

The beam guns were deleted with the addition of the mid upper turret but many early production aircraft continued to exhibit the beam gun hatches until the existing fuselage jigs could be replaced or modified. Shortly after the introduction of the C Mk II turret the rearmost aerial mast was deleted and the aerials slung from the inboard face of the fins. Production aircraft were also fitted with two different size, three bladed wooden propellers, both Rotol fully feathering types. Either 12ft 9in diameter R7/35/54 or 13ft 0in diameter R7/35/55 type were fitted or, as was not uncommon, a combination of both simultaneously.

On 25 October No 35 Squadron received its first B Mk II Halifaxes, R9364:M from Handley Page and V9979:E from English Electric. October had been a fairly successful month for the squadron which had carried out nine raids without loss although two aircraft were damaged in crash landings at base. Bad weather reduced the number of operations to four during November, two Halifaxes being lost.

A third squadron joined the ranks in December, No 10 Squadron relinquishing its Mk V Whitleys in favour of B Mk II Halifaxes. Its first operation coincided with Bomber Command's decision to explore further the practicalities of daylight bombing.

Operation Veracity I was set for 18 December and was to use a mixed force of Halifaxes, Stirlings and Manchesters against the *Scharnhorst* and *Gneisenau* at Brest. Strong fighter cover was to be provided to cover the actual bombing attack and the withdrawal. Despite the intense cold and heavy frost, the weather was excellent and No 35 Squadron's six Halifaxes, having formed up into two sections, were joined by the other two Halifax squadrons. No 10 Squadron's five Halifaxes swung into position first, Wg Cdr Tuck's aircraft having aborted through hydraulic trouble, followed by the six Halifaxes from No 76 Squadron which took up station at the rear of the formation. The route to the target was Lundy Island-Lizard Point-Lanildut on the French coast-Brest. The attack was to be carried out from 16,000ft at 1238hrs but despite the detailed planning some difficulties were encountered.

It had been arranged that the actual marshalling of the entire force was to be done at a point five to ten miles north of Lundy Island, but when the Halifaxes arrived 10 minutes early there was no sign of either the Stirlings or the Manchesters. One of the No 76 Squadron aircraft was forced to jettison its bombs and withdraw through engine trouble at this point but the remaining Halifaxes commenced a wide left orbit. Halfway around the Stirling formation was seen approaching from the east and, despite the fact that there was still some five or six minutes to go before the scheduled departure time, proceeded in the direction of Lands End. Caught off guard, the Halifaxes turned in behind the fast disappearing Stirling which were now only just visible with two stragglers well to the rear. The timing error was apparently realised because the Stirlings suddenly swung west of track. The Manchesters were still not to be seen.

Having reached Lands End the Stirlings turned south for Brest and then made another surprise move by suddenly starting to climb. The Halifaxes were forced to swing to starboard to avoid overtaking the Stirling stragglers and closing in on the main formation. Finally established correctly the two formations proceeded to the target where the Stirlings went in first.

The Halifaxes were in perfect formation, each squadron in sections, 'V' formation, line astern and close in to each other. At a predetermined point the leading squadron went into formation line astern and made for a point just inside the coastline from where the final run-up to the target was made. The Stirlings were heavily engaged by flak and a few fighters and some broke to the right as the Halifaxes, in tight formation, came in on a course directly at right angles to the two battleships lying in dry dock. Despite the heavy and accurate flak the Halifaxes held their formation, bombed and withdrew to their original starting point. As they did so the Manchesters appeared approaching the coast in tight formation.

The leading Halifax, R9367:G, had been hit in the port wing by flak which riddled both port engines with splinters and set them on fire. Wg Cdr Collings was unable to feather the engines but did manage to extinguish the fires. Despite the drastic reduction in airspeed, which was in the region of 110mph, the two wing men managed to hold formation with him until he ditched the Halifax in the sea some 60 miles off the English coast. It continued to float for a period in excess of half an hour and Collings re-entered the aircraft twice during this period, the second time to look for his favourite pipe. The entire crew were rescued that same evening.

A Halifax, V9978:A, in the second section of the No 35 Squadron formation also sustained flak damage to two engines. The port inner failed immediately after leaving the target and was feathered only with difficulty. Shortly afterwards the starboard outer failed and caught fire but this was extinguished. In spite of the damage it reached Boscombe Down safely with the other two Halifaxes of the section holding perfect formation all the way, again at a drastically reduced air speed.

Apart from a small amount of shrapnel damage to some aircraft the only loss had been Collings' Halifax from their portion of the attacking force. Damage to the battleships could not be accurately assessed but bomb bursts had been seen on the stern of both warships, causing a whitish grey explosion.

Heartened by the success of the operation Bomber Command ordered a repeat performance on 30 December. However, due to unfavourable weather conditions in the 3 and 5 Group areas the three Halifax squadrons were left to carry out Operation Veracity II unassisted. Fighter escort was provided by a Polish Spitfire wing who were to cover the Halifaxes from five minutes before the attack right through to the withdrawal. The three bomber squadrons used the same formation as before, six Halifaxes of No 35 Squadron leading followed by four from No 10 Squadron, one had failed to take-off and another aborted during the outward journey due to a glycol leak, and six from No 76 Squadron in the rear. Just before beginning the bombing run the port outer engine of the lead Halifax cut causing it to swing and momentarily upset the tight formation, but they recovered in time to bomb as planned.

The German defences were well alerted this time and the flak gunners put up a concentrated and accurate barrage. Sqn Ldr Middleton's V9979:E went down after being hit in the port wing and L9615:X, hit during the actual bombing

Top and above: L9485, the first production B Mk I fitted out as the trials aircraft for tests with the Boulton Paul C Mk II and K turrets. The latter is just visible as a bulge below the fuselage. L9485 also served as a trials aircraft for a variety of tests, including exhaust flame damping, until damaged in July 1942. Returned to Handley Page on the 8th it was subsequently converted to an instructional airframe, 3362M, and issued to No 4 School of Technical Training on 15 September 1945.

Left: Interior details of the B Mk II. The navigator's table with prone bomb aiming position mattress in the centre. Above is the front turret with gunner's harness and seat hanging down flanked by the ammunition bins. Hot air hoses enter the canvas surround behind the turret. / Flight International

Below: Moving aft, the wireless operator's cabin immediately below the pilot's cockpit. / IWM

Right: The cockpit with standard blind flying instrument panel flanked by the engine instruments. Top to bottom on the centre pedestal are throttle levers, airscrew pitch levers and boost, mixture and blower levers. / Flight International

Below right: Immediately aft, the flight engineer's section with its aft facing instrument panels. / IWM

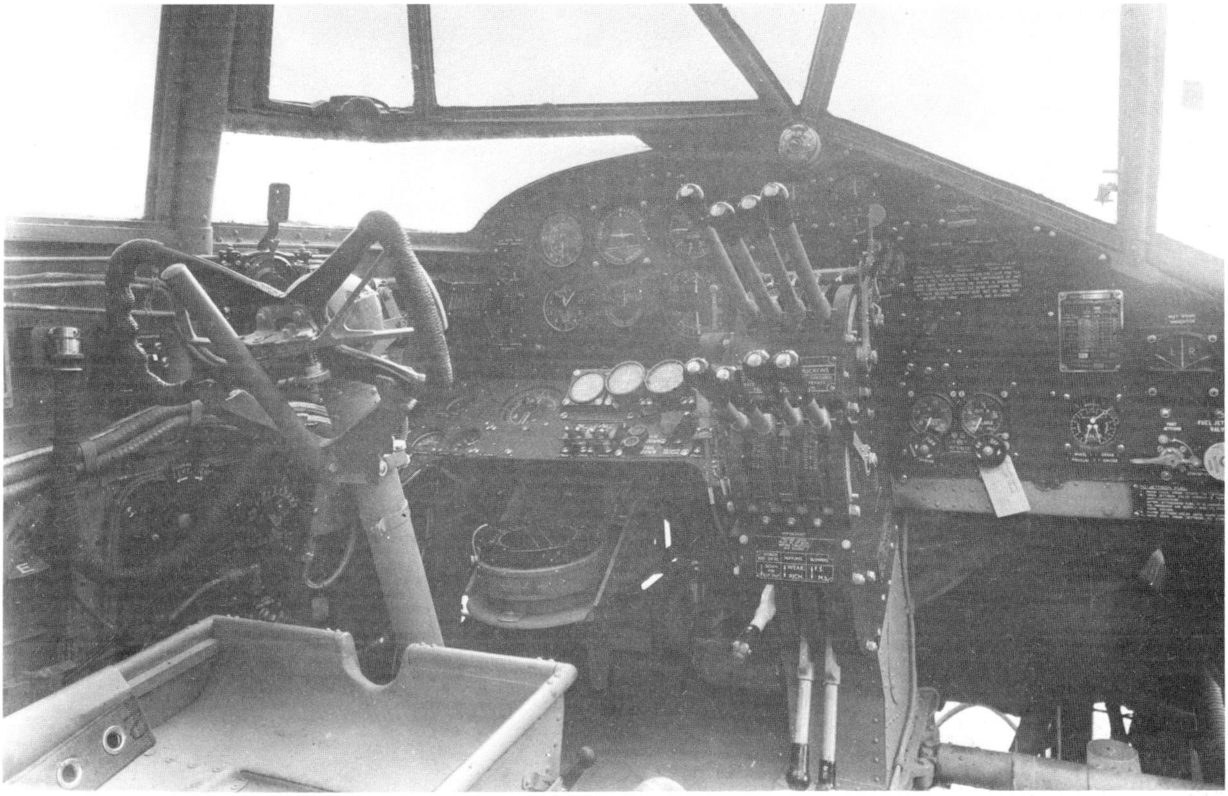

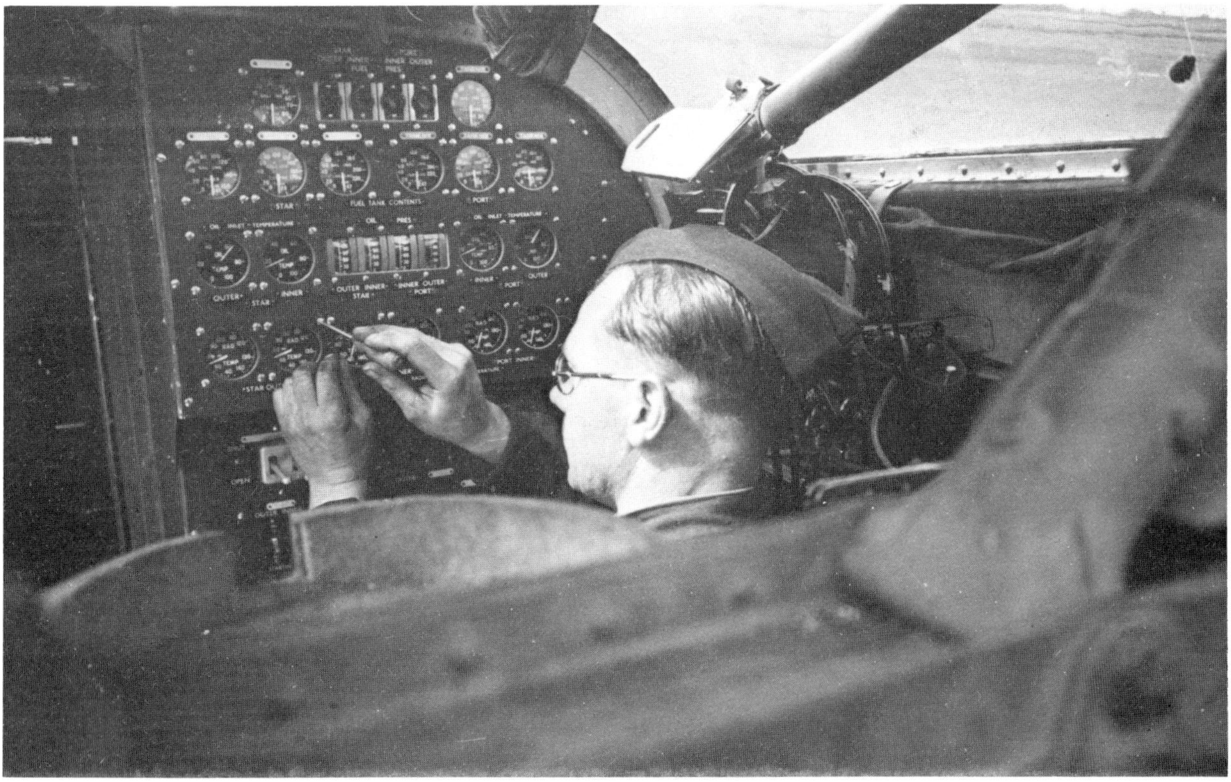
FUEL TANK CONTENTS
STAR
PORT

run, was seen to dive away from the starboard side of the formation. Gliding out to sea with smoke coming from the starboard outer engine it finally ditched some 20 miles from the coast. Two Spitfires protected it from further attack as it went down.

The withdrawal was interrupted by a strong force of enemy fighters which were immediately engaged by the Spitfire escort. One of the No 10 Squadron Halifaxes, R9374, was already badly damaged by flak which had smashed the port outer engine. Unable to keep in formation it was immediately attacked by a Bf109 which riddled it with cannon fire from dead astern and put both inboard engines out of action. Flt Sgt Whyte managed to ditch the crippled Halifax safely in the sea 80 miles south of Lizard Point, he and his crew being rescued by an Air Sea Rescue launch five hours later. Plt Off Hacking's R9370 was also attacked by a Bf109 but the pilot made the mistake of passing directly over the tail of the Halifax and was promptly shot down in flames by the rear gunner, Sgt Porritt. A second Bf109 was driven off by Porritt and the Spitfire escort shot down the next two who attempted to attack the Haifax. Porritt had been slightly wounded in the face and hands during these attacks but still managed to drive off yet another Bf109.

The results of the raid were not encouraging at first glance, three Halifaxes and two crews had been lost and most aircraft had suffered extensive flak damage. However, it had to be realised that the Halifaxes had been the sole attacking force and bore the brunt of some very extensive and well alerted defences.

While Bomber Command digested the results two detachments from Nos 10 and 76 Squadrons were sent north to Lossiemouth for a highly secret operation. Their target was the *Tirpitz* lying in Aas Fjord, Norway. It had been estimated that with the ship anchored only about 50ft from the shore it would be possible to roll some special mines down the sloping side of the Fjord and into the water beneath it. Fitted with hydrostatic fuses, the mines should then go off underneath the *Tirpitz* and rupture the relatively vulnerable lower hull. Starting at an altitude of 2,000ft the Halifaxes had to descend during a timed run so that they reached the dropping point at a height of 200ft. Each aircraft was loaded with four of the special 1,000lb mines which would not quite fit in the main bomb compartment, the Halifaxes being forced to fly with the bomb doors partly open.

The target lay at the extreme range of the Halifax and poor weather severely hampered the operation, 10/10ths cloud covering most of Norway. The four aircraft from No 10 Squadron all failed to locate the *Tirpitz* as did four of the five from No 76 Squadron. The fourth, L9581:Q, lost its port engine during the return flight and even after jettisoning the mines the pilot was forced to ditch three miles off Aberdeen through lack of fuel, the crew fortunately being rescued by boat. The remaining Halifax also failed to identify positively the target but assumed that it was the source of the flak and bombed accordingly.

Despite the poor weather conditions No 35 Squadron was active on five occasions during January. Snow and ice caused considerable trouble for the ground crews who had to keep the aircraft free from these dangerous accretions.

Such was the intensity of the cold that several aircraft had trouble with turrets freezing up in flight and one, L9584:L, became mysteriously uncontrollable three quarters of an hour after take-off but was nevertheless safely landed. It was eventually established that the pitot head had frozen up and the aircraft flown in a stalled condition. Fortunately the stall characteristics of the Halifax were very mild.

January closed with a significant piece of information for Allied Intelligence which stated that the *Sharnhorst*, *Gneisenau* and *Prinz Eugen* were likely to break out from Brest harbour and make a dash through the Channel within the very near future. The subsequent break out by the three capital ships on 11 February has been described many times before. Among the Bomber Command force employed were four Halifaxes from No 35 Squadron all of which failed to attack due to the foul weather conditions prevailing at the time. One sighted the force for a brief moment but lost it again almost immediately. The seven Halifaxes from No 10 Squadron had similar luck, six returning to base without even sighting the ships. The seventh, R9366 flown by Sqn Ldr Thompson, caught a momentary glimpse of a large ship through a break in the clouds and released all its bombs in one stick from 9,000ft but was unable to observe the results.

The 'Channel Dash' episode brought some severe criticisms to bear against Bomber Command and it was in the midst of this situation that the leadersip of the Command was taken over by Air Marshal A. T. Harris who promptly took up its defence in characteristic fashion. On 3 February, using an unprecedented concentration in time and space, a highly successful attack was carried out by 235 bombers against the Renault works at Billancourt, near Paris. The Halifaxes' contribution was restricted to a relatively small force from Nos 10 and 76 Squadrons, principally because all three Halifax squadrons had been screened from operations at the beginning of the month.

The reason for the screening was to allow the Halifax force to equip with TR1335, better known as Gee, a new radio navigational aid of considerable importance. With it aircraft could fix their position with a high degree of accuracy up to a range of 300 miles from base. There was, however, one drawback in that the equipment could not be fitted retrospectively and the Halifaxes had to be replaced by new aircraft specially modified during assembly. This problem was partly to blame for the delay of No 102 Squadron, which had begun to re-equip with Halifaxes during December, in becoming operational. A shortage of Gee-equipped Halifaxes in No 102 Squadron was finally overcome by exchanging W1047, W1048, W1049, W1050, W1051 and W1053 for six fully equipped Halifaxes, R9441, R9442, R9446, R9449, R9488 and R9494, from No 35 Squadron on 9 April. The other three Halifax squadrons had not been inactive during this period, all moving north to Scotland from where they carried out another attack on the *Tirpitz* in Aas Fjord on the night of 30 March.

The previous problems of weather and distance had not changed in any way since the earlier attempt. The Halifaxes crossed to Norway at 1,000ft to avoid detection by the German radar and visibility remained good until the target area was reached where 10/10ths cloud and fog again

Above: **Looking forward from the crew rest station amidships. One of the two heat exchanger units and its ducting is on the right with the escape hatch overhead. Switching for the long range fuel tanks is located beneath the seats.** / Flight International

Left: Looking aft from the same position. Ammunition feed tracks for the rear turret can be seen with the Elsan toilet, complete with black cloth curtain, immediately below. / Flight International

Below left: Through the rear bulkhead door, looking into the rear turret with the gunner's arm rests locked in the up position for egress. Four side mounted Browning machine guns and the gunner's control column and gunsight can be seen. / Flight International

Right: Starting up. Early production B Mk II Series I Halifaxes of No 35 Squadron move out for an operation. / IWM

Below: An early model B Mk II Series I with beam gun hatches and no mid-upper turret. The serial number, L9619, appears in red just forward of the top bar of the letter E. This unusual positioning was a No 10 Squadron idiosyncrasy seen on many of its Halifaxes during the war. L9619, which took part in the squadron's first operation on 18 December 1941, was abandoned over Cumberland on 15/16 February 1942. / IWM

foiled all attempts to locate the *Tirpitz*. The Halifaxes remained in the target area as long as their marginal fuel reserves would allow but they were eventually forced to abort the mission. Most of them jettisoned their four 1,000lb mines in the Fjord while a few donated theirs to the local flak and searchlight batteries which promptly ceased to operate. Losses were relatively high, six out of the 34 Halifaxes failing to return. Fuel problems were acute and most aircraft landed with virtually dry tanks while R9453:K of No 76 Squadron was known to have ditched in the sea but the crew were never found. There is little doubt that fuel starvation accounted for most, if not all, of the other missing Halifaxes that night, two from No 10 Squadron and three from No 76 Squadron.

Improved navigational aids were not the only new items introduced by Bomber Command during the early months of 1942, the 8,000lb high capacity (HC) bomb also made its initial appearance at this time. L9485 had been used for trials with this large type of bomb which was of such proportions that it could not be entirely contained within the fuselage bomb compartment. It projected below the fuselage for about one quarter of its depth and the bomb doors had to remain partly open.

Mr Knivett, the Handley Page representative, assisted with the first trial installation of the 4,000lb version of this weapon. While one of the installation party was working in the cramped confines of the bomb compartment wiring up the new bomb rack, Knivett was inside the fuselage with two of the bomb winches still in place. Four times one of the technicians asked if he could remove the winches and each time Knivett declined saying that there was still plenty of time. A short while later one of the ground crew, who had nothing to do with the bomb installation party, connected up the aircraft's main power supply. The whole Halifax suddenly shook as the huge bomb dropped from its rack and hung, on the quivering strands of the winch cables, about a foot below it. During the routine servicing checks someone had left the jettison bar of the bomb selector box pulled down! It is extremely doubtful if the bomb would have exploded had it broken free and struck the ground but the experience was sobering none the less.

The trials were carried out with both a single 8,000lb installation and a double 4,000lb combination. Despite the bulkiness of the loads the trials showed no measurable adverse effect upon the take-off performance and the general handling characteristics. To ease the drag problem as much as possible a doped canvas strip was used to cover the end of the bomb and the partly open bomb doors. At 0025hrs on 11 April the first 8,000lb bomb was dropped, on Essen, by R9487:A of No 76 Squadron. The captain, Plt Off Renaut, reported one very large explosion, with a momentary glow of dull red and orange colour, on the north-west side of the target area. This was but the first of many.

Knivett was also involved with Leonard Cheshire in an unofficial bombing experiment. Knivett fitted a gunsight to a Halifax so that Cheshire could attempt 'precision' dive bombing. The results were spectacular but far from promising because insufficient allowance was made for bomb clearance and relative dive angle. Cheshire returned with damage to the front bulkhead where the bombs had passed through.

No 102 Squadron operated its Halifaxes for the first time three nights later sending two aircraft to Le Havre. Its second operation, on 27 April, was a bitter experience, two of the three Halifaxes despatched, two to Cologne and one to Denmark, failing to return. The other three Halifax squadrons were also active that night but against a far more distant target — the *Tirpitz*.

Two of the squadrons, Nos 10 and 35, were briefed to attack with mines as on the previous raids but No 76 Squadron was armed with conventional bombs and ordered to bomb the defences. Thirty-two Halifaxes set out from their temporary Scottish bases with one aborting soon after take-off. Visibility was slightly better on this occasion but so also were the defences, active and passive. Several aircraft later reported dropping their mines from the prescribed 200ft near the target, but others had their attempts frustrated by the billowing smoke screens. The defences did not have it all their own way and No 76 Squadron made a considerable impression on them with its bombing attacks. The raid cost four Halifaxes, W1048:S and W1020:K from No 35 Squadron, W1041:B and W1037:U from No 10 Squadron. W1041 was being flown that night by No 10 Squadron's new commanding officer, Wg Cdr D. C. T. Bennett. Most of the crew evaded capture and escaped into Sweden and Bennett himself was back in command of the squadron one month later.

Determined to make maximum use of the force while it was still available, a repeat attack was dispatched the next night by a now reduced number of 24 Halifaxes. The operation cost No 35 Squadron two of its nine Halifaxes (W1053:G, W7656:P) but the other two squadrons operated without loss. Plt Off Whyte very nearly became a casualty when his Halifax, W1057:X, sustained heavy flak damage which caused the flaps to come down. The return journey was made at 110mph and Whyte was just able to reach Sumburgh on the southern tip of the Shetland Isles.

Despite the success of the Billincourt operation and a series of very well executed raids on Cologne, Rostock and Lübeck during April and May, Bomber Command was still subjected to criticism by those who wished to see it disbanded and its forces dispersed to support the needs of the Army and Navy. The use of Gee had greatly aided the accuracy of these raids and the tactic of concentrating the attack within a short period of time had proved most successful, the defences being swamped. Harris decided the time had now come to demonstrate Bomber Command's potential to the full with a display of force greater than any seen before. Three more squadrons had been stood down during April and May to convert to Halifaxes and two of these, Nos 78 and 405 (RCAF) Squadrons, became operational in time to participate in the first of Harris's mammoth raids.

After careful consideration Cologne was chosen as the target and 1,046 bombers dispatched to attack it on the night of 30/31 May. The first wave of the attacking force consisted of Gee-equipped Wellingtons and Stirlings of Nos 1 and 3 Groups who acted as 'pathfinders' by using a high percentage of incendiaries to mark the main aiming points. The second wave followed in the next hour while the third, composed entirely of Halifaxes and Lancasters, attacked during the last 15 minutes of the raid.

Above: W7676:P of No 35 Squadron which replaced W7656:P lost in an attack on the *Tirpitz* in April 1942. A B Mk II Series I with mid-upper turret and single radio mast it was a veteran of many operations, including the 1,000-bomber raid on Cologne. It was lost on 28/29 August during a raid against Nuremberg. */ Real Photographs*

Right: A double 4,000lb bomb installation in L9485 on 11 April 1942. Despite the protrusion no measurable adverse effects were experienced during flight trials. The Lorenz Beam Approach aerial and trailing aerial fairlead are just visible upper right.

One hundred and eighteen Halifaxes, drawn from Nos 10, 35, 76, 102 and 405 Squadrons and 1652 Heavy Conversion Unit, took part in the raid which was an outstanding success. It left a deep impression on most crews, a wing commander from No 35 Squadron stating in his report: '. . . . enormous fires burning in the target area, visibility good, no cloud. Bombs dropped in the target area. The whole centre of the town was in flames and dense smoke from the fires reached up to 9,000ft. The fires were visible from 100 miles after leaving the target area.' A No 76 Squadron pilot reported intense opposition at the coast and the defended belt but over the target itself both searchlight and flak appeared to have been put out of action by the previous attacks. Typical of the bomb loads carried by the heavy bombers were No 76 Squadron's, their 21 Halifaxes delivering 61×1,000lb HE bombs, 16,380×4lb incendiaries and 488×30lb incendiaries.

Losses for the operation, wave by wave, made an interesting comparison. The first wave suffered 4.8%, the second 4.1% and the last, which was the most concentrated, 1.9%. Halifax losses, from all causes, amounted to the remarkably small figure of four, which included one from No 76 Squadron that collided with a Hampden of 14 OTU also returning from the raid, killing several crew members in both aircraft.

Harris, never one to waste an opportunity, launched two further 1,000 plus raids during the next three weeks. The first of these took place on the night of 1/2 June, the target being Essen, the industrial heart of the Ruhr and home of the Krupps works. A permanent industrial haze, combined with a constantly recurring ground mist, made this target an extremely difficult one. Accordingly seven Halifaxes from No 76 Squadron were briefed to attack the precise aiming point, a large shed in the middle of the Krupp works. Twenty Wellington bombers were to pinpoint their position and then release flares so that the entire target area would be illuminated for the fire raisers of the marker force. The remaining 123 Halifaxes joined the main force attack. Halifax losses were again relatively light, only eight failing to return one of which, from No 10 Squadron, ditched in the sea.

The third attack, on Bremen, on 25/26 June followed much the same lines as the Essen attack No 76 Squadron providing eight Halifaxes for the marker force. However, heavy cloud hampered the main force attack and this operation was the least successful of the three. Of the 129 Halifaxes dispatched nine were lost, this figure again including one, this time from No 158 Squadron, which ditched in the sea.

These mass raids produced an interesting, if unsuccessful, experiment by Sqn Ldr Cheshire who decided to find a quicker method of getting his squadron airborne. A fighter type take-off was adopted with four Halifaxes in a diamond formation, the experiment taking place on a day when no operations had been ordered. Everything went well until the formation just became airborne and the leading pilot selected bomb doors open instead of undercarriage up. The Halifax promptly lost speed and Cheshire, flying the rearmost aircraft, found himself approaching its stern rapidly. He throttled back equally rapidly and in doing so his Halifax touched down momentarily on its partly retracted undercarriage. The lead Halifax pulled away almost immediately enabling Cheshire to open up the throttles again but not before he had bent the undercarriage retraction jacks jamming the wheels half up. The rest of the formation landed safely and Cheshire put his Halifax down on the grass as gently as possible. When the damage report went in to Group HQ they were not impressed!

With the completion of the three 1,000-bomber raids the squadrons turned to an intensive campaign against targets in Germany which received a large proportion of 4,000lb and 8,000lb bombs. Carrying bombs of this size produced some very dangerous situations as is typified by the experience of W7761:N of No 35 Squadron. Over the target the bomb aimer pressed the release for the two 4,000lb bombs but the forward lugs on the front one failed to release. Unable to jettison the now precarious load the pilot was forced to fly back to England with it, but the aircraft was very difficult to control and finally had to be abandoned near Harrogate. During its final plunge the Halifax turned over on its back and caught fire, the tenacious bomb being wrenched free in the process and falling within half a mile of the aircraft. The subsequent Court of Inquiry recommended a modification of the emergency release gear!

By contrast to the mass raids of May and June four Halifaxes, two from each of Nos 102 and 405 Squadrons, were dispatched to attack Hamburg on 3 August. This was to be flown in daylight using cloud cover to provide an element of surprise. In view of Hamburg's formidable defences it was perhaps fortunate that all cloud cover ceased at the Dutch coast. Wg Cdr Faquier, the pilot of one of the No 405 Squadron aircraft, spent 90 minutes cruising up and down the coast waiting for the cloud to increase but was eventually forced to return.

The success of the pathfinder techniques applied during the 1,000-bomber raids prompted the formation of a permanent force to carry out these exacting duties. No 35 Squadron was one of the four squadrons chosen to form the nucleus of what was to become the Path Finder Force. The squadron moved to Graveley where it came under the control of No 8 Group now commanded by Grp Capt Bennett. The raid of 13 October is typical of the early techniques employed and provides an interesting comparison with the improved methods used during the Peenemünde raid of late 1943 (see Chapter 6).

Twelve Halifaxes were detailed for the attack on Kiel. Five of them were to act as 'Finders' and lay sticks of marker flares across the target area or, if the aiming point was definitely identified, to act as 'Illuminators' and to drop their flares over the aiming point. Three aircraft, detailed as 'Illuminators', were to light the target area from zero hour plus one to 17 minutes. The remaining four aircraft carried five 1,000lb GP bombs and were to attack with the main force. The operation was most successful and all the Halifaxes returned safely.

The sixth Halifax squadron to be formed, No 103, was part of the attacking force that night. Its career on Halifaxes was as short as its operational activity was intense. Commencing its first Halifax operation on 1 September it attacked 14 major targets in Germany and

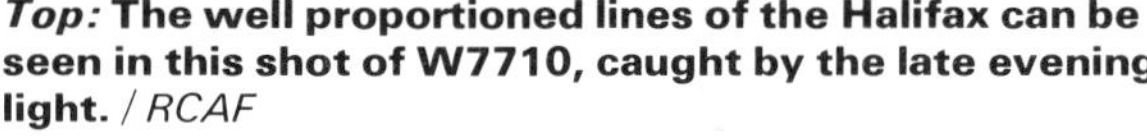

Top: The well proportioned lines of the Halifax can be seen in this shot of W7710, caught by the late evening light. / *RCAF*

Above: The prototype Dowty lever suspension undercarriage installation on L9520 which served as the test bed for the **B Mk V Series I** version of the Halifax.

Right: The standard Messier undercarriage installation.

Italy before its last operation with the type on 25 October. Under the new policy of concentrating aircraft types into groups for maintenance and logistic purposes this lone Halifax squadron of No 1 Group converted to Lancasters. Its tenacity is exemplified by Sqn Ldr Saxelby's experience in W1219 during a raid on Nuremburg on 29 August. During the first bombing run the bomb aimer clearly identified the aiming point, pressed the bomb release but saw no bomb bursts. It was then discoverd that the bomb doors had not opened and the crew spent 13 minutes outside the target area while the doors were pumped open by hand. A second bombing run was then made at 8,200ft and all the bombs released—or so it was thought. A visual check showed a single 1,000lb still in the racks and this was eventually released by the navigator putting his hand through the inspection hole. A further 20 minutes were then spent trying to close the bomb doors. Just as the pilot reported them shut the gauge blew off the top of the hydraulic accumulator partly blinding the wireless operator and covering the other two crew members with oil. Rapid action by the flight engineer prevented further loss of oil with consequent hydraulic failure.

In October a second RCAF squadron, No 408, converted to Halifaxes but Halifaxes with a difference. In late 1941 doubts had been expressed about the continued supply of the imposing British Messier undercarriage units being able to keep pace with the expanding Halifax production. Tests were then made to see if it would be possible to adapt a Dowty lever suspension undercarriage for use in its place; L9520, a B Mk I, was set aside for this purpose. Fitting the Dowty undercarriage required some redesign of the existing hydraulic system but otherwise the conversion was fairly straightforward. Tests were carried out in January 1942 and the new undercarriage proved superior, in certain respects, to the Messier type. Its main advantage was smoother operation over bumpy ground, improving handling during take-off. This change in design was accompanied by a change in designation to B Mk V Series I, the Company type number HP63 being allotted. In all other respects the type was identical with the B Mk II series. Despite its slim proportions the Dowty undercarriage and its associated hydraulic system was heavier than the British Messier installation.

Tailwheel shimmy, a long standing problem with the Halifax, made an appearance during the crosswind landing tests and a converted Dowty tailwheel unit was fitted to L9520. It was tested a few days later but did not entirely eliminate the problem. From the results of these tests it was recommended that further anti-shimmy damping be provided. This recommendation was dealt with immediately and a new damping device was fitted to both production and existing service aircraft within a space of two months.

No 408 Squadron received its first two B Mk V Halifaxes on 11 October and by the end of the month had 13 on charge. Tragically, it lost one of these during a fighter affiliation exercise on 9 November. The squadron was not to retain its B Mk Vs for very long; an order for their replacement by B Mk IIs being received on 30 November. Twelve of the B Mk Vs were ferried to 18 MU, Dumfries, where they were to be modified to B Mk V Series I (Special) standard. For an obscure reason a single B Mk V remained on the squadron's charge for several months.

No 77 Squadron also converted to Halifaxes during October, receiving B Mk II Series I aircraft which were soon recalled and B Mk V Series I (Special) type issued in their place. The withdrawal of the B Mk Vs was only a temporary measure and they were to make a general reappearance within the space of a few months.

Above: **W7710:LQ-R,** *Ruhr Valley Express,* **of No 405 Squadron, the first of the Canadian units to operate the Halifax. R-Robert took part in the squadron's first operation. Flown by Sqn Ldr Thiele it accompanied the CO's aircraft in an attempted daylight raid on Hamburg on 3 February 1942.** / *RCAF*

4 Modifications

'The incidence of accident rate on the Halifax Mk II aircraft increased during 1942 and an analysis of these incidents showed a large number to be the result of rudder overbalance — a feature which has been present in the type since its introduction into the service.'

So begins perhaps the most critical report on the Halifax. As already stated in Chapter 1, the first instance of rudder overbalance occurred during the trials with L7244. The initial flight tests showed that a reduction of 3° in the design rudder angle partially reduced the tendency for the rudder to overbalance and orders for the retrospective modification of all service Halifaxes were issued. The benefits of this temporary expedient were negated to a large extent by two other factors brought to light by the same trials. The limit stops for the rudders was made of a rubber block sandwiched between two metal plates, the latter being gradually deformed by the rudder forces until the rubber was permanently compressed. This allowed the rudder to move over a greater angular distance than originally intended and aggravated the stall condition associated with the overbalancing. The metal limit stop arm, which struck the limit stop, also tended to wear at the point where it was attached to the rudder by a bracket again allowing the rudder more angular deflection than desired. It should be realised at this point that the forces involved here were quite considerable. An accident occurred during side-slip tests in which the top half of one of the rudders broke away due to the force with which the rudder overbalanced and struck the limit stop.

An attempt was made to rectify the overbalance problem by adjusting the range of movement of the balance tab on each rudder. This created some difficulties since the tab was a combined balance-trim tab. Satisfactory adjustment could be made to the balance range but the resultant trim range was insufficient and further improvement became imperative. Wind tunnel tests were made on a complete 1/10 scale model and a partial 1/3 scale model to examine this problem. These revealed that directional instability due to fin stall occurred at about 20° of side-slip and associated with this was a reversal of rudder force required to maintain directional trim due to rudder overbalance. Various modifications were tried including the use of leading edge slats to delay the fin stall but no substantial improvement resulted. The set back rudder balance was cut back and trailing edge chords fitted, as well as tests with three different sizes of horn balance but again with negative results. Finally, various modifications to the rudder balance showed that some form of shielded horn appeared to produce the most promising results. This was achieved by thickening the nose of the rudder to give a bulbous nose effect to that part of the balance which protruded into the slipstream at large angles of attack.

The bulbous noses were fitted to the rudders of L7245 and a series of tests carried out. Since the airscrews rotated clockwise the resultant torque produced a tendency for the aircraft to roll to the left. Under normal circumstances this was not noticeable and even with the starboard engines shut down and feathered, no difficulty was encountered flying on the remaining two engines. However, the most critical condition obviously occurred when the port engines were cut, the natural tendency for the port wing to drop being aggravated by the torque and it was under these circumstances that rudder overbalance occurred. No 76 Squadron lost a very experienced crew in this way on 25 July 1942, when both port engines of their Halifax cut shortly after take-off.

The early tests with L7245 were made with the starboard engines running at the normal cruise setting and both port engines switched off. At 170mph, the rudders began a slight oscillation and violently overbalanced at 160mph, remaining hard over to starboard. Control could not be regained by increasing the speed and at 180mph the starboard engines were throttled back, only then could the rudders be centralised.

For normal flying the bulbous noses had the effect of making the rudders sloppy at all speeds up to 260mph. They were then transferred to L9515 which also had the balance tab movement reduced by 50% thus reducing the available trimming range by 30%. The tests were carried out at 50,000lb auw, with only the port outer engine shut down and the propeller feathered. The full trim range to starboard was required to keep the aircraft straight at 178mph. At 150mph control could be comfortably maintained if 10° of bank were used but below this speed the foot load on the rudder pedals became excessive. There was no sign of overbalance at speeds as low as 130mph although this speed could only be held for a short period. With both port engines off and full trim the foot load became excessive at 140mph.

The overbalance problem had almost been solved but it still remained clear that the trim problem had not. A further series of modifications and tests produced a trim range which allowed the aircraft to be flown on the starboard engines only, at 140mph with 10° of bank and full right

Top: W7773, a standard B Mk II Series I, being air tested by Flt Lt J. R. Talbot, Handley Page's chief test pilot. The bulky asbestos tunnel shrouds, which critically effected performance, are seen here in their unpainted state. Note the hydraulically operated landing light beneath the port wing; it was permanently locked down on this mark and added to the drag problems. / Rolls-Royce

Above: W1008, one of three test aircraft used for propeller trials during the critical period.

rudder, the foot load being zero under these conditions. The rudders, however, remained sluggish at low speeds and further improvement was still considered desirable. It was suggested that some increase in fin area would overcome the sluggishness at low speeds as well as improve the asymmetric handling characteristics. Meanwhile, as a palliative the bulbous noses, officially Handley Page modification 413, were introduced on to the production lines but a considerable delay was experienced in incorporating them retrospectively. The accident rate continued to increase but not all losses were attributable to rudder problems.

A general review of the Halifax's performance during the autumn of 1942 had shown, in the words of the official report,'... that deterioration in performance of the Halifax II aircraft, consequent upon progressive application of external equipment, has augmented to such an extent that the aircraft has become incapable of meeting concurrently the operational requirements of both high loading and high altitude cruising.' If somewhat verbose the meaning was still quite clear — the situation was critical!

The reasons for this fall off in performance were multiple. Since the introduction of the B Mk II Series I Halifax into service engine power had remained static while weight had crept steadily upwards due to the constant additions to the internal equipment and the airframe. Attempts had been made to increase the performance by a series of trials with different types of propeller. These were carried out between February and April 1942 on R9387, W1008 and W1009, but failed to produce any major improvement.

During the early months of 1942 three major changes had been made to the external condition of the Halifaxes then in service; the installation of large asbestos tunnel shrouds over the engine exhausts, the introduction of RDM2A special rough night black finish on the sides and undersurfaces of the aircraft and the fitting of two 4,000lb bombs with the bomb doors only partly closed. Between August and October a series of trials were undertaken which were to have far reaching effects and the results have already been stated. However, the details are worthy of closer examination. The tests were begun using W7801 and during the same month DG221, a fully equipped and operational B Mk II aircraft from No 10 Squadron, was also thoroughly flight tested and examined. The latter aircraft was found to have some small additional items of equipment and showed evidence of bad workmanship and poor servicing. In addition it had a particularly rough coat of RDM2A black finish. The aircraft was test flown with and without the large asbestos tunnel shrouds and the airflow behind these examined with the aid of wool tufts. The results showed excessively turbulent flow over the inboard engine nacelles and wing section which caused considerable vibration of the wing trailing edge. In addition, the aircraft showed a marked lack of directional stability. Take-off tests were made without the shrouds fitted, at an auw of 60,500lb and ground runs lasting 33-37sec recorded. After fitting the shrouds the take-off became critical, the final test run taking $42\frac{1}{2}$sec and the aerodrome boundary was cleared with difficulty only after two previous attempts to become airborne.

In an effort to regain some of the lost performance, tests were made, in collaboration with a Handley Page representative, on W7776 a No 138 Squadron aircraft which had been specially cleaned up. The mid-upper and front turrets had been removed, the resulting aperture in the nose being faired in with what was to become known as a Tollerton fairing. (Tollerton Aircraft Services who made the fairing had been previously associated with Handley Page through conversion of the Herefords to Hampdens.) The fuel jettison pipes, barrage balloon cable cutters and ramps were removed from the wings and all engine nacelle and body leaks sealed. (As early as June 1941 a report on drag trials completed with L7245 had shown, among other things, that the reducion of camouflage paint thickness from .002in to .001in would reduce profile drag from 3.1% to 1.7%. More significant was the fact that leak drag, caused by gaps around the undercarriage, bomb doors, wing/fuselage joints etc resulted in anything from 3% to 12% of the total profile drag.) In addition the whip aerial, the fairing in front of the flare chute, one wireless mast, one navigation blister, the hand rail on top of the fuselage and the carburettor air intake ice guards were removed. Extended radiator shutters were fitted to all four engines. The net gain of these removals was just sufficient to compensate for the speed loss incurred by the use of the RDM2A finish. Tests with a B Mk V, DG237, at Speke aerodrome had shown that a careful application of one coat of this rough night finish over the ordinary smooth black finish reduced airspeeds by an average of 4-5mph and increased the time to 20,000ft by four minutes.

As a result of these trials with W7776 a series of immediate proposals were put forward embracing these modifications. Further immediate cleaning up of the airframe was to include better sealing of the wing and fuselage bomb doors, removal of the second navigation blister, provision of bomb doors capable of completely enclosing large bombs and the fitting of a retractable tail wheel. Long term modifications provided for the introduction of Merlin 23 and 61 engines and the adoption of dropped inboard engine nacelles which, although designed for Merlin 61 engines could also be used for Merlin XX engines.

The inadequacy of the radiators to cope with engine temperatures had been amply demonstrated during the preceding months. It had been found necessary to keep the radiator flaps partly or fully open during operational flights causing a speed loss of 9mph (True) at 15,000ft which, in turn, affected the operational ceiling of the aircraft. Rolls-Royce suggested increasing the radiator exit area and introducing a cruising boost limit of 6lb/sq in. However, the squadrons had already begun applying their own remedial action by cropping the radiator flaps which increased the effective exit area when fully closed.

The results of the trials were sobering in the extreme and in the light of Halifax losses of 10.1% in No 4 Group during August 1942 all squadron operations were drastically reduced for a period of three to four weeks while the aircraft were modified. During this period crews received a welcome rest and underwent additional training. Analysis of the rising casualties among Halifax crews during the autumn had revealed that the number of sorties

Above and above right:
DG221:EY-A of No 78 Squadron, subject of the official investigation into declining performance. It had done 10 operations when selected for testing. The bulky tunnel shrouds had been removed when these photographs were taken.

Left: Modification No 413, the bulbous nose fittings to the rudder leading edge, can be seen here. The sturdy construction of the Boulton Paul E Mk 1 tail turret is quite evident. / *IWM*

Centre right and bottom right:
W7776, ex-NF-L of No 138 Squadron, the Halifax fitted with the first Z fairing by Tollerton Aircraft Services. It served as the prototype for the B Mk II Series I (Special).

Above: W7922:EY-L of No 78 Squadron photographed amidst the December mist during testing at Boscombe Down in 1942. This was a squadron modification to Series I (Special) standard but both the mid-upper turret and the locked down landing gear light have been retained.

Left: The Boulton Paul A Mk VIII turret in its low profile fairing as adopted for the improved Series IA Halifaxes.

made before failing to return was directly related to the number of trips made as second pilot before becoming a captain of a crew. Statistics showed that those pilots who had done less than three trips as a second pilot only completed an avergage of two main target trips before being lost. Those who had completed six trips as second pilot averaged eight operations. Consequently, Halifax pilots were given a series of cross-country exercises and two or three mining operations as second pilots before assuming command of a Halifax and crew of their own. It was perhaps cold comfort but another survey showed that figures for crews who survived being shot down were relatively more favourable for Halifax crews with 29% as against 17% for Stirling and 11% for Lancasters.

The modifications were not instituted to a specific pattern which resulted, for many months, in Halifaxes being seen in varying stages of metamorphosis. For instance W7922, which had been cleaned up by the squadron personnel, was tested at Boscombe Down in December and had most of the modifications applied to W7776. It had a considerably improved performance; maximum operational height had been increased slightly, the service ceiling raised by 1,000ft and the time to 20,000ft reduced by two minutes. This was not the total benefit possible as the aircraft still retained the mid-upper turret, some barrage cable cutters, ice guards on the carburettor intakes and Kilfrost de-icing paste on the leading edges of the control surfaces.

This Halifax was used to test an increased cruising boost limitation of 6lb/sq in and locked mixture control for its Merlin XX engines as had been suggested by Rolls-Royce. This greatly improved the cruising capabilities over the height range from 15,000 to 18,000ft as well as improving the cruising speed, on high supercharger setting, by approximately 20mph up the full throttle height of 17,400ft. It also raised the maximum operational height to 19,000ft.

The degree of modification was by no means limited to the official recommendations. No 76 Squadron's dynamic commanding officer, Leonard Cheshire, did a little extra stripping of his own which amounted to practically everything removable and included the armour-plated door of the flight engineer's compartment. Removal of the mid-upper turret was not strictly a new innovation, some squadron individuals had decided that the speed loss caused by its bulky shape did not warrant the additional protection it provided. Most night fighters attacked from astern, low down, with the bomber silhouetted against the night sky and many crews had expressed concern at the vulnerability of this totally blind area beneath the belly of their aircraft. Sgt G. Coates and LAC F. Layton of No 76 Squadron, with the enthusiastic backing of Wg Cdr Cheshire, produced their own answer to this problem in the form of a perspex blister which fitted over the ventral well hatch position of W7650. This experimental installation was duly tested at Boscombe Down early in 1943.

Tests were already in hand to find a suitable replacement for the bulky C Mk II turret. A Boulton Paul T Mk I turret arrived at Boscombe Down on 22 September 1942, and was fitted to R9436. A compact turret, mounting two Browning No 2 Mk II .5in machine guns, it weighed 1,404lb fully equipped which included 600 rounds per gun and 243lb of 20mm armour plate. A successful series of trials was carried out during October but a far more promising turret was already under test and the T Mk I did not enter production, the prototype being sent to America.

The other turret was a Boulton Paul A Mk VIII. Some eight inches shallower and five inches smaller in diameter than the C Mk II, it was equipped with four Browning .303in machine guns. With 550 rounds of ammunition for each gun and $7\frac{1}{2}$ pounds of 12mm armour plate it weighed only 586lb fully equipped. A built-up metal surround was fitted to the fuselage when it was installed in R9375 and testing took place during October, the turret proving most successful.

A surplus of Boulton Paul A Mk II turrets were modified to this new standard and designated A Mk VIII (Special), this version being fitted initially to the Halifax. By September 1943 stocks of this type had been used up and the standard A Mk VIII was introduced on to the production lines. A more easily distinguished change occurred when the improved B Mk II Series IA Halifaxes entered service. The large metal fairing, with its contour track for the interrupter gear, was removed and the turret lowered some five inches. A simple metal skirt was used to fair it into the top of the fuselage and the normal Boulton Paul electro-mechanical fire interrupter gear installed.

The critical period had been met and overcome. The Halifax still had some difficulties to face during its service career but never again would it have to endure such a trying period.

5 Operations in Germany

With the introduction of the B Mk II Series I (Special) Halifax losses dropped markedly and the type was in time to participate in the offensive against Italy. Only the long autumn and winter nights could provide an adequate cover of darkness for such long range operations. During one of the earliest attacks, on 23 October 1942, Sgt M. Caplan of No 158 Squadron found the defences more accurate than he had anticipated. Having attacked Genoa he was intercepted by two single engined Italian night fighters near Turin. They fired several long bursts of cannon fire at DT521:O damaging the radio equipment and wounding the rear gunner, Sgt M. Danban.

Defences were not the only danger. Wg Cdr B. V. Robinson, DSO, DFC of No 35 Squadron located and bombed Turin on the night of 18/19 November but on reaching the Alps one of the four flares which had failed to release burst into flames causing a fire in the bomb bay. The fire appeared to be spreading and he ordered the crew to bail out. Before he had time to leave the aircraft himself the fire abated and finally extinguished itself so Robinson brought DT488:S back alone, receiving a bar to his DFC for his tenacity. The Italian radio later reported that his crew were safe and prisoners.

Engine failures were still an ever present threat and Wg Cdr W. Fletcher of No 158 Squadron lost the starboard engine of W1091:W shortly before bombing Turin. To complicate matters 40×4lb incendiaries failed to release. Unable to gain sufficient height to cross the Alps, Fletcher turned the Halifax south-west to the Rhone valley and from there flew across France to a point west of Le Havre and then back to base where he landed with visibility down to 500yd. This effort earned him an immediate DFC, the navigator, Sgt H. Kay and the flight engineer, Sgt R. Lewis, each a DFM.

At the beginning of 1943 Bomber Command was almost ready to begin a sustained offensive against Germany when the U-boat crisis in the Altantic forced a temporary diversion of the bomber force to try and relieve the situation by attacking the U-boat pens and their facilities in the occupied French ports of Lorient, St Nazaire and La Pallice. Air Marshal Harris believed this to be a gross misuse of his carefully husbanded force because the pens themselves contained all the necessary facilities and were virtually bomb proof. However, with no other choice Harris dispatched 3,170 sorties between 14 January and 6 April, all of which were concentrated against Lorient and St Nazaire. The two largest attacks were both mounted during February, 466 aircraft attacking La Pallice on 13th and 437 St Nazaire on 28th. During the St Nazaire raid eight Halifaxes from No 35 Squadron formed part of the attacking force and the old problem of engine overheating manifested itself once more.

Sqn Ldr Dean's aircraft, W7877:Q lost its port outer engine at 13,400ft but despite being forced down gradually to 9,000ft the bombing run was continued on three engines. Just after leaving the target area the starboard inner engine failed, flames shooting out of the air intakes and the Halifax slowly lost height to 3,000ft. All preparations were made for ditching while the aircraft continued its flight through heavy cloud, but fortunately the English coast was at last sighted and a homing made on to Harrowbeer airfield. However, the flare path was extremely feeble and Dean landed halfway along the 1,100ft runway, overshot and collapsed the undercarriage on rough ground where the Halifax finally came to rest without causing any casualties among the crew.

The campaign, comprising 14 raids, cost Bomber Command 38 aircraft and nine others destroyed in accidents over England. Harris's point had been proved for, despite the destruction of much of the towns of Lorient and St Nazaire, the U-boats pens, their facilities and the U-boats themselves, remained virtually unscathed. However, the diversification had not prevented the remainder of Harris's force being used against Germany with a series of attacks which were mainly a prelude to the coming major offensive of March.

Berlin was attacked on 16 January 1943, the first time since 1941. A notoriously difficult and dangerous target, it lay well beyond the range of available navigation aids and the Pathfinders, who were to mark the target, had to rely on dead reckoning navigation. Three Lancasters were to drop flares in the target area two minutes before zero hour and by their light five Halifaxes and five Lancasters were to identify the aiming point visually and drop target indicators to guide the main force. Unbroken cloud covered the route across Europe to within 10 miles of Berlin making navigation extremely difficult and the target itself was covered with thick haze. The 201 aircraft of the main force attacked aiming on the target indicators and some very concentrated bombing was achieved by a large portion of the force. No 76 Squadron provided 14 Halifaxes, 'the cream of the squadron' in the words of their diarist, for this raid and all returned safely. Crews reported that the damage done by HE and incendiaries dropped in and

Below: BB324:ZA-X of No 10 Squadron photographed in April 1943 after completing four missions; it is typical of unit modified Series I (Special) Halifaxes. Front and mid-upper turrets, navigation window blisters and fuselage top handrail have all been removed and close fitting exhaust shrouds fitted. However the radio mast and high astro dome remain and the landing light is still locked down. The emblem below the cockpit is a cartoon of a terrier dog's head wearing a sailor's cap with *Wings For Victory*, in white, below it. / *via Darby*

Bottom: In this view it can be seen that the fuel jettison pipes have been removed. A small downwards vision blister has been added below the rear fuselage; immediately aft is the short rod aerial for the Gee set. The dipole aerial for the Monica set projects from the rear of the fuselage. / *via Darby*

around the concentration of target indicators was devastating. Fires could be seen concentrated over the entire target area, the glow being visible from as far away as Hanover during the return journey. The reports were correct but the area the target indicators bombed so thoroughly, lay in the Templehof district and the remainder of the force bombed a widely spread area of the southern suburbs. The next night 187 bombers went back to Berlin, strangely by the same route, but results were virtually no better. Unfortunately, the same could not be said of the losses which was one Lancaster the first night but rose sharply to 22 aircraft the next night with an additional 30 damaged.

Essen received six visits from Bomber Command during the month but the attack on Hamburg on the night of 30/31st was unique. Gee had made a significant contribution to the solving of the navigation problems which had beset Bomber Command since the earliest days of the war. Unfortunately, it was singularly a navigation aid and analysis of bombing errors had also pointed out the desperate need for some form of blind bombing aid.

The idea of a radar navigation aid had been formulated in the late 1930s with tests to determine the optimum wave lengths in early 1939. The introduction of centimetric wave lengths gave the idea new impetus and the first aerial trials were carried out on 1 November 1941, by a Blenheim fitted with a 9cm AI (Air Interception) system normally used for air-to-air searching associated with night fighter tactics, the beam in this case being tilted downward to try to record ground responses. From these early trials ultimately stemmed the 'H2S' set which not only became an indispensable navigation aid but revolutionised the blind bombing technique and gave Bomber Command a much needed boost from 1943 onwards.

One of the problems associated with H2S was the housing of the scanner assembly in a heavy bomber. Because of its capacious fuselage the Halifax was chosen for the trials with the new device and on 27 March 1942, V9977 landed at Hurn equipped with an experimental perspex blister in the position normally intended for a ventral turret. Technicians from the Telecommunications Research Establishment installed the first experimental 10cm H2S set in this blister and the flight trials, after some delays with the magnetron valve fitting, began early in April. The first major test was carried out on 7 June but disaster struck and at 1620hrs V9977 crashed whilst returning to Defford and was completely destroyed by fire. Six leading H2S experts, the entire crew and Sqn Ldr Sansom, a liaison officer, perished with the only magnetron equipped H2S set, a terrible loss from every aspect. By working day and night another magnetron set was completed and installed in a second Halifax, V7711, and trials recommenced at the end of the first week in July. By the end of September the first production H2S set had been fitted to W7808 and service trials had commenced at the Bombing Development Unit. The only drawback was the poor serviceability of the equipment.

The Telecommunications Research Establishment were engaged also in the training of navigators to use the equipment which produced a representation of the ground detail within a limited radius beneath the aircraft on a circular cathode ray tube. The definition was somewhat limited and it required a well trained operator to interpret the picture with any accuracy. However, the distinction between land and water masses was most clearly defined. For this reason Bomber Command chose Hamburg as the trial target for the new device.

The attack took place on the night of 30/31 January 1943 in moonless conditions and with visibility in the target area virtually impossible for visual identification. Six Halifaxes of No 35 Squadron, in company with seven Stirlings from No 7 Squadron, were to mark the target for the main force. Three of No 7 Squadron's Stirlings aborted early in the raid due to H2S unserviceability and No 35 Squadron faired little better. W7875 aborted through mechanical failure and W7872, W7873 and W7874 suffered H2S failures. The remaining two aircraft, W7851 and W7878, succeeded in marking the target using their H2S equipment and, of equal significance, conducting their navigation solely by the aid of this equipment.

Flg Off Brown, the pilot of W7851:N, reported afterwards: 'There was thin strato cumulus cloud over the target with tops at 5,000-8,000ft, as a result of which no ground detail could be seen. The target was identified, however, on special equipment and at $0237\frac{1}{2}$hrs four red flares were dropped at 52° 50' North 09° 09' East from 21,000ft. At 0304hrs four green flares were placed as instructed from 20,000ft followed three minutes later by 16 red/green star flares from the same height. In poor conditions no photograph was attempted and very little was seen.'

Three further trial raids were carried out in quick succession, Cologne on 2/3 February, Hamburg on 3/4th and Turin on 4/5th. The success of the system was established beyond doubt on each of these occasions. However, production difficulties delayed the introduction of H2S in quantity for several months and by the end of May the maximum number of H2S equipped bombers to operate on any one raid did not exceed 18. These problems were finally overcome and by August 840 sets had been produced. Production was one aspect, fitting the equipment another and by 12 October 155 Halifaxes, 225 Lancasters and 70 Stirlings had been equipped and delivered to Bomber Command. However, the normal attrition rate had already accounted for 70 Halifaxes, 50 Lancasters and 29 Stirlings. Despite these delays Bomber Command remained very active.

The operational introduction of H2S albeit in only small quantities, occurred at a most opportune moment for a directive reached Bomber Command HQ on 4 February which stated the main Allied aims were ' . . . Primarily the progressive destruction and dislocation of the German military, industrial and economic system and the undermining of the morale of the German people to a point where their capacity for armed resistance is fatally weakened.' This was accompanied by a selection of targets which were to be attacked, weather and tactical considerations permitting. These compromised U-boat construction yards, the aircraft industry, transport, oil plants and other targets allied to the war industry. In addition, Berlin was to be attacked on occasions when it was likely to have most effect upon German morale as a whole, or, conversely, whenever it would boost Russian

Top: **With both starboard propellers feathered BB324 shows its upper surface camouflage of dark earth/dark green cellulose finish to DTD38A. The smooth black finish was cellulose DTD308 which replaced the old matt black RDM2A. Another paint, dull black DTD314S, was then currently being introduced on to the production lines due to a shortage of DTD308. This aircraft was subsequently lost in an attack against Mulheim on 22/23 June 1943.** */ via Darby*

Above: **DG235 fresh from the production line as a fully equipped B Mk V Series I. It was one of the first two Halifaxes received by No 408 Squadron on 11 October 1942. It was being used by the squadron's conversion flight when the latter was renumbered No 1659 HCU. On 25 November 1942 it reverted to No 408 Squadron where it was modified to a Series I (Special); its condition being typical of this interim standard.** */ IWM*

Left: Sqn Ldr 'Bunny' Buncross's EY-Z, a Series I (Special) of No 78 Squadron which had completed 10 missions. The artwork was done by WO Hugh Burns and the Latin motto — Virtue teaches preparedness — is believed to be that of a New Zealand school. / *H. Burns*

Right: Of indifferent quality but unique markings for a bomber; JB910:ZA-J of No 10 Squadron with 26 missions marked up. / *via Darby*

Below: DG235 passed to Rolls-Royce on 13 December 1942 and was used for four-bladed Rotol propeller tests. On 29 January 1943 it carried out flame damping trials with multi-blister, four fishtail, manifolds at Boscombe Down. It left Rolls-Royce for No 48 MU on 8 March 1944, then went to Handley Page RIU on 19 March 1944, to No 44 MU on 1 September 1944, to No 1667 HCU on 23 September 1944, to No 48 MU on 12 January 1945 and was struck off charge on 1 November 1945. / *Rolls-Royce*

morale. Harris interpreted these instructions in the best interests of his force and its abilities, namely the destruction of the industrial heart of Germany. The time for the first great offensive was not quite right but Bomber Command continued to increase its tempo of attacks and to perfect the techniques associated with the new blind bombing aid and the Pathfinder target marking.

There were still minor problems involved as shown by a report from Sqn Ldr P. Fletcher of No 158 Squadron. He was flying W7865:G over Nuremburg on 25 February and the Pathfinders were late. 'Within a few moments of the first target indicator markers going down everyone sitting around the target pounced on it and you could see everything going down at once. The yellow flares at Speyer were dropped over a wide area. Weather to and from the target was awful.'

The Ruhr Valley, rich in bituminous coal to the extent of 75% of all coal produced in Germany, was the home of the most important heavy industries and metallurgical factories. Its geographical situation was perfect, lying as it did at the hub of the transcontinental road, rail, river and canal routes. It had ready access to major sea ports through a network of waterways, but it also lay nearer to England than almost any other part of Germany, a point well appreciated by the Germans who provided it with formidable defences. Its notoriety had earned it the title of the 'Happy Valley' amongst aircrews.

Bomber Command stood ready to pit its much improved force against those formidable defences, defences which included a comprehensive early warning radar system of Freyas supplemented by Würzburgs for tracking and local plotting associated with ground controlled interception techniques. Radio counter measures, in support of Bomber Command, began in December 1942 when crews were notified that they were allowed to use their IFF sets (a device normally used to identify friendly aircraft by Allied radar) to jam the Würzburg equipment. To jam the Freya sets a device, code-named Mandrel, was fitted to Bomber Command aircraft, Nos 158 and 408 Squadrons being among the first Halifax units to be so equipped. Thus armed Bomber Command began the Battle of the Ruhr, as it became known, on the night of 5/6 March with an attack on Essen.

This city had been raided many times before, accounting for 10% of Bomber Command's total effort during 1942. Flt Lt K. Reynolds of No 158 Squadron was flying DT700:S that night and his description of the attack is most vivid:
'After the first target indicator marker was dropped Essen seemed swamped with Halifaxes. Pathfinder yellow marker was dead on time and the first red target indicator flare burst just after passing over the turning point. Searchlights were in greater numbers than I have ever seen previously. The whole sky leading in to the target was criss-crossed by beams. At first the searchlights were in very large cones and the heavy AA was bursting in the intersections but as the attack developed the searchlights were badly disorganised and useless and the flak less effective. The target was blazing with incendiaries and the flashes from the HEs lighting up the long buildings. I think Krupps really got a pasting.'

Photographic reconnaissance later confirmed that 300 acres of Essen had been severely damaged. Krupps works suffered 10% damage, an encouraging start after so many failures.

Harris sent a message of congratulations to all crews which included a reference to ' . . . giving it a second barrel without pause.' However, the old enemy, the weather, prevented this follow up blow for a week but when it did fall it was equally devastating. The German defences were as tenacious as ever and 23 of the 457 bombers failed to return. Crews were enthusiastic about the success of the raid, No 58 Squadron diarist recording, 'It is reckoned by experienced members of the crew that this was the most damaging raid that they had ever seen.' Bomb damage assessment reports later estimated that 27% of the Krupp factory complex had been badly damaged.

Although not actually lying within the confines of the Ruhr Valley, Nuremburg, Stuttgart and Munich in southern Germany were, along with similar locations, included on the target list. This achieved a wide dispersal of the German defences and thus indirectly aided the Ruhr offensive. No 77 Squadron, recently converted to Halifaxes, suffered its first casualties during one of these raids, JB795:H and DT734:J failing to return from Munich on 9/10 March. Stuttgart was the target the next night then, after a break of nearly a week during which St Nazaire was attacked, Duisburg was attacked on the 26/27th. Sgt G. Vinish, the pilot of DT784, later made the following report which is interesting as an example of the gradually developing use of the Pathfinder techniques:
'Bombed primary target at 0222hrs from 19,000ft on red target marker and a timed run from yellow markers. Visibility fair and bombs were thought to have fallen near red target marker. A good number of fires noted in the target area. Moderate flak encountered but six groups of searchlights were operating in and around Duisburg.'
Berlin had received a heavy attack on 1/2 March which resulted in concentrated bombing and an apparent saturation of the enemy defences. In view of this result the raid of 27/28 March was something of an anti-climax, most of the bombs falling in open country. Some crews found the target but were given a very warm reception from the defences. Sgt C. Surgey of No 158 Squadron was coned by searchlights for eight minutes over the target. After releasing his bombs he took violent evasive action during which a near miss by a flak shell caused W1221:H to turn over on its back and go into a spin. The engines cut but the pilot was able to regain control and restarted them at 7,000ft. During the spin the escape hatch had come open and sundry equipment and personal effects, including the wireless operators watch and silk gloves and the bomb aimer's gloves, were lost. Perhaps the most keenly felt loss was the contents of the thermos flasks which were all smashed.

St Nazaire was raided the next night and then Berlin again. Extremely bad weather severely hampered the operation and results were again disappointing with 21 aircraft lost out of the 578 dispatched. Further attacks on Berlin were deferred until crews could utilise the security of the autumn nights. Other distant targets less well defended were still attacked and on 16/17 April

225 bombers were detailed to attack the Skoda armament works at Pilsen in Czechoslovakia. To cover this operation diversionary raids were made on cities in western Germany, but despite this precaution the Skoda raid was a failure and cost 37 aircraft, including five from No 51 Squadron and four from No 408 Squadron.

New German night fighter tactics were encountered during these raids. Sgt Carrie of No 76 Squadron was piloting DT698:W to Stuttgart on 14 April when a Ju88 approached with all its lights on. The rear gunner hit it with a well-aimed burst which sent it spiralling down with one engine aflame. Immediately a second Ju88 riddled the Halifax with a long burst of fire, mortally wounding one of the crew. These decoy tactics were repeated on many occasions, usually with less favourable results for the victim. Night fighters, however, were only part of the rapidly increasing defences. Heavy calibre flak guns were brought into action which were capable of sustained fire up to 21,000ft. Sgt G. Beveridge of No 10 Squadron had a narrow escape from these weapons during the early hours of 14 May. His Halifax was flying at 18,000ft between Dusseldorf and Cologne when it was caught by searchlights. During the subsequent violent manoeuvres a near miss from a flak burst caused the rudders the Halifax to overbalance and the aircraft turned over on its back. The nose dropped and the aircraft plunged down to 7,000ft before Beveridge could regain control and level out. The mid-upper gunner, no doubt thinking the aircraft doomed, had bailed out. The searchlights once more locked on to HR695:D and shortly afterwards Beveridge jettisoned the bomb load and escaped the blinding fingers of light. Over the Zuid Beveland at 12,000ft the rear gunner, Sgt Compton, sighted a Ju88 500ft above them, 600yd to port and astern, with a searchlight in its nose. Just at that moment another Ju88 was sighted 300yd away on the starboard quarter. Beveridge swung the Halifax to port as the second Ju88 attacked causing it to miss. Compton returned the fire from 100yd range and thought that he hit the Ju88 in the starboard wing. The evasive action caused both Ju88s to be momentarily lost from sight but within a few seconds both of them attacked again from the port the starboard quarters. Compton exchanged fire with the attacker from the starboard quarter, neither finding his mark. A few moments later one of the Ju88s attacked from the port beam and closing to 30yd fired a short burst. This time Compton saw his own fire register on the port engine and nose of the Ju88 causing the former to smoke. In a well timed attack the other assailant struck from the starboard beam closing to 300yd. Two further attacks were made from the port beam and quarter but the Halifax eventually evaded its pursuers and returned safely to its base. Damage was only moderate, being confined to the port tailplane, elevator, rudder, the outboard fuel tank in the port wing and one gun rendered unserviceable.

Even during this period of intense operational activity some squadrons were still able to meet certain social obligations. No 77 Squadron, affiliated with the City of Lancaster, was ordered to take part in the city's 'Wings for Victory' parade on 22 May. Fifty members of the ground personnel took part in the march past while four of the squadron's Halifaxes flew overhead in tactical pairs.

During the raid on Dusseldorf on 11/12 June German night fighters were active in large numbers shooting down 38 of the 783 bombers dispatched. The battle was not entirely one sided and several crews claimed kills that night. Flt Sgt Williams, a veteran Australian rear gunner of No 35 Squadron, was badly wounded in the body and legs by the opening burst from one of two night fighters which attacked his Halifax. Despite his intense pain, he was able to pass directions for evasive action when the second fighter attacked. The turret rotation mechanism had been destroyed by the first fighter attack but Williams managed to open fire on the second attacker which exploded in the air. The first night fighter then resumed the attack and promptly met the same fate as its companion. Williams remained at his post until HR798:A landed back at its base where the turret had to be cut away to release him. For his courage and gunnery ability he received an immediate award of the comparatively rare Conspicuous Gallantry Medal.

Enemy night fighter tactics employed many ruses, an unusual example being the experience of Flg Off R. Fitzgerald's No 77 Squadron crew who were part of a force sent to attack Duisburg on 12/13 May. On the way to the target another aircraft was seen approaching on a parallel course and was eventually identified as a Halifax. On closer examination it was seen to be devoid of nose and mid-upper turrets and was painted black all over with no national markings visible. The mystery Halifax slipped nearer to Fitzgerald's JD110:P its speed being some 25mph faster. No exhaust flames were visible which was in itself unusual for a Halifax and no lights were showing. The captain's suspicions were aroused and he turned into and under the nose of the black Halifax which immediately straightened out as if trying to bring its rear turret guns to bear. Fitzgerald turned his Halifax in again and the other aircraft broke away to port and disappeared towards the coast. Immediately afterwards a Ju88 was sighted, also painted black, but there was nothing to suggest definitely that the two were working together although the black paint rendered observation of both very difficult.

Other dangers lurked in the night skies and HR837:F of No 158 Squadron had just released its bomb load over Cologne on 28 May when it was struck simultaneously by a cannon shell from a Ju88 and a 1,000lb bomb from another aircraft above. The bomb passed through the fuselage and port wing leaving a hole four feet square in the fuselage near the mid-upper turret. It returned safely to base.

After five heavy raids on Duisburg it was considered that sufficient damage had been caused to allow attacks to be concentrated on the two important satellite towns of Oberhausen and Mulheim during June. Sgt F. Mathers was one of the No 77 Squadron pilots that made up the 557 strong force which attacked Mulheim on 22/23 June. He had just released his bombs from 19,000ft when a flak burst put the starboard outer engine out of action. Three minutes later a second flak shell hit the port inner engine. Mathers managed to feather both damaged engines and subdue the fires only to learn that several petrol tanks had also been holed. The mid-upper guns were jettisoned after half an hour due to the severe loss of height. Undaunted, he headed for base deviating from the set course to avoid the heavy defences of Amsterdam and Rotterdam. Shortly after crossing the enemy coast, an hour and a quarter later, he and his crew were beginning to feel that their luck may have changed for the better. A sudden burst of fire from a Bf110 changed their minds, JD110 being raked from stem to stern. The rear turret, the ammunition tracks and the intercom were all damaged. The Bf110 made three more attacks before being shot down into the sea by the rear gunner. Having finally reached base the crew found that the hydraulic system had also been hit and Mathers had to make a wheels up landing, fortunately without injury to anyone.

In view of the rising night fighter menace the introduction of a device, code-named Monica, was welcomed by the bomber crews. This apparatus was a tail warning radar set which produced an audible signal in the pilot's headphones if another aircraft approached from astern. Halifaxes fitted with the device could be easily distinguished by the small dipole aerial protruding rearward from beneath the rear turret. During July the third of four major attacks was launched against Cologne by 653 bombers. No 405 Squadron, now part of the 8 Group Path Finder Force, assisted in the marking of the target on the night of 3/4 July. On the way into the target Sgt J. Phillips' Halifax, NA179:B, was shot up badly by a single engined night fighter, the first burst tearing into the starboard tailplane where exploding cannon shells severed the control rods. Unable to take any evasive action, the defence of the Halifax rested solely with the gunners and an accurate long burst of 800 rounds by Sgt Kohnke, the rear gunner, damaged the night fighter sufficiently to drive it off. Meanwhile, Phillips was having great difficulty preventing the Halifax from stalling because it kept trying to climb. This was partly overcome by tying the control column to the rudder bars with the dinghy rope, but pressure still had to be maintained to hold it forward. In addition to the damage inflicted to the starboard elevator and tail assembly, a cannon shell had passed through the starboard wing causing internal damage. The fuselage and the bomb doors had been shot up as also had the astrodome and the mid-upper turret, the gunner being wounded. Despite the damage and the control difficulties Phillips continued his run in to the target but the bomb doors failed to open due to the damaged hydraulics. Sgt McLean, the flight engineer, tried to pump the doors down by hand but they would not move. During the return journey they finally freed themselves and the crew were able to jettison the three 1,000lb and eight 500lb HE bombs. One 1,000lb bomb had already been jettisoned by hand release-through the bomb doors before they decided to open. The target indicator flares were brought back and the Halifax landed safely, but with considerable difficulty, at its base.

Accounts of combats with night fighters were prolific during this period of intense activity but some were rather unusual. Flg Off M. Sattler's No 405 Squadron crew encountered what was positively identified by both gunners as a Do217 night fighter, during a raid on Montbeliard, on the night of 15 July. Both gunners also recognised British style camouflage and national markings on the aircraft

Above: Flt Sgt D. Cameron and two of his crew pose amidst the damage caused by a 'friendly' bomb which hit HR837:NP-F of No 158 Squadron. It was repaired and completed a total of 11 operations before being posted to No 1656 HCU on 12 April 1944. / *IWM*

Above right: HR782:MH-V, a B Mk II Series IA of No 51

Squadron which collided with a Lancaster at 4,000ft, 10 miles SE of Ossington on 30 August 1943. Two markings features can be seen; the transfer (decal) used to apply the serial number, a common feature, and the dividing line between upper and lower camouflage colours. The latter was common to Handley Page built aircraft. / *IWM*

Top: DT807:KN–R of No 77 Squadron basks in the 1943 harvest sunshine. Like many Series I (Special) Halifaxes the Tolerton fairing is adorned with artwork, a semi nude named Rita. Of the 20 bomb symbols the 9th is an icecream cone denoting at Italian target visited via the Alps. / *IWM*

Above: No 76 Squadron suffered few casualties during the last half of 1943. Flt Lt C. M. Shannon, a West Australian, brought this B Mk V Series I (Special) DK168:G *Johnnie The Wolf* home safely from its 15th mission on 25 July 1943 despite extensive damage. / *IWM*

which attacked them eight times. Sattler carried out a series of violent corkscrew manoeuvres but the Do217 hit the Halifax several times, shooting away one of the bomb carriers, piercing several fuel tanks and wounding the mid-upper gunner, Flg Off W. Anderson, in the left arm. Anderson and the rear gunner returned the fire and eventually the Do217 went into a shallow dive and one engine burst into flames before it hit the ground where it continued to burn.

Night fighter attacks from the region of the blind underbelly of the Halifax had prompted the No 76 Squadron experiment of late 1942. By mid-1943 the growing menace of such lethal attacks prompted other squadrons to take matters into their own hands and No 419 Squadron modified their Halifaxes during August to carry hand operated machine guns in the old fuselage well position.

The dangers were not restricted to enemy action alone. Sgt J. Sugden of No 158 Squadron felt two heavy thuds on HR721:S which he took to be near misses from flak bursts. The whole aircraft shuddered and the rear gunner reported a large hole in the port elevator. After landing the base of a 4lb incendiary bomb was found jammed in the hinges of the tailplane.

During an attack on Stettin Plt Off W. Sherk of No 35 Squadron had a similar experience. Five minutes after marking the allotted target the Halifax was struck by incendiary bombs, one of which smashed through the pilot's escape hatch and set his seat on fire before exploding in the flight engineer's compartment. With the aircraft out of control the pilot gave the order to bail out, but moments later he regained control and cancelled the order. Seconds could mean the difference between life and death and JB785:F returned to base minus two of the crew who had abandoned the aircraft during those first vital moments.

Perhaps one of the greatest fears was that of midair collision, with literally hundreds of aircraft within the near vicinity of a target the chance was always there. Sgt M. Smith of No 158 Squadron guided HR752:T in to a blind bombing attack on Essen. With 9/10ths cloud over the target the Pathfinder aircraft had marked the track into Essen with red and green target indicators and then released sky markers for the main force to bomb on. Smith's bomb aimer released the bombs and the Halifax was turned away from the target only to collide with a Lancaster at 18,000ft. The impact ripped two blades from the port outer engine, which burst into flames, and damaged the wing. Smith was lucky, he managed to extinguish the fire and limp back to base.

During a raid on München-Gladbach HR782 of No 51 Squadron collided with a Lancaster flying a reciprocal course. The damage was severe and the Halifax became uncontrollable at speeds less than 180mph. By a brilliant piece of flying the captain not only reached his base but also successfully landed — at 180mph.

Sometimes danger lurked upon the very airfield itself. Twenty Halifaxes of No 51 Squadron were waiting to be bombed up for a mission when an explosion took place in the bomb dump at approximately 1330hrs on 19 June. Incendiaries caught fire and all personnel were forced to take cover until 1700hrs. During this period a large number of heavy calibre bombs blew up killing 18 people. With no bombs available transport was rushed to RAF Holme to obtain the necessary supplies. In spite of considerable difficulties, by the joint efforts of the ground and air crews of all ranks 14 aircraft were bombed up in time for the mission.

Below: Victim of repeated attacks by a Ju88 night fighter during a raid on Hamburg on 2 August 1943, this B Mk II Series I (Special) JD146:B of No 10 Squadron was brought home by Flg Off J. Jenkins and crew. The Ju88 was dispatched in flames. /*IWM*

6 Further Expansion

The Halifax force continued its steady expansion during 1943, several more squadrons joining the ranks. No 6 Group, which became operational on 1 January, was composed exclusively of RCAF squadrons and the B Mk V Halifaxes, at last available in quantity, were issued principally to this mixed Halifax-Lancaster Group. This eased the maintenance problems since the Dowty landing gear was common to both types. There was, however, the inevitable exception. No 76 Squadron of 4 Group was equipped with the type as well. Based at Linton-on-Ouse the squadron had its B Mk II Halifaxes withdrawn in May and replaced by B Mk Vs but the following month the station itself was transferred from 4 Group to 6 Group.

A further change to the Halifax's external lines occurred around early June when the first of the B Mk II and V Series IA aircraft were issued to the squadrons. Following the review of the Halifax's performance which produced the critical report of late 1942, a series of tests were carried out on two aircraft, L9515 and HR679, incorporating some of the recommendations made in the report.

It had been appreciated that the Tollerton fairing modification was only an interim measure and L9515 was modified to flight test a mock up of the proposed revised nose shape of superior aerodynamic form. Turbulent flow over the inboard wing section had been a prime source of concern and was not entirely the fault of the bulky exhaust shrouds. The positioning of the inboard engines caused a portion of the turbulence and it had been recommended that the engines be dropped relevant to the wing chord. This would have involved major structural changes and an attempt was made to overcome the airflow problem by extending the existing nacelles well aft of the wing trailing edge. The A Mk VIII mid-upper turret also had its bulky surround removed and replaced by a small peripheral fairing.

Having flight tested these modifications on L9515, they were then incorporated on HR679 which was further modified to become the prototype B Mk II Series IA Halifax. The mock-up nose section of L9515 was replaced by a small extension of the fuselage and terminated in a perspex nose. This increased the overall length of the fuselage to 71ft 7in. The criticisms about the marginal power were overcome by installing Merlin 22 engines, rated at 1,480bhp at 12,250ft, in place of the Merlin XX engines. The Gallay radiators and oil coolers, which had proved troublesome, were replaced by Morris single block radiators with series oil cooler. This produced a revised radiator bath shape similar to the type originally fitted to the B Mk I but with a raked back chin. The tailwheel was also made fully retractable.

Thus equipped, HR679 was extensively test flown between December 1942 and May 1943; some of the equipment and modifications were added as the tests progressed. On 28 February it was flown to Boscombe Down where armament trials were carried out with a single Vickers GO machine gun fitted to the nose transparency in a gimbal mounting. Results of the tests were very good and a recommendation was made to incorporate most of the modifications tested on to the production lines. The extended inboard engine nacelles were not included due to the marginal benefit gained compared with the production problems involved. The tailwheel also remained non-retractable. With the introduction of the new mark the bad weather vision panel, in the cockpit starboard quarter light, was deleted.

Due to the inevitable supply problems and the speed with which the modifications could be incorporated on to the production lines (HR748, one of the first B Mk II Series IA Halifaxes underwent normal routine production tests at Boscombe Down in May) many of the early aircraft were fitted with Merlin 22 engines but retained the Gallay radiators with their characteristic cowlings. This produced something of an anomalous situation for, while they were fitted with the lengthened fuselage and new engines, they were still officially Series I (Special) Halifaxes since an Air Ministry order stated quite specifically that the Morris radiator modification was essential to the classification Series IA. Such subtleties do not appear to have reached the squadrons who continued to refer to their improved charges as Series IAs.

One of No 158 Squadron's new B Mk II Series IA Halifaxes, JD246:R, took part in an attack on Bochum on 12 June. Homeward bound, near the border of Germany and Holland, it was attacked by two Bf110 fighters. In the ensuing action two bursts of cannon fire hit the Halifax, one shell going through the port side of the fuselage. Glancing off the control rods it passed between the pilot's legs, went underneath the instrument panel and hit the leads to the Gee and IFF sets causing their emergency destruction detonators to explode. It then struck the bomb aimer, Sgt Dunning, a glancing blow on the scalp before smashing its way out through the perspex nose cone. The rear turret guns were out of action at this stage and the only defensive fire came from the mid-upper turret while the rear gunner called out evasive manoeuvres to the pilot. One of the attackers became a little too enthusiastic and nearly rammed the Halifax and earning itself a good solid burst from the mid-upper turret. It broke off the combat and disappeared. The other Bf110 continued to press home its attacks from dead astern and underneath repeatedly hitting the Halifax. It suddenly changed its tactics and stood off, trying to hit the Halifax when it was about halfway down each corkscrew manoeuvre, which forced the pilot, Sgt C. Robinson, to apply 40° of bank to avoid the enemy fire. After approximately 15 minutes of this the Bf110 broke off the engagement and the Halifax was able to regain its orignal course for home. Robinson received an immediate DFM for his efforts.

The Halifax's old enigma, rudder overbalance, also came under review during this period. Considerable delays had occurred in incorporating Mod 413, the bulbous noses, and the accident rate had increased. Analysis of these accidents indicated that rudder overbalance was a contributory factor and further investigation was recommended. The earlier tests had shown that the overbalance might be cured by fitting a larger fin. However, in view of the delays involved in such a major modification, further tests were made on HR679 and another B Mk II Series IA aircraft, HR727, in an effort to find a stop gap palliative. The latter aircraft was fitted with modified fins of slightly increased area. The bulbous noses were removed from the rudders which also had their leading edges cut back two inches and the resulting gap filled in with additional fin area. The results of the tests only served to show that no simple means of eliminating rudder overbalance was to be found.

A drastically modified fin assembly was therefore fitted to R9534, currently under test as the prototype B Mk III (See Chapter 10). The rudders were standard units without Mod 413, but the leading edge of each fin had been built up to a broad rectangular shape, the increase in area being approximately 40%. Side-slip and asymmetric flight tests were carried out on R9534 between 1 and 19 June, care being taken to repeat the same programme already carried out when the aircraft was fitted with the old style fins.

The new fin and rudder assembly was considered satisfactory although it was somewhat heavy on controls at the high end of the speed range, between 250 and 300mph. Under normal conditions of zero bank, with two engines cut, the rudder power was insufficient to allow turns to be made against the working engines at the best climbing speed or in straight flight. However, for asymmetric flight at minimum cruising speed for comfortable continuous cruising, ie approximately 150mph (IAS), the rudder was sufficient to enable straight flight and turns against the working engines, particularly if aileron were used to assist the rudder. Side-slip tests showed that there was no longer any need to restrict the range of the rudder movement and even when using the trimmers the rudders did not lock over.

An identical set of fins and rudders was then fitted to DK145, a B Mk V Series I (Special), and a similar series of tests carried out. These produced an equally satisfactory set of results, the only adverse comment again being the fact that the rudder controls were a little heavier than usual for the type.

The new fin and rudder assembly, officially Mod 814, was introduced onto the assembly lines as rapidly as possible, the production version varying only slightly from the prototype models. The overall height of the fin was increased by two and a half inches, due to the top and bottom leading edge corners being filled out slightly, and the combined trim-balance tab was increased in chord by approximately one inch. Retrospective modification of Halifaxes already in service presented a major problem but this was overcome largely by the magnificent efforts of the working party from 13 MU, Henlow. Composed of a warrant officer, five senior NCOs and 36 other ranks, they travelled from airfield to airfield modifying 225 Mk II and V Halifaxes in the remarkably short period of three and a half months. Within the next two months they modified a further 277 Halifaxes and in March 1944 they moved to St Davids where they modified a further 60 Halifaxes for Coastal Command.

Bomber Command, despite its growing pains, was making its new found strength felt. Between April and June approximately 11,000 sorties had been made over the Ruhr and the Rhineland, a figure equal to the entire efforts of all the heavy bomber raids made during 1942. Other targets were not neglected and on 19 July an attack was made on the Schneider works, near Paris, taking advantage of the brilliant moonlight to ensure that there were no unneccesary civilian casualties in the surrounding residential areas. A very successful series of photographs were taken of the raid by Sqn Ldr Earthrowe's crew from DK190, this being the first time a daylight camera had been used at night.

The Ruhr campaign drew to a close with a series of attacks on Cologne, four being made between 16/17 June and 8/9 July. The first attack was frustrated by a combination of bad weather and technical difficulties. However, the next three were all very successful and Cologne lay devastated from virtually end to end. Yet even this was to be nothing when compared with what lay in store for Hamburg.

Bomber Command's autumn offensive was aimed at a deep penetration into the heart of Germany. This, in itself, meant that precise target identification and navigation depended entirely upon the H2S equipment. The first major blow was, therefore, directed at Hamburg which, in addition to its importance as a target, had the secondary benefit of providing a well defined radar response on the H2S equipment. Between late July and early August four major attacks were made within the space of 10 days, approximately 8,000 tons of bombs being dropped.

The opening attack of Operation Gomorrah was launched by 791 bombers on 24 July 1943. It was during this raid that Window was first used. Dropped from each aircraft at the rate of one bundle every minute the diffused bundles of metal foil produced radar responses equivalent to a force of 12,000 aircraft thus effectively masking the genuine echoes. Not only was the ground based radar neutralised but also the Lichtenstein sets of the German night fighters. This did not completely nullify the fighters' effectiveness for the glow from the fires of Hamburg served to illuminate the bombers long enough for them to be intercepted. Flg Off J. Jenkins of No 10 Squadron heard a warning from the Monica set which had detected a Ju88 stalking his Halifax. Moments later the fighter swept in to make several rapid attacks before Jenkins' gunners shot it down in flames. The enemy fighter had scored several times during the brief encounter severely damaging the Halifax's tail unit and shooting away portions of both elevators. Cannon shells had ripped through both wings, the port side of the fuselage and the bomb doors. In spite of the damage Jenkins brought the Halifax back safely.

Losses among the 246 Halifaxes were very light, the total losses for the whole operation amounting to only 12. This figure of 1.5% was remarkable, previous percentages for Hamburg averaging out at 5.4% over the past 18 months. The effect of the next two raids, made by 787 and 777 bombers respectively, could not be assessed until 1 August when photo reconnaissance revealed that 74% of Hamburg's closely built up residential areas had been heavily damaged.

The final raid on 2/3 August was a failure. The German defences had been defeated but nature was not subject to man's impositions. Severe electrical storms and icing conditions badly disrupted the mixed force of 235 Halifaxes, 329 Lancasters, 105 Stirlings and 66 Wellingtons, forcing many to jettison their bomb loads over north west Germany or attack other targets. Enemy opposition was negligible and there is little doubt that the majority of the 30 aircraft which failed to return that night fell victim to the elements.

Mannheim-Ludwigshaven was raided on 9/10 August, then on 17 August, 597 bombers were dispatched to attack the experimental research station at Peenemünde, on the Baltic coast. Ironically, few if any of the crews knew the real reason for the attack, German rocket research was highly secret both sides of the Channel.

Operation Hydra was the first occasion on which a master bomber technique was employed on a major raid. Both No 35 and No 405 Squadron were among the Path Finder Force that night. Flt Lt Davidson, flying HR897:F of No 35 Squadron, later reported that the fires were visible from 150 miles away after leaving the target. Visibility was excellent and the railway lines could be clearly seen with one block of the buildngs split open and burning furiously. Another of the squadron's Halifaxes, JB787:G, was being flown by Flg Off J. Jagger who captured the atmosphere of the raid in the brief phrasing of his report.
'Visibility good but smoke screen down west side of perimeter. Identified by red and green target indictors. Red target indicators went down first and flares, white, with them. Two greens went down a little later followed by more greens. These were all well grouped between aiming points F and B. Own greens found this group and then two yellows came down almost immediately after right on this group. HE bang on the target indicator flares. Would have been useful but for the smoke screen. Woods well alight to south west of aiming point F. Fires close amongst buildings. One big sheet of flame went up about 0022hrs and also 0025hrs with billows of flame.'

The attack achieved its aim at the cost of 40 bombers, among them 10 Halifaxes from No 6 Group, three from No 4 Group and two from No 8 Group. The bombing emphasis now swung back to Germany and on 23/24 August the first of three heavy raids was launched against Berlin. The steady increase in the number of heavy bombers at last made it possible to prosecute a winter campaign against the German capital. Any attack on Berlin entailed a minimum flight of 500 miles over enemy territory and this initial series of raids was designed to probe the strength and efficiency of the enemy defences before commencing the main campaign.

Results were not encouraging. The first attack met with partial success despite dummy target indicators dropped by German aircraft to mislead the bombers but losses were high with 57 of the 719 bombers failing to return. Just one week later, on 31 August, 621 bombers set out again for Berlin but despite the precaution of a diversionary raid, night fighters were present in large numbers. This was the first occasion on which flares were dropped, from 20,000ft, to illuminate the bomber stream. No 158 Squadron dispatched 19 Halifaxes for this raid of which four failed to return. Crews reported less interference from ground defences going to and from the target and relatively moderate flak in the target area itself. However, searchlights were plentiful and went into action before the attack actually commenced. Particular mention was made of the new system of defence, '... consisting of continuous illumination of the skies above the target by intensely bright white flares. Crews were of the opinion that they were dropped by aircraft in clusters of a dozen or more at the corners of the target area with a double strip apparently dropped by rapidly moving aircraft around the perimeter of the area and igniting at about 17,000ft and lasting for several minutes. Enemy night fighters were very active...'

The loss of 47 bombers was even more depressing when the results of the raid were analysed. An unexpected wind veer upset the Pathfinder marking and most of the bombs fell 10 miles or more south of the city. The final raid of 3/4 September, made by a comparatively small number of 320 aircraft, achieved slightly better results for the loss of 22 bombers. While material results were meagre the psychological effect on the German population was most marked and the panic evacuation following the raid of 23/24 August was comparable to that experienced in Hamburg.

No sustained offensive was maintained against Ruhr and Rhineland targets during the actual autumn period but a variety of industrial targets were attacked at intervals. Kassel, an important engine manufacturing centre, was one such target which received two heavy raids during October. Flt Sgt McPhail of No 102 Squadron took part in the first of these, on 3/4 October. While circling to land back at Pocklington, the port inner engine fell out of the Halifax, JD467:V. McPhail still managed to make a safe landing and fortunately such occurrences were rare in the extreme.

While the squadrons continued to operate their modified Halifaxes tests continued to try and improve the performance even further. HR756 was set aside for these tests and incorporated the recommendations which had resulted from the Series IA trials. The most radical modification was the dropping of the inboard engines, the nacelles being extended aft of the wing trailing edge. The nacelles were then fitted with modified undercarriage doors

Above: **L9515, test aircraft for the mock-up of the Series IA nose modifications and extended inboard engine nacelles, resplendent in dark earth/dark green with yellow under surfaces and prototype markings. The leading edge slats, although locked and sealed, can still be seen.** / Flight International

Left: **The extended inboard nacelles can be clearly seen. L9515 ended its days as an instructional airframe, 4185M, at No 4 School of Technical Training, being allocated to it on 12 October 1943.** / Flight International

which completely enclosed the main landing wheels when retracted. The air intakes for the cabin heating system were removed from the top of the engine cowlings and fitted underneath the wing near the root. The four Merlin 22 engines incorporating Morris block radiators, thermostatically controlled radiator flaps and six-way exhaust ejector stubs were fitted, the propellers being three-bladed Rotol, Type XHF 53/W units. These were basically standard R7/35/54 units which had had their root shape slightly modified to allow Beaufighter type spinners to be fitted. Apart from a fixed tailwheel and the engine modifications the aircraft was externally similar to the prototype B Mk II Series IA aircraft, HR679.

The prototype B Mk II Series II Halifax, as HR756 was now designated, was thoroughly tested between April and May 1943. The cruising speed was only 9mph faster than the standard Series IA aircraft but the cruising ceiling had been greatly improved to over 19,000ft. The Series IA Halifaxes fitted with Merlin 22 engines had their boost limitation increased to +7lb for weak mixture cruising which gave a cruising ceiling of 16,000ft. Above this height, with throttles fully open, the boost fell off until at 20,000ft it reached +4lb. The significance of this improvement becomes clear when it is realised that the Series IA aircraft, fully laden, were unable to operate in the weak mixture range owing to insufficient power to maintain the minimum speed of 155mph above 18,000ft. They were thus forced to carry out the flights in the rich mixture range, with engines set at 2,650rpm and +6lb boost, resulting in a very high fuel consumption rate. There was very little improvement in the climbing speed but the service ceiling was some 500ft higher and the maximum speed, using +9lb boost, was 264mph at 18,000ft.

Short of putting the Series II Halifax into production there remained only two other alternatives to improve the operating ceiling of the Series IA aircraft. Either the airframe could be further cleaned up, such as the removal once more of the mid-upper turret, or engines would have to be fitted which gave more power at altitude for weak mixture cruising. Production of the Series II aircraft was impractical in view of the trials being carried out with the prototype B Mk III and its impending introduction on to the production lines. Further cleaning up of the Series IA aircraft offered little scope for the necessary improvement and the growing menace of the German night fighter force ruled out removal of the mid-upper turret. This narrowed the opportunity for improvement down to the engines and HR756 was fitted with Merlin 85s in June. These were later exchanged for Merlin 65s but by the time that the tests had been completed the B Mk III had made its operational appearance and retrospective introduction of the more powerful Merlin engines was no longer practical.

Specification B1/39 had been issued in 1939 for a super-heavy bomber but the emergency issues of 1940 had drastically delayed the development associated with this project. Although construction of a prototype was stopped in May 1940 the Air Ministry and the Ministry of Aircraft Production encouraged Handley Page to enlarge their existing Halifax design and the Company designation HP60A was allocated to this project. Most of the B Mk II Series II features were to have been included in the

B Mk IV, as it was designated, along with a new strengthened fuselage floor and an enlarged bomb compartment. However, like the Series II Halifax its necessity was precluded by the B Mk III.

Merlin 24 engines were tested on a B Mk II Series I Halifax, V9985, during July and a series of comparative take-off trials made in conjunction with DK145, a B Mk V Series I (Special). The use of V9985 was somewhat unusual since it retained all the features of the very early B Mk II Halifaxes; nose and tail turrets, beam gun hatches, two wireless masts, two navigational blisters, long chord radiator shutters and triangular fins. The rudders, however, did have the bulbous nose modification. By comparison DK145 was representative of the late Series I (Special) aircraft having been cleaned up and fitted with an A Mk VIII turret in a raised surround, cut back radiator shutters and the new 'D' shaped fins. Because of the drastic differences between the two the results of the trials were all the more interesting.

The Merlin 24 engines had a boost limit of +18lb compared with the +12lb of the Merlin XX engines fitted to DK145. In spite of the use of a higher boost figure of +14lb, achieved by using the boost control cut out, DK145 took 1,010yd to become airborne and 1,330yd to clear a 50ft screen. Using the same take-off weight, 60,000lb, V9985 became airborne after only 540yd and cleared the 50ft mark after 890yd. The unstick speed was also reduced by 12mph.

Other attempts to increase performance were made by trying to improve propeller efficiency. A B Mk II Halifax was fitted with two sets of Wellington Mk VI four-bladed propellers but these caused a reduction in the cruising performance. Further tests were required to establish the climb and level speed performance using a full set of four-bladed propellers. DK145 was again used as the test aircraft being fitted with four sets of 13ft diameter Rotol XH54 propellers which had an identical blade shape to the standard R7/35/55 propellers. (Prior to this test DK145 had 12ft 9in R7/35/54 units on the inboard engines and R7/35/55 units on the outboard engines.) The results showed no appreciable difference in the level speed figures but the weak mixture cruising speed was increased by 2-4mph. The rate of climb, at low altitude, remained unaltered but there was a gradual increase of up to 70ft/min at higher altitudes and the service ceiling was raised by 1,000ft.

Four-bladed propellers, Rotol Type R7/14B5/4, were adopted for use by service Halifaxes and were allocated principally to the B Mk Vs, regardless of which command they were serving. Their use on Mk II Halifaxes was restricted mainly to a few Coastal Command aircraft. DG235, a B Mk V Series I (Special), was used by Rolls-Royce for further tests with four-bladed propellers these units being later transferred to a B Mk II Series I (Special) Halifax, W7783.

One of the features adopted with the Series IA aircraft was the close fitting exhaust shrouds. Flame damping trials, with a variety of shrouds, had begun with a series of tests on L9485 in September 1941. The normal, unshielded, exhaust emitted a feathery orange flame, approximately four inches long, from the fish tail while the rest of the

Above: HR679 incorporated the modifications tested on L9515 but was fitted with a glazed nose cone to become the prototype Series IA. It was also fitted with Merlin 22 engines and Morris single block radiators with revised radiator nacelles. / *IWM*

Centre left: JD300:NP-G of No 158 Squadron fitted with Merlin 22s but retaining the original galley radiators and nacelles, thus making it officially a B Mk II Series I (Special). During a raid on Nuremburg on 10/11 August 1943 the crew claimed a Do217 destroyed 25 miles NW of Ludwigshaven. Between 30 June and 24 December 1943 it completed 28 operations with No 158 Squadron before going to No 51 Squadron. It was later used to test a ventral gun installation at Boscombe Down. / *G. V. Smith*

Bottom left: A close up of JD300 showing the revised nose design. Of the 19 operations marked up, the eighth is an icecream cone denoting a trip to an Italian target via the Alps. / *G. V. Smith*

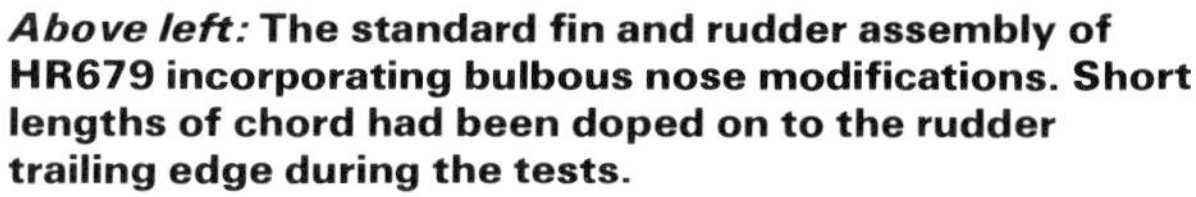

Above left: The standard fin and rudder assembly of HR679 incorporating bulbous nose modifications. Short lengths of chord had been doped on to the rudder trailing edge during the tests.

Above: The modified fin and rudder assembly tested on HR727.

Left: The experimental fin and rudder tested on R9534. Standard 'D' fins varied only slightly from this prototype form.

exhaust pipe glowed cherry red. The bulky asbestos tunnel shrouds, which were to have such a marked effect on performance, were also tested being fitted to the starboard engines for comparative purposes. Their adoption and subsequent removal has already been related, however, their replacement was another matter. With the knowledge of earlier tests on unshielded exhausts it was obviously necessary to find a substitute as rapidly as possible and two B Mk II aircraft, DG221 and W7823, were tested in October 1942 with anti-glow paint and a venturi flame damping extension respectively. Both items failed to achieve the desired result. A multi-blister, four fishtail, manifold was tried on a B Mk V, DG281, in May but despite a slight improvement of the flame damping qualities the type did not meet the required conditions of invisibility. The same aircraft was also used to test a set of close fitting shrouds which followed the outline of the exhaust manifold. These had already been fitted to HR679 and achieved the desired result but they had a marked effect on performance. The maximum level speed was reduced by 2% and the maximum economical cruising speed by 3%. The rate of climb was reduced by 50-100ft/min, the time to reach 20,000ft increased by seven minutes and the service ceiling reduced from 21,000ft to 19,000ft.

Regardless of the drawbacks, the shrouds were a necessary evil and entered production immediately. It was possibly as a result of the rapidity with which they were placed in production that tolerances slipped and badly oversized shrouds crept into the production lines. It was standard procedure for production aircraft to be selected at random and tested. Two such aircraft, a B Mk II JD304 and a B Mk V DK256, were received for testing in July and in both cases the exhaust shrouds were found to be grossly oversized. The ones fitted to DK256 had a butt strap riveted between the half sections of each shroud which increased the circumference of the outlet branch by approximately one and a half inches. Both Halifaxes were thoroughly test flown and the effects of the oversized shrouds carefully measured. DK256 fitted with its original shrouds, then with normal size shrouds and, finally, without any shrouds, respectively, recorded the following rates of climb to 16,000ft; 360ft/min, 400ft/min and 430ft/min. The appropriate service ceiling figures were 18,900ft, 19,400ft and 19,900ft.

Steps were taken to prevent the abnormal shrouds being issued to the production lines and the problem was rapidly eliminated, although a few still slipped through. A B Mk V, LK729, was received for routine testing in November and was found to be fitted with abnormal shrouds. The subsequent report stated that the sub-normal performance of the aircraft was due entirely to the shrouds. Without them the aircraft had a better than average performance.

These difficulties were completely eliminated with the introduction of a four-way ejector and shroud developed from earlier trials, this type being fitted to late production Merlin engined Halifaxes and greatly improved the performance once more.

By November 1943 Bomber Command had expanded its heavy bomber element sufficiently to allow the long awaited campaign against Berlin. Quantity production of H2S had at last been achieved and over 90% of the force were fitted with the equipment. Berlin was attacked on every possible occasion between November and the following February. Treacherous weather conditions and the necessity to restrict raids to moonless nights limited the number of operations during November and December to eight. The first was made by an all Lancaster force on 18/19 November but a mixed force of 395 Halifaxes and Stirlings raided Mannheim in an effort to split the opposing night fighter resources. The ruse was successful but cost the Mannheim force 25 bombers. The wind forecast for the Berlin raid was inaccurate and many bombers arrived over the target well before the Pathfinders and had to circle for up to 15 minutes.

Weather conditions occasionally favoured the Allies and during the next Berlin raid, on 23/24 November, the German night fighter force was grounded by bad weather. The attack was highly successful and losses amounted to 26 of the 764 bombers dispatched.

During November No 419 Squadron carried out some experiments to try and improve their Halifax mid-under gun positions against the intense cold encountered at high altitudes. A few nights later, on the 25th, the squadron took part in a raid on Frankfurt-on-Main and one of their Halifaxes encountered a major 'cold' problem which affected all the crew. LW243:Y was attacked by a night fighter which severely damaged it and forced the captain to jettison the bomb load. The port rudder and the bomb compartment doors were damaged but the starboard wing took most of the night fighter's cannon shells. The inboard engine was hit and the undercarriage doors blown off along with a large piece of the wing. More serious though was the damage to the forward fuselage, the perspex nose cone being blown off and most of the navigator's equipment destroyed. The navigator guided the aircraft home using an old map that he had in his bag but had to lie on the floor of the rest station amidships to try and get out of the icy blast which roared through the length of the fuselage.

No 102 Squadron also took part in the same operation. HX153:P, one of the 22 Halifaxes dispatched, removed part of the airfield boundary fence with its undercarriage but went on to bomb the target. On returning to base the Halifax swung badly to port during the landing but the captain, Plt Off Eddy, managed to retain control and pulled up without further damage.

The next night the main force headed for the same target again but split into two sections, the Lancaster force going to Berlin while the Halifaxes continued on to Stuttgart. The ruse worked and the German night fighter force wasted a considerable amount of time laying flares over Frankfurt-on-Main. By the time that they realised the main target was Berlin they were only able to intercept the last bomber wave.

The Berlin attack of 2/3 December was a complete failure due to winds varying greatly both in strength and direction from those forecast. Unlike the first Berlin raid losses were heavy, 40 of the 458 bombers dispatched failing to return. Foul weather over England caused a heavy loss of life on return from the next Berlin raid but the final two for the year were more successful, particularly the last one. No 76 Squadron crews reported 10/10ths cloud over the target but 19 of their 20 Halifaxes released their bombs on

Top: **Sqn Ldr Alec Cranswick's HR926:TL-L of No 35 Squadron, summer 1943. Cranswick was a pilot of rare skill and an outstanding PFF exponent. Sadly he was killed on the night of 4/5 July 1944, on his 107th mission and his fourth tour, flying a Lancaster.** */ C. Cole*

Above: **HR756 the prototype B Mk II Series II whose principal features were to have been included in the projected B Mk IV. The deep radiator baths, six way exhaust ejectors and Beaufighter type spinners and bulged mainwheel doors can be seen here.**

the sky markers dropped by the Pathfinders. Enemy fighters had been lured away to Leipzig and Magdeburg by spoof raids but the flak defences were more active than usual. Bundles of Window soon disrupted the radar prediction equipment and the German gunners were forced to resort to firing box barrages. Flt Sgt Burcher of No 10 Squadron had one engine of his Halifax set on fire by flak but held his bombing run for two minutes. Having bombed he then extinguished the blaze and turned for home only to lose a second engine before finally reaching an emergency airfield where he landed safely.

Emergency landing facilities had been set up at RAF Woodbridge which opened in August, the first emergency landing by a bomber being LK918:F of No 431 Squadron on 18 November. Flt Sgt King had attacked Ludwigshafen earlier in the evening and landed, short of fuel, at 2320hrs. Another aid, FIDO (Fog Intensive Dispersal Operation) was first put into emergency use the following night when four Halifaxes from No 35 Squadron made an emergency landing at Graveley.

The disruption of the original Lichtenstein night fighter radar by Window caused the Germans to intensify their development of its successor, Lichtenstein SN2. The old equipment worked on a wavelength of 53cm and had a very narrow search beam of 24° while the new equipment was far superior with a beam width of 120° and a wave length of 330cm, the latter not being jammed by Window. Range was also greatly improved but there was one drawback. The minimum range was 400yd which was beyond the distance at which visual contact was normally made. Further refinement of the equipment remedied this on later models. 'Flensburg' was another radar device which could be used to home on to the emissions from the Monica tail warning sets while a third device, 'Naxos', was tuned to home on to the H2S emissions. Equipped with this formidable array of radar aids the German night fighter force joined in a pitch battle with Bomber Command's forces in the new year.

Not surprisingly Halifax losses began to rise during January 1944. No 76 Squadron which had, until the end of the previous year, suffered virtually no losses for several months, lost six Halifaxes in the first two operations in January, plus two more through crashes. No 102 Squadron had an equally black start to the year losing 11 aircraft in the first month, seven of them in one night. Halifax losses in No 4 Group reached an all time peak during January with 11.4% missing out of 544 sorties against German targets and an overall loss of 10.1% out of 613 sorties against all targets. In February the figures fell slightly for German targets to 10.8% of 269 sorties. The overall figure, however, was halved with 5.1% losses from 644 sorties against all targets. The indication was quite clear and an order was issued permanently suspending all B Mk II and V Halifaxes from operations against German targets. In actual fact this only affected four squadrons, Nos 10, 77, 102, and 419. The remainder had already converted to the more powerful B Mk III version which had no such restrictions placed upon it. The ban restricted No 10 Squadron for about two weeks as it began operating B Mk IIIs in March. Nos 102 and 77 Squadrons continued to operate their Merlin-engined Halifaxes until May and

June respectively while No 419 Squadron exchanged its charges for Lancaster Xs in April.

One of No 419 Squadron's Halifaxes was apparently a little reluctant to leave. In the early hours of 22 March JD468:W ditched in the sea. The crew was rescued three and a half hours later with their Halifax still obstinately floating near by, gun fire having to be used to sink it.

Others fell victim to simpler things such as birds. One of No 434 Squadron's Halifaxes, LK907:M a veteran of 18 missions, was being air tested during the late afternoon of 25 February. On board were the crew and three airmen. At about 11,000ft a bird, thought to be a seagull, hit the windscreen directly in front of the pilot, shattering it and causing Plt Off J. Pollard some severe and painful cuts and bruises around the eyes. Unable to see he lost control of the aircraft and Flg Off R. James, the bomb aimer, took over and flew the Halifax back to base. The crew was given the opportunity of bailing out but everyone preferred to stay. With virtually no forward vision and hampered by the strong wind blast in his face James had to rely upon Flg Off Rowe, the navigator, sitting next to him to guide him in. The pilot assisted by passing instructions over the intercom from the rest bay position. The Halifax touched down and bounced high in the air but James kept the wings level until it touched down again. Bouncing twice more it swung off the runway, careered across the grass, over the perimeter track and a dispersal site, before finally coming to rest on a pile of rocks where it started to burn around the starboard inner engine.

All 10 on board clambered out of the wrecked aircraft, a little shaken but suffering from nothing worse than a few scratches and bruises. They were all standing under one wing congratulating each other on their miraculous escape when the ambulance and fire tender arrived. James received a well deserved immediate DFC for his efforts.

Squadrons affected by the ban did not remain inactive, but concentrated on French targets and minelaying. The latter function had been carried out more or less continuously since the outbreak of war. It had been mainly a Coastal Command function until 1942, when heavy bomber groups were gradually equipped with mine-laying gear. Mines suitable for this type of operation had been in production since 1940 and reached a monthly output figure of approximately 1,200 by the beginning of 1943, and 95% of these found their way into enemy waters. Gardening operations, as they were termed, required a high degree of precision for the actual drop and in the early days this meant a timed run, at a few hundred feet, from a known geographic point. Losses were initially low but as the dropping zones became known so the defences took a steadily increasing toll.

During 1943 trials were carried out which proved that it was possible to drop a standard mine from as high as 15,000ft. Due to the necessity of sowing minefields accurately aircraft were kept down to the relatively low altitudes of 5,000-6,000ft. However, with the widespread introduction of H2S during late 1943, crews gained considerable tactical freedom and on 4 January 1944, six Halifaxes laid mines off Brest Harbour from 15,000ft. The technique went one step further with No 10 Squadron dispatching 13 Halifaxes, on 25/26 February, on a

AM 11678

AM.11121.

minelaying sortie, three of them marking the route with flares and then illuminating the dropping zone before laying their own mines.

The intensity of mining operations may be gauged from the following facts. During 1943, 13,776 mines were sown in North-West European waters and another 11,415 in the first six months of 1944. Aircraft losses were 2.1% of the sorties dispatched in return for which Germany lost 175,000 tons of shipping over this 18 month period. The loss of such vital supplies from Norway and Scandinavia forced the Germans to increase their night fighter forces in Jutland at the expense of their home defence network.

The withdrawal of the Merlin-engined Halifaxes from Bomber Command by no means meant the end of their active duties and they continued to give good service in other Commands of the RAF.

Left: Standard production saxaphone exhausts which finally cured the exhaust emission problems. This shot also shows the galley radiator nacelle shape of the Series I (Special), complete with cut back radiator flaps.

Below left: The venturi exhaust system fitted to W7823. The outline of the earlier asbestos shroud fitting can also be seen.

Right: The production problems discovered during routine testing; top, JD304 (oversize); centre, HR679 (standard); bottom, DK256 (grossly oversize).

Below: The lowered engine position, blunt spinners and deep, forward raked radiator nacelles can be seen here.

7 Airborne Operations

The value of glider supported airborne troops as an instrument of war had been demonstrated by the Wermacht in 1940 and the British Government was quick to appreciate the lesson. In October 1940 a flight was formed for glider and parachute experiments. What the Airborne Forces Development Unit, as it was officially christened, lacked in experience was made up in enthusiasm and a wide variety of equipment which included Hectors, Tiger Moths, Whitleys, a Wellington and a Swallow. Specifications for four military gliders were issued in 1940 and the first of these, the GAL Hotspur I, was test flown by Flg Off Davie and Flg Off Kronfeld on 21 January 1941. The second and third Hotspurs joined the test programme in February and March respectively.

During January the mock ups of the Slingsby Hengist and the Airspeed Horsa were inspected and four months later, on 28 May, a very significant conference was held at General Aircraft Ltd. The subject of the discussion was the mock up of the Hamilcar tank carrying glider. The rapid increase in size from the eight-seat Hotspur to this giant in so short a time posed problems with regard to a suitable towing aircraft. Clearly it was beyond the capabilities of the Whitley and Flg Off Pitkethly visited Boscombe Down on 5 June to make a study of the Manchester, Lancaster, Halifax and Liberator aircraft as potential tugs.

The Development Unit at Ringway received its first Halifax, R9435, on 12 October 1941. Used for paratroop dropping trials it was modified by fitting a circular hatch in the bottom of the fuselage well. The first drops, using dummies, were made on 23 October. The static lines proved troublesome. One damaged the dropping aperture when the line and its pack streamed back and jammed under the tailwheel during the landing. The Whitleys had experienced similar difficulties and in November three of them were fitted with tailwheel spats while another, K7220, was equipped with doors to close over the static line attachment. However, while the spat was adopted for the Whitley neither modification proved suitable for the Halifax.

General testing and modification continued but the Halifax proved the most difficult for retrieving the static lines. Eventually a special winch was designed and fitted to overcome the problem. One further modification was made which was to become the distinguishing feature of this version of the Halifax. A circular windshield was fitted to the periphery of the dropping aperture and projected down into the slipstream to provide a region of still air. This allowed the paratroops to drop clear of the aircraft before the slipstream took effect. With this refinement the first live drop was successfully carried out from R9435 by three RAF parachute instructors on 10 December.

During November three more Halifaxes had been received by the Airborne Forces detachment at Ringway. A fifth, R9443, was received the following month and all were modified for glider towing. The towing rig was installed beneath the rear fuselage, aft of the tailwheel, and anchored to frames 45 and 47. In January 1942 it was decided to transfer the test flying programme for the Horsa glider to Snaith in Yorkshire where the manufacturers trials with the Hamilcar were also to take place. Service trials would be carried out at Newmarket. The prototype Hamilcar arrived at Snaith on 29 January and test flying commenced almost immediately.

By the end of May the Halifax-Horsa trials were almost completed as also were the Hotspur trials. The latter included double and triple towing by R9443. Two more Halifaxes, W7719 and W7720, joined the trials programme on 7 June, the emphasis now gradually shifting to the Hamilcar towing. It was not long before the results of the Horsa trials were to be put to the test.

At the time of the German invasion of Norway the Norsk Hydro Plant, at Vermok, was engaged in the production of deuterium oxide. Within one month of the occupation Norway's new rulers were demanding a substantial increase in the output of this valuable commodity. By 1942 their demands had more than trebled, a fact that could not be overlooked by the Allies. If they were to sustain the initiative in the field of atomic research then Germany had to be deprived of this valuable source of 'heavy water'.

An attempt was made to destroy the plant by a bombing attack but the nature of the terrain surrounding the plant and its difficult location made this almost an impossibility at the time. Accordingly, it was proposed that it should be destroyed by a glider assault force aided by Norwegian guides.

This force was composed of 16 volunteer parachutists from 9th Field Company RE (Airborne) and a similar number from the 261st Field Park Company (Airborne). The tug aircraft were drawn from No 38 Wing's detachment which had been specially formed for this operation with a complement of two crews and three Halifaxes. The glider crews were specially chosen for their experience, two being members of the Glider Pilot

Regiment and the other two RAAF pilots. Both parties were to be independent of each other and either was capable of completing the task.

Considerable practice was devoted to long distance towing exercises with fully laden gliders and this provided valuable experience for the operation. In addition, accurate radar homing aids in the form of Rebecca-Eureka sets were to be used, the Eureka sets being placed in an appropriate position by the Norwegian agents prior to the operation.

Given the code-name 'Washington Party' the personnel and aircraft, three Halifaxes and three Horsas, moved to Skitten in Scotland on 17 November 1942. Grp Capt T. B. Cooper, DFC, was in charge of the operation which was scheduled for the night of 19/20 November or the next suitable night during that moon period. Weather conditions were reasonable, at first, on the night in question but the possibility of a deterioration stopping the operation during that moon period made it essential to go ahead according to schedule. A near crisis occurred at the last moment when the additional flight engineer failed to arrive. The deficiency was rectified by the station medical officer who volunteered to fill the vacancy and Sqn Ldr Wilkinson literally handed him a copy of the appropriate instructions and then guided him around the Halifax. Half an hour later the MO joined Flt Lt Parkinson's crew and the operation got under way.

Sqn Ldr Wilkinson's combination was scheduled to leave at 1750hrs, followed 20 minutes later by the second. Each set course individually across the 340-mile North Sea crossing. The first combination made landfall on the Norwegian coast and headed on to the target with some difficulty, the Rebecca set having become unserviceable shortly before and patchy cloud made map reading very difficult. Unable to find the target on the first run in, Wilkinson attempted another search despite the fact that he was flying in thick cloud and unable to climb out of it. With the small fuel reserve diminishing rapidly the combination was forced steadily lower and lower by the severe icing conditions until, just north of Stavanger, the tow rope snapped through icing. Wilkinson managed to nurse his Halifax back to Skitten where he landed with his fuel supply nearly exhausted.

The Horsa was less fortunate and crashed on top of the snow covered mountains at Fylesdalen, overlooking Lyse Fjord. The landing, carried out in a snowstorm, killed eight of the party including the two Army pilots, four others being seriously injured. The party was captured before they could escape and the four injured members were executed by a doctor. The remainder were imprisoned until they were executed by Gestapo on 18 January 1943.

Flt Lt Parkinson's combination came to grief immediately after crossing the coast, the Horsa crash landing in the mountains just north of Helleland. The Halifax managed to clear the range only to crash into another line of hills further south killing the entire crew. Three of the glider's complement died in the crash while the remainder were captured and shot within a few hours.

The operation had been a hazardous undertaking from the start with a long sea crossing and a landfall in difficult and unknown terrain at night. Weather conditions were bad and had hampered both the navigation and the actual target identification. The operation was a bitter failure. The plant was eventually destroyed by agents of the SOE in conjunction with members of the Norwegian resistance movement.

Among the early squadrons established for glider towing operations was No 295 formed at Netheravon under No 38 Wing of Army Co-operation Command. It was equipped with Whitleys and a mixture of Hotspur and Horsa gliders. The Whitleys were used alternatively for glider towing, parachute dropping, leaflet raids and normal bombing duties.

In February 1943 Halifaxes began to replace the elderly Whitleys of A Flight. The Halifaxes operated for the first time on the night of 19/20 February, two being dispatched to attack a transformer station at Distre in France. Despite flak damage DK122 successfully attacked the target but DK123 failed to return. The supply of Halifaxes was very slow and was matched by a similar deficiency in flight engineers, consequently operational activity was limited until six more arrived on 21 April.

On 1 May the squadron carried out a full scale 'operation' when the entire unit, including ground personnel, moved to the new base at Holmsley South in the New Forest. This was highly successful and normal training had been resumed by 3 May. The basic glider towing training employed a fairly simple but precise technique. For take-off the tug aircraft moved forward until the tow rope was taut then the combination moved off, down the runway, in unison. The glider became airborne first, at approximately 70mph, with the tug still on the runway. Once both elements were airborne the glider took up station either just below or above the tug to avoid its slipstream. Whilst on tow the captain of the tug was in command, communication between the two aircraft being accomplished by means of wire woven into the tow rope.

While preparations for the invasion of Sicily were in progress the first substantial quantities of Horsa gliders began to come off the production lines. In view of the fact that they possessed a much greater carrying capacity than their American counterparts, the Waco, it was decided to employ as many as could be flown out to North Africa in time for the assault on Sicily. Operation Beggar involved towing the empty gliders 1,200 miles across the sea, including crossing the Bay of Biscay, to Salé in Morocco. From there it was still another 1,000 miles across the African mainland to the area of Sousse, in Tunisia, where the glider squadrons were assembled. The only available aircraft capable of the task was the Halifax, it being estimated that if the journey was not interrupted by either the enemy or bad weather, the combination should just be able to reach the coastal area of North Africa. Since No 295 Squadron was the only unit equipped for the task, it fell to them.

The crews were sent off on 10-hour cross-country towing exercises to try and provide some training for the operation. Meanwhile, a working party from 13 MU arrived at Hurn on 8 May 1943 to modify 23 Halifaxes to glider tug configuration. The target date for completion of the task was 1 June and despite the loss of two Halifaxes which crashed, the job was completed on time. Also resident at Hurn was the Heavy Glider Maintenance Unit whose task it was to prepare the Horsas for Operation

Left: Operation Beggar gets under way. EB139:NN, an A Mk V Series I (Special) of No 295 Squadron, gets airborne with Horsa LG723. This was the second combination to leave and the Horsa ended up in the sea following tow rope failure. / *IWM*

Below: North Africa, heat and sand. A No 295 Squadron Halifax moves forward to take up the slack in the tow rope and shrouds the Horsas in dust. / *IWM*

This picture: An A Mk V Series I (Special) undergoing routine field maintenance. It is not often remembered that most Halifaxes, like most large RAF aircraft of that period, spent virtually their entire working life in the open. / *IWM*

Beggar. No 295 Squadron collected their charges from Hurn and then towed them to Portreath, on the Cornish coast.

The position of this airfield led to a somewhat nerve racking situation since the runway ended on the edge of the cliffs. This, combined with the fact that the Halifaxes were loaded to capacity with fuel and ammunition, produced some rather hair raising take-offs with the combination disappearing from view and reappearing, when some two to three miles out to sea, straining for height.

The operation began on 3 June when four combinations left for Salé. The first tug, DK138, was forced to return due to the Horsa, DP574, becoming unserviceable. The second combination also encountered trouble, the tow rope parting and the glider ending up in the sea. The crew was rescued, none the worse for their experience, 10 hours later by the Royal Navy. The other two combinations reached their destination safely.

After this the operation proceeded smoothly and 14 combinations reached Salé by 14 June. Considering that the towing was carried out in daylight — a night operation over the distances involved was considered too hazardous — and involved flying within 100 miles of the enemy air bases in south-western France, the combinations had been fortunate in avoiding interception by enemy aircraft for so long. On the 14th two Focke-Wulf Condors intercepted a combination 100 miles north-west of Cape Finisterre.

Despite a gallant effort on the part of the Halifax's rear gunner to defend the combination the Horsa was eventually forced to cast off and ditched in the sea, the tug, DK130:EE being shot down. This time the Royal Navy was not on hand to effect a rescue and the unfortunate glider crew drifted for 11 days before being picked up by a Portuguese fishing boat. By a twist of fate two of the survivors were part of the crew which had ditched on the opening day of the operation.

Apart from the routine modifications applied to all glider tug Halifaxes, ie removal of the nose and mid-upper turret, local strengthening of the rear fuselage and fitting of the towing rig, the only additional item fitted for this operation was set of wire gauze filters to try and prevent the engines ingesting too much of the notoriously fine North African sand. These worked reasonably well but DK197 spent several days languishing in the blazing heat due to a badly fitted filter.

While some of the Halifaxes plied back and forth between England and North Africa others remained to assist in training the Horsa crews. The dynamic Grp Capt Cooper, from HQ No 38 Wing, not content in supervising the action from England, flew out to Salé in EB145 on 3 July. On arrival he learned that a Horsa had broken its tow during the trip from Salé to Kairouan and landed in a ravine, where it was considered a write-off due to its inaccessibility. Cooper, knowing the enormous risks taken by his Halifax crews to provide these precious gliders, obtained a Wellington and a volunteer crew for both aircraft. Landing in the narrow confines of the ravine he successfully towed the Horsa out. On another occasion, when one of the Halifaxes was declared completely unserviceable, he found a volunteer to act as flight engineer and flew the aircraft back to England doing his own navigation while the auto-pilot kept it on course.

Only one other combination was lost by the time the 21st and last Horsa had been delivered safely to Salé on 28 June, although it must be recorded that one of these crashed on landing. The last of the Horsas arrived at Kairouan only a week or so before the invasion of Sicily allowing little time for training with this type. The American Dakota-Waco combinations had also had only a limited period of intensive training and they found themselves handicapped to some extent by their navigation techniques which were inadequate for the task in hand.

On the night of 9/10 July a combined Anglo-American force was launched against Sicily from the six airfields at Kairouan. They were towed by seven Halifaxes and 28 Albemarles of Nos 295 and 296 Squadrons of No 38 Wing, and 109 Dakota aircraft of the United States Troop Carrier Command. Conditions were far from favourable with 30mph winds sweeping across the path of the force. Coupled with the lack of experience of most crews and the difficult nature of the final approach, the force faced disaster.

Of the 137 gliders released, 69 came down in the sea while a further 56 were scattered far and wide along the south-eastern coast. Only 12, part of the force towed by No 38 Wing tugs, reached the landing zone and one, a Horsa, came to rest within 300yd of the vital Ponte Grande Bridge across the Syracuse canal. By dawn the bridge was in the hands of the attackers along with a substantial number of prisoners.

For the next few nights a small number of SAS and reinforcement operations were carried out by No 38 Wing tugs but an attack on Augusta was cancelled at the last minute, just as the crews were preparing for take-off. Last minute cancellations were always a strain, but particularly so in this case since the Halifaxes had been laboriously refuelled by hand using four-gallon petrol cans!

Operation Fustian was the last airborne assault of the Sicilian campaign, the target being the Simeto bridge which controlled the exits from the high ground into the Catanian plain. This was again a combined operation using 107 Dakotas and Albermarles to drop paratroops, while six Wacos and eleven Horsas were towed by Halifaxes and Albemarles. Only five Halifaxes were available, Flg Off Cleaver's aircraft having been written-off and another was unserviceable.

The force set out on the evening of 13 July — a date which retained its bad reputation. Due to a break down in communications the glider force flew straight through a balloon barrage protecting the troop ships off the coast. A short while after flak began to burst around the formation claiming at least two of the Albemarles. As the second of these spiralled down in flames its glider turned for the safety of the coast narrowly missing a collision with Halifax EB139:NN. These losses were a tragic mistake the fire coming from Allied naval vessels who were being attacked by Ju88 just as the glider forces passed overhead. In the target area the enemy flak claimed several victims. Just after releasing its Horsa, EB139 was hit, flak holing the starboard inner fuel tank and putting the port inner engine out of action. Almost simultaneously a Halifax directly ahead disintegrated into a ball of flame from a

Above: DG396:QQ of No 295 Squadron photographed (probably at Kairouan) after a solo trip made on 27 June 1943. This was the Halifax involved in the running fight with eight Ju88s on 17 September. / *IWM*

Below: LL218:T an A Mk V Series IA of No 298 Squadron early in 1944. As with No 295 Squadron, unit codes had not then been allocated, the 40 Halifaxes on strength using individual letters from A to Z then double letters commencing AA. The aircraft letter can be seen marked on the front face of the undercarriage. Note also the wind shield for the ventral dropping hatch. / *J. Stewart-Crump*

Below: In March 1944 LL218 was transferred to No 644 Squadron when the latter formed from C Flight of No 298 Squadron. Coded 2P-N it was one of the six Halifaxes of the coup de main force that spearheaded the airborne invasion on 6 June. Later it was part of the Hadrian towing force which supplied SAS forces in Brittany on 5 August. This shot was taken during pre-invasion training, with a Hamilcar, hence the lack of invasion markings. / *IWM*

Bottom: Afternoon at Tarrant Rushton. Preparations for the final phase of the D-Day airborne assault by Nos 298 and 644 Squadrons; two Horsas, 30 Hamilcars and 32 Halifaxes. On the runway LL402:9U-F is hitched to the first Horsa. On the right, from the front, is No 298 Squadron's 8A-J then No 644 Squadron's LL331:9U-K (both still fitted with three-bladed propellers), LL301:9U-R, LL352:9U-Q, LL328:9U-Y, LL342:2P-L, then No 298 Squadron's 8T-G, 8T-H and 8T-K. All the Halifaxes and gliders are wearing full invasion markings. / *IWM*

direct hit. This was the only Halifax lost that night, its pilot was the veteran Sqn Ldr Wilkinson.

The operation met with mixed success. The gliders achieved the best results, 13 alighting in their correct zones although one of these crashed. The other four failed to reach the dropping zone either through damage at take-off or coming down in sea. Losses were light, apart from Wilkinson's Halifax only 10 Dakotas and three Albemarles were lost. The bridge was taken by a force of 200 men using five anti-tank guns, thus ensuring the advance of the US Seventh and British Eighth Armies in their drive across Sicily.

Although not a success from the airborne side, valuable lessons were learned which were to be applied in the impending European operations. No 296 Squadron remained in North Africa and Sicily for a further three months, for training purposes, while No 295 Squadron returned to England for Operation Elaborate.

This glider ferrying operation to North Africa continued for the next two months during which time only two occasions occurred where lives were lost although several gliders were lost, through various causes, two of them alighting in Portugal.

On 17 September DG396:QQ set out for Salé with Horsa HS102 on tow plus the usual Beaufighter escort. Three hours later the crystal clear blue sky over the Bay of Biscay appeared to be empty, the Beaufighters having returned to base. Plt Off J. Stewart-Crump, the flight engineer, was moving forward from the rest bay section when he sighted some tiny specks in the distance ahead. For several agonising minutes the crew watched as they grew in size and number until they became identifiable as eight Ju88s.

Just as the leading Ju88, prominent by its red spinners, fired a red and yellow Very cartridge the Halifax's navigator spotted four more Ju88s at sea level. The nearest flight of four banked around to starboard while the second group of four climbed away to port, gaining height for an attack on the combination from astern. The glider pilot very gallantly requested permission to cast off knowing that this would be the only hope for the Halifax. However, Flg Off Norman was determined not to lose his charge while the remotest chance remained and ordered the glider to remain on tow. A distant cloud bank had appeared ahead and the Halifax made a bold run for it just as the Ju88s turned in for their first attack.

It was clear that the combination had no chance of making the cloud cover but Norman still refused to abandon the helpless glider crew. The decision, however, was taken out of his hands by the unselfish action of the glider crew who released the tow (they were later picked up by Air Sea Rescue). At the moment that the Horsa dived for the sea the first Ju88 opened fire with its heavy machine guns and cannon. A moment later a flash of flame burst from beneath each wing as two rockets disappeared beneath the gyrating Halifax, two white smoke trails marking their passage. The other three Ju88s moved in from the starboard for a series of concerted attacks with the four Ju88s on the port side.

Norman retained the tow rope streaming out behind the Halifax, hoping that it might deter close range attacks.

Pushing the throttles right through the emergency gate to maximum power he commenced a series of violent evasive manoeuvres, the flight engineer calling out the attacks and the rear gunner keeping up a defensive fire. So violent were the manoeuvres that the flight engineer was hurled bodily in all directions, at one moment pinned against the fuselage by the *g* only to smack his head against the astrodome in the next moment as the Halifax dropped out from underneath him. He also had a fleeting view of the wingtips flexing most pronouncedly upwards only to reverse their aspect as the aircraft shot upwards again.

The tactics were effective and most of the enemy fire, including several more rockets, missed their mark. The enemy flight commander must have felt that the situation called for drastic measures for moments later he carried out a head-on attack. The high closing speed forced Norman to hold his course for fear of a collision if he should break away is the same direction as the Ju88. At 600yd the enemy aircraft fired two rockets which struck the Halifax as the Ju88 swept by in a blur of speed. A length of the starboard inner propeller smashed through the fuselage, shot past the flight engineer's legs, hit the gyro units and dropped on to his platform. An enormous gaping hole appeared in the starboard wing, making visible twisted ribs and the collapsed side of the main fuel tank. Petrol poured out leaving a white trail behind the wing while the stumps of the three propeller blades rotated jerkily. A moment later the engine cowl broke loose and disappeared astern, baring the damaged engine which miraculously did not catch fire. It was obvious that the wing was severely damaged, but Norman was forced to continue violent evasive manoeuvres. The second rocket penetrated the fuselage, burst inside with a bright red and orange flash followed by choking fumes. A large gaping hole in the roof helped to evacuate the offending fumes to reveal the devastation. Emergency rations were scattered, a yellow dinghy pack cover streamed out like a flag and dozens of tufts of woolly material from the upholstery of the shattered rest bay seats littered the floor sticking to patches of hydraulic oil from the burst header tank.

The next moment the area of blue sky visible through the hole in the fuselage turned opaque as the Halifax slid into the protection of the cloud bank. A quick check of the damage ruled out the chance of a landing at Gibraltar with its short crowded runways. The flight engineer's parachute had been shot to ribbons so the only course open was to head for Salé.

After a while Norman edged the battered Halifax out of the cloud and the crew were relieved to find themselves alone except for one of their attackers which was wallowing on the surface of the sea about three miles distant. The Halifax reached Salé and Norman received a well earned DFC for his efforts while Sgt Grant, the rear gunner, was awarded a DFM.

The last combination left for Salé on 23 September and thereafter the squadron began to wind up its Halifax operations in preparation for a change-over to Albemarles. During October the conversion was completed and the last Halifax, DK199, operated with the squadron on the 10th.

The expansion of No 38 Wing into a Group, originally suggested in August 1942, had been turned down. A further recommendation for this expansion was tabled in early February 1943 by the AOC-in-C Army Co-operation Command who controlled No 38 Wing but again this was rejected on the grounds of expense in personnel. However, when the results of the Sicilian operations were assessed it became painfully clear that the suggested expansion was indeed necessary along with a considerable reorganisation in order to provide the required facilities for training.

It was finally agreed that No 38 Wing be expanded to Group status with a structure of nine squadrons, four of Albemarles, one of Halifaxes and four of Stirlings. No 298 Squadron, the Halifax unit, was formed at Tarrant Rushton on 4 November. It had an initial establishment of 17 A Mk V Halifaxes and seven Horsa gliders. Ten crews from No 295 Squadron were posted in to form A Flight while 12 crews from No 297 Squadron formed B Flight.

Although training began with Horsa gliders the squadron's main function was to be centred on the new Hamilcar glider. The largest glider ever used operationally, the Hamilcar first appeared at Tarrant Rushton in the November of 1943 where training with this giant began under the guidance of Grp Capt T. Cooper, DFC and Maj A. Dale, DFC.

The Hamilcar was literally enormous, spanning 110ft and was over 20ft high, its empty weight was 18,500lb — nearly 3,000lb heavier than the all up weight of a Horsa. Designed specifically for transporting heavy equipment, it was capable of carrying a disposable load of 17,500lb which was adequately accommodated within its capacious 1,920cu ft interior.

Bad weather and other problems delayed No 298 Squadron's flying programme and by the end of January 1944 only a very small number of flights had been achieved. However, some idea of the operational efficiency achieved during this limited training can be judged from the take-off times accomplished in Exercise Co-operation. During early February 1944 11 Halifaxes, carrying paratroops, were airborne in $4\frac{1}{2}$min followed by three Stirlings and ten Halifaxes, each towing a Horsa, in 9min 55sec.

A third flight was formed on 5 February 1944, raising the squadron's crew strength to 40 by the end of the month. The additional crews were to form the nucleus of a new squadron. The weather, which had hindered training, finally cleared early in the month and a 24-hour flying schedule was instituted. Progress mounted rapidly and in the two month period ending March 1,200 flights were accomplished, including 400 at night. By 6 June this figure had risen to 2,800.

On 16 March No 644 Squadron formed from C Flight of No 298 Squadron. Half of the latter's 40 crews and Halifaxes were transferred to the new squadron providing an establishment of 18 aircraft and two reserves for each unit.

One of the new techniques that evolved for glider warfare was the use of a few specialist crews trained to land in extremely confined areas, near key points, to obtain a tactical advantage. A special training programme for selected Horsa and Halifax crews was therefore established for this purpose at Tarrant Rushton, under Flt Lt T. Grant, DSO. The technique involved the tug's navigator working out the course for the glider pilot to fly once released, the only additional equipment fitted to the glider being a gyro compass. Although simple in essence, only by constant practice could the required degree of perfection be achieved.

During this working up period the No 38 Group aircraft were fitted with additional navigation aids, Gee and Rebecca Mk II, in preparation for the impending invasion of Europe. Because the serviceability rate of the Merlin 22 engines was approximately four times that of the Merlin XX a decision was also taken to re-equip the Group's Halifaxes with the later mark of engine. Unfortunately, a shortage of Merlin 22 engines slowed down this programme and by March only 23 of the 40 Halifaxes had been refitted.

Three principal glider operations were planned for Operation Neptune, the airborne phase of Operation Overlord, the first of which involved the specialist coup de main force. They were to capture, intact, two bridges, one over the Orne river and one over the Caen canal. These bridges were vital to the success of the main operation as they would provide communication for the 6th Airborne Division with the left flank of the beachead forces. Six Halifaxes, LL335:G, LL355:K, LL406:T, of No 298 Squadron and LL344:P, LL350:Z, LL218:2P-N of No 644 Squadron, each towed a Horsa, the force being responsible for securing these objectives.

The force attacked shortly after midnight, the gliders landing literally on the approaches to the bridges and gaining complete surprise. After a short but bitter fight both objectives were secured despite the fact that the Orne bridge force were one glider short. It had landed eight miles away on a bridge over the Dives river. The six Halifax tugs had also been carrying a small bomb load which they used to attack a large cement factory in Caen, thus temporarily masking the real nature of their mission. To the tug crews' eternal embarrassment the cement factory was one of the few buildings left standing when the Allies finally took Caen.

The main glider operations of the day involved a force of 350 gliders, the responsibility for towing them being equally divided between Nos 38 Group and 46 Group. For their part in Operation Tonga, the first major assault of the day, both Halifax squadrons provided an identical force of 17 aircraft to tow two Hamilcars and 15 Horsas. The Horsas carried mostly six-pounder guns and jeeps while the Hamilcars carried 17-pounder guns and Morris tractors of the Royal Artillery anti-tank unit.

Weather conditions were bad with low cloud and heavy rain but began to moderate over the Channel and improved steadily as France was reached. Patches of cloud, however were still encountered well below the release height of 1,500ft. No 298 Squadron lost three of its gliders during the early stages, two landing in England and a third in the Channel. Heavy flak from the German coastal defences cost them Halifax LL348:M but fortunately the crew survived.

No 644 Squadron fared a little better, losing only two Horsas which both landed in England. The remaining gliders all reached their correct landing zones despite one releasing three and a half miles short and another breaking

Above: The mixed force of A Mk IIIs and VIIs of No 298 Squadron with No 644 Squadron's A Mk IIIs at Woodbridge on 24 March 1945 for Operation Varsity. On the runway are 48 Hamilcars with 12 Horsas at the far end. On the left are No 298 Squadron's NA344:8T-Q, 8A-M, NA347:8A-J, NA568:8T-E and MZ966:8T-K. Unlike the gliders, none of the Halifaxes now wear invasion markings as it was not intended that they should operate from European bases. / *IWM*

loose six miles short. The tragedy of Sicily had not been forgotten and all glider tugs wore the broad black and white distinguishing bands around wing and fuselage which identified them most positively.

Operation Mallard, the third and final phase of the day's airborne assault, was the largest daylight operation ever attempted up to this time and its success vindicated the exponents of daylight tactics. A force of 256 gliders was used, the principal aim being to reinforce all the airborne troops in France, 17 fighter squadrons flying escort. The composition of the glider force for this phase was reversed, each of the Halifax squadrons towing 15 Hamilcars and one Horsa. The Halifaxes towing the Horsas carried an additional load of nine containers which were released in the dropping zone.

This time all the gliders reached the dropping zone safely where a 100% release was achieved. However, enemy tanks were sufficiently close to hit the tugs and No 298 Squadron lost a second Halifax that day. It was forced to ditch in the Channel eight miles off the French coast. Very lights fired from another Halifax circling it drew a naval vessel to the scene to pick up the crew. Thus neither squadron lost a single man during the invasion operations.

Four days later both squadrons were active again over the invasion area, six Halifaxes from each carrying out a re-supply mission to the British airborne troops. Each aircraft carried in its bomb bay a jeep, a six pounder gun and six containers which were successfully dropped from 1,000ft. Experiments with this unique type of load had begun almost exactly one year previously at Stapleton. The two Halifax squadrons maintained these re-supply missions until 27 June, carrying out several specialist operations during the period. These included one by No 298 Squadron on the 17th, four of its Halifaxes dropping a mixed force of paratroops, jeeps and containers to the SAS troops in France. Another special mission worthy of mention was a solo effort by a No 644 Squadron Halifax, LL326:9U-N, which towed a Hamilcar loaded with Spitfire wings to an airstrip on the beach head on 4 July.

With the end of the re-supply missions both Halifax squadrons returned to their former occupation of training, mixed with a fairly large proportion of SOE, SAS and tactical bombing operations. On 14 July LL402:9U-F No 644 Squadron set out for an SOE mission crossing the Channel just before 1800hrs. Sqn Ldr Norman sighted a V1 (flying bomb) coming towards him and altered course to pass close to it, on a reciprocal track. Alerting Sgt Grant, the rear gunner, he ordered him to train his guns beam on and fire on command. Just before the V1 passed them Norman gave the order to fire hoping to lay down a field of fire through which the missile would have to pass. Regrettably, it did just that without visible effect.

Some idea of the weight of work undertaken by the Halifaxes can be assessed from No 298 Squadron's monthly report for August 1944. In addition to other commitments it carried out 156 SOE and SAS missions delivering 999 containers and 146 packages for the loss of three Halifaxes. One of the No 644 Squadron pilots came up with an idea for increasing the payload on SOE missions. By keeping the wing bomb cell doors open a double load of containers could be carried, strapped together, one on top of the other. The idea was soon put into general practice.

The two squadrons operated together again with their first Hadrian (Waco) operation on 5 August when five Halifaxes from each towed the Hadrians to Brittany as part of an SAS operation. Each glider carried a jeep plus three men and ancillary equipment. No trouble was experienced and the mission was successful.

It was during one of No 644 Squadron's SOE operations on 8 August that No 38 Group very nearly lost one of its dynamic leaders. Flt Lt Cleaver had been scheduled to carry out a drop but his bomb aimer and flight engineer fell ill at the last moment. Grp Capt T. Cooper volunteered his services as bomb aimer and Flt Lt Stewart-Crump stood in for the flight engineer. The flight went smoothly until the dropping point was reached where some doubt was expressed as to the correctness of the signal from the ground party. Cleaver left the decision to Cooper who finally elected to go in for the drop, only to be greeted by searchlights and a hail of flak from the trap. By sheer luck Cleaver managed to get LL312 away, without too much damage, and reached base safely.

The Allied armies continued to fight their way across NW Europe and by late September the First US Army had advanced as far as the Siegfried Line, while the Third US Army had established a bridge head over the Moselle. The British Second Army occupied a line along the Albert and Escaut Canals from Antwerp to Maastricht. The enemy had behind them three natural lines of defence in the Maas, Waal and Lower Rhine rivers plus the Maas-Waal Canal to ensure against any northern thrust by the 21st Army Group. Field Marshal Montgomery planned to advance over these three rivers and secure a crossing over the Rhine itself and into the Grave-Nijmegen-Arnhem area. The 1st Allied Airborne Army was given the job of capturing intact and holding the main river and canal crossing.

Nos 38 and 46 Groups' aircraft carried out all the Pathfinder paratroop drops and glider towing plus re-supply missions in the Arnhem sector. The US IX Troop Carrier Command undertook all the main parachute drops and in the Nijmegen-Grave sector were responsible for all tasks except towing the British Airborne Corps Headquarters, this being left to No 38 Group. The Eindhoven sector was also the sole responsibility of the US IX TCC.

Briefing and the marshalling of aircraft at Tarrant Rushton was completed by 1800hrs on 16 September and at 1020hrs the following morning the first combination rolled down the runway, followed by the rest of the assembled force at 45sec intervals. The formation, split into three parallel streams spaced one and a half miles apart, consisted of seven Hamilcars and 13 Horsas from No 298 Squadron and seven Hamilcars and 14 Horsas from No 644 Squadron.

Both squadrons suffered minor mishaps. A No 298 Squadron combination was forced to return after 20 minutes through engine trouble while a No 644 Squadron Halifax lost its Hamilcar through tow-rope failure. The glider fortunately managed to reach the coast. Weather over the target area was fair but hazy near the ground, however, the gliders from both squadrons were seen to land on the north bank of the Rhine. Two of the Hamilcars overturned on the soft ground causing the loss of their 17-pounder guns. Little or no flak was experienced and the Halifaxes returned safely.

Bad weather caused a three-hour delay on the second day of the operation. No 298 Squadron towed eight Hamilcars and eight Horsas and No 644 Squadron seven Hamilcars and eight Horsas. The flak was more intense this time and No 298 Squadron suffered damage to one of its Halifaxes, the navigator being injured. No 644 Squadron escaped flak damage but lost two of its gliders over the Channel, only one of them reaching the coast.

The third day's operations was plagued by the increasingly bad weather and the Halifaxes were delayed for nearly five hours. Finally, at 1210hrs, the first combination was airborne on the final phase of this disastrous operation. No 298 Squadron were towing 10 Horsas, the five Hamilcars that were to have been used having been stood down. Hence No 644 Squadron were left to tow a lone Hamilcar, the one which had broken loose on the first day, in company with 10 Horsas. Weather conditions over the Channel deteriorated slightly then improved over the Continent, but a haze persisted making visibility poor.

Enemy defences had improved greatly and German fighters appeared in strength. Due to a misunderstanding there was no fighter escort for the glider force and some of No 298 Squadron's crews later reported seeing several gliders shot down, but fortunately there were no losses amongst its own charges. Despite damage to two of the Halifaxes all the gliders were released over the correct dropping zone. No 644 Squadron encountered very stiff resistance during the final run in, several Halifaxes being damaged by flak and three gliders failed to reach the dropping zone, two through broken tow ropes. The third combination had reached the Group Rendezvous but the Horsa was hit by flak near the tail and dived towards the ground. The tug pilot, Plt Off McConville, dived Halifax LL305:2P-A with the glider in an attempt to hold its nose up but the tow rope snapped under the strain and the Horsa went straight into the ground.

Arnhem has often been referred to as a tragic failure and the ground battle is outside the scope of this work. However, all things considered, the airborne operation was not a failure despite the final outcome. During the battle the main glider force lifted a force of 4,500 men, 95 guns and 544 jeeps to a position some 60 miles to the rear of the enemy lines and achieved this with a considerable degree of success.

While the Arnhem operation was in progress, one of the Albemarle squadrons, No 296, was withdrawn to convert to Halifaxes, crews being detached in batches to 1665 HCU. Glider towing training with Halifaxes commenced in October when the first of the A Mk Vs arrived from Tarrant Rushton. These were surplus since Nos 298 and 644 Squadrons were in the process of re-equipping with the more powerful A Mk III version. The other Albemarle squadron at Earles Colne, No 297, also converted to Halifaxes again using A Mk Vs from Tarrant Rushton.

Both these squadrons continued their training programme interspersed with SAS, SOE and bombing missions until, in February 1945, their elderly A Mk Vs were replaced with A Mk IIIs. Typical of their SOE operations was the dropping of an agent in the near vicinity of Rotterdam by a No 296 Squadron aircraft. To cover up for the presence of a lone heavy bomber at low altitude a bridge in the city was to be bombed by the Halifax, as a diversion, immediately after dropping the agent. Unfortunately, part of the aircraft's blind flying panel ceased to function at an awkward moment and the Halifax flew right through the city, along the river, at 50ft before the instruments began to operate again.

In March the long awaited Rhine crossing was launched and all four Halifax squadrons readied themselves for what was to be the last mass glider operation of the war. The squadrons were paired off, Nos 296 and 297 operating a force of 60 Halifaxes from Earles Colne while Nos 298 and 644 moved to Woodbridge for the operation with their 60 Halifaxes.

The object was to land elements of the 6th Airborne Division on four landing zones near Wesel, in company with the US Airborne forces, to enlarge the bridgehead that was expected to have been obtained the previous night by the ground forces. The lessons of the previous operations were well appreciated and every possible aid to the precise identification of the various dropping zones was provided. Eureka beacons and compass beacons were set up at the various turning points and immediately prior to crossing the Rhine Eureka beacons and coloured strips with distinctive letter panels were to be set up as a guide.

The Woodbridge squadrons were split into two flights for the operation with Wg Cdr Law-Wright, DSO, DFC, leading 12 Horsa combinations and Wg Cdr Archer, AFC, of No 644 Squadron leading 48 Hamilcar combinations. Nos 296 and 297 Squadrons towed a combined force of 60 Horsas between them. On the night before the operation 50% of the tugs and gliders were prehitched and marshalled along the runway in use, at Earles Colne, for approximately one third of its length. The remaining Halifaxes and Horsas were installed on the perimeter along either side of the main runway.

All the squadrons dispatched their combinations at the appointed time. Weather conditions for once were propitious and the massed formations, composed of 1,500 aircraft and 1,300 gliders, presented an awe inspiring sight. Complete Allied mastery of the air, so vital to an operation of this nature, was evinced by the fact that the German fighters were conspicuous by their absence.

Two tugs of the Woodbridge force returned early with engine trouble and one glider also broke loose soon after take-off. The Channel safely behind them, two Hamilcars parted company with their tugs, through broken tow ropes, one over France and the other near Brussels. Near Goch a Hamilcar lost its tail unit and went out of control, breaking the tow rope and crashing.

Despite the aids a smokescreen along the east bank of the river made it difficult for the glider pilots to pick out their correct landing zones. The main danger was not the flak, which nevertheless claimed quite a few victims, but rather the falling tow ropes and the risk of collision. Apart from one glider of the Woodbridge force releasing prematurely on the west bank of the river, all the others were released over the correct area. Five Halifaxes from the four squadrons were lost through flak and three others were damaged. One of the Halifaxes shot down had already released its glider. No 298 Squadron had the distinction of operating the first A Mk VII Halifaxes to go into action, seven in all, during Operation Varsity.

Arnhem had brought home some pertinent points about re-supply missions and this time instead of one dropping point, six were chosen. In addition, three Halifaxes were specially equipped with extra radio facilities and acted as master supply aircraft to direct these operations. Operation Varsity was undoubtedly a success and marked a fitting end to a type of operation developed to a high degree of efficiency through the long and bitter lessons of experience.

The remaining few weeks of the war in Europe were spent on SOE operations, mainly to Norway and Denmark. However, two final, if somewhat peaceful operations awaited the Halifax squadrons. On 8 May, the day hostilities ceased, personnel and equipment of the 1st Airborne Division were landed at Copenhagen by a force of Halifaxes, Stirlings, and C-46s of the US IX TCC. Subsequent re-supply missions were maintained at intervals throughout the remainder of the month by No 38 Group.

The final airborne operation of the war, aptly titled Doomsday, involved the transfer of 7,000 troops and 2,000 tons of equipment and supplies to Norway by No 38 Group. The object was to land Allied troops, immediately following the German surrender, to occupy Oslo, Stavanger and Kristiansand. Planned to be carried out in four phases between 9 May and the 13th, the weather, as it had done so many times before, proved unfavourable and the operation was delayed 36 hours.

A storm front approaching rapidly caught No 644 Squadron's Halifaxes just before they reached Norway, forcing all but two to turn back. One landed at Gardarmoen but the other Halifax ended up at Fornebu, about four miles south-west of Oslo. Unperturbed at being the first Allied aircraft to land at this aerodrome, Plt Off Barr and his crew unloaded the jeep they were carrying and drove off in it to Oslo. The last supply mission, ending the final phase of the glider operations in Europe, was on 27 May 1945.

Above: **Operation Doomsday. Halifaxes lined up at Gardemoen airfield, near Oslo, during the transition to peace. From right to left are No 644 Squadron's MZ975:2P-U then No 296 Squadron's U-9W, P-7C and T-7C. The remainder cannot be identified.** / *IWM*

8 Operations in the Middle East, North Africa and Italy

The land battles of the Middle East, ever fluid in nature, had taken a serious turn for the worse by June 1942. Tobruk, that symbol of British tenacity, was tottering under the relentless series of blows from Rommel's Afrika Korps. In an effort to glean additional aircraft with which to bolster the already overtaxed Allied squadrons supporting the ground forces, Air Chief Marshal Tedder scoured the Mediterranean while Casey, the Minister of State in the Middle East, again sent a signal to Churchill asking for more heavy bombers. By 22 June it was agreed to dispatch two squadrons of Halifaxes to the Middle East as rapidly as possible.

Accordingly, 'detachments' of 16 aircraft from each of Nos 10 and 76 Squadrons were ordered to proceed to Aqir in Palestine. Great secrecy was attached to the move and No 10 Squadron's diarist records that the force was being dispatched for Operation Barefaced which was to be completed within 16 days. The CO, Wg Cdr Bennett, was told that the squadron was to be used to bomb the Italian fleet. The fact that no one in the Middle East apparently knew of the 'operation' leads one to surmise that 'Barefaced' was not entirely an inappropriate title. Upon arrival the two squadrons were to form No 249 Wing of No 205 Group.

On 4 July No 10 Squadron dispatched an advance party in two Halifaxes, Wg Cdr Seymor-Price flying W1174:G and WO Peterson W7756:L. Seven more Halifaxes, W1151:H, W1172:Q W7697:R W7716:I, W7717:J W7757:W and W7758:Y left the next day staging through Gibraltar to Aqir via Kasfareet. The remaining seven, W1170:U, W1171:X, W1176:Z, W1178:T, W7659:F, W7679:C and W7695:D followed on the 6th. That same day a conference was held at No 249 Wing HQ where it was decided to combine Nos 10 and 227 Squadrons and No 76 with No 454 Squadron for maintenance purposes.

The initial move was not without incident. Just after taking off from Gibraltar, on 8 July, Flt Lt Hacking was forced to turn back and crash landed. The crew was unhurt but W1178 was a write off. WO O'Driscoll was equally unfortunate the next day when he departed in W7695. Unable to locate a landing ground he was forced to ditch in the sea off Alexandria through fuel shortage. The crew, ground crew and passengers completed the journey to shore by dinghy and then proceeded overland to Aqir. Three other Halifaxes were forced to remain at Gibraltar, W1170, W1171 and W7679 all being unserviceable. They were still there when the squadron settled in at its new base on 11 July. The previous day the No 76 Squadron detachment had left Middleton St George, Sqn Ldr Iveson in W7672:E leading seven Halifaxes, W1144:Q, W1156:Y, W1161:O, W1169:S, W7655:C, W7754:F and W7762:D. Wg Cdr Young, in W7755:A, left four days later at the head of the remaining seven Halifaxes, W1148:P, W1149:R, W1177:G, W1183:M, W7664:T, W7671:H and W7702:L.

On arrival at Aqir all personnel were warned to be prepared for an indefinite stay which produced a certain amount of dismay. Apart from domestic arrangements, impending weddings etc, some personnel were not even medically fit for overseas service. Despite these problems the Wing began operations on the night of 11/12 July with a lone attack on Tobruk by a No 10 Squadron machine. The squadron lost its first Halifax to enemy action on 13/14 July during a raid on the same target by four aircraft. Plt Off Drake crash landed W1171 at Almaza due to flak damage sustained over the target, the aircraft being burnt out. Several Egyptian firemen were killed when a bomb burst in the wreckage.

Tobruk was to remain the main target for the next few months. Rommel's Afrika Korps, already hard pressed for essential supplies, were to be denied the use of harbours. Benghazi and Tobruk were the key ports in the forward supply line and while American Liberators attended to the former, Wellingtons and Halifaxes battered Tobruk.

The sudden and, to the squadron personnel at least, unexpected prolonged stay in the Middle East brought problems in the form of a continuous stream of unserviceabilities of one type or another. Hydraulic failures abounded and kept the ground crews busy trying to overcome a variety of problems with the minimum of equipment and spares.

In spite of the almost regular nightly raids on Tobruk losses remained low. No 76 Squadron suffered its first operational loss when W7762:D was hit by flak in the port engine. Out over the Mediterreanean, 160 miles from Alexandria, the starboard engine packed up but the pilot was able to coax the Halifax over the coast at 1,300ft, near Aboukir. He then ordered the two gunners to bail out and they eventually found their way back to base with the assistance of native guides. Unable to locate Burg el Arab aerodrome the pilot was forced to crash land near LG09, fortunately without causing any casualties.

These attacks were moderately successful but haze prevented any definite assessment of damage on most

Above: B Mk II Series I W1176:Z-ZA part of the original No 10 Squadron detachment. It was taken over by No 462 Squadron only to be lost through engine failure on take-off for an attack on Tobruk on 29 September 1942. The crew survived the crash landing. / *IWM*

Below: Fayid aerodrome 1942. A B Mk II Series I W1156:Y of No 462 Squadron has its engines checked. Lack of radio navigational aids and night fighter opposition led to the removal of the Lorenz Beam Approach aerial and exhaust flame dampers. In October W1156 and W7716:B were fitted with dual controls and sent to No 2 Middle East Training School at Aqir. / *IWM*

Right: DT497:E of No 462 Squadron undergoing maintenance at Fayid in August 1942. Overpainting in the area of the aircraft code letter has produced a highlight, obscuring the lower portion of it. / *J. Stanley*

Below right: A No 462 Squadron navigator ground-checks his equipment. The flight engineer's fold down seat can be seen stowed against the fuselage to the left. / *W. G. Russel*

occasions. Engine overheating problems were another headache for the already hard pressed ground crews and Sgt DeClerk's Halifax, from No 10 Squadron, was lost as a result of this type of problem on 5/6 August. Flak damage over Tobruk put the starboard inner engine out of action then, during the return journey, the port outer engine had to be feathered and W7757 began to lose height. The remaining engines began to overheat and he was eventually forced to ditch, the crew fortunately escaping by dinghy. Engine trouble claimed W7754 of No 76 Squadron on 30 August, the aircraft crash landing en route to the target, but again fortunately without loss of life. For these operations the Wing was allocated advanced landing grounds at Kilo 40 and Shallufa (LG224) the latter being permanently manned by Sgt Brinton, a fitter-armourer, and 24 airmen.

September augured well for the Allied armies with the failure of Rommel's offensive. Fuel, the life blood of any motorised army, was still critical and the Axis did everything in its power to improve its supply. Crete was a most convenient staging point for men and supplies, a fact not overlooked by the Allied planners. Heraklion aerodrome was a tempting target being heavily congested with transport aircraft and No 249 Wing was ordered to attack it in daylight on 5 September. Each squadron was to provide six aircraft but unserviceability rapidly reduced the number.

One of No 76 Squadron's Halifaxes failed to take-off due to a glycol leak and another, W1183, lost its starboard outer engine shortly after take-off and returned to base. No 10 Squadron also lost one of its number before take-off but the remainder eventually joined the four from No 76. The formation arranged itself in sections of three with three from No 76 leading, one from No 76 and two from No 10 Squadron in the middle and the remaining three from No 10 Squadron in the rear. Engine failure reduced the number once more, one of the No 10 Squadron aircraft from the second section being forced to jettison its bomb load and turn for home. The remainder made a straight and level run up to the target in perfect half span formation. The bombs were seen to burst amongst the dispersed aircraft and across the runways, causing several fires. The flak defences opened fire but failed to hit any of the aircraft in the first section. The reduced second section carried out their attack from 9,000ft and Flt Lt J. Bryan's Halifax, W1114:Q was hit by flak, going down in flames. Two of the crew escaped by parachute. The other Halifax, W1174:G was attacked by two Bf109E fighters shortly after releasing its bombs. Wg Cdr Seymor-Price managed to evade their second and third attacks successfully despite the extensive damage caused by the first. Cannon shells had ripped open the wing between the starboard engines while flak had punctured the tailwheel and starboard mainwheel, torn several holes in the fuselage and shattered the hydraulics which rendered the bomb doors and flaps unserviceable. In spite of the damage Seymor-Price brought the crippled Halifax back to Fayid.

The leading Halifax of the third section, W7679:C, was seen to go down with the starboard outer engine on fire shortly after bombing. The fire spread along the wing and several parachutes were observed before it hit the ground south-east of Castelli Padiada. The loss of Sqn Ldr Hacking and his very experienced crew was a severe setback to the squadron. Between them they had an accumulated total of 137 operations and were credited with the destruction of two Bf109s and a third damaged. Both of the remaining Halifaxes suffered minor damage from flak and fighters but returned safely.

The following day instructions were received from No 205 Group HQ to amalgamate the two squadron detachments to form a new squadron, No 462 RAAF, which was to be commanded by Wg Cdr D. O. Young, DSO, DFC, AFC. The No 76 Squadron diarist recorded the following comments before the unit lost its identity, '...since the arrival in the Middle East of No 76 Squadron... the 16 aircraft which comprised the squadron have completed 154 sorties without replacement aircraft and the whole squadron, both air and ground crews, are to be congratulated on this fine achievement.'

The squadron number may have changed but the priorities had not and Tobruk appeared on the target list with monotonous regularity. A particularly heavy attack was made on 13 September in support of the combined army and naval offensive. Fourteen Halifaxes took part, without loss, some attacking from as low as 8,000ft and one making 16 runs over the target. The ground and sea forces were not so fortunate and suffered heavy losses.

Engine failures still took their toll, two Halifaxes being lost on 29 September from this cause. The first, W7672:E, was being air tested during the morning and crash landed when the pilot was forced to feather the port engine. The aircraft was burnt out but the crew escaped. The same day W1176:Z left in the late afternoon for an attack on Tobruk but lost its port outer engine at 50ft. At 150ft the port inner also failed and Flt Lt Murray successfully crash landed five miles north-west of Fayid in the desert. The first news the squadron had of the crash was when Murray walked into the watch office to report it.

October brought an addition to the target list and the squadron turned its attention to Crete once more. During one of these attacks, on 10 October, Sqn Ldr P. Warner's Halifax, W1183:M, sustained a near miss while over the target. The shell burst very close to the nose of the aircraft riddling it with splinters which severed all the electrical services in the forward fuselage and put both outboard engines out of action. The navigator, Flt Lt F. Collins, was seriously wounded but after receiving first aid treatment continued his duties. The aircraft had continued to lose height and was down to 1,100ft before the bombs in the fuselage could be released by hand. Warner managed to coax the port outer engine back to life and by jettisoning all the surplus equipment possible got the Halifax back up to 3,900ft, at which height he managed to reach the North African coast. However, the port outer engine failed again and he decided to head for Abu Sueir but the Halifax steadily lost height, due to the weight of the bombs which could not be jettisoned from the wing cells, and a successful force landing was made 12 miles from Dikirnes. The crew escaped without further injury and Collins received an immediate DSO for his courage.

The stranglehold on Rommel's precious seaborne lifeline never ceased and between 6 September and 24 October the

Above: W7671, one of the original B Mk II Series I aircraft of the No 76 Squadron detachment. Previously coded H it has been repainted in Middle East camouflage and allocated the code letter W after being transferred to No 462 Squadron. It was still on charge in September 1943. / *IWM*

Below: No 462 Squadron's W1169:S lands amidst its own personal dust storm. A much modified B Mk II Series I, it has had its mid-upper turret removed. The front turret guns have also been removed and the entire cupola sealed over with canvas. Part of the original No 76 Squadron detachment it had completed 50 operations by September 1943. / *J. Stanley*

Right: S-Sugar's eventual replacement BB331:S resplendent in Middle East camouflage of mid stone and dark earth with night black under surfaces. The rear turret armament has been reduced to two machine guns, indicative of the lack of night fighter opposition. It arrived in the Middle East in May 1943 and had completed 26 missions when photographed. It survived to become part of No 614 Squadron. / *G. Carver*

Below: A Handley Page winch is used to load the bombs into the wing cells of this Halifax. / *RAAF*

Halifaxes carried out 183 sorties against Tobruk. The historic battle for El Alamein began on 23 October and, in common with other desert bomber squadrons, No 462 were allotted battle area targets in support of the ground forces. The first of these night attacks, which were to continue for the next four nights, came on 5 November. Enemy motor transport concentrations were the target and the squadron celebrated Guy Fawkes day in traditional style. Fuka, Matruh, Sidi Barrani, Sollum, Buq-Buq, Halfaya, Capuzzo, the list of target areas was almost as endless as the targets themselves. Nightly the Halifaxes went lower and lower in their unprecedented role of bomber-come-ground strafer. Indicative of their enthusiasm is that bombing heights which began at 9,000ft were down to 5,000ft at the end of the first series of operations and decreased rapidly as time passed. Some crews, not satisfied with 2,700ft, pressed home their strafing attacks from 1,200ft.

The squadron's activities were interrupted by a series of moves, first to Kilo 40 (LG237) from where it carried out a few attacks against Crete and Tripolitania after an enforced period of inactivity due to dust storms. Further moves took it to El Daba (LG09) then on to Bir El Baheira (LG167) in Libya from where it attacked Crete, before moving back to LG237 on 17 December. It then became temporarily non-operational while tour-expired aircrews, which involved about 90% of its strength were sent home and replacement crews brought in. Thus, partly replenished, the squadron moved to its new operational base at Solluch in January 1943.

Targets and priorities had changed somewhat in the intervening period and Sicily now received the squadron's attentions. Six Halifaxes opened the new tour of operations by dropping 29,000lb of bombs on the rail ferry terminal at Messina on 29 January. A repeat attack was made by seven Halifaxes two nights later when 40,000lb of bombs were dropped.

During a lull in the land battle General Montgomery began building up his forces for a further offensive and, in keeping with the policy of establishing local air superiority, the desert bomber forces began a series of systematic attacks against German held airfields. From 23-26 February No 462 Squadron attacked Gabes-West airfield each night. Reconnaissance showed that large enemy troop movements, mainly reinforcements were being made in the Mareth position, south of Gabes, and the squadron turned its attention to these collections of armour and motor transport concentrations. Similar attacks were also carried out against El Hamma, Oudref, Wadi Akrit areas.

During April the squadron's operational efficiency was gradually impaired by an unusually high number of engine failures. Replacement engines were not available on the squadron and on many occasions engines were switched from one Halifax to another in an attempt to maintain a reasonable number of aircraft serviceable. Obviously there was a limit to this process and the point was eventually reached where it was not possible to do any more switching. Finally 60% of the Halifaxes were transferred to 61RSU to await replacement engines. Supplies improved towards the end of the month and the squadron was brought up to strength again. However, a great deal of concern was felt over the comparatively short life of the locally overhauled and rebuilt engines, failures during the first 40 hours being common. In an attempt to ease the strain on the engines the CO Wg Cdr Warner, suggested the removal of the front and mid-upper turrets to decrease the weight, permission being received later in the month.

Attacks during May were mainly concentrated against troop and motor transport concentrations in Tunisia. A second Halifax bomber squadron joined the ranks during the latter part of the month. No 178 Squadron, based at Hosc Raui, was already active with Liberators and began to re-equip with Halifaxes launching its first Halifax operation, two plus six Liberators, on the night of 31 May 1943. No 462 Squadron moved into the same base at the end of May and commenced operations with No 178 Squadron against Italian targets. Wg Cdr Warner, No 462 Squadron's very popular CO, was lost during this period when his Halifax was shot down over the Mediterranean. The aircraft exploded and only the flight engineer survived, landing in the sea and being rescued almost immediately by a British destroyer.

The move to Hosc Raui was not particularly popular and conditions, already primitive, were further aggravated by torrential rains. The continued engine failures were also beginning to create a morale problem. Wg Cdr W. T. Russell, who took over command of No 462 Squadron at this crucial period, recalls the seriousness of the situation in the following words:
'We even had aircraft which, on being collected from the MU after a major overhaul, arrived at the squadron on three engines — one had packed in on the delivery flight.

'Operating over the Mediterranean under these conditions was not conducive to a happy, carefree existence. Invariably the flare path party remained on the scene for an hour after the last take-off to be ready for an early return due to engine failure. With a full load, on hot nights, if an engine packed in there was only one thing to do — unload and return. If you didn't it was a pretty good bet that the added strain on the remaining three engines would cause even more trouble. I still remember one night listening to one gentleman who progressively lost one, two and three engines. He was on his way back and there was a lot of anxious blokes on the ground, as well as in the air, before he limped into an airfield up the road having restarted a second engine to enable him to complete successfully the last few miles.'
In spite of these difficulties the Halifaxes continued to operate regularly. One of No 178 Squadron's had a spirited fight with a Ju88 on the night of 26 July. On the way into the target, the Reggio Di Calabria aerodrome, the Ju88 attacked from astern its first burst raking the fuselage of BB385:Q damaging the intercom and wounding the wireless operator. Continuing its attack it fired a second and third burst inflicting further damage and jamming the port elevator down. The rear gunner fired a short burst registering strikes on the Ju88. Then, as it closed in for the kill, the rear gunner fired one long burst and the Ju88 blew up, falling in flames into the sea. The Halifax managed to limp into Malta where it landed safely.

Night bombing missions in the Middle East had been handicapped to a large degree by the almost total lack of

Above: JP228, one of the fully equipped B Mk II Series IA Halifaxes that began to reach No 462 Squadron after its move to Italy and its change of number to No 614 Squadron in March 1944. It arrived on 28 April 1944 and became P-Peter but was lost on operations on the night of 21/22 August. Note the late model exhaust flame dampers. / *IWM*

Centre right: Ground crew salvage parts from the remains of No 462 Squadron's *Penelope Anne*, a flight commander's aircraft lost in a forced landing. / *W. G. Russel*

Below right: Maintenance between operations was a constant task in the harsh conditions of the Middle East. Powder-like sand filtered into every tiny crevice and metal, baked by the sun, burnt the skin. / *RAAF*

Right: A No 462 Squadron Halifax is moved into position to have its compass swung. With virtually no night navigation aids in the Middle East DR navigation was critical to survival. / *RAAF*

Below: Preparing for the night's operation. A mobile crane unloads bombs under the supervision of No 462 Squadron armourers / *IWM*

navigational facilities. For the most part it was back to the 1939/40 methods of dead reckoning plus astro navigation whenever possible. These problems had been a source of discussion at HQ Middle East for some time and Wg Cdr Russell rapidly put into practice the ideas that had been formulated. Selecting about four of the best crews he made them concentrate on their navigation techniques and on every raid two of them would carry nothing but flares. They were required to locate the target and illuminate it continuously for the duration of the raid which usually lasted from five to 10 minutes. Aircraft times over the target were also concentrated into this time bracket and crews now took a photograph of the aiming point, more to assist with the navigation post mortem than for target damage assessment. Results, and the squadron morale, improved rapidly. This applied also to the ground crews, some of whom had been in the desert for 18 months without a break working under the worst possible conditions. Anyone who served with No 462 Squadron at this time will recall the slightly unofficial but very effective remedial measures which were instituted. An unofficial squadron badge also emerged during this period, a very pugnacious bird wearing boxing gloves.

Representatives from Rolls-Royce, having visited the squadron, instituted changes at the MUs which greatly improved the overhaul of the Merlin engines. Other relief in this quarter came with the arrival of replacement Halifaxes fitted with Merlin 22 engines, 13 being taken on charge by the end of September. Some of them came from No 178 Squadron which ceased its Halifax operations on 7/8 September and converted to Liberators. The Merlin 22s produced an immediate improvement in operational efficiency and a rapid decline in engine changes. Unfortunately, one of the new aircraft was found to have a defective fuel tank, a similar fault affecting the entire batch of Halifaxes in the BB serial range. At 161 MU modified tanks were fitted and by the end of the month eight Halifaxes were back and operating regularly.

For every rule there is usually an exception and W1169:S was just that. It completed its 50th mission during September. It was one of the original No 76 Squadron machines and due to the keenness and efficiency of its devoted ground crew retained its clean appearance and reputation for reliability right through to its last operation.

The squadron spent the remainder of the year prosecuting its new policy of illumination and bombing, attacks being concentrated against Italian and Greek aerodromes during October and November. December marked the beginning of diversionary raids to cover mining operations around Greece and Crete, plus some anti-shipping raids against Suda Bay and Piraeus.

The Christmas festivities were barely over when orders were received to move from Terria, the squadron's base since late September, to El Adem. The move was hampered by a shortage of road transport but the squadron personnel rose to the occasion in true style. In most theatres of war captured enemy vehicles were usually taken over by a central authority but with No 462 Squadron it was a case of 'finders keepers'. The road convoy of squadron vehicles was almost endless in its variety of 'privately' owned German and Italian vehicles. Cpl J. Stanley, an instrument fitter responsible for maintaining the automatic pilots fitted to the squadron's Halifaxes, 'acquired' the first permanent workshop the instrument section had ever had during this move. A mobile caravan-type workshop had been abandoned on the side of the road due to the loss of its wheels. Stanley happened to be driving a semi-trailer with some space left on it and the next vehicle in the convoy was a mobile crane. A quick inspection and an equally quick conference and the instrument section had a workshop at last.

The bad weather severely restricted operations, only 46 sorties being flown during the seven raids mounted in January. Preliminary advice was also received, 19 January 1944, of an impending move to Italy where the squadron would change its role to one of target marking, thus becoming the pathfinders for the entire central Mediterranean night bombing forces. Several crews had been sent to England to learn the new technique thoroughly. The first of these returned during January bringing with them a Halifax fitted with H2S and a Mk XIV bombsight.

February 1944 was hectic in every sense of the word. Only 21 sorties were flown, diversionary bombing and leaflet dropping, but this was no measure of the actual activity. An intense ground instruction course was implemented to teach crews to handle the new equipment and, between this and the operations the squadron began its move to Celone in Italy. The move was completed by 1 March and two days later the squadron was renumbered No 614 Squadron, its old number being allocated to a new RAAF unit in England. Ironically, this change back to an RAF identity came at a time when the squadron was more Australian in numbers and character than it had ever been at any previous time.

Large quantities of H2S and Gee equipment were on hand when the squadron arrived at its new base and it lost no time in becoming operational again. Seven Halifaxes attacked the marshalling yards at Genoa on 11 March and despite the bad weather all bombed from 16,000ft. The next operation, on 15 March, was disastrous; four of the nine Halifaxes sent to bomb the marshalling yards at Sofia failed to return. Very bad weather was encountered and one crew bailed out while a second Halifax crashed. The other two aircraft were presumed to have been shot down. Three more bombing operations were carried out and then the squadron stood down to concentrate on training. Its new policy was outlined in the following directive:
'The squadron will become the target marking force for No 205 Group. It will consist of two operational flights of eight H2S equipped aircraft, each with a training flight consisting of two dual, non H2S, aircraft and four H2S aircraft. Squadron will be brought up to establishment in equipment and ground personnel, non-essential bomber aircraft will be removed and training flight will supply replacement crews. These will be above average No 205 Group crews with experience in night operations and they will be converted on to Halifaxes and trained in target marking techniques on the squadron.'
While training continued the first target marking operation was carried out on 10 April. Eight Halifaxes successfully

marked and illuminated the Plovidiv marshalling yards. Similar tasks followed at a steady pace and successes were enhanced by the extremely low loss rate.

In mid-May the unit moved to Stornara from where it continued its run of successes against a wide variety of targets. Oil was the top priority during June and July and no effort was spared to deny the enemy this vital commodity. Three of the squadron's Halifaxes acted a route markers for mine-laying operations in the Danube on 1/2 July, this somewhat devious method being very successful in slowing the movement of oil by river transport. Five nights and 10 operations later No 614 Squadron was called upon to mark Fuersbrunn airfield for a mixed bomber force of Wellingtons and Liberators. Nineteen enemy aircraft were destroyed and the remaining 50 immobilised by the heavy cratering to the runways and surrounding area. The raid was not without loss and in addition to 10 Wellingtons and two Liberators a single Halifax, JP287, fell victim to the enemy night fighters. The next day the American Fifteenth Army Air Force encountered no opposition in that area and a message of appreciation was sent to No 205 Group by General Twining.

Despite the original policy statement, No 614 Squadron began operating a few of its Halifaxes on purely bombing duties, these accompanying the normal Pathfinder Halifaxes. Target allocations moved northwards spreading gradually east and west during August and on the 3rd eight Halifaxes marked the marshalling yards at Valence, in France, for a force of 55 Wellingtons and 22 Liberators. A few nights later the squadron aircraft were active over the infamous Ploesti oil refineries in Rumania, the operation costing two Halifaxes and several other crew casualties.

Operation Dragoon, the invasion of southern France, opened on 15 August and the Mediterranean Allied Strategic Air Force was heavily committed in support of this battle. As a preliminary to the operation No 614 Squadron marked the docks at Genoa and Marseilles on the 13th and 14th respectively. The next day it marked the Valence aerodrome but the resulting attack was a failure due to thick haze which covered the target. Firmly established the ground forces made no more immediate demands upon the MASAF and No 614 Squadron turned its attention to other targets. The last five operations of the month were in direct support of the Eighth Army in Italy with three attacks on German divisions at Pesaro and two on marshalling yards, Balogna and Bovenna, in the battle area.

Losses were not restricted to operations and JN912, on a training flight from Catina, was forced to ditch in the sea. The Halifax turned on its back and the dinghy failed to inflate. One of the passengers, LAC Isaacs, and the wireless operator swam for the shore some 20 miles distant. Isaacs staggered ashore 19 hours later and alerted the Italian Marines who rescued the wireless operator. He had accompanied Isaacs to within one mile of the shore only to die from sheer exhaustion immediately after his rescue.

During September the squadron received its first four Liberators, all of the No 205 Group squadrons being converted to the type over a period of several months. The change-over was dictated by the fact that the Liberator would be more compatible with the numerically superior USAAF element of the MASAF. Halifax operations continued unabated and on 16 October 1944 Zagren East marshalling yard was marked by the squadron's first Halifax-Liberator force. Recognition for the squadron's Pathfinder duties finally came through during the month and authority was received for selected crews to wear the distinctive PFF badge.

On 31 October two Halifaxes were detached to assist the Balkan Air Force by marking dropping areas for SOE flights operating over Yugoslavia. This was the start of a series of operations in support of the BAF either by marking or by dropping supplies. These in turn progressed to attacks on troop concentrations and aerodromes and daylight bridge-busting operations. Typical of the latter was an attack by three Halifaxes and a Liberator on the main bridge and a subsidiary pontoon bridge at Matesevo on 19 December. The bombing was carried out from between 7,000 and 8,000ft and Halifax JP134 made six runs across the target dropping a 1,000lb bomb each time. The third bomb fell alongside the bridge on the eastern side of the river while the sixth hit the entrance to the bridge on the south side, removing part of the approach. The remainder hit the road badly cratering it. Sweeping in from 3,200ft the Halifax's gunners sprayed 2,500 rounds of machine gun fire into a line of 50 motor transports strung along the road and camouflaged with tree branches. Three vehicles burst into flames and several others were damaged. The same night six more of the squadron's aircraft, five Liberators and a Halifax, attacked the marshalling yards at Sarejivo West, again without loss.

The rapid tempo of operations gave No 614 Squadron little opportunity to operate in its intended capacity as a Pathfinder squadron except for three very accurate marking operations against bridges in Northern Italy in late December 1944. Duties varied mainly between bridge-busting and the odd supply drop the squadron rapidly developing a great talent for the former. Bad weather kept the aircraft grounded for 12 days during late January 1945 but at the first opportunity they were out again in force with a successful attack against the marshalling yards at Udine. The next few weeks were spent attacking targets in northern Italy plus some supply drops to Yugoslavian partisan groups.

Finally, on 3 March 1945, JP280 carried out the squadron's last Halifax operation, an attack on Port Marhamo oil storage depot as part of a diversion for some mining operations. The Halifax had left No 614 Squadron but it was still to be seen in the skies over the Balkans as will be related.

9 SOE Operations

The Special Operations Executive was formed to promote and organise sabotage against the enemy from within his own territories. The supply of the manpower and the means to achieve this end was largely the responsibility of the RAF. No 419 Flight, later renumbered No 1419 Flight, carried out this task most successfully, with its few Lysanders, from August 1940. Twelve months later the increasing demands for its unique talents led to its expansion into a full squadron, the unit being redesignated No 138 (Special Duties) Squadron. The Lysanders became A Flight while Whitleys formed the new B Flight.

Among the requests received by the SOE was one from the Polish Home Army who wanted supplies and equipment to be dropped to them. This posed a problem since the distance involved was far beyond the practical range of a Whitley. To overcome the problem a small number of Halifaxes was allocated to the squadron and the initial Polish volunteer crews began to arrive early in October 1941 on completion of their conversion course on to the type. Three Halifaxes were modified by the Airborne Forces Establishment as a trial lash up upon which the official Handley Page modifications could be based. One of these conversions was completed by 28 October for No 138 Squadron as requested by the Directorate of Technical Development and the Directorate of Operational Research. The modifications included fitting a circular hatch in the bottom of the fuselage well and a winch to retrieve the static lines of the parachutes. In addition a short faired mast was fixed, just forward of the tailwheel, to the underside of the fuselage to deflect containers that were swept back as they entered the slipstream. To protect the tail-wheel and prevent the static lines becoming entangled with it, a simple sheet metal fairing was wrapped around the front and both sides.

Operation Ruction, the first of many clandestine trips to Poland, was flown by Wg Cdr Rudkowski on the night of 7/8 November 1941. The aircraft was L9612 a modified B Mk II Series I. The load consisted of three instructors, and their equipment, who were to be dropped to a reception party, from the Polish Home Army, at a point west of Warsaw. After successfully completing the drop powerful headwinds were encountered during the return journey and Rudkowski realised that they would be unable to reach England with their dwindling fuel reserves. Instead he made for neutral Sweden where a forced landing was made, the aircraft being destroyed by fire after ground looping. The crew escaped injury and Rudkowski and his navigator, Flg

Off S. Krol, were back with the squadron early in the new year.

Early operations to Poland followed a route over the North Sea to Denmark, then along the Baltic coast to a point between Danzig and Kolobrzeg and then inland on a southerly heading. The shortest distance involved was approximately 800 miles to a dropping zone in Pomerania, while to Warsaw itself was 1,000 miles. The Warsaw flights, with their round trip of 2,000 miles, were barely within the Halifax's range, even with long range tanks, if a margin for emergencies was to be allowed. Payload suffered accordingly and was reduced to approximately 2,400lb.

Typical of the extremes involved was the Polish attachment's third operation to Poland on 6 January 1942. Foul weather existed for most of the journey and the round trip took 14 hours, the Halifax landing with virtually dry tanks. February was accompanied by its usual winter savagery and on several occasions crews were forced to return early due to severe icing conditions. The weather improved in March and operations commenced again and continued until May when a temporary halt had to be imposed due to the short summer nights.

During March the squadron had moved, along with its Polish attachment, to Tempsford in company with the second Special Duties squadron, No 161, which formed in February. The nucleus of its personnel gained their initial experience within No 138 Squadron. The activities of the Polish attachment were not confined solely to PHA needs and they also carried out supply drops to Norway, Austria and Czechoslovakia. It was during an operation over Austria, on 20 April, that the Poles lost their first crew.

In September the longer nights allowed a resumption of supply flights to Poland. The suitability of the Halifax for SOE operations was exploited further as soon as sufficient aircraft could be diverted from the main Bomber Command priorities. No 161 Squadron received its first, W1046, on 6 October and two more on the 18th. The use of heavy bombers for SOE operations was still something of a luxury and both squadrons were required to assist the main bombing offensive when not engaged in their clandestine duties. A further duty fell to them with the formation of No 511 Squadron in October 1942. This was a transport squadron and came into being at a time when every possible unit capable of undertaking transport duties was engaged in ferrying supplies to North Africa in support of the forthcoming British offensive in Libya. Due to a shortage of Liberators the Halifaxes were attached to temporarily fill the gap, W1229, DT542 and DT543 from No 138 Squadron arriving at Lyneham on 2 December. The situation continued for approximately six months, the Halifaxes being used principally on the supply run to the Mediterranean. No 161 Squadron's Halifaxes joined the operation when DG244:Y and DG245:W were dispatched to the Middle East, via Malta, on 6 December.

Even transport duties were fraught with danger and the Polish attachment lost Flg Off Dobromirski and his crew in DT542 at Malta on 17 December. The Halifaxes were attached to No 511 Squadron only for specific flights, returning to their normal duties between trips.

SOE operations by No 161 Squadron using Halifaxes, which now equipped B Flight, were started on the night of 14/15 January 1943. The summary for the month of January is fairly indicative of the normal type of SOE operations and the margin of success involved. Out of 16 operations three were completed, five partly completed, five not completed due to no reception committee at the dropping point, two were abandoned and one Halifax failed to return. Each trip usually involved more than one task and the composition of the loads varied greatly. For example on No 161 Squadron's first operation, Flt Lt Prior's DG245 carried two agents, 15 pigeons and four containers of coffee. Four hours after take off he returned to base having mapread his way across France at 1,500ft to the dropping point only to run into thick cloud which extended right down to ground level. By contrast, on the night of 25/26 January, the same crew and aircraft left Tempsford at 2203hrs with a load of six containers, leaflets, two agents (more commonly known as 'Joes'), and a package. They crossed the French coast at Cabourg at a height of 2,000ft and set course for Loire. Having located it they then mapread to Givors and from there to the appointed dropping point. The reception party flashed its coded signal and the Halifax released its six containers from 1,000ft, these being seen to drop close to the ground party. Phase one of the mission completed, Prior headed DG245 towards the next dropping point, mapreading at low level all the way. Having positively identified the pinpoint, the 'Joes' and the parcel were dropped from 800ft.

The Halifax landed back at base at 0528hrs after a trip of nearly seven and a half hours, mostly at low level over occupied territory, and relying mainly upon the crew's ability to mapread at night.

This squadron's first loss also followed what was to become a familiar pattern. DG285:X departed for a mission over France on the night of 15/16 January, the load consisting of four containers, one parcel, 20 pigeons and some leaflets. The next day a message was received from the French underground that a four engined bomber had been found burnt out four miles south of Rennes. The bodies of the seven crew members were amongst the wreckage. It was not determined whether the Halifax had fallen to flak or fighters but in either case the low altitude at which the aircraft operated gave little hope of escape by parachute.

Operations into Poland became steadily more hazardous and the Polish contingent of No 138 Squadron suffered a disastrous series of losses in two successive operations,

seven Halifaxes out of 16 being shot down. Those that returned were so badly damaged that they had to be returned to the manufacturers for extensive repairs. Only two fully serviceable Halifaxes remained available. As a result of these heavy losses suffered in early 1943 the old route was abandoned and a more northerly one, over Sweden, selected. This increased the distance involved by up to 160 miles which meant that only during exceptionally good weather, and with great difficulty, could the Polish manned Halifaxes keep up their hazardous supply runs.

Early 1943 brought a small expansion of the SOE force and No 1575 (SD) Flight was formed at Tempsford on 21 May. It used a nucleus of officers from No 161 Squadron and was equipped with four Halifaxes and two Venturas. This small unit was posted to North-West Africa to undertake operations in the Mediterranean area. The first two Halifaxes, EB140 and EB141, departed for Maison Blanche on 11 June. EB142 and EB143 followed eight days later by which time the other two Halifaxes had carried out the unit's first operations, over Sardinia and Corsica respectively, from their base at Blida on 13 June. Although the unit confined its operations mainly to Corsica, Sardinia and Italy, occasional trips were made over southern France, EB141 making the first of these on 19 June.

On 6 August EB141 crashed, fortunately without loss of life, and just one month later, on 7 September, Ventura AE881 failed to return from an operation. Two further Halifaxes were lost in crashes during the brief life of this unit, EB197 on 9 September and EB188 on the 20th, but again fortunately without loss of life. Two days later the flight was disbanded and all personnel and aircraft posted to the newly formed No 624 Squadron.

Another SOE squadron already existed in the Middle East. No 148 Squadron, a Wellington equipped bomber unit, had four Liberators on its charge, AL510:W AL506:X, AL509:Y and AL530:Z. These Liberators were engaged in SOE operations and continued their task as an independent unit after the squadron was disbanded in December 1942. No 148 Squadron was resurrected as a Special Duties unit and reabsorbed the four Liberators, the first Halifaxes arriving on 18 February. By 13 March the squadron had moved to its new base at Gambut dispatching the first sorties, HR680:D and Liberator AL510, three days later. The Liberators were to prove a useful addition since the squadron had only a small number of Halifaxes, 10, and a replacement priority of one per month.

Another move took the squadron to Derna on 3 April and a very successful series of operations were carried out from there over Greece and the Balkans. Reports received from the partisan forces gave high praise to the almost uncanny accuracy of these supply drops.

Like most Middle East-based squadrons living conditions for No 148 were poor and the supply of spares, containers, parachutes etc was far from satisfactory. Not to be overcome by such difficulties, ground crews became very adept at working near miracles to keep the precious supply of Halifaxes available. The following account is typical of this ingenuity but by no means an isolated case.

On 15 June 1943 a Halifax was brought in with damage

to the fuselage, wing and tailplane on the port side. The main box formers had been damaged and normally the aircraft should have been transferred to 161 MU at Fayid. This would have meant losing the Halifax for at least a week at the peak of the moon period which was the time of maximum activity. The engineering officer, Plt Off Fuller, undertook to have the aircraft serviceable within three days. The ground crew were very keen to tackle the job and rigged up temporary lights using old car headlamps and starter batteries. New stringers were made from sheet metal and, as no salt bath was available, the metal was normalised by blow lamp and oil. A rudder was taken from another Halifax which had already lost its engines to keep three other Halifaxes flying. The repairs to the fuselage and wing took 863 rivets and by working double shifts, day and night, the Halifax was fully serviceable within 36 hours. The normal routine 40-hour inspection had also been carried out at the same time.

Despite such problems the squadron kept up a steady series of operations and during August delivered, to the partisan forces, 1,957 containers and 2,079 packages plus 70 agents. The total weight of supplies was just short of 264 tons. Allied intelligence placed considerable value on these operations, estimating that to counter them 50,000 Germans were immobilised in Greece, Albania and Yugoslavia.

After moving to Tocra on 1 September No 148's activities for the month consisted of leaflet raids over Tripolis, Novplion, Argos, Xylokastron, Lamia, Volos, Larissa, Salonika and Athens. While the danger from night fighters and flak was less acute in operations over Greece and Yugoslavia, crews faced additional hazards from both weather and terrain. Accurate drops to partisan forces often meant flying into deep valleys between mountain peaks. Wg Cdr Blackburn had a particularly frightening experience on 19 October whilst dropping containers at low altitude in the Greek mountains. One container hung up but the parachute opened pulling HR680 into a sudden nose dive. Blackburn managed to pull the Halifax's nose up in time and turned away, out over the Gulf of Corinth, the parachute finally pulling the container and the bomb rack free. The parachute then became entangled in the tail unit before finally parting company. Undeterred, Blackburn returned to the dropping point and completed his mission.

Dangers from weather were always present. WO Fortune was flying BB344 through mountainous country in foul weather on the night of 10 December. Just as he was changing places with the second pilot the Halifax entered a vicious down draft which turned it over on its back. The entire crew ended up on the ceiling along with some incendiary flares which burst into flame and set fire to the surrounding kit bags and the fuselage. Grabbing the control column, Fortune heaved back on it as best he could from his unusual position. As the speed built up he forced full aileron on and managed to roll the Halifax out of its inverted dive at a height of 4,000ft. The surrounding mountains towered another 4,000ft into the night sky. The fire extinguished and all the burning kit bags jettisoned Fortune continued on to the dropping zone but failed to locate the reception committee. Returning to base very short of petrol he made an emergency landing in a strong crosswind, the Halifax swinging badly. Due to the change of attitude and lack of petrol the port engines did not respond and the Halifax ran off the runway, pulverised a parked Spitfire, turned over on its back and burst into flames. Miraculously, the crew escaped without serious injury.

The Middle East-based SOE force gained strength with the arrival of No 1586 (SD) Flight at Tunis in November. This unit, with its establishment of 10 crews, three Halifaxes and three Liberators, was Polish in its entirety. The Polish element of No 138 Squadron had received a boost when No 301 (Polish) Squadron was disbanded on 7 April 1943, some of the personnel being transferred to its strength. This provided sufficient crews for the Poles to form a new unit, No 301 (SD) Flight, in July. The difficulties of operations to Poland was partly alleviated by the allocation, in October, of three Liberators which had a greater range than the Halifax. This small number was insufficient to cope with the work load and it was decided to transfer the flight to Italy, the Allied invasion having made suitable bases available. For security reasons the flight's number was changed to No 1586 (SD) Flight.

No 1575 Flight's successor, No 624 (SD) Squadron, formed at Blida on 7 September and begin operations on the night of 22 September, EB154:A going to Italy and BB444:D and EB196 going to Corsica. The squadron dispatched a detachment to its advanced base at Protville on 1 October. Three Halifaxes from No 138 Squadron joined the No 624 Squadron machines at this base to carry out a very special secret mission before returning to England on 11 October. Two ground crews moved to Malta with EB197 on 15 October for an operation over Czechoslovakia but two days later it was replaced by EB154, the former being due for an inspection.

The No 624 Squadron detachment moved to Sidi Amor on 16 October continuing to operate from this base until the whole squadron finally moved to Brindisi, via Tocra, in late December. With No 1586 Flight it became part of No 334 Wing. Operations resumed on 4 January 1944, and 93 missions were carried out by the end of the month 72.5% being successful. The operations were a mixture of leaflet drops over Yugoslavia, Albania and Italy plus some agent and supply drops. The squadron suffered its first loss on 1 February when BB444 crashed at the dropping point, only the rear gunner surviving.

A change of policy occurred during February and No 624 Squadron was ordered back to its old base, the first aircraft leaving for Blida on the 8th. Once established again the squadron concentrated the remainder of its wartime operations over France. Its place at Brindisi was filled by No 148 Squadron which moved in from Tocra on 22 January. In conjunction with No 1586 Flight it concentrated its operations over the Balkans and central Europe. Arms drops were made in increasing numbers to Poland.

One of No 148 Squadron's earliest operations from Italy involved a large supply drop to partisan forces in Yugoslavia. The original dropping point was overrun by the Germans late in the day and a new one was nominated 15 miles away. Eleven Halifaxes were dispatched and the first six completed their task successfully. Plt Off Leleu was next and having guided JP239:C up to the dropping point began to unload his containers. At this point he saw other parachutes showering down on the target and accompanied by coloured parachute flares. Looking up he saw several aircraft overhead with their navigation lights on. It was only then that he realised that he was caught in the middle of a German paratroop attack and, in is own words, 'got the hell out of there fast'. The remaining Halifaxes reported no reception lights when they arrived.

During the early part of 1944 most of the SOE squadrons began to receive Mk II or V Series IA Halifaxes to replace their ageing Series I (Special) machines. Most SOE Halifaxes also carried reduced crews but those operating with No 1586 Flight were drastically reduced to two pilots, a navigator and a dispatcher, possibly in an effort to keep payloads as high as possible. Loads varied but on an average the gross disposable load was around 7,000lb-7,4000lb compared with 5,000lb for the Liberators. A typical load is shown broken down as follows:

15 containers   4,624lb gross, 2,824lb nett
29 packages   2,058lb gross, 1,458lb nett
Nickles   230lb gross,   230lb nett
Total disposable gross load 6,912lb

The number of agents averaged two or three but was occasionally as high as five. By contrast, No 624 Squadron operating over France carried up to 15 agents at a time.

During the early months of 1944, No 624 Squadron increased its activities over France, the number of missions per night varying between 12 and 14 and occasionally going as high as 19. The loss rate remained encouragingly low. It also undertook a series of paratroop tasks for the USAAF during May which earned a letter of appreciation from General Ira C. Eaker.

On 15 July the squadron learned that it was to convert to Stirlings and Wg Cdr Stanbury collected the first of these from 144 MU on the 28th. Eight Stirlings were on charge by 19 July but despite conversion training the Halifaxes continued to operate regularly over France. However, as new Stirling crews arrived the surplus Halifax crews were transferred to No 148 Squadron. The first mixed Stirling Halifax operation was flown on the night of 29 July and by August the squadron was fully operational with Stirlings. The last Halifax mission was carried out by Flg Off F. Driscoll in JN896 which failed to return on 13 August.

The short summer nights had restricted the activities of the Brindisi based Halifaxes and drops were made to Yugoslavia and northern Italy only. Losses were normally very small on an average although No 148 Squadron lost four Halifaxes on 3 July. After this losses, still small in number, became consistent and were related directly to the increased Axis defences and the steadily worsening weather conditions. But worse was yet to come.

On 1 August 1944, the Warsaw uprising began and the PHA came out into the open seizing a large section of the city from the German occupation forces. This action caught the SOE forces off balance at first and it was not until the night of the 4th that a major supply effort could be made. Both No 148 Squadron and No 1586 Flight flew missions to Warsaw that night. Conditions were catastrophic. Dense smoke from the burning city billowed up obscuring the flares of the reception points. The close proximity of the German and Polish forces made it essential to use absolute precision when dropping the supplies .This, in turn, meant that the aircraft were forced to fly between 300 and 400ft and No 148 Squadron lost four of its Halifaxes on the first night.

As the battle progressed the German flak defences were increased along the route the supply aircraft were forced to follow, culminating in a very heavy concentration over Warsaw itself. Crews were sometimes forced to fly as low as 100ft to get below the line of fire of the flak batteries. Losses were heavy and one pilot from No 148 Squadron reported seeing five aircraft shot down over the city itself during a mission. The Halifaxes which returned were usually so badly shot up that they required extensive repairs. On 16 August the following message was received by No 334 Wing from the GOC Warsaw, General Bor-Komorovski. 'The gallant effort of your airmen has enabled us to continue our struggle. Fighting Warsaw thanks heroic airmen and sends them her highest appreciation. We bow with deepest reverence before fallen crews.' A message was also received from Air Chief Marshal Slessor praising the courage of the No 334 Wing crews.

The Polish Flight had been in the worst possible position when the uprising began due to the attrition rate suffered in previous operations over Yugoslavia and Italy. This applied not only to crews but also to aircraft and No 148 Squadron lent any Halifaxes that it could spare. However, its own losses prevented more than a token effort and the cumulative losses of this period exhausted the general Halifax reserves in the Mediterranean area. On receipt of an urgent request from the PHA HQ, the Air Ministry ordered 10 Halifaxes to be withdrawn from Bomber Command and transferred immediately to No 334 Wing. Unfortunately these aircraft were equipped to Bomber Command requirements and needed to be stripped of a considerable amount of equipment. It was also necessary to modify the interior to take static line attachments for freight dropping through the fuselage well hatch. All this took time and the first nine arrived at Brindisi between 30 August and 1 September. Despite this No 148 Squadron carried out 116 supply missions and No 1586 Flight 80 during August.

Further supplies of aircraft to No 334 Wing were held up through the dispatch of some Mk V Halifaxes which, on arrival at 144 MU, were found to be due for a major overhaul and inspection. They were also fitted with Merlin XX engines which had to be changed for Merlin 22s before they could be cleared for operations.

Tragically, less than half of the precious supplies dropped reached the PHA, the Germans and the raging fires consumed the remainder. Bad weather set in during late September and by the time that it had cleared the Polish forces had capitulated.

In October No 148 Squadron received instructions that daylight operations would be permitted whenever possible. Flying conditions were much harsher during the day due to the turbulence caused by the sun heating the barren

Left: JP121, a production B Mk II Series IA. The majority of Halifaxes from the JP serial block were allocated to the Special Duties squadrons. / *C. Cole*

Below: Italy 1944. Loading up a late model Series IA Halifax of No 148 Squadron with 15 containers for a supply drop to Yugoslavian partisans. On the left is FS-E, possibly JN956. / *IWM*

Below right: The wreckage of L9612 photographed the morning after its crash in Sweden near Tomelilla in Scania. In the left foreground is the tailwheel complete with its sheet metal fairing fitted to stop the parachute static lines from fouling it. / *T. Olausson*

mountains. Towering cumulo nimbus clouds, magnificently beautiful but dangerous in the extreme, were also a daily feature of the landscape. Most crews considered the increased accuracy of the drops justified the rougher conditions. One drawback was that the dropping point markers were harder to distinguish in daylight but this was eventually overcome by the use of smoke flares. The increased accuracy can be judged by a message received during October from a Balkan partisan group thanking the crew for dropping the supplies right in the yard of their headquarters. Another, somewhat tongue in cheek, wished to remind the Halifax crews that it was only necessary to drop the supplies in the area marked by the smoke flares and not to extinguish the individual smoke flares with the containers.

One member of the crew definitely preferred daylight drops despite the rougher ride, this was the dispatcher. His duty was to push the supplies through the well hatch and since they were stacked in the rest bay during take-off he had to move them aft for dropping after the aircraft became airborne. On night operations this meant working in almost total darkness so that no light showed through the hatch. To prevent the chance of falling out he was usually attached to the static line rail by a rope from his parachute harness. Timing was critical and all the packages had to be stacked near the hatch ready to be pushed out with the minimum of delay. Because bags dropped without a parachute had a longer trajectory they had to be dropped first. As soon as the green light came on, on the dispatcher's panel, the chuted containers were pushed out as rapidly as possible until it went out. The Halifax was then out of the area and had to make another run if there were any supplies left. Often odd shaped bags would not go through the hatch cleanly and the dispatcher would have to jump on the particular article to push it through. A good dispatcher and his assistant, usually the wireless operator could drop half a ton in three seconds. The actual final run up to the dropping point was the responsibility of the bomb aimer. The Halifax would begin its run over the target with the bomb doors open, flaps partly down and engines throttled back while the bomb aimer called out corrections and finally releasing the containers in the bomb bay. It was on his signal that the dispatcher dropped the fuselage load.

The Poles continued their night operations to Czechoslovakia, Austria, Yugoslavia, Bulgaria and Crete as well as 20 drops to the PHA behind the German lines. On 7 November the strength of No 1586 Flight was finally brought up to that of a full squadron and it was renumbered No 301 (SD) Squadron. It made its last supply drop to Poland on 28 December, further flights being banned by the SOE due to the Soviet offensive in Poland.

No 148 Squadron received a couple of Stirlings during November and then, in December, received orders that it would be converting to Liberators. As none of these had arrived the squadron continued its Halifax operations making a particularly successul drop to the Russian forces in January 1945. The Russians were highly impressed. Despite the winter conditions the missions continued throughout January and several agents, some female, were dropped along with a jeep and supplies to partisans in northern Italy.

On 28 February No 301 Squadron was transferred to transport duties due to the rapidly declining requirements of the SOE. This reflected the general situation in Europe, No 624 Squadron having disbanded on 24 September 1944. This left only No 148 Squadron which now found itself acting in direct support of the final army operations in Italy, thus keeping it occupied until VE day. Its first peacetime operation was the dispatch of five Halifaxes to Yugoslavia to evacuate POWs. Finally, on 23 May 1945 it made its long overdue conversion to Liberators, the Halifaxes being ferried to 144 MU at Maison Blanche in North Africa.

10 Development of the B Mk III

Among the Halifaxes retained by Handley Page for development work was a B Mk II, R9534. In late 1942 it was fitted with four Bristol Hercules VI engines, with two speed superchargers, rated at 1,615bhp for take-off. At this stage of its career R9534 had undergone the cleaning up process applicable to the Series I (Special) configuration, including the bulbous nose rudder modification, but it still retained its C Mk II mid-upper turret.

It was delivered to Boscombe Down in early March 1943 where it underwent a rigorous series of tests. The rear boxes of the intermediate wings required some strengthening and were redesigned, being fitted with continuous stringers. During the sideslip and asymmetric flight trials the normal rudder deficiencies were noted and also some aileron snatch. To overcome the latter a set of experimental ailerons was fitted.

In May the experimental 'D' fins were fitted and test flying began with these on 1 June. Four days later the prototype Halifax B Mk III, as R9534 was now designated, was involved in an unfortunate accident. During the morning the aircraft was prepared for a test flight and the pilot, having run up the engines, called for the chocks to be removed. The starboard one jammed and one of the RAF ground crew moved forward to release it but misjudged the distance and was struck by the propeller seriously injuring him.

The new fin and rudder combination was acceptable for use on Mk II and V aircraft but due to peculiarities associated with R9534, the rudder was found to be rather too heavy with the existing aileron control. The ailerons themselves were too heavy to allow any appreciable bank at high speeds and the rudders on their own were also too heavy to be of much assistance in putting on bank. In view of this the ailerons were redesigned with a bulbous nose modification similar to that applied to the original rudders. An additional geared trim tab was fitted to the starboard aileron and the fixed balance tab of the port aileron was replaced by a broad chord geared trim tab.

On 17 July intensive flying trials began, a retractable tailwheel having been fitted immediately prior to the tests. The Halifax had already completed 85hr 40min flying when these trials began and was flown for an additional 67 hours during which time the airframe gave some trouble due to general deterioration. The first production B Mk III, HX227, flew on 29 August and was delivered to Boscombe Down on 12 September having done only 3hr 55min flying. The H2S blister was removed and the engine air intakes replaced by a strengthened type prior to commencing test flying. It retained its non-retracting tailwheel and was fitted with full standard operational equipment. Its engines were Bristol Hercules XVIs which differed from the Hercules VI engines only in having fully automatic carburettors.

Routine and intensive flying was done by two attached crews sent from operational squadrons. In addition R9534 was flown on occasions by test pilots and pilots from No 4 Group. Ground maintenance was done by ground crews attached from operational squadrons. Between 27 August and 7 September R9534 was mostly away from base being flown by No 4 Group crews, the routine 150-hour inspection being done in the field. It was returned to Handley Page after a total of 44 flights, during which it logged 66hr 35min flying time, for examination and rectification of the wing structure.

HX227 was flown between 14 September and 22 October for a total of 45 flights, logging 150hr 10min in less than five and a half weeks. The official report was most enthusiastic. It read, '. . . the aircraft was far better as regards maintenance and reliability than was expected from previous experience of four engined aircraft and the intensive flight trials were completed in less time than has been taken for any other four engined aircraft.'

Experiments were carried out with two types of air scoops during September and the Bristol Open Scoop type replaced by Vokes Modified Internal Tunnel type which bestowed a relatively meagre 3mph to the weak mixture cruising speed but added a very significant 1,000ft to the cruising ceiling. The all up weight was cleared to 63,000lb although portion of this was taken up by additional fuel, total capacity being raised to 2,688gal. Each wing still contained six fuel tanks but the number two tank was transferred to the centre section of the wings and provision made for additional long range fuel tanks in the outermost wing bomb cells. The main six tanks held 1,806gal, the two new tanks each held 96gal and the three fuselage long range tanks 230gal each.

Some minor difficulties with vibration had occurred and this was traced to the rear turret balance flaps. It was partly cured by packing out the deflector flaps. Movement of the turrets, especially the rear one, effected the controls considerably and a large amount of trim had to be used to keep the aircraft straight. In violent evasive actions, at speeds below 190mph, response to the controls was good although the rudder was heavy. At high speeds the rudder and aileron heaviness experienced with R9534 was again encountered. The modified bulbous nose ailerons which cured the condition were not available for the initial production aircraft and these machines were delivered with standard ailerons.

The use of the more powerful Hercules radial engines completely restored the Halifax's performance and production of the new mark got under way rapidly. In addition to HX227 three other production Halifaxes were retained for trials work, HX226, HX229 and HX238. The production aircraft differed from the first one, HX227, only in having a retractable tailwheel fitted.

The first batch of B Mk IIIs was issued to four squadrons in November, among them being the oldest Halifax unit of all, No 35 Squadron based at Graveley. Mr A. H. Atwood was the chief servicing engineer for Bristol's at the time and he had the task of lecturing to the pilots, both in the air and on the ground, on throttle handling techniques. These differed markedly from those associated with the Merlin engines. Cabin heating provided some problems, ample quantities being provided by the inboard engines but distribution was difficult to control. The final version was christened with the station name, becoming known as the Graveley Heating System.

No 466 Squadron received its first B Mk III Halifaxes on 3 November 1943 and four days later HX244 crash landed after the undercarriage locked half way up due to the aircraft sinking back on to the runway during take-off. No 433 Squadron also suffered an early loss. Shortly before noon on 19 December HX345 took-off with a new crew on board, turned over on its back and plunged down onto HX277 which was parked at dispersal. Both aircraft burst into flames and the crew of five was killed along with one of the four ground staff personnel working on HX277.

A mobile H2S fitting party visited the four B Mk III equipped squadrons during December fitting sets at the rate of one a day. Modified Vokes air intakes were also fitted during this period by the unit ground crews.

No 466 Squadron began operations on 1 December, 12 Halifaxes being dispatched to lay mines off Terschelling. Of a slightly more aggressive nature, four of 35 Squadron's new B Mk III Halifaxes took part in the attack on Frankfurt on 20/21 December. One of them failed to return, HX270:M apparently falling to the enemy defences. A second, HX328:J, caught fire when a target indicator exploded as it was preparing to land. Sqn Ldr J. Sale, DSO, climbed the burning Halifax to 2,000ft and bailed out five members of the crew. The mid-upper gunner was unable to jump as his parachute had been destroyed by fire so Sale calmly landed the blazing aircraft and taxied it off the runway. The Halifax exploded when he and the gunner were some 200yd away. The only casualty was the rear gunner who fractured one of his ankles after bailing out. For his cool-headed action Sale was awarded a bar to his DSO.

Such losses were, of course, not the fault of the aircraft and crews were impressed with the performance of the new mark. No 466 Squadron joined in the Berlin offensive with 15 of its improved Halifaxes on 29/30 December and executed its part in the mission without loss.

Expansion of the B Mk III Halifax force was relatively rapid and by mid-January 1944 nine squadrons were operational with the type. Prior to receiving its Halifaxes

No 466 Squadron had operated Wellingtons and apart from three or four B Mk IIs for training purposes it was equipped with B Mk IIIs from the start. In other squadrons the transition was slower and they operated a mixture of B Mk IIs, Vs and IIIs. No 35 Squadron sent 10 B Mk IIs and a lone B Mk III to Berlin on 20/21 January 1944 but next night sent nine B Mk IIIs and four B Mk IIs to the same target. By contrast No 51 Squadron received sufficient B Mk IIIs for its C Flight to become the nucleus of a new squadron, No 578. No 158 Squadron went through a similar process and No 640 Squadron was formed from its C Flight.

Improved aircraft were not the only additions to the Halifax squadrons and from December 1943 onwards supplies of Visual Monica, more popularly known as Fishpond, became available. This new version of the tail warning device, as the name suggests, gave a visual indication, on a cathode ray tube, rather than the original aural system.

The old version of Monica had lost much of its effectiveness due to the high concentration of aircraft within the bomber stream which caused it to be activated almost continuously. Professor Bernard Lovell came up with the idea of using a second plan position indicator, operated from the H2S set, which gave a radar picture of any aircraft nearby. Other bombers, since they were moving at approximately the same speed, appeared as slowly moving blips. Fighters, on the other hand, were readily discernible by their relatively rapid movement across the screen. Within two weeks of formulating the idea a working model had been produced for bench testing and shortly afterwards a test set was ready for installation in an aircraft. Within three weeks the set was installed in a B Mk II Halifax, BB360, and tests had begun. By July Fishpond was in production.

Experimental work with the B Mk III Halifaxes continued and tropical tests showed that engine temperatures were excessive. To overcome this spinners and fans were fitted to the port outer and starboard inner engines of HX226. The 18-bladed fans were attached to the spinner back plates and revolved at the same speed as the de Havilland Type 55/18, semi-flared, propellers. The tests were only partly successful and in July a fully operational B Mk III, LW125, was sent to Khartoum for tropical trials.

During 1941 an investigation had been made into drag problems associated with Halifaxes. Part of the report made a study of methods of increasing the all up weight and stated that 60,000lb could be achieved without further structural modifications. However, to increase this figure to 65,000lb would necessitate an increase in wing span to keep the take-off distance and cruising ceiling within resonable limits. To achieve the increased span it was proposed to extend the wing centre section but this would have entailed a considerable amount of redesign work and produced production delays which were not tolerable at the time. The solution eventually proved to be relatively simple and the additional span was achieved by extending the wings at the tips. A B Mk II Series IA Halifax, HR845, was fitted with the revised wing tips, which increased the span to 103ft 8in, and tested at Boscombe Down in January 1944. The rate of climb was increased by

Above: R9534 in its initial form after being fitted with four Bristol Hercules VI engines. It still retains its Series I (Special) nose and the bulky C Mk II mid-upper turret. The use of orthochromatic film has made the yellow prototype marking, roundel outer ring and under surfaces appear black. / *IWM*

Right and below: Two views of R9534 prior to May 1943 when it was fitted with 'D' fins. At the time that these photographs were taken it was already designated as the prototype B Mk III and had been fitted with the shallow A Mk VIII four gun turret. / Flight International

R9534

Above: After a four Halifax mining operation on 2 January 1944, No 433 Squadron sent 10 of its new B Mk IIIs to Magdeburg on 21 January 1944, the squadron's first bombing mission. HX283, seen here still fitted with Bristol open scoop air intakes, took part as BM-A and failed to return, thus becoming the unit's first operational loss. By contrast its successor HX268:A survived 62 missions and was pensioned off to an HCU. / *C. Cole*

Below: The experimental 'D' fins fitted to R9534. Production model fins varied only slightly from the ones seen here.

Bottom: HX226, one of three production B Mk III Halifaxes retained for experimental work.

70-120ft/min, service ceiling by 800ft, maximum weak mixture cruising speed by 7-10mph and the cruising ceiling by 1,700ft. No time was lost in introducing the new wing extensions on to the production lines and by February the first revised models were in service.

The first production B Mk III to undergo routine testing by the A&AEE personnel was checked over between 4 and 9 January. HX339 was representative of the very earliest production aircraft having short span wings and B Mk II type ailerons. The aircraft passed all tests satisfactorily but the oil coolers proved to be a little too efficient and seven inch circular blanks, made from dural plate backed with felt, were fitted to the centre of the forward face of each cooler. Without the blanks the oil congealed causing the temperatures to rise with a corresponding drop in oil pressure. This modification became standard for all B Mk IIIs and in some instances it was even necessary to increase the size of the blanks.

Bomber Command losses in the Berlin attacks were not light at any time and every effort was made to reduce the effectiveness of the defences. Three spoof raids were made on Dusseldorf, Kiel and Hanover in an attempt to cover the Berlin raid of 20/21 January 1944 but the ruse failed and German night fighters penetrated the bomber stream soon after it crossed the enemy coastline. Halifaxes were out in strength that night and for Nos 51 and 578 Squadrons it was their first operation since equipping with B Mk IIIs. Flak was only moderate over Berlin but three of No 466 Squadron's Halifaxes were damaged. However, Halifax losses formed only a small fraction of the 35 aircraft missing from the night's operation.

The following night the process was reversed and while the main force attacked Magdeburg a small force of Lancasters went to Berlin. HX283:A of No 433 Squadron failed to return and HX272:N ditched 50 miles from the English coast. These were the squadron's first losses. The next raid on Berlin, on 27/28 January, produced the highest losses of the year with 33 of the 530 bombers dispatched failing to return. Undeterred Bomber Command was out in force again the following night. Despite extensive diversions an estimated 150 night fighters were waiting for the bombers over Berlin and losses were the highest yet recorded, 46 of the 680 bombers being lost. No 466 Squadron crews had to battle their way to and from the target losing three of the 12 Halifaxes which actually reached Berlin. Two others were attacked twice by night fighters and three more sustained attacks up to 100 miles from the target. The bombers returned again the next night and for the cost of 33 of the 540 aircraft dispatched made a successful, concentrated attack.

The moon period prevented any further attacks until mid February during which period another five Halifax squadrons became operational with the B Mk III version. The first attack on Berlin for the month was also the largest to date. The bombers set out on 15 February and followed a devious route, across the North Sea and down the Baltic, arriving over Berlin in a compact group. The attack lasted 38 minutes, an average of one bomber every three seconds, and this effective concentration in time was reflected in the lowered loss ratio of 43 out of 891 bombers.

The war of bluff and counter bluff was now being bitterly waged, sometimes with success and sometimes with drastic failure. Three nights after the very successful Berlin raid, Leipzig was attacked by a force of 823 bombers but despite decoys and diversionary raids, including a last minute change of direction by the bomber stream, 78 aircraft failed to return. This raid had been in support of a directive, issued jointly to the RAF and the American 8th Air Force on 29 January, stipulating the destruction of key installations in the German fighter airframe and ball-bearing industries. Leipzig was one of the chief commercial and manufacturing cities in Germany and of particular importance to the aircraft and chemical industries. Night fighters investigating intruder operations over Dutch airfields had accidentally met the main bomber stream as it crossed the coast. From then on they attacked throughout the rest of the operation. One of No 466 Squadron's Halifaxes had a running fight with three Ju88s for a considerable portion of the journey before finally shaking them off. An incorrect wind forecast badly disrupted the navigation and most bombers arrived early at the turning points where they were forced to orbit, at least four being lost through collisions. Twenty others were seen to go down in flames before reaching Leipzig where early arrivals caused a dangerous situation by having to orbit until the Pathfinder target indicators went down. Despite the difficulties and heavy losses a concentrated attack finally developed and the target was badly damaged.

On 29 February LW650 was put through routine tests by the A&AEE personnel and in most respects was a standard B Mk III. However, it had a 0.5in Browning machine gun fitted in the ventral blister. Production of H2S equipment could not keep pace with the rapidly expanding bomber force and experiments which had started unofficially 18 months before finally culminated in an official ventral gun installation. Some minor criticism was made of the actual stowage of the gun which was some 45° on the beam and caused unnecessary drag. Tests with this type of installation had been made at Boscombe Down on DJ300 in late 1943 but it was not until the shortage of H2S sets occurred in February 1944 that it was adopted for general use. The installation, even at the expense of H2S, was popular with crews and many were disappointed when their Halifaxes were eventually fitted with H2S sets. Some squadrons made further modifications to improve the efficiency of the position which, incidentally, required an additional crew member. No 429 Squadron found that removal of the seat improved the gunner's field of vision greatly, while No 431 Squadron went a step further and installed twin machine guns when they received their B Mk IIIs in March.

On 2 March the second B Mk III Halifax to be tested from Handley Page's initial production batch was checked over. LV907 was passed as being up to standard for workmanship but slightly above average in performance. Perhaps this helped it in its subsequent operational career for it completed 128 missions and survived the war. Four Halifaxes, all B Mk IIIs, are known to have completed 100 or more operations, although many others came very close to the magic figure. LV907 did all of its operations with No 158 Squadron; No 578 Squadron's pair, LW587 (104) and MZ527 (105) celebrated their 100th jointly with an

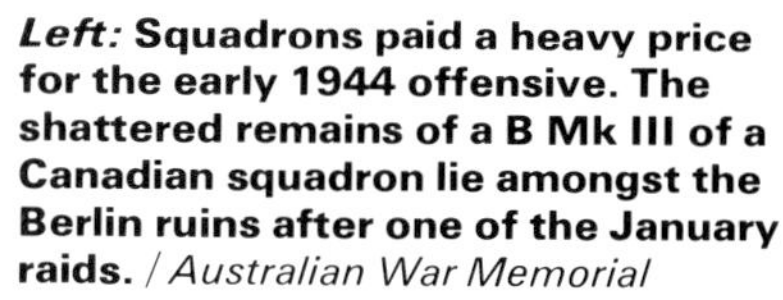

Left: Squadrons paid a heavy price for the early 1944 offensive. The shattered remains of a B Mk III of a Canadian squadron lie amongst the Berlin ruins after one of the January raids. / *Australian War Memorial*

Centre left: January 1944 brought heavy fighting and heavy losses for No 466 Squadron. HX312:HD-K was one of the aircraft that failed to return from the Magdeburg raid of 21/22 January. / *RAAF*

Below: Losses meant replacements. A B Mk III takes-off for a test flight; no codes have yet been applied. / *IWM*

Right: The crew of No 466 Squadron's LW516:HD-K prepare for a mission. Left to right: Sgt W. K. Handley; Flt Sgt K. S. Oaks; Sgt R. E. Tickell; Plt Off T. C. Drake-Brockman; Flt Sgt J. C. Scott; Sgt D. V. Westley; and Flt Sgt M. W. G. Pointon. Kilfrost de-icing paste has been applied to the leading edge of the rudders. / *RAAF*

Below right: Bombing up X-Xray, a No 466 Squadron B Mk III, for a raid on Berlin. The long range fuel tank is just visible in the forward section of the fuselage bomb compartment. / *Department of Air*

attack on Kamen on 3/4 March 1945. LV937, an ex-No 578 Squadron Halifax, did its 100th with No 51 Squadron.

Bomber Command continued its intensive bombing campaign throughout the remainder of February and March. Stuttgart, Schweinfurt and Augsburg were attacked in rapid succession between 20 and 25 February. The Augsburg raid was a spectacular success, over 60% of the target being devastated by this one raid. Stuttgart received two further visits in early March and then, on the night of the 24/25th, Berlin was attacked for the last time in the current campaign.

The same long Baltic route was used as on the previous raid and diversionary sweeps were made to confuse the night fighter controllers. Again an unforecast strong northerly wind badly upset the navigation and the bomber force was scattered over a wide area. Berlin was a very difficult and dangerous target under any conditions and, due to its sprawling suburbs, gave a very poor H2S response. Those aircraft not fitted with H2S found conditions practically impossible and another sudden, unpredicted change in the wind caused many aircraft to stray into the heart of the Ruhr defences on the return trip. Out of 726 bombers dispatched that night 72 failed to return.

On 30/31 March the last heavy raid of the winter was made by a force of 795 bombers against Nuremberg. It was a memorable last raid for it precipitated the largest night fighter battle of the war and the worst reverse suffered by Bomber Command. Weather conditions over the North Sea precluded the use of any large scale diversion but 50 Halifaxes layed mines in the Heligoland Bight in the hope of drawing some of the night fighter force away from the target area. However, these were ignored and the night fighter controllers grouped their forces at Bonn and Frankfurt-on-Main where they were ideally positioned to intercept the bomber stream. An unpredicted high velocity wind at altitude—a jet-stream as it later became known—upset navigation badly and the bomber stream spread out in a broad band north of the actual track. High cloud cover, predicted to cover most of the route, disappeared over Belgium and the bombers were exposed to the light of the half moon which silhouetted them against the lower cloud banks.

The high scores achieved by some German night fighter crews have been questioned many times but it does not take much imagination to see how they were achieved. Leutnant Martin Beker of I/NJG 6 was airborne in his Bf110 that night and made his first radar contact, just after midnight, with a group of Halifaxes east of Bonn. Ten minutes later the first Halifax fell to his guns and within the space of the next 30 minutes he shot down a further five. Short of fuel he was forced to land but took-off again later and shot down a seventh bomber over Luxembourg. Thirty burning wrecks were counted by one RAF crew between Aachen and Nuremberg and it is estimated that at least 50 bombers were shot down before reaching the target. Out of the 93 Halifaxes dispatched that night 30 failed to return, No 51 Squadron alone losing six plus one more which crashed on return killing the crew.

Plt Off C. J. Barton was flying his 19th mission that night at the controls of LK979:E, a No 578 Squadron Halifax. Seventy miles from the target a Ju88 night fighter attacked putting the intercom out of action with its first burst of fire. An Me210 then joined the attack and damaged one engine. By this time all of the Halifax's turrets were out of action and the night fighters continued to press home their attacks. Due to the failure of the intercom a signal was misinterpreted by the bomb aimer, navigator and wireless operator who bailed out. Despite the loss of this highly essential part of his crew and being cut off from the remaining members, Barton continued on to Nuremberg where he released the bombs himself. As he turned for home the propeller of the damaged engine flew off and at about this time it was discovered that two of the petrol tanks had been damaged and were leaking. Without any navigational aids and hampered by the loss of one engine and strong head winds Barton successfully circumnavigated the heavily defended areas and crossed the English coast 90 miles north of his base. With petrol almost exhausted the remaining engines cut leaving him with only one running and at too low an altitude to allow his crew to bail out. Ordering the flight engineer and two gunners to their crash stations he made a last attempt to clear the houses over which he was flying. The Halifax crashed at Ryehope, near Sunderland, killing Barton but his three companions survived. For his tenacity and courage Barton was awarded a posthumous Victoria Cross, the only Halifax crew member to receive this rare award.

The entire operation cost Bomber Command 95 aircraft, with 11 others damaged beyond repair. A tragic loss especially when it was realised that the attack was so scattered that it caused little damage.

As the battle of the Ruhr tapered off Bomber Command had already committed part of its force to a series of experimental attacks against French railway marshalling yards. If these proved successful the campaign was to be expanded, the attacks being in direct support of the forthcoming invasion of Europe which was scheduled for June. The first of these attacks was made against the marshalling yards at Trappes on 6/7 March. The main aiming point in this type of attack was the locomotive running sheds and repair depots. Mosquitos of the PFF carried out the marking using 'Oboe', a precision blind bombing radar device. The main bombing force of 263 aircraft was split into two phases, the Halifaxes attacking last.

The weather improved steadily as the target area was approached and many crews reported that after crossing the French coast it was possible to see the first phase of the attack being carried out. By the time the Halifaxes reached Trappes the second phase of the marking had just begun, the first cluster appearing to fall right on the aiming point. Visibility was such that the lake 700yd north of the aiming point could be clearly seen. All of the 142 Halifaxes dispatched bombed the primary target without loss, the majority of them within a seven minute period. The last aircraft over the target, 20 minutes after zero hour, reported that the engine sheds, now partly cleared of smoke, appeared to have suffered considerable damage. In all 1,258 tons of bombs were dropped and Trappes

Above: May 1944 and quieter times. The crew and ground crew of LW497:MH-W, *Winsome WAAF* of No 51 Squadron, take time out to pose for a photograph. / *G. V. Smith*

Left: The ventral gun installation was popular with crews and many were not happy to lose it for an H2S installation. These two No 425 Squadron B Mk IIIs show both types of fitting. LL596:KW-U has a single 0.5in machine gun in its ventral bulge while MZ454:KW-S has a standard H2S fitting. / *RCAF*

Above: **NR147:KW-L runs up its engines against the brakes, waiting for a green light from the chequered mobile tower on the right.** / *RCAF*

Below: **Tholthorpe and off duty crews watch No 425 Squadron's MZ620:KW-T taxi out. The Canadians were undoubtedly masters of the exotic artwork! The signboard on the ground bear the warnings HATCHES and FLAPS, essential reminders before take-off.** / *RCAF*

remained out of action for approximately five weeks.

By 11 April similar targets had been attacked on 13 occasions, involving 2,513 heavy bomber sorties. Most of these were carried out by the Halifaxes of Nos 4 and 6 Groups. In order to create the maximum damage possible bomb loads consisted of a mixture of 500lb and 1,000lb bombs. For example, on these raids the normal bomb load of a B Mk III Halifax, not fitted with H2S, was nine 1,000lb and six 500lb bombs. Losses remained almost negligible with one exception, the raid on Tergnier on 10/11 April, when 10 Halifaxes were lost out of a force of 157. By contrast all of the 122 Halifaxes which attacked the marshalling yards at Ghent that same night returned safely.

The success of this type of operation had become obvious by the end of March and 80 of the most important rail centres had been selected for attack by the Allied Air Forces. Thirty-seven were allocated to Bomber Command and the remainder to the US 9th Air Force, the British 2nd Tactical Air Force and the Air Defence of Great Britain (ADGB) fighter forces. The principal objective was to reduce the capacity of the complex French railway system to the minimum, thus denying the German forces the tactical mobility that would be so essential for defence against the Allied landings. By the time the invasion got under way 51 of the targets had been heavily damaged, 25 severely damaged and four only superficially damaged.

The last attack in the series was, by coincidence, against Trappes marshalling yards, 2/3 June. However, unlike the first raid in March night fighters were waiting over the target and aided by moonlight and flares attacked the bombers. Losses were the highest suffered for the whole campaign, 16 of the 128 bombers dispatched failing to return.

No 466 Squadron lost two of its 15 Halifaxes and a third was severely damaged by a Me210. The pilot, Flt Lt J. Stevens, managed to nurse the battered Halifax back to base despite losing height until almost at ground level at one stage of the journey. Plt Off B. Bancroft of No 458 Squadron had his Halifax even more extensively damaged by a Ju88 night fighter. The intercom and all the instruments were damaged and the hydraulics, allowing the bomb doors and flaps to come down. A gaping hole the full width of the fuselage and three feet long was smashed in the floor. The radio operator's position had a large hole torn out of the fuselage, both turrets were put out of action and one of the petrol tanks punctured. A fire broke out in the rear of the bomb bay but Bancroft managed to keep the Halifax under control while Plt Off Fripp, the navigator and two other surviving members of the crew subdued the flames with fire extinguishers. With no compass Bancroft steered a homeward course using the North Star and landed at Hurn airfield.

The attacks on marshalling yards required only part of the Bomber Command forces and the remainder were employed in a coincidental series of raids on enemy aircraft industrial targets, including the French airframe and engine factories.

Friedrichshafen was a very important industrial centre situated on the shore of Lake Constance and produced aircraft and tank engine gearboxes as well as radar equipment. On 27/28 April a raid was made by bombers from No 1 Group, the target being marked by Lancasters and Halifaxes of the PFF, and a concentrated attack was delivered which caused extensive damage. One of the No 35 Squadron Halifaxes was attacked by a night fighter both on the way into the target and on the way out, the second attack setting the aircraft on fire amidships. Blinded by the smoke the pilot, Plt Off R. Peter, finally managed to pull the Halifax out of its spiral dive at 3,000ft. Two members of the crew had bailed out but both of the gunners, who suffered minor burns, had had their parachutes destroyed by the fire. The wireless operator had lost his parachute out of the forward escape hatch when the other members jumped. With the Halifax wallowing badly Peter turned back and ditched it in Lake Constance. The dinghy was fortunately undamaged and the crew paddled towards the neutral shore of Switzerland, enjoying a ring-side seat view of the last phase of the raid.

Every effort was made to reduce the German potential for retaliation within the area marked for the coming invasion. During May two of the largest German military camps were attacked by Bomber Command. The first was an all Lancaster raid on Mailly-le-Camp, a similar force attacking the camp at Bourg Leopold, in Belgium, eight nights later. However, the latter attack was called off by the Master Bomber due to marking difficulties and only half the bombers attacked. A second attack was made on the same target by a mixed Halifax-Lancaster force on 27/28 May and caused widespead devastation.

As the time for the invasion drew near the scope of the targets was varied to include the German early warning systems and during the first week in June Bomber Command launched attacks on navigational and wireless telephony stations in the intended assault area. These small targets were difficult ones and the enemy's old friend, bad weather, hampered the attacks. Ferm d'Urville, on the Cherbourg peninsula, was the headquarters of the German intelligence service in north-west France. Solid cloud enshrouded the target and the Halifaxes were forced to rely upon sky markers for the bombing. Many crews later expressed doubts as to the success of the operation, their pessimism being borne out by the reconnaissance report. A few nights later, in better conditions, a second attack was made by No 5 Group and the target was obliterated.

By 6 June the German radar and signals network had been sufficiently disorganised to ensure that it would not compromise the element of surprise which was to mark the opening of the invasion.

Less successful was the campaign against the German coastal batteries of Hitler's vaunted 'West Wall'. Although some sites were still under construction there were 49 gun batteries known to be capable of engaging the invasion forces in the chosen assault area. To avoid any chance of indicating where the invasion might be made diversionary attacks were also made on batteries outside the prescribed assault area.

This campaign, a joint Allied effort, began on 10 April and continued until the eve of the assault. The main problem was the fact that only 1,000lb bombs were available and against the heavily armoured guns and concrete casements they had little effect. However, most of the vital ancillary equipment was destroyed and many of the gun sites were severely handicapped on the day of the invasion.

11 Full Production

The Halifax was designed to take full advantage of Handley Page's well tried and proven split construction and unit assembly methods. The entire aircraft was divided into a dozen major assemblies which allowed far more operators to work on each assembly than would normally have been possible. This not only speeded up production but also made transportation and repair far easier.

It was this production technique which enabled Handley Page to utilise the services of other engineering companies, many of them new to the aircraft field, when the Air Ministry gave the order to proceed with mass production of the Halifax. A manufacturing group of companies, the first to be devoted to heavy bomber production, was established with Handley Page as the consultant head. Each member of the group had its own direct contractural agreements with the Ministry of Aircraft Production, Handley Page acting as technical advisers and providing, except in the case of English Electric, the jigs.

The first to join the Halifax production scheme was the English Electric Company who were already linked with Handley Page by its construction of Hampdens for the latter. Instructions were received from the Air Ministry on 22 February 1939, to proceed with the necessary planning for the production of 100 Halifax bomber airframes and the manufacture of the necessary jigs. Unlike the later members of the manufacturing group, English Electric jigged and tooled the Halifax to suit their own production techniques.

This initial order was followed by a revised one for 200 Halifaxes on 30 April 1940. Initially the undercarriages were manufactured at the main Preston works but this was later transferred to the Company's new premises at Low Moor, Bradford. The main assemblies of their first Halifax were transported to the final assembly sheds at Samlesbury airfield on 24 June 1941, where they were married up and the aircraft test flown on 15 August. After checking and thorough testing it was ready for delivery on 20 September. By 31 December seven B Mk IIs had been delivered.

The other participants in the Halifax production programme were Rootes Securities Ltd, at Speke, the Fairey Aviation Co Ltd, at Stockport, and the London Aircraft Production Group. The latter consisted of the London Passenger Transport Board, Park Royal Coach Works, the Express Motor and Body Works, Chrysler Motors and Duplex Bodies and Motors.

To help establish the production techniques Handley Page supplied English Electric with a pattern aircraft, R9538, and the London Aircraft Production Group with two others, R9539 and R9540. These three Halifaxes were completed, to the appropriate standard, in addition to the total number of aircraft ordered. To maintain a consistent standard of production one Halifax from each hundred produced by these firms was flown to Handley Page's aerodrome where they were thoroughly test flown. Any deficiencies were then notified to the firm concerned and the necessary remedial action taken.

Production of the Halifax, as already stated, was based on the progressive assembly of major components which were, in turn, constructed into sub-assemblies. The fuselage was built from four sections constructed of light alloy monocoque with 'L' and 'V' section formers connected by 'L' section stringers. The nose section, containing the main crew accommodation, joined the centre section just aft of the wing leading edge.

This mid-section was built up integrally with the main wing section which extended outboard to the inboard engines. The remaining portion of each wing was divided into two sections, the first of which extended to a point just inboard of the outer engines. The mounting of the outboard engines on to the final wing section was radical for its time.

The third fuselage section extended from the wing rear spar line to a point just forward of the tailplane. The final section carried the rear turret and the attachment points for the cantilever tailplane which was secured by four bolts. The tailwheel mounting was anchored to the front face of the tailplane spar.

Handley Page had designed their split construction method to speed up production but their ingenuity was not limited to the final production aspects. One of the largest bottlenecks in aircraft production was the translation of scale drawings of components into the full sized article. By studying methods used overseas Handley Page eventually produced an efficient system whereby the original component was drafted full size on a sheet of half hard 16swg aluminium and then photocopied. The technique was termed photolofting. The 8ft 0in by 4ft 0in sheets of aluminium were first coated with four very thin applications of cellulose lacquer, duck egg green in colour. From the paint shop they were transferred to the lay-out section on the floor above, this one room covering a floor area of 7,500sq ft. A special silver solder pen point was used to inscribe the detail on the sheets, producing a fine black line. The finished sheets were then passed to the

Left: Early production B Mk II Series I Halifaxes on the final assembly line at English Electric's Preston works. In the background is the Hampden final assembly line. */ English Electric*

Below: 27 October 1942 and DJ980, a B Mk V Series I, leaves the Stockport factory of Fairey Aviation Co Ltd the first of many Halifaxes from this sub-contractor. */ Fairey Aviation*

Above: B Mk II Series I (Special) Halifaxes lined up awaiting delivery after air testing at Samlesbury airfield where final assembly of English Electric produced aircraft took place. The first four aircraft are JB889, '91, '93 and '99. The mid-upper turrets are Boulton Paul A Mk III (Special) type, which were modified A Mk IIs. / *English Electric*

Left: Glazing the cockpit shell on a sub-assembly line. From the production series Mk II Series I (Special) onwards the horizontal glazing, just forward of the pilot's windscreen, was faired in with a metal panel. Note that the aircraft behind has not yet had the panel fitted and the original round cornered opening is still visible. / *English Electric*

Above right: The cockpit top shell is married to the front fuselage assembly. / *Fairey Aviation*

Right: The centre section, heart of the Halifax's construction, is lowered on to a production line mobile trestle. / *English Electric*

photographic section for recording on quarter plate glass negatives. These were then reproduced as enlargements on suitably sensitised metal sheets with consistent accuracy. This method ensured that all components were interchangeable whether produced by Handley Page of any of the other firms.

Another special process was introduced when H2S became a standard fitting on the production lines. The actual blister was manufactured from perspex and due to its size began life as four sheets of this material joined together. This composite sheet was then placed on a specially heated metal table. By covering the perspex sheet with a felt blanket the temperature was raised to 170°C, this being continued until the perspex became soft and pliable. From the table it was then slid over a female mould and the outer edges securely clamped with a series of wooden bars. The mould was then evacuated until a vacuum of 15-20in of mercury was reached. The sheet of perspex was slowly drawn in until it took up the shape of the mould. Within three minutes the completed blister was ready for removal and trimming.

After being test flown by a company test pilot the Halifaxes were usually delivered to a Maintenance Unit. From there they were dispatched to the various squadrons or units, usually by ATA (Air Transport Auxiliary) pilots. For delivery to overseas theatres of operation the process usually included an additional step, namely a Ferry Transport Unit. No 301 FTU at Lyneham received its first four Halifaxes, two for conversion training of the ferry pilots and two for dispatch, in September 1942.

Halifaxes passed through regularly during the next two years and very few failed to reach their destination. Among those that did not was DT493 which force landed in Portugal on 8 October 1942, through engine failure. Capt J. Stagnes of Ferry Command and his crew escaped unharmed while the aircraft, complete with its secret equipment, was destroyed by fire. Six months later BB322, en route to the Middle East, force landed in Spain on 10 April at San Fernando, again without loss of life. Others, however, were less fortunate and BB377 ditched 300 yards off Bournemouth Pier on 6 January 1944, taking the entire crew down with it.

The unit closed down in March 1944 and the Halifaxes were then handled by No 1 Ferry Unit at Pershore, this new unit absorbing 301 FTU and its servicing wing.

1942 had marked the beginning of the intensive production programme for the Halifax and the London Aircraft Production Group delivered their first B Mk II in January, while Rootes Securities delivered theirs just four months later. Rootes produced only 12 B Mk IIs before concentrating exclusively on the B Mk V variant. Fairey's commenced production of the B Mk V at their Eastwood Park factory, in Stockport, and delivered their first aircraft on 27 October. Like Rootes they concentrated exclusively on this mark until the introduction of the radial-engined variants. Within 18 months Fairey's were producing 34 Halifaxes a month.

Production alone was not enough and when the Halifaxes entered service a suitable site for a repair depot had already been chosen. Known as Rawcliffe, it adjoined the civilian airfield called York aerodrome. The need for an efficient repair organisation had been foreseen and the on site repair and modification policy practised by Handley Page in peace time naturally applied to the Halifax. This was put to the test on 31 March 1941, when L9486 made a wheels up landing in the middle of Linton-on-Ouse aerodrome.

The organisation was formulated by Handley Page, the Civilian Repair Organisation and the Ministry of Aircraft Production. The first hangar was ready for occupation in July, albeit roofless, and Mr E. W. Pickston with a staff of 29 arrived from Handley Page's Cricklewood plant. From a very modest beginning with its single 200ft by 100ft hangar it was to grow to a complex of six hangars covering an area of some 200,000sq ft.

By the end of 1941 it was apparent that the existing facilities would not be able to cope with the expected increase in damaged aircraft and a second site, known as Water Lane, took shape on the far side of the aerodrome. From similar beginnings to its sister site it too grew, eventually becoming a complex of nine hangars of somewhat larger proportions than those at Rawcliffe.

Damaged Halifaxes classified as category 'B' ie too badly damaged to be repaired at their own base, were shipped to the repair sites by the lorries and trailers of No 43 Group. Already inspected and their degree of damage assessed the Halifaxes were stripped of damaged components, new parts fitted and general repairs carried out. The extent to which a Halifax could be repaired is indicated by the work carried out on LK660. Badly damaged over Berlin it had to have a new port outer mainplane, port tailplane, port inboard flap and a new section in the rear fuselage. If an aircraft was too badly damaged it was dismantled and salvagable components used to reconstruct less badly damaged aircraft.

When the Water Lane site commenced in September 1942 final assembly work of the complete aircraft was carried out there, detailed assembly being confined to Rawcliffe. In mid-1941 the depot employed 100 people with an additional 50 doing on-site repairs at the various bomber stations. The final employment figure rose to 2,700 of whom 350 worked on other airfields. The number of vehicles also increased from a modest two, a 5cwt van and a three-ton lorry, to over 90.

In addition to repair work the depot also undertook certain major inspections and North African based Halifaxes were flown in direct from the Middle East for this purpose, 240 being received by the end of hostilities. Liaison with the RAF was very close and during one three month period 11,500 man hours were worked by the depot's civilian personnel on RAF maintenance and repair work.

By the end of the war the depot had repaired or overhauled and flight tested over 2,000 Halifaxes. Its safety record was broken only by two minor accidents neither of which caused serious damage nor injury. On the first occasion on a Halifax overran the runway and struck the boundary fence while the other involved a Halifax which taxied into soft ground and stood up on its nose. No damage was incurred and it was righted and flown away.

During the peak period the collective Halifax production facilities comprised 41 factories and dispersal units

Above: With glazing and painting completed, and D/F loop in place, the nose assemblies wait to be moved on to the main assembly line for marrying up with the centre sections in the foreground. Note that unlike the English Electric production schedule the wing sections have not yet been painted. / *Fairey Aviation*

Right: The pregnant profile of the Halifax in embryonic form. One more huge, vacuum moulded, perspex blister for the H2S scanner is lifted from its mould. / *English Electric*

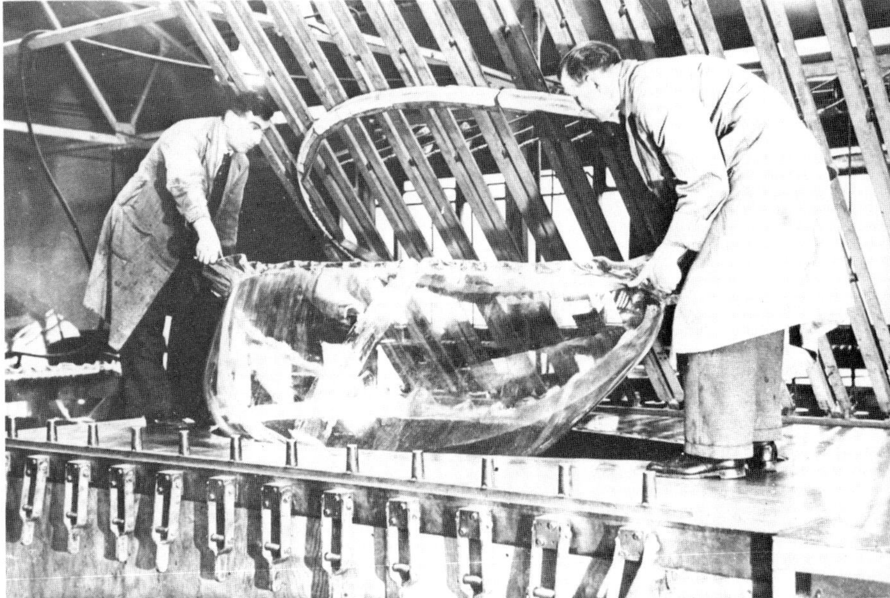

Above: The final assembly line at Stockport where outer wing sections, engines and propellers are added as each airframe moves steadily along. In the foreground is NA579, a Mk III; the serial number is repeated on the wing leading edge inboard of the engine and partly obscured by the propeller. It is also chalked on the upper rim of the engine cowling. The fin assembly in the foreground bears a small 'T' shaped marking made up of two manufacturer's plates. These only appeared on the starboard fin, regardless of the manufacturer. / *Fairey Aviation*

Top right: The extent to which repair work was undertaken is shown in this photograph of a B Mk III undergoing flight testing prior to repainting. The outer wing panels, rear fuselage, fins and tail plane are all unpainted salvaged components. Rudders, elevators, ailerons, flaps and engine cowlings are new components, painted in undercoat. The repair work to the outer wing skinning and the replacement of both wing tips suggest that the aircraft was modified, during repair, to late B Mk III standard.

Right: Having received its clearance from the production test pilot, LV833, a B Mk III, waits delivery to an MU prior to issue to a squadron. This aircraft was allocated to No 466 Squadron early in 1944. / *Flight International*

occupying a floor space of 7,500,000sq ft. It was supported by 600 sub-contractors and employed 51,000 people. One complete Halifax per working hour was achieved from the group effort, while on an individual basis for example English Electric produced two aircraft per day consistently.

With the end of the war in sight, production contracts were cut back, in some cases drastically. English Electric's last order for 350 Halifaxes, placed on 22 May 1944, was progressively reduced to 175 in July 1945 and then to 25 shortly afterwards. It delivered the last of its Halifaxes in December 1945. As the Halifax order was cut back English Electric commenced construction of the de Havilland Vampire delivering the first of these in April 1944. Although a sub-contractor this firm produced more Halifaxes than any other constructor, including Handley Page.

The last Halifax from Rootes Securities factory at Speke underwent flight tests on 9 July 1945. At the controls was Flt Lt J. R. Palmer who had been the resident company production test pilot since 1939. On 5 October the last of Fairey's 661 Halifaxes left the production lines and was delivered on 17 October.

The Halifax continued in production longest with Handley Page who were the only ones to manufacture the A Mk IX version. Production of this mark commenced in November 1945 and the last one to be delivered to the RAF, RT938, was taken on charge just 12 months later, 26 November 1946.

Above: **October 1945. Mr Sam Moseley, Chief Test Pilot, receives the clearance papers from Mr Pinder, Chief of AID at Stockport, prior to test flying A Mk VII, PN343, the last Halifax built by Fairey Aviation.**
/ Fairey Aviation

12 Conversion Training

The introduction of four engined bombers into RAF service had produced several difficulties, among them flying training. Initially, this problem was overcome to some extent by posting experienced operational crews to the first heavy bomber squadrons. No 35 Squadron carried out its own early conversion training as detailed in Chapter Two. However, as more Halifax squadrons entered service the task grew beyond the practical capabilities of the already fully occupied operational squadrons and in late 1941 No 28 Halifax Conversion Flight was formed at Leconfield.

Its Halifaxes were drawn from Nos 35 and 76 Squadrons, the first aircraft arriving in October. A few more were received over the next two months among them being L7245 which was allocated to the unit on 1 November. Having only just been repaired by Handley Page's after an accident in October it was not to last much longer being written off in a landing accident in the following February.

Although this temporarily alleviated the problem it was obvious that further expansion was necessary and in December 1941 a decision was made to establish a new system of one Heavy Conversion Unit per Group plus one Conversion Flight of four aircraft per squadron. For No 4 Group No 1652 HCU was formed at Marston Moore on 2 January 1942, while No 102 Squadron formed its Conversion Flight five days later. Within a month Nos 10, 35 and 76 Squadrons had followed suit, No 78 Squadron joining the ranks with its Conversion Flight a month later.

The standard training programme allowed for approximately 20 hours instruction and covered all essential aspects as follows:

Dual controls were fitted to most of the Halifaxes and this greatly facilitated the training. For the most part the object of the Conversion Flights was to give advanced training to new crews, but occasionally operational crews from the parent squadron were attached for refresher courses.

Training had its element of danger as would be expected, but the accident was not always the fault of the crew under training. No 35 Squadron Conversion Flight lost L9568 on 7 May 1942 when it was struck amidships by W1051 which had just landed after an operation. Fortunately, the crew of W1051 escaped injury as did the guard in L9568 but a third Halifax, L9607:Z was damaged by splinters from the propellers of W1051.

Failure of the tailwheel box casting caused the tailwheel to collapse, usually at an awkward moment, and was not an infrequent occurrence. No doubt the large number of heavy landings to which the training machines were subjected increased the chance of this type of failure.

The three 1,000 bomber raids in mid-1942 brought many of the instructional Halifaxes back on to operations temporarily. For the most part they were flown by instructors but some were crewed entirely by pupils. No 102 Squadron Conversion Flight provided aircraft for all three raids and on the Bremen operation sent three Halifaxes. One was flown by an instructor and the other two by pupils one of whom had just completed his first solo on the type.

The aircraft allotted to the Conversion Flights were generally not new. Bomber Command was still struggling to expand its heavy bomber force and training units, essential though they might be, were a luxury in many respects. The usual practice was for the older aircraft to be

Familiarisation flight	30min	Dual, draining fuel tanks and midair	
Dual circuits and landings	180min	changeover	60min
Solo Circuits and landings	30min	Solo	30min
Dual check and overshoot	30min	Dual instrument flying	60min
Solo	60min	Solo	30min
Dual check and three-engined		Dual instrument flying	60min
handling	120min	Solo	30min
Solo	60min	Dual instrument flying	60min
Solo	60min	Dual, take-off with full bomb load,	
Dual check and two-engined		cross-country and tank	
handling	60min	changeover	120min
Solo climb to 12,000ft and bomb		Dual check including three-engined	
door operation	90min	overshoot and landing	60min

Above: A B Mk II Series I from one of the early conversion units. The fin flashes and fuselage roundel date the photograph as pre-1942 and this narrows the choice to No 28 Halifax Conversion Flight or No 1652 Heavy Conversion Unit. / *K. G. Beetson*

Left: R9430, a B Mk II Series I with mid-upper turret removed, from 1658 HCU undergoing single engine handling tests at 9,000ft. Conventional codes were adopted by this unit when the general expansion of HCUs occurred. Note also the use of spinner colouring for Flight identification. / *IWM*

passed on to the Conversion Flights as new aircraft arrived to replace them. This led to some operationally-tired examples finding their way to the training units. The practice was an unfortunate one but unavoidable for obvious reasons and many a station engineering officer shook his head in dismay at the first inspection of a new arrival.

Two more conversion flights were formed in June 1941, Nos 158 and 408. The early experiences of the former are representative of the problems facing these early training units. The first Halifax to arrive was R9373, from No 78 Squadron. When the log books were checked it was found to be three and a half hours off a major overhaul. Disheartening in itself, it was made worse by the fact that the flight still did not have any heavy equipment or maintenance stands. Despite these shortages a detailed inspection of the Halifax began next day and revealed two cracked front plates, a cold air intake no longer attached to anything in particular and both main tyres needed changing. The next day's batch of arrivals included a similar specimen.

In keeping with Bomber Command's expansion programme a further review of advanced training facilities took place during 1942 and a decision was made to disband the conversion flights and amalgamate their resources to form heavy conversion units. Thus Nos 103, 408 and 460 Squadrons' conversion flights existed only briefly before being absorbed into the HCUs.

Initially many of these HCUs had a mixture of types, Halifaxes, Manchesters, Stirlings and Lancasters, in varying proportions but within a few months they had been resolved into units containing, for the most part, only one type. In the case of the Halifax this categorisation went one step further and No 1667 HCU became the B Mk V specialists being equipped throughout with this mark of Halifax although other HCUs did have small numbers of the type.

Throughout 1943 the number of HCUs steadily increased, many of them moving to satellite stations where they would neither impede nor be impeded by the resident operational squadrons. Each group allocated a base station and its satellites for use by the HCUs associated with it ie in No 42 Base Station was Marston Moore (No 1652 HCU), its satellites being Rufforth (No 1663 HCU) and Riccall (No 1658 HCU).

The mortality rate amongst both aircraft and crews was not insignificant and it is a sobering thought to realise that a very high percentage of aircrews lost during World War II fell victim during their training. This should not be construed to mean that the training programmes or equipment were in any way lacking but rather that in the pressing needs of wartime both men and machines were forced to take calculated risks.

While some aircraft succumbed after a brief period there were always others to prove the exception to the rule. A veteran B Mk I L9534, originally allotted to No 76 Squadron on 15 June 1941, passed successively to No 28 Halifax Conversion Flight, No 1652 HCU and No 1659 HCU before being struck off charge on 20 September 1945. DT733, a B Mk II, was also sent to an HCU starting its career as a training aircraft on 21 January 1943. It

completed well over 1,000 hours during which more than 250 pupil pilots flew it with varying degrees of skill. During one 36-hour period it was airborne for nearly 20 hours. On another occasion a routine 50-hour inspection was completed on a Wednesday and by the following Tuesday it was back for the next 50-hour inspection. Only once was it grounded and then only through a minor accident which caused some buckling to the port main flap shroud. Another veteran B Mk II was W1046 which had clocked up 690 hours' flying time by October 1944.

The handling to which these training Halifaxes were subjected was, naturally, very varied and did not always stay within the prescribed limits. The results were sometimes fatal as was the case with W1009 which crashed through structural failure following violent fighter affiliation manoeuvres on 22 February 1944. Others were written off in landing accidents or taxying accidents. Others fell victim to 'stuffed' clouds such as JD417 which dashed itself to pieces on the hill tops near Trevor, Caernarvonshire, on 3 September 1944. The crew were all RAAF personnel.

The object of the training was to equip crews with the knowledge and skill to meet the enemy on equal terms. Sometimes the enemy could not wait. On the night of 28 April BB255 was practising circuits and landings when a Ju88 night fighter attacked it from behind hitting the starboard fin, wing and outer engine with its cannon shells. Fortunately, the pilot managed to land the damaged Halifax safely. Others had to meet the test in other ways. A No 1658 HCU Halifax, DJ549, was on a night cross country exercise when everything went wrong in rapid succession. With one engine feathered, one with the constant speed unit of the propeller disabled and a third engine running rough the pilot made an emergency landing at RAF Finmere. Despite the rough-running engine cutting during the approach the pilot landed the Halifax safely.

No 1658 HCU had two cases, one fatal, of propeller failure on its elderly B Mk I Halifaxes. The propeller blades were suffering from metal fatigue and tended to part company with the rest of the engine which usually resulted in the reduction gearing being torn out. The unit changed them for wooden bladed propellers and no further trouble was experienced. A further propeller change, but on a much larger scale, occurred on 17 April 1942 when No 1664 HCU began to fit all its Halifaxes with four-bladed propellers. No 1667 HCU followed suit during the first week in May. Originally it had been intended to fit the four-bladed propellers to the outboard engines only but the decision was rescinded and they were fitted to all engines.

The aircraft strength of an HCU was usually far in excess of a normal bomber squadron, in some cases the daily average of serviceable aircraft was as high as 40. Not surprisingly, the turn over in aircraft was proportionately higher and No 1656 HCU's monthly summary for July is fairly representative of most; BB221, BB261 written off due to crashes; HR837, JD307 damaged in taxying accidents; W7705, W1224 and DT675 written off due to deterioration beyond repair. Monthly flying times for No 1667 HCU reflect the intensity of activity 2,039 hours being achieved during July and 2,107 hours the next month.

Above: EB151:OO-R of No 1663 HCU gets airborne from Rufforth. This was an all B Mk V equipped unit. */IWM*

Below: Many a veteran ended its days at an HCU. This B Mk II, HR916, was brand new when photographed. It subsequently went to Cunliffe Owen (25 June 1943), No 405 Squadron (20 July), No 35 Squadron (22 September), No 428 Squadron (31 January 1944) No 1659 HCU (13 March), No 1669 HCU (21 November) and was finally struck off charge on 21 February 1945.

Bottom: A very special Mk VI Halifax, RG815 *Mercury* of the Empire Radio School, photographed during its Australian/New Zealand tour of 18 September 1946. The location appears to be Amberley in Queensland. */D.R.Neibling*

Although an aircraft was written off it did not necessarily mean that its usefulness was ended; some were converted to instructional airframes. No 1666 HCU devised a special series of training aids using portions of time-expired Halifaxes. During September a Halifax nose section was installed in the Ground Instructional School. Completely backed out and fitted with a black out door at the rear, the Night Vision Section installed lighting representing a full moon, half moon and starlight. Bomb aimers under training were then able to do their switch drills under near authentic conditions, a master panel fitted outside the fuselage being monitored by an instructor. This project was so successful that the engineering section of the Ground Instructional School set up a similar nose section to check out flight engineers and pilots. This particular nose section was modified to a B Mk III standard in view of the imminent arrival of this type on the unit.

By December 1944 the length of the training course had increased to five weeks, one week ground instruction and four weeks flying training. Flying hours had doubled compared to the syllabus used by the conversion flights in 1942. Total hours now amounted to 41 composed of 7.5 dual and 15 solo by day and 4.5 dual and 14 solo by night. During the summer 10 to 11 crews a week were posted in but this figure usually dropped to about seven during the winter.

One specialist unit was 1674 HCU which trained crews for Coastal Command, each course usually lasting about three weeks and comprising 45 hours flying during which special attention was paid to radar aids and Leigh Light techniques. On 31 October the organisation of RAF Aldergrove was changed and No 1674 HCU became a training wing with the status of an operational training unit. Many armament experiments were carried out at Lough Neagh Ranges. This was the first bombing range where crews could carry out low level bombing at night, using radar homing and Leigh Light techniques, and receive an accurate assessment of their errors. Throughout its career this unit had a very good safety record and relatively few aircraft and crews were lost.

Among the other specialist training units was the Path Finder Force Navigation Training Unit which had been created in April 1943. It received its first two aircraft, a Stirling and a Lancaster, on 10 April and its first Halifax two days later. W7808 was an ex-No 35 Squadron Halifax and one which had taken part in the H2S development programme. At the time of the unit's transfer to Warboys in June it had an establishment of six Halifaxes, four Lancasters and four Stirlings. Among the half dozen Halifaxes were W7874 and W7875, two of the No 35 Squadron aircraft used for the first H2S attack of the war. With the standardisation on to the Lancaster in No 8 Group the Halifaxes and Stirlings were gradually phased out.

The B Mk III version of the Halifax reached the HCUs in late 1944 and was quickly phased into the training programme. Their greatly improved performance was welcomed by all particularly as B Mk Is and early model B Mk IIs were still in daily use. This did not, of course, make them any the less prone to accident and they appeared on the monthly summaries of damaged and destroyed aircraft along with their elders.

The course of the war with victory a distinct possibility produced a reduction to the already well stocked training programme and this was reflected by the HCUs. A decision to retain the Lancaster as the prime postwar bomber saw many HCUs surrender their Halifaxes in favour of the Lancaster but on a smaller scale. No 1667 HCU which operated a four flight system gave up its large establishment of Halifaxes but only 28 Lancasters were allotted against a unit establishment figure of 32. Several Halifax HCUs soldiered on well into mid-1945, No 1652 HCU, the oldest in No 4 Group finally disbanding on 25 June.

The postwar use of the Halifax for Airborne Forces work ensured that No 1665 HCU, which had trained crews for No 38 Group, continued its existence even though its title was modified to 1665 Heavy Transport Conversion Unit. Similarly No 1659 HCU changed its designation to that of an HTCU and both units moved from Linton-on-Ouse to Dishforth where they disbanded, in July 1946, and amalgamated with No 1332 HTCU. The Operational Refresher Training Unit at Matching converted to an all Halifax unit early in 1945 and took part in the No 38 Group exercises until its disbandment early in 1946.

No 1385 HTSCU at Weathersfield received its first Halifax in March 1946. Concerned with teaching the art of supply and heavy equipment dropping, plus glider towing, the unit received its first intake of crews in April, the 12 coming directly from their HCU course at Linton. It was decided to use A Mk VII Halifaxes exclusively for training and in May the A Mk IIIs were ferried to Edzell for disposal. The following month instructions were received for the unit to amalgamate with No 1333 TSTU at Syerston. No 4 course was the last to be trained at Weathersfield and No 5 course was diverted to Syerston when No 1385 HTSCU moved in early in July, losing its identity and becoming a flight of No 1333 TSTU: No 1333 TSTU eventually gave way to No 1332 HTCU in January 1948 and shortly after the unit was renamed No 241 OCU.

The Halifax also served with several advanced training schools which ran specilaist courses. It had been intended that the Empire Air Navigation School should have an establishment of 20 Lancasters. However, a review in January 1945 replaced these with 18 B Mk III Halifaxes, two Lancaster B Mk Is, a Mk XVI Mosquito and a Mustang. Conversion of the schools pilots on to the Halifaxes took place on the unit, the first four B Mk IIIs arriving on 6 February.

Progress was fairly rapid and No 6 course left for its first navigation exercise to Gibraltar, in three Halifaxes, on 28 March. There were, of course, the inevitable losses and one of the unit's Halifaxes was written off on 10 April. Excitement was not lacking in these long range wartime exercises and on 22 April a crew reported sighting a vapour cloud from a U-Boat's schnorkel device.

The cessation of hostilities allowed far wider range of exercises and on 30 May Wg Cdr J. C. Halley, DSO, made a survey trip to Iceland, this new destination being added to the school's curriculm as also was Bari, in Italy.

Some very long range liaison flights were made by the

school's Halifax NA279:C which and been christened *Capella*. It departed for South-East Asia on 15 June with Sqn Ldr H. R. Hall, DFC, in command and returned to Shawbury on 28 July after a very successful trip. The aircraft used for these liaison trips were drawn from No 3 Flight which maintained two B Mk III Halifaxes, *Capella* and *Kitty*, two Lancasters, a Mosquito, two Ansons and a Proctor. No 1 Flight had 19 B Mk III Halifaxes and No 2 Flight 21 Wellington Mk XIIIs, these being used for the advanced navigational training. One of the Halifaxes, NA553, was disposed of to Halton, to become instructional airframe M5633, in September due to rogue characteristics.

In January 1946 a considerable effort was put into preparing the two No 3 Flight Halifaxes, PN441 and PN189, for a liaison flight to Burma and India, one of the Lancasters being readied for a flight to South Africa at the same time. The two Halifaxes departed at 0600hrs on 14 January, going via Malta and Cairo West. They returned on 10 February and both crews spoke highly of their aircraft's performance throughout the trip.

The school lost two Halifaxes in the space of two weeks, NP952:T crashing while attempting an overshoot on three engines on 21 February. On 8 March Flt Lt Gilbert's crew of eight were forced to abandon PN387:N when some difficulty was encountered with aileron control while returning from a navigation exercise to Gibraltar. The crew all bailed out safely and Gilbert ditched PN387 in the sea, escaping with some lacerations to his face.

On 26 May another liaison mission was dispatched, under the command of Wg Cdr R. T. Billett, to the Middle East and the Mediterranean returning on 27 June. The purpose of the flight was to enable personnel at the various units to have the opportunity of seeing the Halifax's latest navigational aids and hearing lectures by the various members of the crew. In addition each leg of the flight was made using pressure pattern flying and grid navigation, two new techniques currently being evaluated.

The success of this flight prompted further tests by six Halifaxes and a Lancastrian who left Shawbury on 30 July and returned 13 days later. Flying via Gibraltar they went to Castel Benito, over the Sahara Desert to Khartoum, down the Nile Valley to Cairo and then returned via Castel Benito and Gibraltar. The 10,000-mile flight was done using pressure pattern flying and grid navigation.

Another of the five Empire schools established under joint sponsorship of the Air Ministry and the Dominion Governments was the Empire Radio School at Debden. In June 1946, a B Mk VI Halifax was delivered from 48 MU and was joined in July by another, RG815. Christened *Mercury*, RG815 was a specially equipped flying classroom and had already been thoroughly tested by the Wireless and Electrical Flight at Farnborough who gave it its flying clearance on 29 May. It was delivered to RAF Pershore as a special radar equipped aircraft on 7 October 1945, and a civilian team of specialists had prepared its extensive electronic equipment prior to its being dispatched to Canada. On its arrival its was sent to Namoa and Churchill for winterisation trials and while at the latter location the nose perspex cracked at a temperature of −35°C.

The Empire Air Navigation School received another special Halifax, ST814, in November 1946. Christened *Sirius* it was to outlast its contemporaries. It completed several liaison flights as well as some interesting flights to Iceland. In August 1947 the school disposed of its last Halifaxes but retained *Sirius* for the test and development duties.

On 3 November Flt Lt W. Higgins flew *Sirius* on Wind Finding Trials to Malta and Gibraltar but this was to be one of its last flights. In January 1948 it was disposed of to No 45 MU. The Empire Radio School had also phased out most of its Mk VI Halifaxes during the same period but in February 1948 received ST806 from No 29 MU. *Sirius* arrived from No 45 MU in June and both Halifaxes continued in service until September when they were finally disposed of.

The last Halifax to be used for training purposes served with No 1 Parachute Training School. The school had used several A Mk IX Halifaxes for paratroop training but a shortage of servicing personnel caused them to be replaced by Dakotas. However, when the unit moved from Upper Heyford to Abingdon there was a revival of interest in military paratrooping as opposed to relying purely on assault transports to deliver troops into battle. A few A Mk IXs were taken on charge in January 1950 and RT936 survived its companions to be finally written off in April 1953. With its passing the Halifax servered its last connections with the RAF.

Above left: **Looking forward inside *Mercury* which was fitted out as a flying classroom.** / *E. C. Darby*

Left: **Another special Mk VI, ST814 *Sirius* of the Empire Air Navigation School.** / *A. J. Jackson*

13 Coastal Command Operations

In 1942 Coastal Command began a much needed expansion of its long range anti-submarine force. The Sunderland squadrons, which had for so long borne the brunt of these duties, were at last supplemented by American Liberators. To boost further this meagre force, temporary detachments of Halifax and Lancaster squadrons were made to Coastal Command, from Bomber Command.

On 24 October 1942, Nos 158 and 405 Squadrons received orders to forward an operational detachment to RAF Beaulieu where they would be placed under the command of HQ Coastal Command. These detachments were to be completely self-sufficient, No 158 Squadron sending five B Mk II Halifaxes and No 405 Squadron, 15.

Within three days of receiving its orders No 405 Squadron had commenced operations, three of its Halifaxes carrying out an anti-submarine patrol in the Bay of Biscay area. In addition to this type of duty the Halifaxes were responsible for convoy escort work and anti-shipping strikes both at sea and in ports along the enemy coast. The transition from night bombing to the greatly varied day duties does not appear to have presented any great problem to the crews.

November proved to be a busy month for No 405 Squadron and on the second day one of their Halifaxes sighted a submarine. Much to the crew's regret it submerged before they could attack. On 11 November two of No 405 Squadron's Halifaxes were dispatched to patrol in the Bay of Biscay and one of them surprised two motor vessels refuelling a submarine. Bringing his Halifax down to 900ft Plt Off Colledge attacked with machine gun fire and bombs. One salvo of bombs fell short but the rest found their mark and Colledge's gunners added to the chaos with a steady stream of fire, one of the motor vessels eventually raising a white flag.

Another submarine was sighted on 24 November but dived before it could be attacked. Sgt Wober of No 405 Squadron was more fortunate two days later. Sighting a convoy of two destroyers escorting two motor vessels he carried out a determined attack. The heavy defensive fire from the ships made accurate bombing impossible but the Halifax's gunners were given ample opportunity to saturate the targets with machine gun fire. That same day Sgt Symes, of the same squadron, sighted two submarines but these proved too elusive and both crash dived. Shortly afterwards one of the Halifax's engines failed and Symes was forced to feather it and turn for home. A second engine

began to lose power and Symes was barely able to reach St Eval where he attempted a forced landing. After touching down the Halifax bounced off the runway and burst into flames, all the crew escaped except Sgt Farnum who was seen to be trapped in the mid-upper turret. With complete disregard for their own safety Symes and Sgt Nichols, the flight engineer, made their way back into the blazing aircraft. After considerable effort they managed to extricate Farnum and escaped by cutting a hole in the side of the fuselage with the crash axe. Immediately afterwards the Halifax exploded and was totally destroyed by fire.

The month's activities ended with a very determined attack, on the 27th, by Flt Lt Palmer and his crew on a U-boat which was being escorted by two motor vessels. Bringing his Halifax down to 50ft Palmer attacked out of the low morning sun with a stick of six depth charges. These fell short and he turned the Halifax in again for a second attack. This time he straddled U-263 with three depth charges but the concentrated fire of the escort vessels prevented him from making an accurate assessment of the damage.

Daylight attacks were carried out occasionally against French harbours, mainly at Bordeaux and Gironde, and while more in the nature of nuisance raids their value could not be ignored.

No 158 Squadron's detachment returned to Bomber Command in December but No 405 Squadron continued to operate with Coastal Command until 1 March 1943. This service was broken only by a temporary grounding of the Halifaxes for one week, in January, for what is described in the unit records as serious engine breathing difficulties.

Coastal Command was not to lose the Halifax's services for it already had two full squadrons of its own. No 58 Squadron relinquished its Whitleys for Mk II Halifaxes in December 1942 and No 502 Squadron followed suit in January. Both squadrons were operational by 23 February. These two squadrons entered service at a time when improved radar aids were at last becoming available. Servicing crews began fitting ASV Mk III search radar to the Halifaxes in February and most aircraft were equipped with it by May. An additional radar aid, code-name Boozer, was also fitted, this equipment indicating whether the aircraft itself was being subjected to enemy search radar.

While the main U-boat operations were centred in the

Atlantic it was realised that the key to their operations lay in the Bay of Biscay. The introduction of the Metox search receiver in the U-boats did much to nullify the advantages of Coastal Commands early 1.5m ASV equipment and it was hoped that the new Mk III equipment and Boozer might offset this. Another German tactic, not so easily countered, was the introduction of long range fighters which began operating in increasing numbers over the Bay of Biscay from late 1942.

Early in April a No 58 Squadron Halifax was out on a lone patrol at 2,000ft over the Bay of Biscay when the captain sighted seven Ju88 fighters about one mile off the starboard bow and 500ft lower. The enemy fighters quickly manoeuvred themselves between the Halifax and its escape route and then closed in for the kill. The captain jettisoned the depth charges and climbed to 3,000ft in an attempt to reach the little cloud cover that was available. For the next 47 minutes the Ju88s kept up a ceaseless series of attacks, coming in one at a time from different sides while the others made feints to draw the Halifax's fire. Only three times did they press home their attack in force and ran into the controlled and concentrated cross fire from the Halifax's turrets. Two Ju88s departed trailing thick brown smoke from an engine and a third broke away after machine gun strikes were seen to register on the engine cowls. The remainder either lost heart after this, or were running short of fuel, for they also broke off the engagement. After landing back at base the crew examined BB276 and found that the only damage was a bullet hole through the tailplane and three dents on one of the turret fairings.

On 7 May, No 58 Squadron opened its score when one of its Halifaxes attacked and sank U-663. This feat was repeated four days later, U-528 being the victim this time. Of a slightly more passive nature was a leaflet drop to Spanish fishing vessels on 20 May by three of the Squadron's Halifaxes. The presence of these reputedly neutral vessels so close to the Allied shipping movements into and out of Gibraltar could not be risked. The leaflets warned that after 31 May any vessels found other than close to their own shores would be bombed, a threat that was carried out on an least one occasion.

On 15 May Wg Cdr Oulton scored No 58 Squadron's third kill for the month when he sank a grey and brown camouflaged U-boat. Approaching out of the sun he swung HR746:M around to starboard and began his run in from 1,000yd while the navigator opened fire with the nose gun. Six Mk XI torpex depth charges were dropped and the Halifax's gunners raked the U-boat with machine gun fire. The depth charges were well placed and as the spray subsided the U-boat suddenly jerked upwards the whole forepart rising vertically out of the sea. A large light blue oil patch appeared ahead of the bow and greenish white water surged out from around the stricken vessel. Two minutes after the attack began U-463 slid beneath the sea. The next day HR774:R intercepted and sank the Italian submarine *Tazzoli*.

U-boats did not always succumb so readily as U-463 as Wg Cdr Oulton discovered on 31 May. Having sighted U-563 travelling on the surface he began stalking it, using cloud cover to bring his Halifax into a position for an attack. The Halifax finally broke cloud at 3,000ft, four miles from the target. It was only then that a second U-boat was sighted dead ahead but within seconds it had crash dived. Oulton never hesitated and went straight for U-563, his navigator opening fire with the nose gun at 1,000yd. Swinging to starboard, the final run in was made at an angle of 30° to the U-boat's track and six depth charges were dropped across it. As the spray subsided Oulton brought the Halifax in again from dead astern, the navigator again laying down a concentrated fire, and three more depth charges were dropped. When the depth charge plumes subsided the U-boat was seen to be laying beam on to the sea surrounded by a large quantity of oil and a great deal of wreckage. Oulton circled at 3,000yd, weaving and varying height, while his gunners raked U-563 with machine gun fire. The U-boat's crew managed to man a cannon mounted just abaft of the conning tower but they were cut down by the Halifax's guns. By now the U-boat was moving slowly in small circles with a heavy list to starboard. Twice more the Halifax's gunners raked it with machine gun fire but it was still obstinately afloat when Oulton received the recall order to base just one hour and 10 minutes after he had first sighted it.

As he turned HR774 for home another of No 58 Squadron's Halifaxes, DT636:J, appeared and dived to attack the crippled U-563. Oulton tried to warn the other pilot to take his time but was unable to make contact. The depth charges fell short but produced a fresh gout of oil and white vapour. Finally, Oulton summoned the assistance of a No 10 Squadron Sunderland to finish the kill. It was in turn, joined by a No 228 Squadron machine and between them the two Sunderlands sank U-563.

The value of even the single .303in calibre machine gun in the nose of the Halifaxes had been well proven during the early months of 1943. It was felt that a heavier calibre machine gun would improve matters and during the summer experiments were carried out by No 58 Squadron with an American 0.5in machine gun mounted in the nose of their Series IA Halifaxes. The trials were successful and by 1 December over half the aircraft in the squadron had been fitted with these weapons.

Tactics as well as weapons underwent some changes during these early months and patrols were sometimes flown by as many as four Halifaxes in a group with one leading. Two of No 502 Squadron's aircraft, in company with two Sunderlands and a Liberator of No 19 Squadron, USAAF, destroyed a pack of three U-boats on 30 July testifying to the soundness of the new tactics.

It came to the notice of Bomber Command that the Coastal Command Halifaxes were operating at over the permissible maximum all up weight of 60,000lb and a request was made, via Coastal Command HQ, for a report on the handling characteristics. Flg Off McClintock carried out the test from St Eval on 11 June using a No 502 Squadron Halifax which had had its engines modified to give +14lb boost. Despite a take-off weight of 61,400lb, McClintock found the handling characteristics no different from normal and made a favourable report. However, HQ 19 Group took their own views in to account and authorised the removal of certain items of armour plate to keep the weight within the 60,000lb limit.

On 25 July another test was carried out, this time with

HR815/G of the Coastal Command Development Unit, to establish the Halifax's maximum endurance. The engines were again modified to give +14lb boost and 350lb of armour plating was removed reducing the all up weight to 61,570lb. Orders were given to Wg Cdr J. Halley to fly the aircraft at the lowest possible engine revolutions, 1,800, at an indicated airspeed of 140kts and to land with two hours' petrol remaining in the tanks. All the normal operational equipment was retained plus a full crew and a fuel load of 2,732gal. The Halifax landed $14\frac{1}{2}$hrs later at Boscombe Down, where the remaining fuel was carefully measured. The results gave a maximum endurance figure of just over 16 hours. It was therefore recommended that 13 hours should be the normal operational endurance for Mk II Halifaxes fitted with long range tanks, and 12 hours for those fitted with only the three additional tanks in the bomb bay. During October a further test was carried out by the CCDU from Gibraltar and the Halifax remained airborne for 18 hours.

Throughout the months of April, May and June a steady series of changes had occurred to the U-boat transit tactics. No longer able to traverse the Bay of Biscay submerged during the day and on the surface at night, they were forced to fight their way out into the North Atlantic on the surface. Twin and quadruple 20mm cannon mountings were fitted and they travelled in packs for mutual protection. These tactics were successful at first and Coastal Command had to revise its own tactics to overcome this temporary advantage gained by the U-boats. Closer co-operation between Coastal Command aircraft and the special Naval Escort Groups was instituted and soon improved results were gained.

On 30 July this new system produced what was perhaps the most outstanding action of this phase of the war at sea. A Liberator of No 53 Squadron sighted three U-boats, one of about 540 tons and two of about 1,200 tons. In accordance with the new policy the Liberator began to home in other aircraft and a Catalina arrived on the scene shortly afterwards and was dispatched to lead the 2nd Escort Group to the scene. Within a short period of time the Liberator was joined by further aircraft, two Halifaxes of No 502 Squadron, another Liberator and a Sunderland. The Halifaxes were carrying the new 600lb bombs which could be dropped at higher altitude than the depth charges and with the aid of the normal bombsight.

The U-boats maintained a steady evasive action, keeping close together at all times, and put up a very determined defensive fire. Flg Off Biggar took his Halifax down to 1,600ft and burst through the wall of cannon fire to deliver his attack but the bombs fell wide. The Halifax's elevators were damaged by flak and Biggar was forced to withdraw and return to base. Flg Off Van Rossum took his Halifax in for an attack out of the sun and dropped three bombs from 3,000ft from dead astern. One of the bombs exploded close to U-462 and it began to circle slowly to starboard with smoke billowing from abaft the conning tower. Meanwhile the Sunderland attacked and sank U-461 while the U-boats were concentrating their fire on one of the Liberators which made a very gallant, low level attack. Shortly afterwards Van Rossum made another attack on U-462 causing further damage and 15 minutes later it settled on an even

keel and sank leaving 40 survivors in the sea. The remaining U-boat, U-504, fell victim to the Naval Escort Group which arrived in time to join the battle.

In early August a sudden and dramatic change occurred to the U-boat tactics. They no longer attempted to fight their way out on the surface but reverted to their earlier policy of lying submerged by day and surfacing for essential functions only at night. Crippling losses had been inflicted during the preceding week by Coastal Command, losses that could not be sustained indefinitely.

The usefulness of the rocket projectile as an anti-shipping/submarine weapon was not overlooked as a possibility for the Halifax and between late September and early October JD212, a Mk II Series IA aircraft, underwent compatability trials at Boscombe Down. Four RPs were fitted to a strut braced carrier each side of the fuselage. The results showed a reduction of 6-8mph on the maximum speed and 5-7mph on the cruising speed, but otherwise no deleterious effects on handling. Despite the results the project was not continued.

The increasing size and frequency of the Ju88 packs met with some success during August and No 58 Squadron lost three of its Halifaxes to these marauding long range fighter packs. This loss was severe enough but was further aggravated when one Halifax crashed in bad weather and another was forced to ditch in the sea due to engine failure. Five aircraft in nine days. These losses were offset to some degree by the sinking of U-221 on 27 September by one of the squadron's Halifaxes.

The aggressive attitude of the two squadrons was not limited to shipping alone. On 8 October, HR983:R of No 58 Squadron was on a routine patrol when the pilot spotted a Blohm und Voss Bv222 flying boat. He bought the Halifax in for an attack from the port quarter, allowing the navigator to open fire at 600yd with his single machine gun in the nose transparency. The Halifax then broke away to port giving the rear gunner an opportunity to fire, and then dropped astern. Moving over to the starboard quarter, the mid-upper gunner and the navigator then opened fire. The Bv222 maintained a steady course and took no evasive action, returning the fire with cannon from the two dorsal turrets and each beam position. Strikes were seen on the fuselage and hull of the enemy flying boat which was painted duck egg blue all over. Finally, with its rear upper turret position silenced, the Bv222 increased its power and drew away from the Halifax.

Both squadrons had been operating from either St Eval or Holmsley South during 1943 and on 5 December they were notified to move to St Davids, a new station recently opened in Pembrokeshire. The reason for the move was to concentrate three Halifax squadrons in one area under a single station organisation. The third squadron was No 517, which would be stationed at Brawdy, a satellite of St Davids. No 517 Squadron was a meteorological squadron formed from No 1404 Met Flight and received its first Halifax on 1 December while still at St Davids.

Meteorological flights over the sea had begun in 1940 and came under the control of Coastal Command in 1941. In 1943 the units responsible for these duties were increased to squadron strength and No 518 Squadron was formed at Stornoway in July. The first of its Met Mk V

Halifaxes, DG288 and DG250 arrived on 7 July and operations began on 15 September. Ten days later the squadron moved to Tiree.

These meteorological flights were most essential to the prosecution of the war in the air, particularly over Europe. Reconnaissance flights were dispatched west and south west, out over the Atlantic from the Western seaboard, north from Scotland, south from Iceland, west from Gibraltar and out over the North Sea from the east coast of England. Their purpose was to obtain barometric pressure, temperature and humidity readings plus weather, cloud and wind velocity data.

No 518 Squadron's duties were typical of the other squadrons. This particular flight pattern was code-named Mercer, a single Halifax setting out each day on a track of 265°T to a point 700nm from base. Positions along the track were given station numbers at 50nm intervals and the aircraft would fly a series of step climbs and descents, crossing each station at a predetermined height, or more correctly pressure level. Sea level pressure readings were taken every 100nm and at the end of the 700nm leg a circular climb would be made to approximately 20,000ft. The aircraft would then fly due east for 500nm and make a circular descent to sea level and then returned to base at 1,500ft. It was crucial that the pilot should fly the aircraft at exactly the right height and follow the other instructions given by the meteorological observer on board. As the weather pattern was constantly changing it was essential that the observations be transmitted back to base every half hour. This involved a certain element of risk since the flights were made in daylight and there was always a chance of the enemy homing in on the radio signals.

As the information was received from the various aircraft it was correlated with local observations and the results passed to all commands via the teleprinter link. It was on the basis of this information that the weather predictions were made for Bomber Command's operations over Europe.

The work was seemingly unspectacular and it was only by realising the crucial importance of the information obtained that crews retained the very high standards required. Regardless of the weather conditions these flights had to be carried out, often when all other aircraft were grounded. In 1944 No 518 Squadron flew sorties on all but two days of the year, these missions being scrubbed only after several attempts. On one of the two days in question LK966:P was scheduled for the normal 0430hrs departure but the mission was scrubbed twice due to ice and snow. It was rescheduled for 1100hrs but after two attempts to get airborne, both of which ended with the Halifax skidding off into the frozen grass, the mission was finally called off.

A third meteorological squadron, No 520, was formed at Gibraltar in September but did not receive its first Halifax, LK997, until February 1944. In October 1943 two training units were set up to handle the conversion of Halifax crews to Coastal Command requirements. No 1674 Conversion Unit was formed at Aldergrove and was responsible for training crews for the two general reconnaissance squadrons. No 518 Meteorological Squadron was screened from operations and used as an OTU for training crews for its own specialist duties. The first course commenced on 30 October and within five months 60 fully trained crews were produced for the loss of only one crew. The squadron also managed to carry out a small number of operations during the same period.

Halifaxes equipping the meteorological squadrons were Mk Vs, Cunliffe Owen at Eastleigh carrying out the special modifications applicable to these duties. These modifications, to a certain extent, were the product of experience, No 518 Squadron sending the first of its Halifaxes to Cunliffe Owen for additional special modifications in December 1943. Eventually a standard modification was established which promised a degree of accuracy previously unknown in meteorological flying. However, the very urgency of the task in hand, coupled with the reduced manpower available, forced the squadrons to accept a limited modification initially. As a result, fully modified Halifaxes were not available in quantity until early in the summer of 1944. No 518 Squadron sent LK688:D to Gosport on 14 December to undergo some initial modifications, radar and AYD being fitted. To help overcome the delays already mentioned these sets were made at Gosport and supplied direct to the squadron.

A well equipped station in a Halifax provided the meteorological observer with comparative comfort. The nose gun was removed and the additional instruments fitted in the nose section immediately forward of the navigator's position. Radio altimeters enabled accurate measurement of sea level pressure to be made, both by day and by night, while a special instrument which protruded from the starboard side of the nose section recorded air temperature and humidity. Gee, or Loran, and an air position indicator greatly assisted the high degree of navigational precision required and also allowed measurement of high level winds above cloud. Low level wind measurement became more accurate with the introduction of a B3 drift meter and bad weather homing facilities were improved by the fitting of ASV Mk II.

There remained, however, one major problem. The Merlin XX engines displayed a strong dislike for the long range sorties and action was taken to refit the Halifaxes with Merlin 22 engines. While some improvement was obtained the problem was never entirely overcome. This probably accounted for some of the eight Halifaxes lost by No 518 Squadron during 1944. Another danger was discovered by Sqn Ldr Young and his crew. Having nearly exhausted the fuel in the long range tanks fitted in the bomb bay the pilot called for the flight engineer, Sgt Jones, to switch over to the main tanks. As this was done all four engines cut simultaneously and LK966 dropped like a stone towards the sea 1,500ft below. As he struggled to keep the Halifax airborne Young made two rapid requests, 'Switch the bloody things back again', and 'Full boost'. The engines fortunately responded in time. This type of occurrence may well have accounted for some of the other missing Halifaxes.

A new type of meteorological flight was begun on 24 February 1944, when LK692:M set out to fly a triangular course code-named Bismuth. The first leg was a track of 270°T from base for 550nm, then on to a track of 045°T for 400nm before turning on to a direct course for base. The usual readings, climbs and descents were made at

Above: LK966:P, a Met Mk V Series IA of No 518 Squadron photographed over the Caledonian Canal. It was issued to the squadron in January 1944. On 8 January 1943 an official order was issued that all Halifaxes diverted for Coastal Command duties would be finished in extra dark sea grey on upper surfaces with white sides and under surfaces. On 9 February 1943 a further order stipulated white for all front and side views, including engine cowlings and spinners, with upper surfaces in extra dark sea grey. Serial numbers were to be light slate grey with codes in red. LK966, however, appears to have used black for its code letter. Transferred to No 520 Squadron at Gibraltar it became Q-Queenie and lost following multiple engine failure off Portugal on 24 November 1944. The crew were rescued unharmed. / *W. Diamond*

Below: Sister aircraft LL296:S of No 518 Squadron shows the unit practice, at this time, of using only a single letter code, again in black. / *W. Diamond*

the various points. This trial flight was also used to measure the increase in performance with the mid-upper turret removed. The squadron continued to fly both types of flight for the remainder of the war.

No 517 Squadron moved from St Davids to Brawdy during February, its Halifaxes going to Gosport for modification. A third meteorological squadron, No 520 based at Gibraltar, also began operating Halifaxes, receiving LK997 on 6 February.

The change of tactics by the U-boats in late 1943 was rapidly met and overcome by Coastal Command. Equipped with parachute flares the two general reconnaissance Halifax squadrons, Nos 58 and 502, continued their war against the U-boats at night. On 2 January U-445 was attacked and damaged by one of No 58 Squadron's Halifaxes, while another of the squadrons aircraft damaged U-415 three days later. The difficulties inherent with this type of attack are shown by the following account.

Sqn Ldr J. Grant of No 58 Squadron was carrying out a night patrol on 14 January. Flying at 1,000ft he made an initial radar contact at a range of 12 miles but lost and regained it several times during the next few minutes until, finally, a steady contact was achieved from a height of 600ft. The parachute flares were dropped at just under two miles range and a fully surfaced U-boat, travelling at 12kts, was sighted at one and a quarter miles range. At the crucial moment the radar contact was lost once more and Grant was forced to take HR741:H down to 200ft. The U-boat's crew opened fire with cannon and machine guns, fortunately initially against the flares in an attempt to extinguish them. As the Halifax closed to within half a mile the U-boat crew turned their fire on it, narrowly missing the port wing. Grant's navigator gave a spirited reply with the single machine gun while six depth charges were released from a height of 100ft. Explosions were seen to occur along the starboard side of the U-boat and one minute after the attack began it had stopped moving. Sporadic fire continued to come from the U-boat and was returned by the mid-upper and rear gunners of the Halifax. Fourteen minutes later contact was lost and despite dropping five more flares no further trace could be found of the U-boat. The official Admiralty comment was: 'Insufficient evidence of damage'.

An equally frustrating brace of attacks was made by Flg Off F. Culling-Mannix of No 502 Squadron on the night of 28/29 January. Having picked up a radar contact, a timed run was made and two parachute flares dropped. After a further 20 seconds two 600lb anti-submarine bombs were then dropped from 1,400ft. The radar operator assessed that the target had passed slightly to port but before anything could be done a second contact appeared on the screen. Culling-Mannix successfully homed on to the second contact and illuminated a U-boat with some flares. Pressing home his attack, he dropped two more 600lb bombs this time using the Mk VII bombsight. The U-boat was thought to have been straddled by the bombs but nothing further was seen after the attack.

So the endless pattern continued for the next few months, the tempo increasing steadily as the Allied invasion of Europe loomed nearer. As always the meteorological squadrons maintained their constant lonely routines, two further routes being introduced code-named Epicure and Nocturnal. The dangers of these long solo flights is illustrated by the loss of LL144 of No 517 Squadron on 6 June. At 0733hrs a report was received at base that the Halifax was returning with engine trouble. This was followed by a series of dots and dashes which finally faded. At 1230hrs the aircraft was presumed overdue and the probable ditching position plotted at a point approximately 700 miles off Lands End, 400 miles west of Cape Finisterre. Dispatched to search the area LL295:H was forced to return through engine trouble but the search was continued by other Halifaxes from the squadron who were assisted by Catalinas of No 202 Squadron. It was one of these Gibraltar-based Catalinas which finally located the survivors at 1100hrs on 7 June. No 19 Group immediately requested the diversion of a naval vessel to rescue the crew. At 2129hrs LL220:F of No 517 Squadron made contact with the dinghy and dropped six Bircham Barrels and two dinghy radios which were retrieved by the survivors. Half an hour later another of No 202 Squadron's Catalinas joined LL220 and continued the lonely vigil after the Halifax left for its base at 2330hrs. At 0310hrs on the morning of the 8th it was joined by another of its companions and both Catalinas continued to circle ceaselessly until the first Catalina was finally forced to leave. Rescue, in the form of an American destroyer, arrived and retrieved the crew at 0825hrs, a little over 48 hours after they ditched.

By July 1944, Nos 58 and 502 Squadrons were carrying out three types of operations; anti-submarine patrols in the English Channel and the Bay of Biscay, mainly by night, anti-shipping strikes along the French coast of the Bay of Biscay, anti-shipping and armed reconnaissance in the Channel Islands in support of the armies in Normandy. Between 18 and 30 July three attacks were carried out on the harbour of Granville as it was believed that the enemy were passing reinforcements from St Malo through it.

Throughout late July and August the two squadrons were predominantly engaged in anti-shipping patrols in the Bay of Biscay and along the northern coast of Brittany. Beaufighter strike wings severely harassed the enemy's small force of destroyers, sperrbrechers, auxiliaries and torpedo boats which plied these waters desperately trying to escort the German supply convoys. Forced to an almost standstill by day the enemy sought the cover of darkness to mask its movements, only to be singled out by the lone Halifaxes and attacked under the very noses of the shore defences.

The audacity of these Halifax patrols is exemplified by Flt Lt D. McLeod's action on 3 August. The No 58 Squadron Halifax set out for an anti-shipping patrol close inshore along the coast of Brittany. Successfully avoiding the fire from the coastal batteries at Les Minquiers, south of Jersey, McLeod eventually picked up a radar contact which, in turn, lead to a visual sighting of five E-boats. Sweeping in to attack he released his stick of bombs across the formation scoring a definite hit on one. The attack was not entirely one sided and the Halifax brought back a 10in hole in its port wing. These last months also witnessed the final anti-submarine successes, both honours going to

Top and above: JD212, a B Mk II Series I (Special) — no Morris block radiator modification — used for compatibility trials at Boscombe Down. Four rocket projectiles were fitted each side on rails slung beneath the inboard wing section.

Below: LK688:Y3-H of No 518 Squadron shows its four-bladed propellers. The mid-upper turret has been removed and full codes marked in light slate grey. In December 1943 this Met Mk V Series IA was coded 'D' when it was sent to Gosport for radar installation, one of the squadron's first aircraft to be so modified. By February 1945 it was coded as shown here. / P. J. R. Moyes

No 502 Squadron which damaged U-413 on 8 June and sank U-981 on 12 August.

The closing days of August proved to be somewhat of an anti-climax as suitable targets could no longer be found in French waters. Both squadrons moved to Stornaway, in the Outer Hebrides, and commenced anti-submarine patrols. September passed slowly without incident and a distinct rise in morale was noted when, on 4 October, the two squadrons were notified that they would be concentrating on night anti-shipping duties in future. Their patrol area in general would be the Skaggerak and Kattegat but they were to concentrate on the shipping lanes between Oslo, Kristiansand South and the Danish ports. These shipping lanes not only carried Germany's last important sea traffic, bringing urgently needed supplies of raw materials, but were also the focus of the troop traffic from Oslo to the western front.

On 6 June a new weapon had been added to the anti-shipping Halifaxes' armoury, the 250lb and 500lb mc bombs, fitted with an air burst pistol, had caused both material damage and casualties from the shrapnel effect of near misses. The two squadrons continued to use these weapons against their entire range of targets and they were to prove highly effective for night anti-shipping attacks. The replacement of the old Mk VII bombsight with the more sophisticated Mk XIV also greatly improved the accuracy of the attacks.

October was a busy month and Nos 58 and 502 Squadrons, now operating in conjunction, made 27 attacks; but as was usual with night operations results were hard to assess. One exception occurred on 25 October when one of No 58 Squadron's Halifaxes set a merchant vessel and its escort on fire with a single stick of bombs. The flames were still visible at a range of 20 miles. One other item of significance during the month was the receipt of approval to operate the Halifaxes at an increased all up weight of 63,000lb. As a result the standard bomb load was increased from five to six 500lb mc bombs.

The increasing pressure placed on their already strained shipping supply lines forced the Germans to attempt stronger counter measures to the Halifaxes and a marked increase in night fighter activity was soon noted. The Halifax crews countered this by flying at lower altitudes, a certain degree of experimentation being involved before the optimum altitude of 200ft was arrived at. German night fighters were sighted as low as 500ft but they showed an understandable reluctance to attack at lower altitudes. They preferred, instead, to shadow the Halifaxes and await more favourable opportunities.

Twelve attacks were made during November for the loss of the indomitable McLeod and his crew on the 29th. A radio report was received stating that they had just attacked a 4,000 ton ship in the Kattegat, estimating two hits, but nothing further was heard from them.

The weather, always a fickle ally, prevented the normal anti-shipping patrols being carried out, on occasions, during December. Not to be deprived of their prey, the Halifaxes used these opportunities to attack shipping anchored at Kristiansund and to bomb Aalesund along the central Norwegian coast.

Occasionally the Halifaxes became victims of their own style of tactics as Flt Lt Davison of No 58 Squadron found out on 13 January 1945. At about 1940hrs, at a point 20 miles north-west of Gothenburg in neutral Sweden, his Halifax was suddenly illuminated from above by four parachute flares and simultaneously coned by intense light flak from several ships. Davison immediately dived JP329 down to 450ft and turned to port but a quick succession of flak strikes on the port engines caused a sudden loss of power which resulted in a violent side-slip. Davison managed to level the aircraft out but it continued to sink and the rear fuselage struck the sea, tearing off the ASV cover, the lower half of the starboard fin and rudder and portion of the port fin and rudder. Thinking that a ditching was inevitable he closed the throttles but the Halifax rebounded into the air and the second pilot slammed the throttles and pitch levers fully open. Frantically retrimming the aircraft Davison somehow managed to keep it flying on an even keel. The radar operator reported that an explosion had occurred in the ASV set, blowing a large hole in the top of the fuselage and starting an intense fire which spread rapidly from the mid-upper turret to the rear escape hatch. While the wireless operator transmitted an SOS and turned the IFF to the distress setting the radar operator tackled the blaze and finally extinguished it after five hectic minutes.

Davison managed to coax the battered and badly vibrating Halifax up to 1,000ft whereupon the blaze broke out again with increased severity. Both gunners, the radar operator and the flight engineer spent 10 minutes trying to get the blaze under control, the rear gunner finally extinguishing it with the contents of the Elsan toilet. Meanwhile the navigator had given the pilot, somewhat optimistically, a course for base but the Halifax again ran into a hail of flak. Taking what evasive action that he could, Davison finally broke clear and nursed the Halifax up to 1,500ft where a closer inspection was made of the damage. The port inner engne was feathered and the port outer fluctuating badly. The radio, Gee set and ASV were out of action as also were the DR compass, the airspeed indicator and the artificial horizon.

The situation was critical and Davison, having gained another precious 500ft of altitude, turned the Halifax towards Gothenburg and the relative safety of Sweden. The reception was a hail of flak which prompted the jettisoning of the bomb load and the firing of the distress cartridges. Unable to locate an aerodrome JP329 was turned out to sea once more but the port outer engine finally failed completely and the aircraft began to break up. Ordering the crew to bail out, Davison turned the Halifax away from the lights of the town and just managed to clear the top of a hill but hit some high tension wires, struck a tree and plunged into a river, breaking the ice on impact. Miraculously Davison survived.

During February the first of the GR Mk III Halifaxes began to arrive and the two squadrons were quick to exploit the advantages of the new aircraft which featured, among other things, an increased bomb load capacity of nine 500lb bombs. The Met Mk III version did not reach the meteorological squadrons until March and they continued to soldier on with their Met Mk Vs.

The extremes of weather in which these meteorological

HALIFAX G.R. MK II
MERLIN
APRIL 1945

Left and below: A GR Mk II Series I (Special), again no Morris block modification, photographed shortly before the war's end. In the rear view it can be seen that the armament has been stripped off which may account for the lack of a radar housing beneath the fuselage. Note also the pronounced division between the upper surface camouflage colours. The lack of codes and general condition of the paintwork and propeller blades indicates that the aircraft had seen little flying duty.

Above: JP328:BY-H of No 58 Squadron. A fully equipped GR Mk II Series IA, it retains standard Bomber Command camouflage despite its Coastal Command duties. This anomaly was not unusual for GR squadrons during the late war period as they were principally on night shipping attacks. /*P. J. R. Moyes*

squadrons were expected to operate has already been mentioned. Even routine air tests were required on occasions to be flown in appalling conditions, two of No 518 Squadron's Halifaxes being lost through such conditions on 16 August 1944. The cloud base was only 100ft but the two Halifaxes took off only to collide directly over the base, the wing from one landing quite close to the mess where about 800 men were having dinner. The second pilot of one of the Halifaxes was Flt Lt Revilloid, a cousin of the Czechoslovakian president of the government in exile.

Typical of the operations undertaken in bad weather were the experiences of the crew of LK688, now coded H, of No 518 Squadron. The Halifax set out on a routine mission on 10 February 1945, spending the first hour flying through very unstable air temperatures, clear ice collecting on the wings at 1,000ft. The ice continued to thicken, the cockpit canopy turning opaque and electrical discharges began to weave their fantastic patterns over all the protrusions on the Halifax. Two hours later a great flash lit up the aircraft followed immediately by a loud explosion as lightning struck. Despite a fuselage full of smoke no major damage could be discerned except for the starboard undercarriage, which was hanging down, and the total absence of the trailing aerial. The rear gunner reported a flapping noise in his vicinity, which turned out to be the main aerial no longer fixed to the DE fairing but flapping between the fins. The weather continued to deteriorate, severe hail being experienced at 18,600ft plus a constant series of dangerous cumulo nimbus clouds. Overcome by the severity of the conditions the Halifax was eventually forced to return to base, one engine failing en route.

As the war entered its final weeks the volume of traffic increased as the enemy attempted to withdraw troops and equipment from southern Norway. Both of the anti-shipping Halifax squadrons found themselves heavily engaged during this period, No 58 Squadron carrying out 55 attacks during March alone. April produced an all time record of 101 attacks, from the combined efforts of both squadrons, which cost the enemy 5,998 tons of shipping sunk for the loss of four Halifaxes. This same month No 502 Squadron received a message of congratulations from the AOC, Coastal Command, for sinking more than 25,000 tons and damaging 50,000 tons of shipping since January. Even allowing for discrepancies in accurately assessing the shipping tonnages the figures are still impressive. The Ministry of Economics estimated that the blockade by the Halifaxes operating in the Skaggerak and the Kattegat severely reduced Germany's imports from the Scandinavian countries at a crucial time.

May commenced on the same tempo of operations and then, suddenly, the shooting ceased and the war was over. However, while the more lethal aspects had been removed

operations continued at the same pace. Between 9 and 23 May No 58 Squadron carried out 41 operations. Both squadrons were engaged upon unarmed anti-shipping reconnaissance in their old hunting grounds of a few days before. The object of the flights was to report, by wireless, to the Naval OIC at Copenhagen all enemy shipping movements so that the navy could check on the large number of Germans ships known to be fleeing from Russian held territory.

The traffic was as diverse as it was numerous, craft of all descriptions being sighted even down to barges and house boats packed to capacity with troops. Except for one isolated instance none of the Halifaxes was fired upon. Two of No 58 Squadron's Halifaxes experienced engine trouble and landed at the former German occupied aerodrome at Aalborg West, in Denmark, where they were joined by another of the squadron's Halifaxes. Wg Cdr Ingle, the squadron engineering officer, arrived by air on 15 May with a maintenance party and spares, all the Halifaxes returning via Grove, in Denmark, on 18 May.

Both squadrons were disbanded with effect from 25 May 1945, No 58 Squadron receiving a final tribute from the AOC 18 Group, in which he expressed his sincere appreciation of the '…magnificent work carried out by your squadron against the main supply of the enemy between the resources of Norway and the battle zones on the Continent'.

The Halifax had disappeared from Coastal Command as an anti-shipping weapon but it was to soldier on for many years in the meteorological role.

Anti-Submarine Operations by Coastal Command Halifaxes during World War II

27 November 1942   U-263 damaged by J of No 405 Squadron

7 May 1943   U-663 sunk by S of No 58 Squadron

11 May 1943   U-528 sunk by D of No 58 Squadron (shared with other units)

15 May 1943   U-463 sunk by HR746:M of No 58 Squadron

16 May 1943   *Tazzoli* sunk by HR774:R of No 58 Squadron

31 May 1943   U-563 sunk by HR774:R and DT636:J of No 58 Squadron (shared with other units)

30 July 1943   U-462 sunk by S of No 502 Squadron

27 September 1943   U-221 sunk by B of No 58 Squadron

2 January 1944   U-445 damaged by A of No 58 Squadron

5 January 1944   U-415 damaged by R (HR983?) of No 58 Squadron

8 June 1944   U-413 damaged by F of No 502 Squadron

12 August 1944   U-981 sunk by F of No 502 Squadron

14 Development of the B Mk VI and VII

During the night of 5/6 June Bomber Command launched a series of attacks against 10 coastal batteries in preparation for the now imminent invasion. Each target was to be attacked by a force of approximately 100 heavy bombers. The first began at 2335hrs against Fontenay-Crisbecq and was followed 15 minutes later by an attack on the battery at St Martin de Varreville by the remainder of the No 1 Group force. Both attacks were hampered by solid cloud and rain. The third attack began at 0030hrs and was carried out by No 6 Group Halifaxes but again 10/10ths cloud obscured the target and few of the 16-18 500lb bombs carried by each aircraft hit the target.

The second phase of the attacks began at 0320hrs when 101 of the 110 Halifaxes dispatched by No 4 Group bombed the battery at Maisy without loss, an Me 210 and a Fw190 being claimed as damaged. Cloud cover, which had hampered the earlier raids, had partly broken up and this resulted in a far more accurate attack. The No 5 Group Lancasters which attacked the La Pernelle battery at 0335hrs were not so lucky and the target escaped damage. By contrast, No 6 Group Halifaxes successfully attacked the Houlgate position shortly afterwards.

The four remaining targets were all located within close proximity to the landing beaches and for this reason the attacks were timed for just before dawn to provide maximum benefit to the landing forces. The first of these, Longues, was attacked by a Lancaster force but again weather conditions hampered the attack and damage was negligible. This battery survived a further attack by American bombers, at dawn, plus a bombardment by the naval forces off shore. At 0435hrs the Mont Fleury battery was bombed by 101 Halifaxes from No 4 Group but despite some damage the single 122mm gun continued firing until captured by the ground forces. The final two attacks were carried out by Lancasters against Pointe du Hoe and Ouistreham but these also met with little success.

Although the Bomber Command attacks failed to achieve their primary objective, the 5,200 tons of bombs dropped, plus those from the 1,361 Fortresses and Liberators and approximately 200 medium bombers which attacked before the actual landings, did much to disrupt the efficiency of the installations and their crews.

While these raids were in progress an elaborate series of deceptions were being perpetrated by a mixed force of heavy bombers. Over the sea Lancasters and Stirlings created ghost convoys with the aid of Window while over France Halifaxes and Stirlings simulated airborne landings at various points. Eleven Halifaxes of Nos 138 and 161 Squadrons, in company with four Stirlings of No 149 Squadron dropped dummy paratroops near Yvetot. Fitted with ingenious devices, the dummies landed amidst the sound of machine gun and rifle fire. A similar drop was made by three Stirlings of No 149 Squadron near Maltot, while a lone Halifax of No 138 Squadron and 15 Stirlings of No 90 Squadron made another dummy airborne drop near Marigny.

With the initial landings established the Allies were quick to ensure that the immediate German reserves, stationed between the Seine and the Loire, could not be brought into action by 7 June. While fighter bombers harassed the forces themselves a series of heavy bomber attacks were made on key road and rail centred in this area during the night of 6/7 June. Relatively small forces, similar in size to those used against the coastal batteries, were employed against Vire, Chateaudun, Lisieux, Argentan, St Lo, Caen, Coutances, Conde-sur-Noireau and Archeres.

Lancasters attacked Vire just after midnight and two hours later 107 Halifaxes of No 4 Group bombed Chateaudun with equal success. St Lo, 20 miles behind the beach head, was also allotted to a No 4 Group Halifax force. No 78 Squadron dispatched 28 Halifaxes for this raid which was carried out from 3,000ft. The bridge at Coutances was attacked by portion of the Halifaxes from No 6 Group, one of No 420 Squadron's aircraft scoring a direct hit, while the remainder bombed Conde-sur-Noireau.

To aggravate the already badly disrupted rail system, four rail centres near Paris, Achires, Juvisy, Palaiseau-Massy and Versailles-Matelet, were attacked on 7/8 June. All four targets were heavily damaged but the enemy defences, almost negligible in the beach head area, claimed 28 of the attacking 337 bombers. No 78 Squadron's crews pressed home their attacks from 2,800 to 3,000ft, losing three of their Halifaxes at Juvisy.

To widen this state of disruption 16 raids were carried out between 13 June and the 30th against rail congestion points. Losses were generally light but the defences, especially on the deeper penetration raids, took toll of 3.6% of the attacking force.

The 28 June raid on Metz was met with strong opposition and WO H. McVeigh's No 433 Squadron Halifax was attacked four times. He evaded the first three attacks but his Halifax was hit, while in a corkscrew turn, on the fourth occasion. The starboard fin and rudder were shot off ar 1 the starboard elevator damaged. The starboard wing was also badly damaged, the flap, aileron and wingtip being smashed. The aircraft went into a tight spin at 13,000ft and McVeigh ordered the crew to bail out. Two members had abandoned the aircraft when McVeigh managed to regain control and levelled off at 6,000ft.

Shortly after setting course for England the port inner engine failed but McVeigh managed to nurse LV839 back to Woodbridge. He was fortunate in choosing this emergency landing airfield with its extra long runways as it was necessary to land the badly crippled Halifax at 155mph in order to keep the damaged wing up.

On 14/15 June Bomber Command had commenced a series of attacks against troop and ordnance concentrations immediately behind the battle area. Most of these were nocturnal but the attack on the concentration of armoured vehicles at Villers-Bocage on 30 June was carried out in the last light of evening. The target indicators were accurately placed and the master bomber's instructions were clear and precise to the 100 Halifaxes of No 4 Group. Only a small amount of heavy flak was encountered and this died down as the attack developed and only two aircraft were seen to go down.

Somewhat appropriately two new squadrons joined the battle during June, Nos 346 and 347, both manned by French personnel. They commenced operations, literally within a few days of forming, but completed only one operation with their B Mk V Halifaxes, without loss, before being withdrawn for re-grouping with B Mk IIIs.

Another addition to the Halifax force was not so easily discernible. This was the B Mk VII version which, like its predecessor the B Mk III, evolved as an interim model.

The B Mk III version of the Halifax was the end result of the need for increased engine power and in most respects was basically a B Mk II airframe adapted for radial engines. The potential of using even more powerful engines resulted in a redesign of the B Mk III to take Hercules 100 engines which delivered 1,675bhp for take-off and 1,630bhp at 20,000ft. The fuel system, apart from the tanks themselves, was completely revised and pressurised to accommodate injector type carburettors. A permanent 150gal fuel tank was fitted in what had previously been the optional long range tank position in the outboard wing bomb nacelle, and the original No 6 tank enlarged and renumbered No 7. The tanks were also grouped with one group per engine Three 230gal long range tanks remained a standard optional fitting for the bomb bay. Oil tanks, one to each wing, were located between the inner and outer engine nacelles in the leading edge of the wing. These were divided in two by a partition, each portion containing 32gal.

Externally there was little to distinguish the B Mk III from the B Mk VI the latter having some slight variations to the engine cowlings. A B Mk III aircraft, LV838, was selected from Handley Page's production line and extensively modified to the new standard to become the prototype B Mk VI. It was delivered to Boscombe Down for evaluation and testing on 5 February 1944. Fitted with de Havilland three bladed, type 55/18 semi-flared, propellers of 13ft diameter, it underwent climb and level speed performance checks. The more powerful engines allowed an increase in the all up weight, for take-off, to

65,000lb. The tests were quite straightforward and LV838 recorded a service ceiling of 20,000ft, taking 45 minutes to reach this altitude. The maximum rate of climb was 900ft/min while the maximum speeds in weak and rich mixture cruising were, respectively, 252mph and 270mph (TAS).

An attempt was made to better these performance figures by fitting de Havilland experimental three-bladed, Type 55/10 fully flared, propellers of 13ft diameter. However, these failed to produce any significant change in performance. The four Hercules 100 engines used in these trials were replacement units incorporating a small modification but otherwise were no different from the original engines.

A serious set back occurred with the shortage of Hercules 100 engines and as a stop gap palliative Hercules XVI engines were fitted to the modified airframes. The Air Ministry allocated a new mark number to this version which became the B Mk VII. A second B Mk VI appeared from Handley Page's original B Mk III batch, LV776, which was delivered to Bristol's on 29 February. Apart from these two B Mk VI aircraft the first production aircraft, were not destined to leave the production line until June.

In the meantime, production of the interim version, the B Mk VII, continued rapidly and authority was received by No 6 Group to re-equip No 426 Squadron with this version as from 15 June. A similar authorisation was received a few days later for No 432 Squadron to re-equip with the type as from 20 June. The last 15 Halifaxes of Handley Page's B Mk III batch, which had produced the two B Mk VIs, were completed as B Mk VIIs. All 15 were delivered to No 426 Squadron on 16 June.

Since the new aircraft were fitted with H2S the squadron crews were a little perturbed at first at losing their B Mk IIIs with the ventral gun positions. However, the increased performance of the new aircraft soon overcame their reluctance and within four days the crews were ready for their first operation, a daylight raid on St Harten.

No 408 Squadron, which had relinquished its Halifaxes for Lancaster B Mk IIs in July 1943, began to re-equip with the new B Mk VII Halifax just 12 months later, B Flight being completely converted by the end of the month. Apart from a few B Mk III Halifaxes it used the B Mk VII version exclusively for the remainder of the war. With the exception of a few B Mk VIIs issued to No 415 Squadron, the use of this particular mark of Halifax was restricted to the three squadrons mentioned, Nos 408, 426 and 432.

With the mopping up of the last vestiges of resistance in the Cherbourg peninsula on 1 July, the Allies were able to turn their full attention to the problem of relieving the serious congestion of the bridgehead area. The task was not easy since the Germans, despite serious handicaps, stubbornly held fast to a line of well sited defensive positions throughout the bocage country and around Caen. The very nature of the countryside, with its series of massive banked-up hedgerows providing natural anti-tank obstacles, favoured the enemy and the Allied commanders feared that unless a rapid breakthrough was made the whole campaign might be seriously impaired as it had done in Italy. The light and even medium bombers could not deliver a sufficient weight of bombs in a single attack to blast a path through the German defences. Thus Bomber Command was given the task of assisting General Montgomery's frontal attack on Caen.

Originally timed for 0420hrs on 8 July, bad weather intervened once more and the mixed Halifax-Lancaster force of 467 bombers attacked Caen at dusk on 7 July instead. Escorted by a strong force of fighters, the bombers attacked an area two and a half miles long by one mile deep some 6,000yd ahead of the foremost British positions. The only opposition came from the ground defences in the southern sector of Caen. The attack was highly successful and by the evening of 8 July British troops had reached the northernmost suburbs. Unfortunately the bombing had been a little too effective and the heavy cratering and fallen masonry in the narrow streets halted the armoured forces who were trying to reach the Orne bridges. The Germans destroyed all the bridges and established a new defensive system in the industrial suburbs of Vaucelles.

While the intention had not been fully achieved the application had been proven and General Eisenhower approved the subsequent use of Bomber Command and the 8th Air Force for two similar operations, Goodwood and Cobra, designed to smash outlets through the German positions for both the British and American forces in the lodgement area.

Some 2,019 heavy, medium and light bombers were committed to Operation Goodwood. American heavy bombers were assigned three areas, two to the rear and one on the eastern flank of the enemy positions, while the medium and light bombers of the Allied Expeditionary Air Force were to attack three specific pinpoints. Bomber Command crews were given the task of attacking five areas on a line directly in front of the Allied positions which were only about one mile away to the north.

At 0545hrs on 18 July this highly complicated aerial operation began with 235 bombers attacking Colombelles from low level, completely saturating the target area in a precision attack. The smoke still shrouded the target when, 20 minutes later, a second force of 232 Halifaxes and Lancasters swept in for a low level attack on the enemy positions around the Mondeville steel works just south of Colombelles. The master bomber changed the aiming point from time to time to ensure that the target area was completely saturated and crews were highly confident of the results. Losses were light and not all due to enemy action. No 429 Squadron lost a Halifax when LW127 was struck by bombs from another Halifax overhead, completely removing the starboard side of the tailplane and causing it to crash in the target area.

While the Colombelles attack was in progress the road and rail junction at Sommerville was receiving the attention of 105 Halifaxes from No 4 Group, accompanied by 125 Lancasters of No 1 Group, who delivered a very concentrated low level attack. Twenty minutes later, coincidental with the Mondeville raid, a mixed Halifax-Lancaster force of 242 bombers attacked Mannerville. Cagny, a strong point to the rear held by the 21st Panzer Division, was the final target for a force of 106 bombers which attacked successfully at 0620hrs. In the remarkably short time of 35 minutes, 5,000 tons of bombs had been dropped for the loss of nine bombers which included a Halifax from No 76 Squadron and one from No 578 Squadron.

Bad weather yet again interceded in the enemy's favour and after rapid advances the ground forces became bogged down in a sea of mud when heavy rain fell on the 20th. The same bad weather also hampered the American Operation Cobra but most objectives were taken and the American forces at last gained a foothold in Brittany. This produced a new requirement—to prevent the transfer of German reinforcements from the British sector to meet this new emergency. The Second British Army, ordered the make a strong attack in the Caumont area, was to be supported by a force of 693 Halifaxes and Lancasters plus 500 light and medium bombers of the AEAF. Six objectives were detailed for attack on 30 July but bad weather resulted in only three receiving any appreciable weight of bombs. Even these limited results assisted and within a few days the enemy had been driven back to Villers-Bocage and Beny-Bocage thus securing the threat to the American flank.

The next major action by Bomber Command in direct support of the ground forces, on 7/8 August, called for an unprecedented and daring night attack on five aiming points along the flank of the projected advance. Great care was taken not to endanger the nearby First Canadian Army which was to make a night assault on Falaise. Low cloud and smoke which quickly obscured the target markers led to the master bombers cancelling most attacks soon after they began and only about 660 of the 1,000 bombers dispatched actually attacked. The attack on May-sur-Orne by the Halifaxes of No 4 Group was curtailed after three minutes but they managed to drop 427 tons of bombs during this brief interlude.

One final close support operation awaited Bomber Command. On 14 August General Montgomery gave the order for Operation Tractable to begin—the daylight assault that was to cut through the German lines at Falaise and link up with the American Third Army thus isolating the German Seventh Army.

Seven strong points were detailed, all within 2,000yd of the Canadian positions. For once the weather was favourable and visibility excellent, some crews pressing home their attack from as low as 2,000ft. By 16 August the Canadians were in Falaise. With the advance once more mobile, Bomber Command's direct assistance was no longer required.

In addition to the immediate tactical needs of the ground battle, Bomber Command was called upon to make heavy attacks on the isolated garrisons and strong points left behind in the coastal regions.

Some attacks were carried out to meet naval requirements such as the small force of No 6 Group Halifaxes which bombed the E-boat and U-boat pens at Boulogne in daylight on 15 June. Brest was attacked on 14 September by a force of 53 Halifaxes from No 4 Group but this time as part of the campaign to sink the block ships being prepared to deny the port facilities to the Allies when they inevitably occupied it.

The delay in securing sufficient harbour facilities had seriously impeded the flow of supplies to the Allied forces and an approach was made to No 4 Group, by the 21st

Above: A B Mk III of an unidentified RCAF squadron stands at dispersal with its starboard outer engine still feathered. The artwork is a bikini clad female holding two pistols and wearing a stetson. The word *Hellzapoppin* tops a bomb log showing 64 missions. The aircraft letter 'H' is marked on the front face of the undercarriage. / *RCAF*

Below: Summer 1944 and a pair of No 420 Squadron's B Mk IIIs bask in the sunshine. In the background is LW676:PT-Y with 40 operations marked up on its nose. Having joined the squadron on 29 February 1944 it eventually passed to No 1659 HCU on 16 October 1944 and was eventually struck off charge on 16 July 1945. LW380:PT-B, nearest the camera, has an almost identical score with 39 operations marked along side the legend *Achtung! Gallopin' Buzzard*. The artwork is a bat-winged buzzard clutching a bomb. / *RCAF*

Right: Operation Goodwood in progress on 18 June 1944 and LW217:HL-F, a B Mk III of No 429 Squadron, is hit by bombs from another Halifax. The squadron was attacking Mondeville on the outskirts of Caen. With its entire starboard tailplane assembly smashed away it crashed in the target area. / *IWM*

Army Group HQ, to deliver urgently needed supplies of motor transport fuel to Brussels-Melsbrook airfield. The Halifax's spacious interior was well suited to the task and in the eight days from 25 September four squadrons, Nos 77, 102, 346 and 347, transported 431,800gal of fuel to Belgium.

Brest was proving a tenacious obstacle and 334 Halifaxes and Lancasters dropped 1,200 tons of bombs on this target on 25/26 August. Despite this and other attacks it was not captured until 18 September. By Hitler's orders Le Havre, Boulogne and Calais were declared fortresses and their defenders were to resist to the last in the tradition of the Brest defenders. Two successful raids were made on Le Havre but bad weather disrupted the one on 8 September. The following day a raid by 272 Halifaxes from No 4 Group was aborted due to solid cloud which extended from 12,000ft down to 1,500ft. The next afternoon a small force of 69 Halifaxes from No 4 Group returned and made a successful spot attack on the gun battery. This was followed almost immediately by an all out attack employing 930 heavy bombers from all Groups who dropped 4,700 tons of bombs. When they departed a vast pall of smoke and dust hung over the target. The next day 218 Halifaxes and Lancasters returned for an equally successful attack and 10 hours later the garrison surrendered to the two Allied Divisions assaulting the positions.

The success of the Le Havre battle led to similar requests for assistance from Bomber Command. Boulogne was attacked by a mixed force of 742 bombers on 17 September and No 76 Squadron crews, who were at the tail end of the attack, reported that the target was well and truly hit. Boulogne surrendered on 22 September. Calais received similar treatment between 20 and 28 September, the raid on the 27th being made at low level. Integrated with these attacks were two against the fortified areas protecting the long range guns at Cap Gris Nez. On 29 September the garrison capitulated as did the Calais garrison the next day.

The campaign against enemy communications had also continued unabated during this period with attacks on 18 rail centres in the six week period from the beginning of July. The bulk of the early attacks were made by the Lancaster-equipped Groups as No 4 Group was preoccupied with attacks against V1 sites. Thus the Halifaxes did not participate until 18 July when they successfully attacked Vaires, heavily cratering the main sidings and severing the Paris-Meaux through line in several places. Ground fire was intense, both en route and at the target, and many Halifaxes sustained minor damage. A No 466 Squadron Halifax was severely damaged by a flak shell which burst in the fuselage and Flt Lt P. Finley found that he could get no response from either the rudders or the elevators of MZ313. With every indication that the aircraft might break up at any moment he ordered the crew to bail out. The mid-upper gunner later reported that the Halifax's back must have been broken because he could see the tail unit swinging from side to side as he floated away. Plt Off R. Evans, the bomb aimer, remained with Finley and they attempted to get the Halifax back to base. By sheer physical effort they managed to keep it flying straight and level and had reached the Dungeness area off the English coast when they were finally forced to give up the struggle and bailed out just before MZ313 broke up in mid-air.

No 4 Group's next daylight railway target was Hazebrouck on 6 August but it returned to night operations for a very successful attack on Dijon on 10/11 August. Following hard on the heels of this raid part of the Halifax force returned a few hours later to bomb the railway bridge at Etaples. The intense activity of this period is epitomised by the No 429 Squadron diarist who recorded that it was not unusual for the squadron to operate against two or three targets simultaneously, one set of crews taking off while the next set were being briefed etc.

Six days after the invasion forces waded ashore, Hitler's much-hinted-at secret weapon, the FZG 76 (V1), finally made its appearance on the night of 12/13 June. Due to the campaign of the previous months against the permanent V1 launching sites the start was a dismal failure, only 10 flying bombs being launched. The War Cabinet met that same day and formulated a directive which would allow Bomber Command to attack these sites as and when bombers could be spared and providing it did not compromise the needs of the Battle of France. The launching, two nights later, of 250 V1s led to General Eisenhower issuing a directive on 16 June. Flying bomb targets were to be given first priority over everything other than any urgent tactical requirements of the armies in Europe.

Prior to 6 June the task of eradicating 'Noball' targets, as they were called, had lain with the medium and fighter bombers of the AEAF and the US 8th Air Force. The major portion of the task now fell to Bomber Command who diverted a considerable number of heavy bombers to it. Target priorities were split into four categories, large sites, supply sites, standard (permanent) sites, and modified (prefabricated) sites. The Germans held a distinct advantage insomuch that by the time that the heavy bombers were committed, the large sites and the permanent sites had lost their significance. Most firings were now conducted from the prefabricated sites which could be erected then removed at relatively short notice. Thus the Allies were forced to adopt the wasteful but unavoidable campign of attacking all sites. A sustained day and night offensive was instituted to offset the delays caused by the prevailing bad weather.

Eisenhower's directive was but a few hours old when a mixed force of 108 Halifaxes and Lancasters attacked the site at Domleger that night. The solid overcast led to some pessimism about the results but reconnaissance photographs showed that both Domleger, and the lauching site attacked under similar conditions the next night, had been put out of action.

Bad weather hampered operations for the next two or three days but finally cleared sufficiently, on 22 June, for an attack on Siracourt, one of the permanent sites. This was the first daylight raid of any significance for the Halifaxes of No 4 Group. Fifteen Halifaxes of No 466 Squadron led the 100 strong force into the target. Heavy flak greeted the force and Sqn Ldr J. McMullan's LW166 was shot down just short of the target, only four parachutes being seen to emerge. The master bomber instructed crews to bomb

Above: **Bombing up No 426 Squadron's aircraft for a mission. A bomb carrier is stacked against the wheel in the left foreground. OW-G is a B Mk VII, possibly NP775.** / *RCAF*

Below: **Plt Off Eric Schuman, DFC, and crew beneath A–Apple of No 466 Squadron. On the right is the squadron engineering leader Flt Lt 'Nick' Nicholls, an Irishman who came to the unit during his third tour. He would fly with any crew and was awarded a DSO.** / *T. Eagleton*

visually for a start but he soon ordered the accompanying No 105 Squadron Pathfinder Mosquitos to mark the target. These target indicators were not seen by many crews and only one from No 158 Squadron aimed on them, the rest bombing on Gee fixes or the bomb bursts seen through the broken cloud cover. Several of this squadron's Halifaxes orbited the target area trying to identify the site but heavy flak from the south eastern Boulogne defences and a position south of the target curtailed this, five aircraft being damaged.

On the night of 23/24 June a far more successful attack was made, in good weather for a change, on a supply site near Oisemont. A few hours later a force of Halifaxes from No 6 Group made an equally successful attack on the site at Bonnetot while No 4 Group Halifaxes attacked the one at Noyelle-en-Chausse. That same night No 4 Group Halifaxes were engaged in an attack on Le Grande Rossignol.

The changing emphasis to daylight attacks was welcomed by most crews. Allied air supremacy was virtually complete during daytime, German fighters only venturing into the forward areas at night where they met with some success due to the twilight conditions prevailing at that time of the year. Bomber losses diminished appreciably with the daylight raids.

Trained for night operations, Bomber Command crews were not generally versed in formation flying and continued to operate in their streams as at night. However, one of the oldest Halifax squadrons, No 76, tried formation flying in vics of three, spaced at two wing span intervals, and stepped up in line astern. This squadron pioneered other tactics during the night operations of this period. These consisted mainly of very rapid changes of height. After bombing from the usual height of 17,000-20,000ft a dive would be made to about 2,000ft, in a period of about six to seven minutes, at a computed airspeed of over 300mph. Near the coast level speed was increased to an IAS of 250mph followed by a steep climb to cross over the light flak defences and then back down to sea level. Following the first experiments the squadron diarist noted 'These tactics had been suggested by the squadron for a very long time against much opposition and it is pleasing to note how successful they were.'

Attack followed attack, some squadrons putting up two raids in one day. The keenness of some crews may be judged by Flg Off N. Gordon's efforts. No 427 Squadron was part of a force detailed to attack the Ferme-du-Grande-Bois site in the early morning of 28 June. Immediately after take off, at a height of 500ft, the port inner engine of LV988:P failed but Gordon continued on to the target. After the attack Flt Lt Shannon in MZ757:Y escorted him part of the way back until four Spitfires appeared and took over. Shortly after Gordon's Halifax lost its starboard outer engine but happily he made a safe landing back at base.

At the end of June the permanent sites were removed from the target priority list and attacks were concentrated throughout July against the modified sites. The size and nature of these made them extemely difficult to locate in bad weather or at night, even when employing Oboe-equipped Pathfinder aircraft.

Among crews operating at this time was a very special veteran who completed an operational tour with No 425 Squadron on 15 July. 'Vickie' was the squadron mascot, a stuffed bunny sent from Ottawa and received on Easter Day 1944. Given the rank of Flight Officer (after all she was a female bunny!) and made an 'Operational Overseer' she had completed 16 operations by 1 June, with 11 crews booked to take her on future operations. On her 35th and final operation, an attack on Nucourt, she carried a special message for the people of the district. It read, '*14 Juillet, (Bastilles) 1944. France combatante vous envoice par les Canadiens Francais de l'Escadrille Alouette, ce symbole de liberation.*' Attached to a French flag it was dropped from the aircraft before reaching the target. No 425 Squadron's co-tenant at Dishforth, No 426 Squadron owned a Totem Pole which had a difference of opinion with a Halifax that overshot the runway on 19 July. Damage was fortunately light to both parties.

Some targets required several attacks before they could be definitely declared destroyed and a far more positive result was achieved against the actual supply dumps which fed the individual sites. Typical of this type of operation was a series of five attacks on the suspected supply depot at Foret de Nieppe. The first of these was a daylight attack on 28 July by the Halifaxes of No 4 Group. Oboe-equipped Mosquitos led each separate formation in, the first group of six Halifaxes bombing with the leading Mosquito and the next six when they were abreast of the smoke columns which surged up from several large explosions. Early the following morning the same crews repeated the performance, Foret de Nieppe receiving its fifth and final raid on 6 August.

From the end of July attacks against modified sites were left entirely to the US 8th Air Force while Bomber Command continued its campaign against the supply depots and the large construction works believed to be associated with the still-to-be-experienced A-4 (V2) rockets.

During one of these attacks, against Bois de Cassan on 4 August, Flg Off R. Simpson of No 466 Squadron was leaving the target area when his Halifax was hit by flak, slightly wounding the bomb aimer and severing the rudder control rods. The rear gunner, Sgt D. Brown, found that he could steer manually by manipulating the severed rods but a more positive form of co-ordinated control was needed for a safe landing. An attempt was then made to repair the rods with wire cut from the trailing aerial but this proved ineffective and Simpson was finally forced to order the crew to abandon HX275:S.

The destruction of the supply dumps and the means of transportation produced the first positive reduction in the number of V1 launchings and the campaign proceeded to the next logical step with an attack on the main assembly complex, the Opel factories at Russelheim, near Mainz. On 12/13 August 287 Halifaxes and Lancasters attacked the target in the face of moderately heavy flak and the persistent attention of night fighters who appeared in force towards the end of the operation. Damage was confined to the storage, loading and dispatch facilities in the south western area of the complex. The price was 20 heavy bombers. A second raid completed the task but the Halifaxes were busy over France that night.

Daylight raids were preferred as has already been stated but they tended to bring home the operational risks in vivid detail. No 466 Squadron was attacking Coquereaux on 9 July when Flt Sgt Burrows' Halifax was hit by flak five miles west of the target. He continued his run and bombed but moments later MZ368 exploded, five or six parachutes miraculously appearing from amidst the smoke and wreckage.

With the overunning of the V1 sites in the Pas de Calais, the task of the heavy bombers ceased and the campaign ended with a note of appreciation to No 4 Group from the Air Council on 12 September:

'... To convey to you their warm appreciation of the part played by your Command in defeating the enemy's flying bomb attacks on this country. The continuous and heavy bombing of the experimental stations, production plants, launching sites, storage depots and communications which has been carried out by your Command not only imposed on the enemy a prolonged and unwelcome delay in the launching of his campaign but effectively limited the scale of effort which he was able to make. This notable achievement has added one more to the long list of successful operations carried out by Bomber Command.'

Above: **Artwork supreme! MZ896 QB-O, a B Mk III of No 424 Squadron taxies out for take-off with one crew member standing in the mid-ships escape hatch. Photographed on 13 November 1944, its bomb log stood at 57 missions.** / *RCAF*

15 Bomber Support Operations

In 1940 the war of radio counter measures began, principally, with the disruption of the German radio navigational beams used to guide their bombers to British targets. From these small beginnings a never ending struggle grew. A small unit, the Wireless Intelligence Development Unit, was expanded to squadron strength in December 1940 becoming No 109 Squadron. For the next two years it used its Wellingtons and Ansons in the development of radio counter measures and radar aids. In July 1942 the squadron split, A Flight becoming No 1473 Flight and B flight becoming No 1474 Flight, while No 109 Squadron proper re-equipped with Mosquitos to become the first Oboe specialists in No 8 Group.

By January 1943, No 1474 Flight's work reached sufficient proportions to warrant its expansion into a full squadron. Thus No 192 Squadron was formed on 4 January being given the distinguishing 'Special Duties' suffix. Its equipment consisted of seven Mk Ic and nine Mk X Wellingtons, three Mk IV Mosquitos — and a Tiger Moth. Officially the Wellingtons were to be phased out and replaced by Halifaxes but shortages at that critical stage of the war delayed the process. Although two Mk IIs, DT737 and DT735, were received on 9 and 15 January respectively, it was July before the next, DK246, arrived. In the interim the Halifax's capacity and long range capabilities were utilised to ferry ground crews out to the squadron's detachment at Blida, in North Africa.

The first Halifax operation proper came on 2 June when DT735 carried out a patrol off the Dutch coast, in the Hook of Holland area, to Alkmaar. An eighth member was added to the crew, a 'Special Operator', who monitored the electronic search equipment installed. A second mission took DT737 to a point south-west of the Scilly Islands on 12 June, again searching the ether for German radio signals.

Several other operations were flown over the western approaches of the Bay of Biscay, to the Brest peninsula, Nuremburg and Dusseldorf. On the missions over Germany the Halifaxes joined the main bomber stream to search for German radar and radio signals. The special operators logged each signal intercepted, noting its basic characteristics or, if necessary, making a recording of it.

Following this pattern the Halifaxes continued their patrols for the next few months. Norway came under surveillance during this period, a detachment of one Halifax and two Wellingtons operating from Lossiemouth in Scotland.

No major co-ordinated radio counter measures system for the direct support of Bomber Command existed at this period of the war. Individual defensive aids such as Monica, Window and Mandrel had been introduced into the main force groups but to accomplish anything worthwhile their use had to be co-ordinated. Window could be used fairly freely without losing too much of its value and Monica by nature was an individual device. However, Mandrel, the offensive jammer on the German early-warning radar frequencies, was by far the most sophisticated aid available over enemy territory and, if properly exploited, could protect an entire bombing force. The decision to co-ordinate these efforts finally reached fulfilment on 8 November 1943, with the creation of No 100 Group. The old title of Special Duties was deleted and all squadrons in the Group were called 'Bomber Support' squadrons.

No 192 Squadron lost its first Halifax in an unfortunate accident on 18 November. Flg Off Israel and his crew had been detailed to join the main bomber stream going to Ludwigshafen but due to a delay were too late and returned to Foulsham. During the landing something went wrong and DK244 crashed, bursting into flames and killing several members of the crew.

Having already moved to Feltwell from Gransden Lodge in April, No 192 Squadron then moved to Foulsham on 25 November, where it was placed under the control of No 100 Group. Radio counter measures was a double edged sword and while the squadron continued its passive listening watches it also began a very active career of electronic jamming in support of the main force bombing raids. Lack of aircraft, which had long delayed its expansion, was finally overcome early in January 1944 when Mk III Halifaxes began to arrive. The Wellingtons, however, lingered on.

Typical of a night's operations by the squadron were five sorties dispatched on 1 May. One Mosquito, DZ376:M, was sent to Mannheim, a single Wellington, LN398:A, patrolled off the northern coast of France between Boulogne and the Cherbourg peninsula, and three Halifaxes undertook radio-radar searches in co-operation with Bomber Command attacks on railway targets in France and Belgium; LW624:T went with the bombers to the area south of Malines, LW613:W made a lonely trip to a point 70 miles north-west of Toulouse while the main force attacked the city's railway installations and MZ501:P accompanied the bombers to Lyons.

The first major success of No 100 Group was the operation in support of the Normandy landings. Three Halifaxes, LW613, LW621:Q and LW624, patrolled throughout the period of darkness along a route between Tonbridge and Yeovil maintaining a Mandrel screen to mask the activities of the Air Borne Forces. This success led to a much wider exploitation of the Mandrel screen and No 199 Squadron's Stirlings were enlisted to supplement these activities.

The Allied advances of August overran most of the German night fighter bases in France and made the position of those in Belgium and Holland precarious. The loss was not confined to bases alone for the Germans were also forced to relinquish their early warning radar installations along the Calvados coast and the Brest peninsula. Bomber Command was thus able to approach northern German targets, across the neck of Denmark, using the Mandrel screen to conceal its activities. Size, however, was a problem but this apparent disadvantage was rapidly turned to an advantage.

When only minor operations were in progress the Mandrel screen would be used in conjunction with a small force carrying Window. At an appropriate time the latter would burst through the Mandrel screen and release the Window thus simulating, on the German radar, a heavy raiding force. German night fighters would be scrambled to meet this ghost force causing the waste of precious stocks of fuel and sowing confusion amongst the German controllers. The element of doubt created by these spoof raids was perhaps the greatest benefit, for suspicion caused delay while the night fighter controllers made certain that the raid was genuine and this, in turn, cost the fighters themselves any tactical advantage they might otherwise have enjoyed.

Bad weather which hampered the Allies so much during the closing months of 1944 also had its advantages. On 3 September LK781:Y was sent out under cover of the weather on a daylight patrol to within 120 miles of Sylt. The Lossiemouth detachment was also very active during this period and five Halifaxes carried out patrols off the Norwegian coast from Kristiansund to the Lofoten Islands.

A second Bomber Support squadron came into being on 8 September, No 171 Squadron being formed from the third flight of No 199 Squadron at North Creake. The intention was for it to equip with Halifaxes but it continued to operate Stirlings until the Halifaxes arrived in force. The first operation, one Halifax and three Stirlings, took place on 23 October. The following day No 171 Squadron began ferrying its Halifaxes, it now had eight, to St Athan where Mandrel equipment was fitted. The squadron's first operation with this equipment was carried out on 20 November. One of the four Halifaxes scheduled for the operation aborted due to magneto trouble but the other three, NA106:X, NA110:Z and LK874:C, were successful. The latter Halifax, LK874, had been attached to No 199 Squadron on 22 August for instructional work on the Mandrel installation so that those crews going to No 171 Squadron would have completed their training in advance. This particular Halifax was also fitted with a multi-Mandrel installation and underwent tests at the Telecommunications Flying Unit at Defford before

returning to squadron duty. It failed to return from an operation on 16 April 1945.

Part of No 192 Squadron's activities centred around German rocket weapons and during October special patrols were made off the Dutch coast between Walcheren and Texel to try and locate signals believed to be associated with these missiles.

A somewhat unusual crew took MZ564:X of No 192 Squadron to Walcheren Island to watch the breaching of the sea wall at Westkappel on 3 October. The captain, Wg Cdr Donaldson, was accompanied by Air Commodore R. A. Chisholm, DSO, DFC, who acted as second pilot while Wg Cdr Willis, DSO, DFC, acted as bomb aimer. The purpose of the flight was to record any enemy radio telephony in connection with the attack by the 259 Lancasters. Three other aircraft accompanied them on this daylight mission, a Halifax and two Lightnings — the latter being temporarily on the squadron's strength.

The next night MZ706:P and LW623:S went to Saarbrucken to investigate enemy VHF telephony while MZ795:V recorded VHF and D/F centimetric signals. A fourth Halifax, MZ932:Z, patrolled the Kattegat while main force bombers sowed mines off the Danish coast. This particular Halifax's job was, in addition to recording enemy VHF telephony, to locate the coast watcher stations, automatic homing equipment being fitted for this purpose.

No 192 Squadron continued to specialise in signals investigation and jamming for most of its career but occasionally it joined the other squadrons in the Group to perform Window-Mandrel operations. It carried out the first of these on 9 October, MZ706 and LK781 going to a point midway between Heligoland and Wilmshaven where they dropped Window to create a diversion for the Bomber Command force operating that night. Such diversions, however, were few and in November it continued with its investigation of the enemy coast watcher stations, the equivalent of the British Observer Corps system, to try and determine if they were being used in connection with the inland flak patrol. On several occasions radio buoys in the North Sea were also investigated to see if they were associated with the launching of V1s. There was something almost prophetic about a lone V1 which passed over the squadron's base on 3 January.

A third Halifax squadron, No 462, was posted to No 100 Group in December, moving to Foulsham that same month. The intention was to make No 462 Squadron a radar counter measures squadron, the Halifaxes to be fitted with the latest equipment designed to jam not only radar transmissions but also wireless and radio telephony. This naturally involved a considerable amount of modification work which could not be done quickly. As an interim measure the squadron continued to operate on spoof sorties, commencing its first missions on 1 January 1945.

Having been a bomber unit the crews of No 462 retained a certain urge and on the Stuttgart operation of 7/8 January each of its Halifaxes carried two 500lb bombs. The practice spread rapidly to the other Halifax squadrons within the Group, which from February included No 199 Squadron, and eventually lead to an elaborate deception technique. The Window force would simulate a normal bomber attack complete with Pathfinder type pyrotechnics and a spoof Master Bomber using No 5 Group radio frequencies.

The first of No 462 Squadron's modified Halifaxes arrived from St Athan on 15 February but the supply was slow, the first RCM operation not being flown until 13 March. These specialist aircraft were distinguishable by the two tall radio masts, offset to port, on the upper fuselage and the suffix 'G' to their serial numbers. Only eleven of these Halifaxes had been taken on charge by the time hostilities ceased.

In the meantime the squadron continued its spoof activities with a double 'attack' by eight of its Halifaxes on 22 February. For this type of operation the Window force came out from the cover of the Mandrel screen and dropped sufficient metal foil to stimulate a reaction from the German night fighter controllers and then withdrew behind the screen again. A little later, as the night fighters were being recalled to their assembly beacons, the Halifaxes emerged once more and made another Window drop. The resulting confusion disrupted any efforts to present a co-ordinated defence.

The following night No 462 Squadron returned to the Ruhr for another spoof raid, in the Neuss area, again operating without loss. However, a further repeat performance over the Ruhr the next night cost the squadron four of 10 Halifaxes. On this occasion the spoof force were operating alone and had to bear the brunt of the resulting night fighter force attack.

One of No 192 Squadron's Halifaxes had a harrowing experience during February but survived to deliver some important information. On the night of the 19th, Flg Off Dutton was routed to the Bohlen area to search for possible enemy centimetric transmissions in the 3,000-4,000mc band. While on the way to the target area one of the engines of NA242:D failed but Dutton continued the mission. Later, on leaving the target area, the Halifax was subjected to 15 attacks over a period of 90 minutes. Among the assailants, some of whom were not identified, were a Ju88, a Bf109 and a jet fighter. The Halifax survived the attacks and landed safely at Manston. The mission had been very successful. WO Coulton, the special operator, having obtained the first reliable information to be gained on enemy centimetric radar transmissions.

No 4 Group's Halifaxes were not the only ones to suffer at the hands of night fighter intruders on 3 March, three of the Foulsham based Halifaxes being shot down in the circuit area by a Ju88. The intruders were also successful over North Creake and No 171 Squadron lost NA107:T but the crew fortunately escaped by parachute. The only other survivors were three of the crew from No 192 Squadron's LV255:G which had been caught with its navigation lights on.

Techniques grew steadily more sophisticated and spoof raids reached a very high standard of efficiency. On 10 April orders were received by No 462 Squadron to provide 10 Halifaxes to cover a main force attack on Leipzig. While three Halifaxes operated on RCM duties the seven strong Window force preceded the main bomber force. Just before reaching Leipzig the Window force branched off towards Berlin dropping foil to simulate the main force. This was done to raise the enemy night fighters to the north of Berlin, where they could be engaged by Mosquito intruders, and to draw others away from the real target and the attacking main force bombers.

The rapidly approaching end of hostilities produced a 10 day lull in operations and none of the Halifax squadrons operated during this period. Then, on the night of 2/3 May Bomber Command launched its last large scale offensive of World War II. No 8 Group sent 126 Mosquitos, in two waves, to attack Kiel while a further eight attacked Eggebeck airfield and six others Husum airfield. No 100 Group dispatched a mixed force of 161 Halifaxes, Mosquitos, Liberators and Fortresses to a wide range of targets for a variety of tasks. Of the four Halifax squadrons No 462 Squadron sent six aircraft to the Flensburg area for a Window operation and four others to Kiel for RCM duties. Each of the Halifaxes carried five 500lb bombs for good measure. The other Foulsham based squadron, No 192, dispatched 14 Halifaxes and five Mosquitos, six of the Halifaxes going to Kiel for RCM duties and the other 10 dropping Window in the Flensburg area.

Both of the North Creake squadrons put up a maximum effort, No 171 Squadron operating four Halifaxes on Mandrel-Window operations over Flensburg, 12 more on similar duties plus bombing over Kiel and two other Halifaxes for the same duties in the Schleswig area. No 199 Squadron outdid itself by putting up 21 Halifaxes, two of them flown by crews borrowed from No 171 Squadron. Five of the Halifaxes carried out Mandrel-Window operations in the North Frisian Islands, one returning early due to compass failure. Ten others joined the Mandrel-Window bombing operations over Kiel and six carried out a similar task in the Schleswig area. All of the 16 Halifaxes carrying out bombing were loaded with eight 500lb bombs each. Two of this force, RG373:T and RG375:R failed to return, thus becoming the last operational Halifax losses of the war.

With the cessation of hostilities the four squadrons carried out routine training flights for a while. One of No 462 Squadron's Halifaxes flew members of the Allied Commission to Flensburg and returned carrying several passengers including a Luftwaffe colonel for interrogation.

On 25 June Exercise Post Mortem began and all four Halifax squadrons participated. The object was to simulate large scale raids on the former enemy territory so that an assessment could be made of the efficiency of the German raid reporting system. The exercise continued until early July with aircraft of Nos 1, 3, 8 and 100 Groups participating. The results showed that Bomber Command's techniques had been so successful that in nearly every case plotting of the main force was incoherent, scattered and unreliable. The final words of the report were pertinent to No 100 Group, their brevity masking a wealth of meaning, 'On the whole there appears no defence against the most effective jamming of the Mandrel and Window forces.'

On this very satisfactory note the Halifax squadrons disbanded over the period of the next few weeks, their task most definitely completed. However, this did not mark the end of the Halifax's service with No 100 Group. No 192 Squadron, which disbanded on 22 August 1945, became the nucleus of the Radio Warfare Establishment the Flying and Servicing Wing forming at Foulsham while the HQ, Technical Wing and Y Wing formed at Swanton Morley. An advance party moved to the unit's new location at Watton, in Norfolk, during September. On 6 October the first group of aircraft arrived, 15 Halifaxes, 10 Mosquitos, three Fortresses, an Oxford and a Ju88, albeit that they were three days in advance of the official movement order from No 100 Group.

On transfer to Watton the unit came under No 60 Group, Fighter Command. By mid-October it had an establishment of 24 Halifaxes, eight Fortresses, 12 Mosquitos, three Ansons, an Oxford and a Proctor. With such a large number of aircraft three sets of codes were issued, the Halifaxes being allocated V7-A to H, then J to Q, U3-S to Z. The Fortresses were given U3-A to H and the Mosquitos 4S-O to Z.

Above: A rare bird; PN451/G was a specially modified B Mk III of No 100 Group. Because of the nature of this group's work few photographs exist. The twin aerials of the high powered radio jamming device, code named Air Borne Cigar, can be seen on top of the fuselage. The incomplete daylight tactical markings on the fin are the yellow stripes used by No 462 Squadron.

16 Final Operations in Europe

From late May to late July 1944 Bomber Command found itself committed to the tactical needs of the invasion forces in France and thus did not carry out any attacks against German cities. Activities over Germany itself were restricted to oil targets in the Ruhr and some concern was felt over the respite being afforded the vast German industrial system which had already demonstrated its capacity for recuperation. Accordingly the strategic bombing offensive recommenced on 23/24 July with an attack on Kiel and 30 major raids had been completed, against 18 targets by the end of September.

Kiel received three more raids, the defences taking an increasing but relatively small toll of the bombers during the second and third attacks. The fourth was, however, an outstanding success the 499 bombers, mostly Halifaxes from Nos 4 and 6 Groups, destroying large sections of the eastern port area with its naval dockyards, arsenal and marine stores. Kiel was removed from the target list for the remainder of the year. Hamburg, so terribly battered the preceding year, reappeared on the target list and was attacked by No 6 Group on 28/29 July, No 408 Squadron taking its new B Mk VII Halifaxes into operation for the first time.

Attacks against the German oil industry had surged and ebbed throughout the preceding war years. Finally, within a few days of the Normandy landings, both British and American bomber forces were allocated a series of priority targets aimed at crippling the German oil industry.

Lancasters attacked the first of these targets on 12/13 June and four nights later a mixed force of Halifaxes and Lancasters bombed the Fischer-Tropsch plant at Holten (Sterkrade). Flak and night fighters provided strong opposition and nature provided an additional complication — solid sheet cloud at 7,000ft which extended upwards to 10,000ft. This quickly swallowed up the target indicators and crews were forced to aim on any glow which filtered through. Losses were high, 32 aircraft failing to return and many reported attacks by night fighters who found conditions ideal for their purpose, above the clouds. Plt Off Sargeant's No 466 Squadron Halifax was attacked by a Fw190 and then a Ju88, both of which caused minor damage, but a third night fighter fell to the Halifax's gunners.

By the end of the month the emphasis shifted and from July to September the Ruhr synthetic oil plants were given precedence. The only divergence occurred in August when the fluid nature of the ground battles required attacks on storage depots, dumps and refineries in occupied territory.

The initial Bomber Command attack on Bottrop-Welheim was made by No 4 Group Halifaxes on 20/21 July while No 3 Group raided the Meerbeck plant. Not all squadrons were operating at full strength that night due to the V1 campaign commitments, No 466 Squadron sending only six Halifaxes, 12 others being dispatched to attack the V1 installations at Ardouval. The German defences were extremely active, eight Halifaxes failing to return. No 51 Squadron lost one of its aircraft under rather tragic circumstances.

Just after completing its bombing run MZ581:C6-C was very badly damaged, the port fin and rudder being shot away, the mainplanes and fuselage severely holed and the rear turret buckled. It was some time before the starboard rudder would function properly and even then Flg Off H. Jowett had to be assisted by the bomb aimer, Flg Off B. Cosgriff, to hold the aircraft on an even keel. Jowett attempted to make an emergency landing at Woodbridge but the Halifax hit some trees and both he and Cosgriff lost their lives along with the mid-upper gunner. The remainder of the crew escaped from the burning wreckage.

Some crews were pursued from the target area to the Channel during the return flight. Harassed by flak over the target Plt Off P. Wilson of No 466 Squadron had his Halifax trailed by two night fighters which attacked from time to time without success. They finally disappeared over the Dutch coast but moments later an Me210 attacked out of the darkness but again without success. Despite the heavy defences, ground haze and the use of dummy fires the attack achieved its purpose and the northern part of the plant was badly damaged.

A few nights later No 4 Group attacked the Wanne Eickel plant with devastating results despite thick haze which obscured the target but not the target markers. The ground defences inflicted some minor damage but no bombers were lost. Several fighters were seen but no combats resulted due partly to the cloud cover and partly to the use of a new form of Window designed to jam the latest night fighter radar frequencies.

The temporary divergence to attack storage depots ceased with the 18/19 August raid on Reime-Ertvelde. The same night an attack by 234 Halifaxes on the Sterkrade-Holten plant marked the start of a new series of raids against the Ruhr-based synthetic oil plants. Sufficient damage was caused to warrant no further attacks against this target until late September.

No 4 Group dispatched 243 Halifaxes to attack the Homberg-Meerbeck plant on 27 August, making Bomber Command's heaviest raid yet committed to a single oil target. It was also the first daylight raid made by British bombers on Germany, in force. In addition to the heavy fighter escort a single Mosquito accompanied them to make an immediate assessment of the resulting damage. The newly formed No 462 Squadron made their operational debut on this raid and for Flg Off A. Lane it was nearly his last. Having lost the port outer engine before even crossing the enemy coast he continued on to the target despite having to fly at a reduced altitude. Over Homberg his Halifax ran into the double danger of being singled out by the flak and running the gauntlet of the bombs showering down from above. Finally, with a second engine put out of action by the flak and the main target obscured Lane was forced to bomb the docks on the east bank of the Rhine.

The target was heavily damaged and losses were nil. Having established the precedent Bomber Command pursued its daylight campaign with vigour and during September 11 raids were made against Ruhr synthetic oil plants. These were divided into two series, Kastrop-Rauxel, Kamen, Nordstern (attacked twice), Wanne-Eickel, Dortmund and Schloven-Buer forming the first phase. The heaviest losses were seven aircraft on the first Nordstern raid and four over Wanne-Eickel but the total figure of 18 out of the 945 bombers employed was not excessive. The only partial failure was the first Nordstern raid thus requiring the second attack, two days later, on 13 September.

During the first raid Flg Off J. Currie's No 77 Squadron Halifax was hit by flak five minutes before bombing. The starboard outer engine was damaged and a considerable oil leak occurred making it impossible to feather the propeller. Despite the subsequent loss of height the crew elected to continue and bomb as planned. During the final run up to the target MZ710:E was hit repeatedly by flak which inflicted some 200 holes, set fire to the dinghy, disabled both the DR and magnetic compasses and the radio. Just after bombing one fuel tank in each wing was punctured and the port inner engine hit removing one cylinder. Height was lost steadily down to 3,500ft but the Halifax managed to escape the flak at the Dutch coast. This height was maintained across the North Sea but just before reaching Orfordness the starboard outer propeller and reduction gear flew off damaging the starboard inner propeller. Despite the loss of one engine and two others only providing partial power Currier was able to maintain sufficient height to reach the Woodbridge area, three Spitfires which had taken up station in the target area remaining as a comforting escort throughout. The endeavour nearly ended in disaster when Currie made his approach, skimming the tops of the trees, on to an experimental runway but a series of yellow flares diverted him at the last moment and he was able to turn on to the correct runway. The port inner engine cut over the boundary fence but the landing was completed safely. The Halifax's old problems of insufficient power and poor asymmetric handling were things of the past.

The second series of oil raids, made in late September, were nearly all disrupted by the vagaries of weather.

Typical of these was the Bottrop attack on the 27th. Solid cloud obscured the target and most crews were forced to make a timed run from a navigational fix. During the long steady run one of No 432 Squadron's B Mk VIIs, NP692:K, was hit by flak wounding the pilot, Flt Lt Woodward. He nevertheless held the bombing run steady while the bombs were released only to have a stick of bombs from above fall past the nose of NP692, barely missing it. The Halifax went into a dive with 30° of bank on and Woodward slumped over the controls. Flg Off D. McLennon, the wireless operator, managed to pull him out of the seat while Flg Off C. Hay, the navigator, got the aircraft under control again. Woodward's parachute was beyond use and his condition made it impossible for him to jump in any case so Hay headed for England and Woodbridge and the rest of the crew elected to stay with the aircraft and assist him. Hay had some difficulty locating Woodbridge at first but eventually found it.

The captain attempted to take over for the landing but his condition was too critical and Hay decided to attempt it himself. The sole B Mk II Series II Halifax, HR756, now attached to the Bomb Ballistics Unit, was sent up to guide NP692 in and to assist Hay with instructions. Formating on NP692, Hay was talked down to a very smooth landing but the speed was too high and the Halifax rose again then dropped back again heavily, the engines catching fire as it came to a halt. The crew all escaped. Tragically Woodward succumbed to his injuries the following day.

September also marked a change of command, control of Bomber Command reverting from SHAEF to the Combined Chiefs of Staff. Under SHAEF's control Bomber Command had shown itself capable of a great variety of tasks, daylight raids were now established as both possible and profitable and precision attacks an accepted capability. The German petroleum industry and its storage facilities remained the first priority. Transportation systems, armoured vehicle production and storage areas, and motor transport construction plants stood second on the list. SHAEF retained the right, however, to be able to call upon Bomber Command for any urgent requirements to support the ground battles.

The increasing threat from the Schnorkel equipped and closed cycle U-boats produced a request from the Admiralty for an attack on their bases at Bergen, in Norway. Halifaxes made the lengthy seven and a half hour round trip in daylight on 4 October. Weather over the target was clear with good visibility and a concentrated attack was delivered. Two large explosions were seen and a pall of smoke remained visible up to 100 miles away on the return journey. Considerable damage was done to the workshops and shipyard facilities and four U-boats, U-92, U-228, U-437 and U-993 sunk. No fighter opposition was encountered and only slight flak experienced.

Weather again proved the decisive factor and during October restricted the number of oil plant attacks to five by Bomber Command and four by the US 8th Air Force. Bomber Command restricted its attention to the Ruhr and launched a double daylight attack on 6 October against Schloven-Buer and Sterkrade-Holten.

The Schloven-Buer raid was carried out using a group formation for the first time, No 76 Squadron leading the vanguard. A heavy fighter escort, mainly of Spitfires, guarded the second force of 126 Halifaxes detailed to put Sterkrade-Holten out of action. Every effort was made to ensure that the force arrived in a compact group and 33 Pathfinder aircraft were on hand to provide a well laid and sustained series of target markers. A concentrated attack developed in the face of strong ground defences and reconnaissance later confirmed a high degree of damage to the target. Only three Halifaxes were lost but more than 70% of the bombers sustained flak damage.

The next day No 4 Group were called upon to attack Kleve, a town ahead of the advancing ground forces and source of a possible threat to the flank of the 21st Army Group. Bomber Command had already expended some effort to assist with the final assault on Walcheren, the heavily defended island at the mouth of the Scheldt Estuary, the gateway to Antwerp. It lay below sea level and was protected from inundation by a massive sea wall and a system of dikes and embankments. The intention was to breach the sea walls and flood out the defenders.

No 76 Squadron crews enthusiastically reported a most successful and accurate attack. The next day 358 Halifaxes and Lancasters went back again and pounded 11 gun positions. A final attack by No 5 group on 30 October completed the work and the ground forces once more took over the task, the German garrison surrendering on 3 November.

Immediately following the Walcheren attacks came an order for all groups of Bomber Command and the US 8th Air Force to prepare for a maximum effort attack on the enemy defences along the River Roer, half an hour before the Allied ground offensive opened. Bad weather delayed the operation for five days but finally, on 16 November, the heaviest tactical bombarment to date broke loose on the enemy. While American heavy bombers blitzed the front line positions, 1,188 Halifaxes and Lancasters attacked the fortified base towns at Heinsburg, Julich and Duren. Halifaxes hit Julich with 1,946 tons of bombs raising huge pillars of smoke which towered to 8,000ft. A large portion of the town was devastated and the road bridge across the Roer effectively removed. All three raids were highly successful and losses amounted to a modest four, none of them Halifaxes.

Between October 1944 and May 1945 Bomber Command achieved the climax of its strategic bombing offensive. As a weapon it had at last fulfilled its ambition, new techniques, new aids, new weapons and an endless supply of well trained crews gave it a flexibility and a striking capability never before achieved. In the last three months of 1944 a greater weight of bombs was dropped than the total tonnage for 1943. During this period the last battle of the Ruhr was fought with outstanding success, some 61,000 tons of bombs being dropped during 14,254 sorties. The cost was less than 1%, only 136 bombers were lost.

The Dortmund raid of 6/7 October was the opening gambit of this winter offensive against the heart of Germany. After Dortmund came Bochum then Duisburg received a double blow. On 14 October 1,063 bombers attacked during the morning, lighting the way for a repeat raid the same night. Flak was intense and 14 of No 158

Squadron's 27 Halifaxes sustained damage but fortunately none was among the 15 aircraft which failed to return.

Many of the same squadrons took part in the second attack made by 1,065 bombers. In both cases a greater weight of bombs were dropped than on any previous occasion in attacks on German industrial cities. Enemy defences were less active during the night raid and only six aircraft failed to return. Some, however, had harrowing experiences. During a visual inspection after bombing a hole seven feet by two feet was seen in the bomb doors of a No 415 Squadron Halifax. A single 1,000lb bomb had failed to drop with the rest of the bomb load and parted company during some evasive manoeuvres when the bomb doors were closed.

No 462 Squadron lost a Halifax which crashed at base due to flak damage and could have lost another but for the tenacity of its pilot Flt Sgt Cockerill. Coned by searchlights just short of the target, the Halifax was hit severely and the pilot was wounded in the left eye. Momentarily losing conciousness he recovered in time to bring the aircraft back on to an even keel and complete the bombing run. The return trip was nightmarish, fire breaking out in one engine and at one stage the aircraft was illuminated by night fighter flares. Unable to see the instruments, Cockerill had one of the crew call out the readings and he successfully got the Halifax back to England where he made an emergency landing at Manston. Reports also came in from many crews of jet night fighters. Reports of this nature were to increase over the next few months and culminate in a disastrous daylight encounter over Hamburg in March 1945.

Essen, a target long familiar to crews, received two raids in quick succession. The first was a major attack by a force of 1,055 bombers. Pathfinders laid sky markers over the heavy cloud covering the target, enabling approximately 90% of the bomber force to attack. Times had changed and the losses were less than 1%, although two badly damaged Halifaxes, one from No 78 Squadron and the other from No 466 Squadron, barely managed to reach base. Of the eight that failed to return that night two, a Halifax and a Lancaster, were lost in a mid-air collision near Aachen.

On 25 October, 771 Halifaxes and Lancasters returned to Essen for a daylight attack and sky markers once more enabled a high degree of destruction to be made to the Krupp works. Homberg was also attacked that same day and one of No 420 Squadron's aircraft gave an admirable demonstration of the Halifax's sturdy construction. Over the target area Flg Off Glover's LW386:A was hit by several 1,000lb bombs, some of which passed between the engines of the port wing, carrying away fuel tanks numbers one and three, while another struck the starboard elevator close to the rear turret. Miraculously the Halifax did not go out of control and Glover brought it back safely.

It was then Cologne's turn, a triple blow being delivered within a period of four days. It was during the second raid, a night attack on 30/31 October, that, in addition to reports of jet night fighters, a crew from No 158 Squadron described how they had seen a rocket projectile come up from the ground and then travel horizontally across the Halifax's track before trailing off. More references to jet night fighters appeared in the crew reports for the following night's raid on Cologne.

Left: A B Mk III of No 578 Squadron, high over the target in daylight, is caught by the camera of a sister aircraft. / *K. G. Beetson*

Below: The crew of No 51 Squadron's LV937:MH-E pose for the camera after completing *Expensive Babe's* 100th mission, an attack on Osnabruck on 6/7 December 1944. Left to right: Flt Lt R. Kemp; Flt Sgt A. C. Townsend; Flt Sgt J. D. Silberberg; WO R. J. Williams; Sgt E. S. Hawkins; Flt Sgt R. T. Jackson; and Flt Sgt F. Thwaites. The Halifax in the background bears a previously unrecorded daylight tactical marking — an all white fin. / *J. D. Silberberg*

Left: Another high scorer. Sqn Ldr T. E. Eagleton, DFC and Bar, poses with his crew in front of No 466 Squadron's LW172:HD-F after the aircraft's 91st operation in March 1945. The crew had just completed their first tour and Eagleton his second. LW172 did 96 operations before crashing in fog at Driffield, killing the entire crew. For part of its career it was flown by Flt Lt Dave Shannon, DFC, the A Flight commander who eventually became CO of the squadron. / *T. E. Eagleton*

Below left: A No 640 Squadron B Mk VI displays its artwork. The lack of bomb symbols indicates that it is a new aircraft. The starter battery cart is plugged in ready for start up. / *RAAF*

Above: NP763:H7-N, a B Mk VI of No 346 Squadron with partly completed codes; only the letter N had been outlined in yellow and the unit emblem (a white rabbit on a blue and orange disc outlined in crimson) was missing. Free French Air Force fuselage roundels and fin flashes are carried, the same crimson shade being used for the code letters and the daylight tactical markings. A late arrival on the squadron it took part in the final mass Halifax operation of the war, the attack on Wangerooge on 25 April 1945. It ended its days in storage at No 29 MU High Ercall and was sold for scrap on 14 February 1949. / *ECP Armées*

Below: PP165:L8-P of Groupe 1/25 *Tunisie* wearing its *Moonlit Bison* badge immediately above the name C. Brachet, starts up its engines. A B Mk VI, it was formally handed over to the French Government on 31 October 1945, one of 64 which were transferred between this date and 21 August 1947. (RG490, '91, 92, '500, '09, '10, '11, '13, '40, '43, '45, '47, '48, '60, '61, '62, '63, '86, '87, '90, '94, '95, '600, '05, '06, '07, 09, '19, '20, '24, '25, '45, '46, '47, '53, '55, '61, '68, '70, '703, '05, '52, '88, '89, '816, '18, '19, '21, '23, '28, '42, '44, '45, '46, '52, '68, '69, '74, ST795, '97, '99, '800 and PP165.) It still retains its former No 347 Squadron daylight tactical markings, a crimson diamond, with code letters outlined in yellow. It served with the squadron from August 1944. / *ECP Armées*

31 October had a special significance for No 425 Squadron. 'Vicki' that illustrious veteran had given 'birth' in early October to four offspring, two daughters 'Mich' and 'Marie', two sons 'Gerry' and 'Jos'. All five were posted to 22 OTU, 'Vicki' as an instructor and the rest as sprog aircrew. All were then posted back to the Alouette squadron as sergeants and commenced operations. 'Vicki' received a well earned DFC and was repatriated to Canada with effect from 12 October. Her final words of wisdom were, 'Now get some in, kids'.

Four days later the squadron was plunged into gloom when MZ831:Z failed to return from the raid on Bochum. Reputedly Sergeants 'Mich' and 'Gerry' were among the missing crew but they mysteriously reappeared several days later. Another Halifax from the squadron nearly met a similar fate over Bochum when a load of incendiaries hailed down upon it, causing 37 holes but fortunately no injuries. Severe damage was done to both wings, the aileron controls, flaps, elevators, rudders and the trailing edges of the wings and tailplane. The oil and fuel lines to one engine were severed and it burst into flames but the blaze was fortunately overcome by the extinguishers and the aircraft limped back to base.

Many a derogatory remark had been passed concerning the single, hand operated, Vickers gun in the nose cone of the Halifaxes but it proved its worth to a No 429 Squadron crew over Oberhausen on 1 November. As the Halifax turned for home an Fw190 swept in for a frontal attack on MZ474:B but Flg Off R. Herbert, the bomb aimer, opened fire with the Vickers gun sending the fighter down in flames to crash on the ground far below.

German jet night fighters would also appear to have suffered at the hands of two No 427 Squadron Halifax crews that same night. Conditions were favourable for the enemy with a full moon and clear skies above a solid layer of 10/10ths cloud. At 2045hrs the tail gunner of LV945:F sighted a jet fighter well astern but it disappeared. A few moments later another jet fighter appeared about 800yd away and the tail gunner instructed the pilot to dive towards the clouds and opened fire as the range decreased to 600yd. The glare from the jet increased greatly as it followed the Halifax through the turn. Moments later the glow turned to flames as the rear gunner's fire struck home sending it spinning down to burst against the ground. The pilot, bomber aimer and flight engineer confirmed its destruction.

At precisely the same time, but several miles distant, the flight engineer of LW130:U also sighted a jet fighter on the port beam and slightly higher. The pilot put the Halifax into a corkscrew dive towards the cloud cover as the fighter, now identified as an Me163, closed in firing as it came. The mid-upper and rear gunners returned the fire with long bursts. The enemy fighter pressed home its attack to approximately 200ft before bursting into flames and dropping vertically through the cloud. The crew did not see the aircraft hit the ground but considered that it was destroyed. They were quite positive about the identity of their attacker and if they were correct then it is the only known instance of the use of this radical jet, or more precisely rocket, fighter operationally at night.

The list of targets grew longer as the weeks passed and most raids were successful. Then, out of the thick fog of Saturday morning, 16 December, the German Fifth, Sixth and Seventh Panzer Armies burst through on a front stretching from Monschau to Echternach. The Ardennes offensive had begun. The ground fog continued for days greatly hampering Allied tactical air support and both Bomber Command and the USAAF were forced to attack communications centres, Duisburg, Munich and Ulm, on 17/18 December. As weather conditions improved the blows moved closer to the battle front and Trier was attacked in daylight on 19, 21 and 23 December.

Other attacks on communications centres, rail, road and water had already begun in November and were delivered against an elongated strip bounded on the west by the Rhine and on the east by a line joining Hamburg, Hanover, Würzburg and Ulm. The success of this difficult to prosecute campaign was marginal at first. The Germans had only been able to gather sufficient supplies, equipment and troops together to launch their Ardennes offensive at the cost of civilian and other, low priority military traffic. Despite a none too promising start the campaign was continued throughout the remaining months of the war and finally achieved its desired effect.

Oil targets, neglected during October, received increased attention, eight daylight and six night attacks being made during November. The success of this type of target was more readily assessable than those of the communications category. Its success had a direct bearing on the Ardennes offensive and indeed made an impact on all fronts. Production had struggled to make a remarkable recovery during October and November but by December it began to taper off and continued to decline rapidly throughout January. The effect would have been achieved earlier but during December tactical requirements absorbed a larger proportion of Bomber Command's efforts and only two daylight and three night attacks were made.

The new year brought with it the sureness that the end of the war with Germany must be near. During those closing months nearly one fifth of the total tonnage for the entire war, 181,000 tons of bombs, was dropped by Bomber Command. Losses remained at less than 1% and far more danger now seemed to exist from midair collisions in the congested skies than from the German night fighters.

Flt Lt R. Sledge of No 578 Squadron had successfully attacked Hanover on the evening of 5 January 1945. Twenty minutes later, at 13,000ft, another Halifax was seen simultaneously by the mid-upper and rear gunners to be converging on RG367 from above and behind. Its approach was so rapid that neither of the gunners had time to warn Sledge and the first thing he knew of it was the shuddering impact as it hit the port wing outboard of the engines, badly damaging the whole wing section. The port aileron was rendered useless and at the same time the flaps came down 30° which did little to assist Sledge as he fought to pull RG367 out of its spiral dive to port. Eventually, by sheer physical force on the control column, full right rudder and by throttling back the starboard outer engine, he managed to regain control and level out. The only way that he could now keep the aircraft on a rough course for home was by keeping the starboard engines throttled back and varying the settings of the port engines and rudder trim. Münster provided a warm welcome for the battered Halifax and Sledge somehow managed to turn north, regaining his original track. His troubles were still not over as the Halifax was again hit by flak over Nijmegen and became almost uncontrollable. The end was near and over Maas the IFF set was switched to distress while the wireless operator tried repeatedly to contact base but without success. As the Halifax passed south of Antwerp, into the Ghent area, the crew bailed out and the battered aircraft crashed nearby in a cabbage patch.

Saarbrücken, a choke point on the German supply routes to both the Ardennes sector and the southern front received a not insignificant share of the 7,000 tons of bombs dropped on transport targets in January, three main force attacks being made in 24 hours. During the night attack on 13/14 January the Halifax's sturdiness was established for all time.

Flg Off A. Wilson of No 51 Squadron had bombed the target and was on the way back to base when his Halifax collided with another aircraft, nine feet of the nose section being chopped completely off. Miraculously the four engines continued to function perfectly despite some propeller damage caused by pieces of wreckage. The aircraft plunged down to 1,500ft before Wilson could regain control and get it back up to 11,000ft again. The loss of so much of the fuselage produced a serious trim problem and it was hardly surprising that MZ465:MH-Y should stall and dive again. However, Wilson managed to master its idiosyncrasies and was eventually able to hold the Halifax steady at 7,000ft. The radio had also remained serviceable and the wireless operator managed to get out an SOS before being forced to shut down the equipment due to shorting, blue sparks playing around the fuselage.

The five remaining members of the crew, the navigator and bomb aimer had perished with the nose section, were frozen by the icy blast of air which tore through the fuselage as the Halifax battled along. The few pieces of fuselage skinning which had been bent around, over the shattered nose section, gave little protection from the elements. Most of the instruments had been put out of action including the airspeed indicator and the DR compass. By a superb piece of airmanship Wilson nursed the battered aircraft back to England where he made a successful landing without causing further damage.

The highest proportion of Bomber Command's efforts still went into attacks on industrial centres and the bad weather of January only lent weight to this campaign, deferring as it did raids against the smaller oil targets. Ludwigshaven, Hanover, Hanau, were all attacked in turn and then Magdeburg received its second full scale attack on 16/17 January. The bomber force was composed mainly of Halifaxes and No 76 Squadron, the orginator of many new tactics, opened the attack well before the main force. The object of the exercise was to draw off any night fighters from the Pathfinder aircraft following behind and was most successful. The last area raid of the month was the attack on the Zuffenhausen district of Stuttgart on 28/29 January. It was, in effect, a double raid, one portion of the force bombing the jet engine production facilities while the remainder bombed the nearby marshalling yards.

The January attacks had been dominated by a triple theme which was to continue for the remaining months of the war; attacks against industrial capacity, fuel and transport, which included communications. The emphasis on communications targets remained in ascendance principally because the shrinking perimeter of German occupation was now virtually confined to Germany itself. Thus strategic and tactical requirements overlapped and attacks on cities now fulfilled a double role as the fighting drew closer. Some cities not previously included on the list of targets fell under the blows of Bomber Command due to their new significance. Mainz, never previously attacked because it had no significant industrial capacity, now assumed a new value because of its geographical position in relation to the proposed ground campaigns. The initial raid of 1/2 February was by a force of 292 Halifaxes from Nos 4 and 6 Groups. Lancasters and Mosquitos of No 8 Group marked the target, which was partly covered by cloud, with ground markers and the initial force of Halifaxes aimed on these. However as the attack developed so did the cloud cover and sky markers were dropped to enable the rhythm of the bombing to continue unabated. Ground defences and a few night fighters were active but had little success and severe damage was done to the town.

During the first week in February, when preparations were being made for the new Allied offensive, the Second Tactical Air Force and the American light and medium bombers were committed to an intensive series of attacks against enemy rail and road complexes. The aim was to deny the Germans the opportunity to regroup their forces when the initial attack was made towards Kleve on 8 February. To precede the artillery bombardment by 1,000 heavy guns, Bomber Command launched two successful attacks on the night of 7/8 February against the key centres of Goch and Kleve. The Luftwaffe made an appearance over Goch and lost an Me410 to a Halifax of No 466 Squadron for its efforts.

NA175 was not so fortunate and a Ju88 damaged it so badly that the crew had to take to their parachutes. Sgt B. Peckham, the rear gunner, was the last to leave and saw the enemy night fighter firing at the crew as they descended so continued to fire his own guns until the ammunition was exhausted, then bailed out himself. His hasty exit did not allow him to see the results of his last burst of fire but the crew later found out that the Ju88 had been damaged and crash landed safely on a railway line but the unfortunate pilot was killed moments later by a train.

German night fighters had better luck during a Bomber Command attack on Worms on 21 February. At the debriefing one of the No 158 Squadron crews reported seeing a Halifax go down with one engine on fire and explode on the ground. One minute later, at 17,000ft over the target area, a second Halifax 300yd away was shot down by what was believed to be an Me410. No 102 Squadron also took part in the raid using 13 of their new B Mk VI Halifaxes.

A close watch was kept on the progress of repair work in Mainz and on 27 February a daylight raid was made by Halifaxes who systematically devastated the target. Crews reported it as a routine operation, a remark which showed quite significantly that Allied air supremacy had indeed been secured.

Oil targets had by no means been neglected during this period over 25% of the efforts of Bomber Command being devoted to this purpose and 14,000 tons of bombs were dropped during February. The scope of targets had widened and now embraced not only the synthetic oil plants but also benzol plants and crude oil refineries which were attacked along with oil storage depots. The campaign reached its climax during March when plants not already destroyed were systematically eliminated.

Kamen, a Fischer-Tropsch plant, received four raids within eight days. Fairly heavy damage resulted from the first three but not sufficient to ensure that production could not be resumed within a few weeks. No 4 Group was ordered to carry out an immediate attack on the night of 3 March. The raid was most successful with good marking and accurate opening bombing which provided natural aiming points for the remainder of the Halifax force. Opposition was only minor and crews returned feeling satisfied with the accuracy of the raid. However, German night fighters, virtually absent over the target area, were waiting over the British bases for the returning bomber force.

As Flg Off Strachen made his final approach to land at Lissett an Me410 raked MZ917 with cannon and machine gun fire causing serious damage and wounding the rear gunner. Fortunately Strachen was able to complete the landing safely. Another of No 158 Squadron's Halifaxes, PN437:X, was being flown by Flt Lt C. Rogers who was less fortunate. Diverted because of the intruder activity his Halifax was shot down in flames near Sledmere Grange. Two more of the squadron's Halifaxes were attacked over the Wash but managed, not without difficulty, to extricate themselves. Eleven of No 466 Squadron's aircraft had landed when the intruders appeared over Driffield shooting down NR179 and NR250, two of the six Halifaxes still airborne. The 22 Halifaxes from No 10 Squadron were all diverted to Leeming, Skipton-on-Swale and High Ercall but HX332:V was intercepted and shot down in the Knaresborough area, only two of the crew escaping. No 77 Squadron diverted four of its Halifaxes but one was intercepted near the base by an Me210. It closed to within 500yd and fired a burst which severed the intercom and put the rear turret out of action, slightly wounding the rear gunner. The pilot managed to evade any further attacks and returned to the circuit area. Although all lights had been extinguished and Flying Control could not be raised a landing was attempted in view of the rear gunner's injuries. The first approach was unsuccessful but NR210:Z was landed safely the second time. The two French squadrons were also subjected to attacks and No 346 Squadron lost NR229 over Croft but the crew escaped by parachute. No 347 Squadron was less fortunate NA680 being shot down near Cranwell and NR235 at Sutton-on-Derwent, near York. With the exception of the pilot, Sqn Ldr Terrien, the rest of the crew escaped from the latter aircraft.

A few intruders returned again the next night and a single Ju88 shot up No 425 Squadron's base at Tholthorpe but without causing any damage. These last gestures were little more than the death throes of the German night fighter force and already the Allied Air Forces were beginning a slow reduction in strength in preparation for the end of hostilities which was inevitably near. No 578 Squadron flew its last operation on 13 March and officially disbanded three days later.

The oil war continued and Bomber Command's smallest target, the Mathias Stinnes benzol distillation plant, was attacked on 15 March in daylight. One of No 102 Squadron's new B Mk VI Halifaxes, RG498:N, was badly damaged by flak over the target. The starboard fin and rudder were shot off and both elevators jammed but Flt Lt W. Dick managed to fly the Halifax back to Manston where he made a forced landing. The aircraft caught fire and was completely destroyed but the crew escaped unhurt.

The threat from the new prefabricated Type XXI U-boats had been realised late in 1944 and the Admiralty lost no time in pressing for attacks on the assembly yards. These began in November 1944 and increased in intensity until they reached devastating proportions during March and April 1945. Hamburg and Bremen were the principal recipients and it was during a heavy daylight raid on the former, on 31 March, that Bomber Command had its one and only heavy engagement with German jet fighters.

A few minutes before 0900hrs the last wave of the 460-strong bomber force approached the target. The mixed force of Halifaxes and Lancasters from No 6 Group were late and the fighter escort had already withdrawn when approximately 12 Me262 fighters from III/JG7 tore into the formation. The battle lasted 12 short minutes but eight bombers, three Halifaxes and five Lancasters, were shot down. One of the Lancaster pilots later reported seeing five Lancasters and one Halifax shot down in the space of two minutes. One of No 425 Squadron's crews in NR231 also reported seeing rockets used but possibly not all the Me262s were fitted with the deadly R4M rockets. This undoubtedly saved the bombers from further destruction but the effect of the Me262s closely grouped four 30mm cannon still took a grim toll. Three of the Halifax squadrons each lost a single aircraft, No 408 Squadron NP806, No 415 Squadron MZ922 and No 425 Squadron MZ418. Four Me262s were claimed as destroyed.

With April came a further reduction in Bomber Command effort and strategic area bombing ceased as such, only 21 major raids being made in April, little more than half of which were night operations. Only 35,000 tons of bombs, about half the previous month's figure, were dropped and the largest single portion of this went on naval targets, harbour facilities and shipping. Railway centres, oil and tactical targets absorbed the remainder.

Leipzig was one such target lying, as it did, in the path of the Allied ground forces. It was attacked in the last light of evening on 10 April, a strong fighter escort being provided. Opposition was however mild, only a small amount of flak being encountered and this was visually aimed. A few isolated jet aircraft were seen in the target area and the crew of NP937:T from No 425 Squadron claimed an Me163 as probably destroyed. The mid-upper gunner first sighted the enemy fighter attacking a Lancaster 500yd away and opened fire whereupon the Me163 was seen to stall and fall on to its back then go down in a steep dive. Three other members of the crew verified the claim.

It was unfortunate that the B Mk VI Halifaxes should at last arrive in significant numbers too late to play a major

Above: **RG590:R-H7 of Groupe 1/25, formerly a No 346
Squadron aircraft which was transferred to the FAF on
31 October 1945. It retains its former unit markings but
all armament has been removed.** / *ECP Armée*

role in the offensive. Nos 346 and 347 Squadrons became fully operational with the type on 4 April and No 158 Squadron began operating theirs on the 18th during a mass raid against the military installations and gun batteries at Heligoland. The Me262 fighters again appeared during this operation and Flg Off Halle of No 425 Squadron was disturbed to find his Halifax, already on three engines, only 700yd from three of these potent fighters. To his relief they did not attack MZ425:U possibly being short of fuel or ammunition.

The last major operation for the Halifaxes was another 'naval' target, the coastal gun batteries on Wangerooge island in the East Frisians. A mixed force of 482 Halifaxes, Lancasters and Mosquitos from Nos 4, 6, 8 and 100 Groups were dispatched and 468 attacked. Fighter cover was provided by 10 Spitfire squadrons from No 11 Group and the Oboe-equipped Mosquitos marked the aiming points. Weather conditions were good with no cloud and visibility excellent. A highly concentrated and accurate attack developed in spite of accurate heavy flak from the nearby islands of Spiekeroog and Langeoog, and the eastern and western extremities of Wangerooge. Fighter opposition was restricted to a single, almost prophetic, appearance of a lone Me262. However, the enemy defences still claimed several aircraft and damaged at least three others. Two Halifaxes were seen to collide on the way in to the target and these were presumably No 426 Squadron's NP820:W and No 408 Squadron's NP796:M. A third Halifax failed to return, NP921 from No 347 Squadron and this possibly fell victim to the flak as did two others from No 76 Squadron. Two Lancasters were also seen to collide on the way out from the target.

For the main force crews of Nos 4 and 6 Groups this was their last operation and it came as something of an anti-climax for many. On 7 May German representatives signed the document of unconditional surrender at 0141hrs and the same day No 4 Group was transferred to Transport Command. No 6 Group began converting Nos 408 and No 425 Squadrons to Lancasters as they were to return to Canada with six other squadrons to train as part of 'Tiger Force' for operations against the Japanese. Four other squadrons remained in Bomber Command to serve with the Armies of Occupation and No 426 Squadron converted to Liberators and joined Transport Command.

Most squadrons spent their last days before converting to transport types dropping now unwanted stocks of bombs in the North Sea. One particular duty was carried out with a distinct air of pleasure — low level sightseeing tours of the former German targets. Three routes were laid down: route A — base, Emden, Bremen, Hamburg, Kiel, Heligoland, Egmond, Cromer, base (859nm); route B — base, Lowestoft, Rotterdam, Krefeld, Essen, Munster, Egmond, Cromer, base (680nm); route C — base, Lowestoft, Antwerp, Bonn, Dusseldorf, Dortmund, Munster, Egmond, Cromer, base (745nm). The pleasure came not from the sight of the desolation and destruction but rather from the opportunity of showing their passengers, the ground crews, the end result of their years of hard work.

Both of the French squadrons, Nos 346 and 347, remained under the control of Bomber Command and completed similar bomb dumping duties plus some temporary detachments for transport work in France. On 18 June, 14 Halifaxes from each squadron took part in the fly past over Paris. Finally, flying officially ceased on 6 October and a few days later both squadrons returned to France taking with them their Halifaxes, presented to France by the British Government.

Above: **L8-N taxies out for take-off with some of its crew standing in the escape hatches. The daylight tactical markings of the two former French squadrons were eventually removed and black fins with normal tricolour markings on the rudder outer surfaces substituted.** / *ECP Armées*

17 Operations in the Far East

In August 1943 No 1577 Flight was formed for the purpose of carrying out extensive trials with the Halifax Mk V and the Lancaster Mk III in India, the unit to operate under the control of No 221 Group. Four crews were assembled at Lyneham on 1 September with Sqn Ldr J. H. Leyland, DFC, and Bar as commanding officer. The three other captains, whether by design or chance, were a representative cross section of the Commonwealth forces, Flt Lt Middleton RAF, Flg Off Richardson RAAF and Flg Off Stewart RCAF.

The first of the two Halifaxes, DK254, arrived on 3 September but the unit moved to Llandow the following day due to the lack of facilities at Lyneham. The two Lancasters, JA903 and JA904, were waiting for them on arrival but it was another four days before DK263 was available to complete the Halifax contingent.

Engine installation on both of the Halifaxes required a good deal of work to bring them up to the necessary standard and the ground crew worked away at this problem for the next week. A civilian repair team arrived from Handley Page's during this period and replaced the original fins on each aircraft with the new 'D' shaped type. Finally, on 26 September, the flight left for India staging through Portreath, Rabat Salé, Castel Benito, Cairo West and then direct to Karachi. The two Lancasters arrived on 5 October, DK254 on the 6th and DK263 the next morning. All four spent the rest of the month at Salboni undergoing minor inspections and air tests.

On 1 November the two Halifaxes and Lancaster JA904 took part in a 'Bulls Eye' exercise to Calcutta. This was the start of a series of tests and miscellaneous duties all designed to provide information on operational efficiency under tropical conditions. For this reason most of the tests were kept to normal duties such as meteorological flights. On 3 November DK254 took off in blazing heat at 1500hrs, loaded to an all up weight of 60,500lb, and climbed to 19,000ft. This performance was repeated on 17 December at an all up weight of 62,000lb and with the local temperature five degrees hotter. The Halifax again performed well reaching 17,200ft in just under an hour. Just one week later DK263 was tested at 62,000lb, taking only 1,200yd to become airborne and reached 20,000ft, a creditable performance.

The serviceability of all four aircraft was hampered by lack of spares, the ship carrying these having caught fire and sunk. However, the success of the trials so far brought a more definite line of duty and on 5 December the flight was notified that it would act on transport duties but was on no account to undertake combat operations.

The flight settled down to its new duties but had to operate under some very primitive conditions. Flg Off Stewart completed the last 700 miles of a return flight from Karachi in DK263 on three engines due to an oil leak in the starboard engine. Not all problems occurred in the air and DK254, in company with one of the Lancasters, spent an uncomfortable time at Quetta while refuelling was carried out from four-gallon cans.

The large 'D' fins fitted to the Halifaxes proved something of a problem in local conditions. The large fin area caused the aircraft to weathercock quite pronouncedly and since most runways in India were aligned badly out of wind most landings were made cross wind, a nightmare which brought DK254 to grief on 3 January. The Halifax had just returned from Bombay and as usual had to make a cross wind landing. At the last moment it swung badly and hit a pile of sand bags, collapsing the port undercarriage. This was the flight's first accident in 800 hours of flying.

Far more serious was the accident involving DK263 on 26 January at Kamptee, near Nagpur. The Halifax was on a routine flight from Bombay and had a full crew on board plus two of the ground crew, five passengers and 66 bags of mail. The strip was only 600yd long but on two engines Flt Lt Middleton did not have much choice. He managed to land the aircraft safely but was not aware of the 80ft drop into a river bed at the end of the strip. The Halifax struck a hole with its starboard wheel near the end of its landing run and cartwheeled into the river, landing on its back. Nine people were killed but miraculously the remainder were all off the serious list within a few days.

The flight moved to Mauripur on 7 May and changed its duties once more, now being used for glider towing trials. Four Horsa and two Hamilcar gliders were provided for the task but these still had to be erected. It was early June before HH974, the first Hamilcar, was ready for towing trials. The flight now expanded to include Dakotas and Curtis Commandos but was devoid of Halifaxes although action was inhand to fill the gap. On 15 October the Air Ministry allocated two Mk III Halifaxes, NA642 and NA644, for general handling trials in the Airborne Forces role which included glider towing, paratroop and equipment dropping. The two Halifaxes were ferried out to India by two No 38 Group crews with Sqn Ldr A. G.

Above: A modified B Mk III of No 1341 Flight, PN369:A, displays its additional D/F type fairing beneath the rear fuselage, virtually the only external evidence of its radar investigation capabilities. Standard Bomber Command Europe camouflage is worn, only the roundels have been replaced by SEAC type. / *IWM*

Below: A jeep and 9-pounder artillery piece loaded into the bomb bay of Halifax R-Robert. This is a similar installation to that tested on NA692 and NA644 of No 1577 Flight. / *J. Stewart-Crump*

Norman acting as flight commander. They arrived on 10 November, the day after the Lancasters officially ceased their attachment.

No time was wasted and on 15 November NA644 commenced towing trials with the Hamilcar. The Halifax responded very well and engine temperatures were well within the prescribed limits despite the high ambient temperatures. The Horsa towing trials suffered a temporary set back when LH237 crashed from 50ft on take-off while still on tow behind NA644. Examination of the wreckage showed that the basic cause of the accident was failure of an aileron hinge bracket. This led to a more detailed inspection of the other gliders and all were found to be suffering from wood shrinkage.

The glider force was supplemented early in January 1945 by the arrival of several Hadrian gliders and a solitary Waco CG13A, KK791, a scaled up version of the Hadrian and the only one to be taken on charge by the RAF. Trials with these new gliders got under way and on 25 January NA644 carried out a twin Hadrian towing test. Several record distance flights were carried out during the next few months, NA642 towing two Hadrians, KH898 and FR767, on the first leg of a trip to Bhita on 24 February. The combination landed at Maharajpin for the night, this being the longest twin Hadrian tow on record. On 9 April NA644, under the command of Flg Off Bretherton, DFC, towed the CG13A from Mauripur to Bihta nonstop, a track distance of 1,200 miles. This was believed to be the longest glider tow carried out in India. These trials finished in April, the Halifax, Dakota and Commando aircraft all having been found quite suitable for the task were now to devote their time to glider ferrying and heavy equipment dropping.

A second Halifax unit, No 1341 Flight, arrived in India in May but its duties were of a slightly more aggressive nature. The first Halifax of this unit arrived at Digri on 13 May and by the last day of the month a total of five, PN369, PN370, PN371, PN381 and PN382, were on strength. Authority had already been received during May for C Flight of No 159 Squadron, who operated Liberators from the same base, to amalgamate with No 1341 Flight. This C Flight consisted of specially equipped Liberators used for investigation of enemy radar transmissions, the same duties as the Halifaxes were equipped for.

The special operations carried out by No 1341 Flight were arranged and authorised by the RCM section of ASCEA and although relatively few in number the operations usually involved long flights in anything but good weather. The Liberators operated three missions during the last week in June making lengthy flights to Bangkok, Sabang and Penang. The severity of the tropical weather conditions can be judged by the fact that Flg Off Smith was forced to spend five hours of the 20hr 20min flight to Penang at 500ft without the aid of an automatic pilot.

The Halifaxes joined in the four operations flown during July, Sqn Ldr Hughes flying a mission to Port Blair on the 21st and Flt Lt Morgan visiting the same target on the 26th. Although these flights produced no significant new information on Japanese radar they did serve the dual purpose of providing information on enemy troop movements. Although there was little operational activity the Halifaxes were not idle, carrying out transport duties for No 159 Squadron to their Liberator detachment based on Akyab Island on the west coast of Burma. The flight carried out its last missions on 1 August, Flt Lt Morgan and WO Painter each flying a Halifax to the Port Blair area. For the remainder of the month the Halifaxes and Liberators performed special transport operations as ordered by ACSEA.

With the close of hostilities the flight turned its talents to a more peaceful occupation, supplying stores, medical supplies and petrol via the 'Hump' route into China. The return flights were perhaps the most rewarding for the crews who carried a very special cargo, ex-POWs. Despite the shortage of spares the Halifaxes were kept flying and continued to operate under the control of No 117 Wing until the flight disbanded on 30 October 1945.

No 1577 Flight had remained active during this period, a detachment of one Halifax and one Dakota at Bihta alone had ferried 43 gliders over a route of 320 miles during an eight week period. Two notable tows were achieved during this task, a fully laden Horsa and a lightly laden one being towed nonstop 750 and 950 miles respectively.

Such flying duties had their moments of tribulation. On 6 June 1945, NA644 took off at an all up weight of 54,000lb towing a Hamilcar, laden to 26,000lb, to tow it to Chaklala. After 50 minutes a hydraulic failure caused the Halifax's undercarriage to come down, breaking the mechanical locks. In spite of the additional drag the combination reached Nawabshah where they landed safely. After repairs the combination set off once more the next morning only to have the hydraulic system in the Halifax fail again just as it got airborne. Unable to retract the undercarriage the situation was critical and could easily have ended in disaster but for the skill and cool headedness of the tug pilot, Flt Lt Northmore and the glider pilot, Flg Off Winnington. Between them they managed to complete a circuit of the airfield at 50ft and land again safely. After returning to base for repairs NA644 returned to complete the tow to Dhamial on 9 June.

The somewhat reluctant NA644 redeemed itself with a record tow from Nawabshah to Chaklala, a distance of 593 track miles, with a Hamilcar. This has thought to be the longest tow ever made by this type of combination. Apart from this aspect the flight also provided some very useful information on cooling and fuel consumption in Halifaxes under tropical conditions, the combination flying at 5,000ft in an average temperature of 31°C.

After months of waiting an 8,000lb bomb beam and electro-magnetic releases arrived at Chaklala on 7 July. This was fitted to NA644 and on 11 June loading trials with a jeep and gun were made, the detachment moving to Dhamial to begin dropping tests. The first of these was made by Flg Off Bretherton two days later, the jeep and gun being dropped from 1,000ft at an indicated air speed of 130mph. A parachute malfunction resulted in the gun making an unarrested descent which caused it to be a write off but the jeep made a perfect landing. Further trials using NA642 were quite successful.

With the cessation of hostilities in Europe it had been intended to transfer some of the No 38 Group squadrons to

Above: **This side elevation shot shows just how far this type of load projected into the slipstream.** *J. Stewart-Crump*

Below: **Although of poor quality this rare shot shows a tropicalised A Mk VII, NA4--, of No 298 Squadron early in 1946. The freight pannier, dropping hatch and lack of glider towing hook show the change of role from** Airborne forces work to pure transport duties. SEAC roundels and fin flashes have been applied over standard European camouflage. The flight call sign letters DP are white and the aircraft code letter P (just visible on the original print) aft of the fuselage roundel is red. The letter is repeated beneath the port wing tip (and possibly the starboard one). / *N. Gray*

the Far East for glider operations against the Japanese. No 1577 Flight had proved the feasibility of glider operations under tropical conditions and on 6 July the first nine tropicalised A Mk VII Halifaxes of No 298 Squadron left Tarrant Rushton for India. A second wave of eight Halifaxes left on 13 July followed by seven more on 18 July.

All of this squadron's aircraft were fitted with freight panniers and to facilitate this modification to the new A Mk VII Halifaxes intended for the Far East, a pattern aircraft had been loaned to the maintenance units at Hawarden, Kinloss and High Ercall. The initial panniers were the flush fitting type with a 3,000lb capacity and in order to fit them the bomb doors were removed and stowed in the fuselage. Within a short period these were replaced by the enlarged 282cu ft type with an 8,000lb capacity, these panniers projecting well below the fuselage.

During August, while the remainder of the squadron continued to arrive at Raipur, the Halifaxes undertook their first commitments under the control of ACSEA. These consisted of transporting passengers and freight and collecting the squadron's stores which required flights to many of the airfields throughout India and Ceylon. The freight varied from stocks of vegetables, unit tools and refrigerators to medical supplies and equipment, rocket projectile rails and parachutes. Passengers included members of the 44th Airborne Division, medical teams and miscellaneous personnel. In all, during the execution of these duties some 473hours' flying time was logged, approximately 50,000lb of freight and 250 passengers were carried. Weather conditions throughout were typical of the south-west monsoon — chronic!

In September the squadron began transferring from Airborne duties to transport work, gradually taking over the commitments of No 1341 Flight. The squadron used one of the flight's Halifaxes to fly the first 'Hump' run into China, Dum Dum (Calcutta) to Kunming, on 3 September. The aircraft returned three days later carrying six ex-POWs. A repeat trip was flown on 10 September using a No 298 Squadron Halifax carrying 2,000lb of freight, in this case petrol, mail packages and six passengers. Several trips were also flown to Singapore and then on 30 September four Halifaxes and six crews moved to Alipore to begin a regular scheduled transport run into China. Four regular trips were made each week using two different routes; Monday and Thursday they flew Dum Dum, Kunming, Chung King, Hong Kong, Shanghai, Hong Kong, Dum Dum; Tuesdays and Fridays they flew Dum Dum, Pigu, Hong Kong, Dum Dum.

During the early part of October, despite the heavy rain and violent tropical thunderstorms, the service never failed to complete a scheduled trip although some delays were incurred. As the aircraft became due for minor routine inspections three modifications were carried out, the TR1196 was raised, the hot air ducting blanked off and a water tank installed in the rear stowage area of the fuselage. All armament, now superfluous, was also removed at the same time. Spare parts, the bane of No 1341 Flight continued to make life difficult for the servicing personnel, a situation which was to continue for several months.

The squadron's scheduled runs were increased during October by the addition of a new route which was divided into four sections, stage I was base, Magpur, Dum Dum, Nagpur; stage II was Nagpur, Santa Cruz, Mauripur, Santa Cruz; stage III Santa Cruz, Dum Dum, Nagpur and stage IV Nagpur to base. A single Halifax left the base every Monday, Wednesday and Friday, Nagpur on Tuesday, Thursday and Saturday, Santa Cruz on Wednesday, Friday and Saturday, Nagpur each Thursday, Saturday and Monday.

Mindful of the increasing passenger needs the squadron modified NA397:L during November. The interior was stripped of any remaining surplus equipment and seating for 24 people was fitted. Thus converted NA397 was flown to No 229 Group HQ, at Delhi, for inspection and then to Chakiri for further inspection where it was left. While waiting for approval to carry out further conversions the squadron, as an interim measure, removed the armour plating, ammunition boxes and towing gear from the remaining Halifaxes and fitted eight safety straps in the rest bay of each aircraft. These interim modifications proved useful when the squadron moved to Digri in December, 800 personnel and 245,461lb of freight being transported by the Halifaxes.

Just as the squadron was getting thoroughly organised for its transport duties a change of command at No 228 Group also produced a change of role back to airborne training. However, one last major commitment befell them on 14 January 1946, the transportation of 100 hospital cases from Bilaspur to Mauripur at the rate of 16 a day, two Halifaxes being supplied for the task. The remainder of the squadron continued with the training programme.

In March famine threatened certain areas of India and the squadron took part in Operation Hunger. Each Halifax carried 50×80lb bags of rice in the freight pannier and an identical load in the fuselage. The rice carried in the fuselage was air dropped at specified dropping zones and the 4,000lb in the pannier deliveried to a central location. By a bit of judicious juggling the load was increased and Halifaxes dispatched on 17 March carried 6,000lb internally plus the usual 4,000lb in the pannier. Two days later the figures rose by 2,000lb when it was discovered that the fuel load could be reduced to 1,500gal allowing 12,000lb of rice to be carried, 6,000lb internally and 6,000lb in the pannier. By the time the operation ended on 31 March the squadron had completed 80 sorties lifting 887,415lb of rice, 360,670lb of which had been air dropped.

April brought a continuation of the famine and Operation Hunger II was put into force. The squadron was again committed to these mercy missions completing 81 sorties and delivering 949,260lb of rice, 456,550lb being air dropped.

At the end of this operation the squadron returned to a more normal routine of training with jeep drops but in July its role was once more changed. It was given the somewhat imposing title of Bomber, Airborne Support and Heavy Equipment Dropping Squadron. A dual control Halifax PP372:W, was allotted to assist with training and practice bombing-come-equipment-dropping until the unit was finally disbanded in December. Many of the squadron's Halifaxes were then struck off charge locally.

This brought to an end RAF Halifax operations in the Far East, No 1577 Flight having disbanded in May and its sole remaining Halifax struck off charge locally.

18 Cargo Carrying and Civil Use

The Halifax's capacious interior ensured that it was used for other than its intended primary role of heavy bomber. The SOE squadrons were the first to exploit this potential to some degree with their agent and supply dropping sorties over Occupied Europe. The temporary detachment of some of their Halifaxes to No 511 Squadron for emergency freighting duties in December 1942 has already been mentioned. Although used temporarily for this purpose these Halifaxes had no special modifications other than those required for their more clandestine duties.

A more positive conversion was made at No 144 MU, Maison Blanche. In addition to other commitments this unit was responsible for maintenance and repairs to Middle East based Halifaxes as well as dispatching working parties to locations as far afield as Italy for this purpose. Several time-expired B Mk II Halifaxes which had seen service with Nos 148, 178 and 462 Squadrons were modified as freighters to carry Merlin, Twin Wasp and Hercules engines or a Spitfire fuselage. These were carried semi-externally between sheet metal side plates which projected downwards from the bomb bay. (It is interesting to note that it was not until April 1946 that official trials were made with NA137, at the AFTDU, fitted with external engine carriage gear.)

The first of these conversions was made around March 1944 and by August four Halifaxes had been modified, among them being W7845, W7847 and W7849. During October the first of these had completed 300 hours flying and was due for a major overhaul. An almost identical figure was achieved by the combined efforts of all four Halifax freighters during November. The total weight of freight carried amounted to 284,000lb and included 20 Merlin engines, 13 Pratt & Witney engines and 93 passengers.

The value of the Halifax's freighting capabilities had also finally reached the point in England where a positive start was being made to exploit this advantage and on 31 October 1944 a signal was received by No 246 Squadron allocating it four Mk III Halifaxes. These were given the title of the Halifax Development Flight and became C Flight, A Flight being equipped with C87s and B Flight with Yorks. During December a study was made to see what would be the best arrangement for the carriage of passengers and on the 13th NA683 left on a trial trip to Cairo. Although still in the experimental stages the flight was asked on 19 December to undertake a special flight to India. It began operating regularly in January 1945, NA683 leaving Lyneham on the 17th on the UK-Istres-Cairo service. This was the first time that a Halifax had undertaken this scheduled service, the next run, on 21 January being made by NA769.

Two more Halifaxes were taken on strength, LW547 and LW548 and a third, NA177, was cancelled before it could be physically allotted. Instructions were received for LW547 to carry out an experimental trooping flight to Karachi with 10 passengers and kit plus two Bristol Aeroplane Co representatives to advise on engine operation. These orders were amended the next day and the Halifax finally left carrying 4,000lb of freight, the passenger seats being detached and stacked.

Just as the flight was getting into a routine of operations it was transferred to RAF Merryfield on 12 March and attached to No 187 Squadron. This squadron had only formed on 1 February and was to have had an initial establishment of 25 C Mk III Halifaxes as the freighter version was now designated. Its purpose was to carry out small scale trooping to India and the Halifax Development Flight was to be serviced and maintained by the squadron. This was the second Halifax transport squadron to be formed, No 96 Squadron having been officially established at Leconfield on 30 December 1944.

The reasons for initially placing a Transport Command squadron within a Bomber Command group were justified for maintenance reasons alone. In addition Leconfield, which had accommodation for two squadrons was being used only by No 640 Squadron at the time. No 96 Squadron was a lodger unit and it was intended to transfer it to a Transport Command station at a later date. Flying personnel consisted of tour-expired crews from Bomber Command and included a fairly high percentage of RAAF personnel. The squadron was allocated 25 C Mk III Halifaxes but in the event only a few were received.

These Halifaxes had been converted from standard B Mk IIIs by removing all armament, the mid-upper turret, the H2S scanner and its housing, the Monica set and the tri-cell chute for the flares. With their interior stripped bare the Halifaxes could handle either freight, nine stretcher cases or passengers. For the latter, eight seats could be fitted in the rear fuselage and a further six passengers could be accommodated in the rest bay amidships.

Training flights began soon after the first of No 96 Squadron's Halifaxes arrived, RG422, RG423, RG425 and RG428, on 7 and 8 January. Notification was received on 2 February that the squadron was to eventually be sent

Above: NA195, seen here in April 1945, was originally a B Mk III allotted to No 10 Squadron on 29 November 1944 and coded ZA-F and later 'R'. Transferred to Leconfield on 27 February 1945 it was converted to C Mk III configuration (the flush fitting 3,000lb container is discernible as a slight bulge, framed by the two sets of propellers, behind the Window dropping tunnel). Flush riveting was used and glossy black applied to all side and lower surfaces. It passed to No 45 MU on 7 April 1945 and was struck off charge as Cat E2 on 5 March 1947. / *IWM*

Centre left and below: V9985, the early model B Mk II (twin aerial masts, no mid-upper turret, beam gun hatches and teardrop blisters over the navigator's windows) retained for trials work with bulged bomb doors.

Above: A close up of the freight pannier of LV838. Hercules 100 engines were fitted when the aircraft was converted to Mk VI configuration and several tests were made using cooling fans as seen here. They were not adopted for production aircraft.

Below: LV838, converted from a B Mk III to serve as the prototype C Mk VI, fitted with the first 8,000lb capacity freight pannier. Note the lack of prototype markings and the standard night camouflage. / *IWM*

to the Middle East to replace No 267 Squadron. Another two Halifaxes, MZ458 and MZ464:Q, were received in February but MZ464 was lost in a crash on the 25th, near Brantingham three miles north of Brough, killing the crew of four and the two passengers.

In mid-March both No 96 and 187 Squadrons received orders to re-equip with Dakotas and the Halifaxes already on charge were disposed of, most going to No 10 Squadron and then to 29 MU at High Ercall. The Halifaxes of the Development Flight continued to operate their freighting runs to the Middle East until the end of March and the unit was disbanded on 3 April 1945.

This by no means signified the end of the Halifax as a pure transport aircraft. Testing of a standard B Mk VI Halifax had continued at Boscombe Down during January and February, TW783 being flown at an increased all up weight of 68,000lb and with the centre of gravity at the after most limits. A thorough test was made under all flight conditions and during a full limit dive the aircraft began pitching and could not be made to exceed 300mph (IAS) even when using full nose heavy trim. The cause was due to the loss of fabric from the starboard elevator, the fabric attachment strings having apparently chaffed against the rib flanges through ballooning on the top surface near the leading edge. At the time this was thought to be an isolated case and not attributable to the increase in the all up weight. Engine failure at low airspeeds posed some problems and after trying several flap settings it was recommended that 20° be used for take-off and that they should not be retracted until a good margin of speed and height had been attained. Two modifications were also recommended to improve handling characteristics following engine failure. The rudder balance tab gearing was increased and the rudder trim wheel moved from the left hand side to the right hand side of the pilot's seat making it more accessible.

Both of these modifications were incorporated on LV838 which had now been converted to serve as the prototype C Mk VI. In addition the rudder angular movement outboard had been limited to 18° instead of 20°. The same equipment was removed as for the C Mk III version. In addition the bomb bay doors were removed and a 272cu ft freight pannier fitted to the lower fuselage which gave the Halifax a decidedly pregnant profile.

The practicability of fitting such a bulky item stemmed from the early Halifax operations with 4,000 and 8,000lb bombs. A B Mk II, V9985, had been fitted with a set of bulged bomb bay doors which completely enclosed the large bombs and trials carried out in January 1943 showed no adverse effect to the handling characteristics. The new pannier bore a very close resemblance to the bulged bomb compartment doors being almost identical in dimensions and contours.

The presence of the pannier had little effect upon the handling characteristics which were similar to a standard B Mk VI but the asymmetic handling qualities were improved by the rudder tab gearing modifications. Rudder forces were lighter and allowed reductions in the minimum flying speeds, under asymmetric conditions, of about 15mph in the case of engine failure after take-off and about 50mph in the case of steady flight with two engines dead on

one side. The rudder trimmer was very powerful and one full turn of the wrist was sufficient to apply full trim. This led to some instances of overtrimming which were initially mistaken for rudder overbalance and pilots were cautioned to exercise care. During the dive tests the elevators again shed some fabric as had happened previously with TW783. A new set of strengthened elevators was fitted which incorporated holding down plates to prevent the fabric coming away from the metal skin of the nose. No further trouble was experienced after this.

Due to the fact that it might prove impossible to jettison the cargo a series of test were made with one and two engines cut. Results showed that the Halifax could be flown straight and level at 160mph (IAS) using two divisions of aileron trim. At speeds below this very mild rudder overbalance occurred but could be easily overcome by exerting a small foot load and by adopting a small amount of bank. Alternatively by applying 10° of bank from the start the speed could be reduced to 135mph (IAS) without any overbalance occurring. At this speed full rudder trim, full aileron trim and a medium foot load were required. For general flying over the speed range from 180 to 230mph (IAS) the aircraft was found to be easy and pleasant to fly.

Coincidental with these trials was a series involving another B Mk VI conversion. In this case, however, PP225 exhibited a far more radical degree of modification. All turrets had been removed and a tail cone fitted which increased the overall length to 73ft 7in. The removal of the rear turret required a half a degree reduction in the tailplane incidence to allow for the forward movement of the centre of gravity. The elevator trim range was also decreased as was the downward movement of the elevator itself from 19° to 17° while the upward range was increased by 2° to 27°. The trim tabs were set at 2° upwards relative to the elevators at neutral setting.

Resplendent in green and grey camouflage with light blue undersides PP225 began its initial trials at Boscombe Down on 4 April, these continuing until the 27th. Handling tests were made at weights of 50,000lb and 68,000lb and in most respects the C Mk VIII, as it was now designated, behaved like a standard B Mk VI except that it proved impossible, at either loading, to induce a normal stall with flaps and undercarriage up due to the lack of elevator power. The elevators failed during dive tests and were replaced with the strengthened type as fitted to LV838 but these in turn failed after eight dives up to speeds of 320mph (IAS). A new set was fitted and no further difficulty was encountered. Rudder trouble was experienced under asymmetric conditions but subsequent trials on 25 and 26 May after incorporating the same modifications as were applied to LV838 eliminated the problem. However, although this reduced the minimum speeds at which control could be regained following an engine failure at take-off, either clean or with undercarriage and flaps down, the speeds were still considered to be high. It was therefore recommended that if an outboard engine failed on take-off when the undercarriage and flaps were down that the corresponding engine on the other side should be cut and the aircraft landed straight ahead.

The first production C Mk VIII, PP217, was delivered to the Air Transport Tactical Development Unit on 9 June

D.

C.

Left and below left: A converted B MK VI PP225 which served as the prototype C Mk VIII. Finished in day bomber camouflage of green, grey and light blue, it lacks any form of prototype marking.

Below: PP217 the first production C Mk VIII. Delivered to the Air Transport Tactical Development Unit on 9 June 1945 it was involved in a minor landing accident at Ringway on 30 November 1941. It passed to No 297 Squadron on 13 January 1947 then to Sky Taxis Ltd on 16 December 1947 and finally to London Aero Motor Service Ltd. / *A. J. Jackson*

Bottom: PP329:GR-P which was posted to No 301 Squadron on 21 February 1946. Camouflage of green/grey/blue with codes in pale grey and serial numbers in black were standard for C Mk VIIIs. The Polish emblem appears just behind the flight call sign letters on the nose. PP329 was sold to Payloads Ltd on 23 September 1947 having received its C of A on the 9th. It became G-AKBR and changed ownership several times. / *R. Riding*

Above: PP311 never saw squadron service being loaned to BOAC on 26 August 1946 for training purposes. Registered G-AHYI it was eventually sold to Anglo French Distributors and re-registered G-AIID. / R. Riding

Below: G-AGZP, the first of many Halifaxes to be placed on the civil register. It eventually passed to BAAS then to Alpha Airways who based it in South Africa as ZS-BTA. It carried every conceivable type of cargo from fruit to refugees. / A. J. Jackson

and began an intensive series of handling and general service trials which continued throughout the remainder of the year. A minor landing accident at Ringway on 30 November necessitated repairs which kept it out of action until 18 January 1946.

The type had, however, already proved itself and in November 1945 No 301 (Polish) Squadron was notified that it was to re-equip with C Mk VIII Halifaxes. Training lectures on Hercules 100 engines began in December. Currently equipped with Mk III Warwicks the squadron was employed on freighting operations to Oslo, Istres, Naples and Athens. Its sister unit at Chedburgh, No 304 (Polish) Squadron, had also been notified that it was to exhange its elderly Mk XIV Wellingtons for Mk III Warwicks in November but on 11 January this order was amended in favour of C Mk VIII Halifaxes.

No 301 Squadron, who expressed its pleasure at renewing acquaintanceship with the Halifax, was given priority and the first 18 aircraft were allotted direct to it. No 304 Squadron took over all the transport commitments during this period. It was intended that re-equipping should take place at the rate of five aircraft a week but delays held up this schedule, Flt Lt K. Twardawa ferrying in PP221 from 45 MU on 15 January 1946, a second arriving on the 17th and a third on the 29th. With typical Polish enthusiasm the squadron began rounding up any pilots and flight engineers with four-engined aircraft experience their 'bag' eventually including one from No 45 Group who was currently serving at Dorval in Canada. By the end of the month 33 crews were on strength and fully trained.

An urgent request to HQ No 46 Group produced a further six Halifaxes in February and nine more by the end of March. Flt Lt Rusiecki made No 301 Squadron's inaugural flight in PP328 to Hassani, a similar attempt previously having failed due to engine failure which forced the aircraft to return. Regular route work began on 15 March with a service to Naples each Saturday and one to Athens each Tuesday and Thursday. However, due to repatriation of squadron personnel and political reasons an order was issued on 9 April stating that all flying by the squadron was to cease with effect from 17 April. This was later rescinded and training flights were continued but no aircraft was permitted to land outside the British Isles. Any aircraft currently at Continental locations were to be collected only if arrangements had already been made.

No 301 Squadron's operational career with the C Mk VIII Halifax was thus virtually stillborn, only 15 flights being carried out including the inaugural flight. No 304 Squadron, who had surrendered all their flying personnel with four engined experience to No 301 Squadron, never became operational with the type, the first Halifaxes arriving in May. However, both squadrons continued a very active training programme, No 304 Squadron averaging approximately 140 hours per month. Accidents were few, PP236 being damaged in a heavy landing after hitting a ditch shortly after being transferred from No 301 Squadron in June. One serious accident occurred on 23 August when PP232 stalled whilst banking around the circuit at 900ft and crashed at Green Farm killing the crew. Instructions were finally received ordering the cessation of flying with effect from 21 November and

both squadrons were disbanded with effect from 10 December 1946.

Thus these two squadrons were the only ones to use the C Mk VIII Halifax and after their disbandment the task of freight and passenger transportation was integrated into the duties of the Halifax squadrons of No 38 Group. The C Mk VIII Halifax had, however, by no means disappeared from use. Two, PP326 and PP327 had been loaned to BOAC in October 1945 producing an anomalous situation since the type was not in service with the RAF at the time. During the following three months some very extensive flying was done carrying freight and mail on an experimental service to West Africa with the object of testing for maximum utilisation. Over a period of two months the two Halifaxes logged some 2,000 flying hours, averaging 205mph on the cruise. Results showed them to be suitable for medium range operations carrying 10 passengers and 3,500lb of cargo.

The first privately owned C Mk VIII Halifax to appear on the British Civil Register was sold, along with a B Mk III, in February 1946. The C Mk VIII, PP336, was purchased through Thomas Cook and Son Ltd on 25 February and collected from 29 MU at High Ercall. The buyer was His Highness the Maharajah Gaekwar of Baroda, the well known race horse owner who required a speedy means of transport for his family and staff from India to his new headquarters at Newmarket. The Halifax was granted a Certificate of Airworthiness on 20 March and registered as G-AGZP. Sqn Ldr E. A. Hood and a special crew from British American Air Services flew the Halifax to Bombay and back in an air time of 56hr 30min for the 10,749-mile trip.

The B Mk III Halifax mentioned before was also a private purchase, Mr G. N. Wickner a former ATA pilot buying it to transport his family and other expatriate Australians home. Granted its C of A on 16 May and registered G-AGXA it became the first of two Mk IIIs to appear on the civil register, the other was G-AJPG, alias NA684, which was used by the College of Aeronautics at Cranfield. Wickner completed his trip to Australia in 71 hours flying time having left Hurn airport on 26 May and touched down at Mascot airport, Sydney, on 26 June. The Halifax was subsequently sold to Air Carriers Ltd and re-registered VH-BDT. It made only one trip, in June 1947, but limped back to Sydney with the port outer engine feathered. It was never used again and was finally gutted by vandals.

Meanwhile BOAC had decided to go ahead with its programme of using Halifaxes for its West African services to bridge the 12 to 14-month delay before the introduction of its Avro Tudor IIs and issued a contract for 12 modified aircraft. Accordingly 14 C Mk VIII Halifaxes were allotted to Short Brothers and Harland Ltd, at Belfast, who undertook the necessary modifications to the passenger role after Handley Page had made the structural adjustments.

The cabin was fitted with 10 Rumbold (IP) semi-adjustable seats, eight being equally spaced side by side on the main floor level with two, one behind the other, on the port side at the same floor level. The fuselage walls were finished in two shades of beige while the seats and carpet

BOAC
G-AH

WALTZING
MATILDA
G-AGXA
VH-AEF

Above: Falkirk, **G-AHDU**, subject of the official naming ceremony for the BOAC Halton fleet. The colour scheme was to DTD Spec260A (one coat grey primer, Type S, one coat aluminium). Lettering was BOAC blue, or, alternatively, Marine Blue DTD Spec62A, edged in gold. The anti-glare panel was Night Black DTD Spec314. / *BOAC*

Left: **G-AGXA**, the second Halifax on the civil register photographed in Australia during a fund raising effort for the RAF Benevolent Fund and the RAAF Welfare Fund. / Sydney Morning Herald

Below: A rare photograph of **G-AGXA** after its sale to Air Carriers Ltd. Allocated the Australian civil registration **VH-BDT**, it still retained its British registration at the christening ceremony at Bankstown, performed by the New South Wales Premier's wife, on **6 March 1947.** / *G. Carver*

ACCESS DOOR
TO FUEL
DISTRIBUTING COCKS

Left: Looking forward in the stewards' galley with its compact installation of equipment. The two small doors above the main spar give access to the crew's quarters. / *Short Brothers and Harland*

Below left: Looking forward in the Halton passenger cabin towards the stewards' galley. / *Short Brothers and Harland*

Below: G-AHYH as *Air Merchant* of the Lancashire Aircraft Corporation. It was one of the C Mk VIIIs loaned to BOAC in 1946 (PP271, '272 and '281 in July and PP261 in September). / *A. J. Jackson*

Bottom: One of the Airtech Ltd tanker conversions using a Regent Oil Co 1,350gal lorry tank slung underneath the fuselage.

were in standard BOAC livery blue. Individual lights, a stewards' call button and oxygen equipment were provided at each passenger position. The main interior lighting came from three roof mounted fittings while a single window, approximately 12in by 15in, at each seat position provided natural lighting. A large passenger door was provided on the starboard side near the tailplane, a small vestibule for hats and coats isolating it from the main cabin proper. Toilet facilities were fitted in the extreme rear of the fuselage. A well equipped pantry, in what had formerly been the midships rest bay position, was screened from the passenger cabin by means of swinging doors. The transparent nose cone was replaced by a metal fairing and fitted with a door on the port side which gave access to a small freight compartment, the main freight being carried in the fuselage pannier.

Delivery of the aircraft to BOAC began in July and the type was officially named 'Halton' during a christening ceremony at Radlett on the 18th. Lady Winster, wife of the then Minister for Civil Aviation, carried out the ceremony with G-AHDU naming it *Falkirk*.

A limited service commenced in September but after six weeks the aircraft were grounded due to a hydraulic fault and returned to the manufacturers for repair and the fitting of de-icing equipment. Of the other two C Mk VIII Halifaxes delivered to Shorts Brothers, PP226 was apparantly not converted and PP238, according to the Company records, was delivered to the French Air Force on 17 March 1947. This may well have been purely on a loan basis for it carried the civil registration G-AHWM and Handley Page received it once more on 4 July before passing it to the RAF. It eventually reappeared on the civil register as G-AJZY.

With the rapid ending of the C Mk VIII's service career Handley Page were able to put a batch of these virtually brand new aircraft up for sale at Radlett in 1946. Six of them were acquired in July by Dr G. Humby who founded London Aero and Motor Service Ltd the aircraft being ferried to the Company's base at Elstree where they were converted for freight carrying. Their successful utilisation led to an order for a further 10 C Mk VIIIs. In the meantime the original six were reduced to four by the loss of one in the sea, off the Belgian coast, in September and the need to 'cannabalise' G-AHZM for spares. The same problem, shortage of spares, led to the demise of two of the new batch of 10, G-AIWO and G-AIWP.

The immediate postwar boom assured the Halifaxes of LAMS and other companies were well occupied and business flourished. The soft fruit trade provided a constant source of charters during the summer season and LAMS alone were handling 500 tons a month by mid-1947.

BOAC's Haltons commenced a London-Karachi service in July 1947 and on 1 September a trans Sahara London-Lagos service was also started. Six services a week were operated on the latter route and it was while on this run that they were finally withdrawn, in May 1948, and put up for sale.

The list of civil operators had meanwhile grown to include LAMS, British American Air Services, Alpha Airways, Air Freight, Chartair, Eagle Aviation, Bond's Air Services, World Air Freight Ltd, Lancashire Aircraft Corporation, Westminster Airways, Skyflight and Petair. Overseas they were operated in France, South Africa and Pakistan. In addition to the C Mk VIII and Mk IIIs already released several batches of Mk VI Halifaxes were also put up for sale but most were purchased for spares, principally by Lancashire Aircraft Corporation.

By 1948 the boom had passed its peak and many feared that the resulting slump would eliminate many of the operators. Then, on Monday 28 June 1948, the greatest aerial supply operation in history began. Operation Carter Patterson or, as it became more popularly known as, the Berlin Air Lift was an attempt to keep the city of Berlin alive by the delivery of all its requirements by air. Food, clothing, materials, fuels both solid and liquid, literally every conceivable item had to be delivered by air. The RAF and the USAF between them bore the brunt of the task for the first three weeks but it soon became obvious that it would require even greater resources than these if it were to continue and succeed. Stocks of available commodities gradually diminished despite the supply flights and it was at this point that the independent British civil operators were invited to join in the air lift.

The offer was made on Sunday, 1 August and an initial force of 12 aircraft, nine Dakotas, one Hythe, one Liberator and one Halton, were quickly assembled. Three days later the Halton, from Bond's Air Services, in company with the Liberator, from Scottish Aviation, carried out the first of the civil operations into the beleauguered city, landing at Wunsdorf airfield. Within days other operators joined the civil air lift and by 21 September the civil fleet had doubled in size. In addition to other aircraft Halifaxes/Haltons arrived from Bond's, Eagle Aviation and Skyflights.

To the civil operators fell the task of supplying the entire liquid fuel needs of Berlin, not only domestic and industrial but also those of the Occupation Forces. This was not, however, their entire contribution and bulk food stocks such as flour, salt and fish were carried also. The carriage of such a corrosive item as salt required heavy anodisation of the airframe and several Halifaxes and Haltons were specially treated for this purpose.

By far the largest single operator of Halifaxes was the Lancashire Aircraft Corporation and in September it agreed to provide six Halifax freighters and six Halifax tankers for the air lift. The six freighters were actually the Company's entire current operational fleet being used to carry milk supplies from Belfast to Blackpool. Extensive overhauls were needed and the first two flew to Wunsdorf on 15 October. The six tankers were developed from standard RAF Halifaxes and thus had to be specially modified to meet the civil licensing requirements.

The civilian force had grown rapidly and Wunsdorf could no longer satisfactorily handle it so various operators began to disperse their aircraft to other airfields. Bond's Air Services moved part of its force to Fuhlsbuttel, Hamburg's former airport, where it was later joined by BAAS while LAC moved its Halifaxes to Schleswigland on 22 November. The move to Schleswigland, near Kiel, was not a particularly popular one as, apart from the size of this dispersed site with two miles separating the parking and loading points from the briefing and canteen facilities, it

Above: **LAMS** royal blue and white **G-AHZJ**, photographed at **Stanstead** prior to application of its name *Port of Marseilles*. **One of the original six company machines it was lost in a crash on 19 August 1947.** / *R. Riding*

Above: **Another European operator of C Mk VIIIs was SANA, F-BESE *Ker Goaler* was formerly G-AKGP.**
/ *A. J. Jackson*

Below: **Of poor quality but an interesting example of just how much sheer bulk a Halifax could handle. The load is a Humber car, complete with packing crate, slung beneath a BAAS freighter.**

also lacked the ground based radar aids so essential for bad weather operations. This meant installing special airborne navigation aids so that the aircraft could operate under all conditions.

The Foreign Office also made a request during December for all LAC Halifaxes to be used as tankers. Other operators also gradually converted their aircraft for tanker operations and an improved tanker conversion appeared at this time. The Regent Oil Company made available a supply of 1,350gal lorry tanks and Airtech Ltd fitted these directly to the belly of the Halifaxes in place of the standard panniers, metal fairings being used to streamline them into the main fuselage contours. Three 250gal aircraft fuel tanks were fitted inside the fuselage and interconnected with the external tank to provide a total actual capacity of 2,050gal with 50gal airspace. Two $2\frac{1}{2}$in external drain cocks enabled the entire load to be taken on, under pressure, in 14 minutes. Discharge time was approximately the same. This load gave a disposable weight of approximately 14,750lb of fuel oil and the Ministry of Civil Aviation had already granted a dispensation for the Halifaxes and Haltons to be operated at an increased landing weight of 59,000lb. Winter operations, with their associated necessity for increased fuel margins in case of diversion, kept the payload down to 1,500gal of fuel oil. The onset of winter also removed the previous policy of 'daylight only' operations for the civil operators and gradually a 24-hour schedule was instituted.

A chronic shortage of spares meant that even minor accidents usually resulted in an aircraft being scrapped and nine Halifaxes were lost in this manner during the period of the air lift. Most occurred on the ground at Schleswigland and Tegel. G-ALBZ was lost in such circumstances, being involved in a ground collision at Schleswigland on 10 May 1949. Others were more serious, G-AJZZ which crashed near Schleswigland on 22 March killed three of the crew of four and G-AKAC crashed in the Russian zone north of Tegel on 29 April killing all four on board. It was ironical that in some instances crews who had fought their way through Berlin's notorious defences to destroy it a few a scant years before should now battle to reach the same target to sustain it.

Due to the high priority given to the 'wet lift' LAC, in addition to the 16 aircrews based in Germany, also provided a maintenance team 100 strong. All maintenance other than major overhauls was done on the spot in Germany on a 24 hour basis. Periodically the Halifaxes would return to the Company's principal home base at Bovingdon where major overhauls or Certificate of Airworthiness renewals were done. Part of the work carried out at Bovingdon was the fitting of Rebecca sets which were ruled as mandatory as a homing and approch aid for aircraft on the Berlin run.

On 23 January LAC celebrated its 100th day on the Berlin Air Lift by carrying 100 tons of fuel oil into the city. By April fuel oil supplies carried by all the civil operators reached a figure in excess of 400 tons a day.

Finally, at midnight on 11/12 May 1949, 318 days after it commenced, the blockade of Berlin ceased as abruptly as it began. Within a relatively short period of time the civil operators were withdrawn. On 12 July Schleswigland was closed and LAC, BAAS, Scottish Airlines and Westminster Airways ceased to operate. A little over one month later Fuhlsbuttel also closed and with it went BAS, Eagle Aviation and World Air Freight. The following day, 16 August, the civil air lift officially ceased.

The Halifax/Halton operators would look back on their efforts with a considerable degree of satisfaction having completed 22,576.23 flying hours during 4,653 freight and 3,509 fuel sorties by Westminster Airways, LAC and BAAS's fleet of tanker aircraft. These utilisation figures, which averaged out at 311 tons per day, were the highest of any type used by the British civil operators and included only the flying hours used directly on operations. Individually some of LAC's efforts serve to give an idea of the intensity of operations achieved. On 3 July the Company made 26 round trips into Berlin in a period of 14 hours and in one week a single Halifax was airborne for 96hr 7min. Although far higher than normal it is worth noting that another Halifax averaged 48 hours flying each week constantly for over a period of five months. Many of the Halifax crews, both ground and air, produced equally outstanding records.

Throughout the period of the air lift 41 Halifaxes and Haltons had been used as follows: LAC 13; BAS 12; Westminster Airways 4; Eagle Aviation 4; BAAS 3; World Air Freight 3 and Skyflight 2. At the time the air lift ceased the final current Halifax/Halton fleet stood as follows: at Schleswigland were 10 Halifaxes of LAC, two of BAAS and two of Westminster Airways while at Tegel, Eagle Aviation had two.

While the air lift had been in progress a few Halifaxes had continued charter operations principally concentrating on bulk cargo such as the 17ft ship's propeller shaft carried by World Air Freight Ltd. Weighing more than six tons it was loaded at Ringway on 10 April, an 8,000lb bomb beam being borrowed from the RAF for the purpose. LAC's station manager at Bovingdon, Wg Cdr Collings, borrowed a bomb beam again from the Transport Command Development Unit at Brize Norton to enable one of the Company's Halifaxes to carry out an almost identical task in July. World Air Freight, who had moved from Stanstead to Bovingdon in late February managed to obtain several similar charters such as heavy mining machinery.

However, such charters were relatively few and for many of the operators a decline set in from which most never recovered. There were several reasons and ironically the Berlin Air Lift which had given them renewed life at a critical time also served to produce the circumstances which now brought about their demise.

With the bulk of the heavy charter aircraft committed to the air lift the contractors had grown accustomed to using the medium class of aircraft such as the Dakota. In addition Halifax operating costs had risen since the middle of 1948 principally due to the increased cost of engines which before the air lift had been available for almost the break-up salvage price. Due to the large number of engines used on the air lift the supply had diminished rapidly and by 1949 a reconditioned engine cost up to £1,200. Many operators had also hoped that the dispensation for the increased landing weight of 59,000lb would remain in force

A nostalgic moment as Lancashire Aircraft Corporation's *Air Voyager* is flagged away in the *Daily Express* sponsored air race of September 1950. The end of an era. / Flight International

but they were to be disappointed and the original figure of 57,000lb was enforced once more. The increasing emphasis on passenger charters also helped the attrition of the heavy charter force. It was now obvious to most operators that the cost of conversion for such traffic was not a practical proposition due to the increased operating costs as compared to the relatively small number of passengers that could be carried per trip. Westminster Airways did attempt to enter this field with one of its three aircraft fitted with 10 seats plus cargo space for approximately 4,000lb of freight.

With such doubtful prospects facing them many operators were not prepared to go to the expense of renewing the Certificate of Airworthiness for their various aircraft. By October 1949 the Halifax/Halton fleet had dwindled considerably, LAC had four immediately available with seven others on stand by, BAAS had two available, Westminster Airways three, World Air Freight one, Eagle Avation three and Bond's Air Services five with two stood off.

None of the Halifax/Halton fleet was available when there occurred a revival of the soft fruit carrying charters. A price cutting war kept a few operating a little longer, charges dropping from the average figure of £85 per hour during the air lift days to about £45 per hour. In the face of direct operating costs of about £40 per hour this was little short of financial suicide.

The end was inevitable and most of the Halifaxes and Haltons found their way to Squires Gate, Woolsington, Bovingdon and Southend where they suffered the ignominy of being reduced to metal ingots. A few lingered on and LAC's G-AKEC *Air Voyager* made a final public appearance in September 1950, at the *Daily Express*-sponsored air race. Capt A. N. Marshall flew it around the course from Hurn airport to Herne Bay at low level to achieve 24th place at an average speed of 267mph. Eagle Aviation were still operating G-AIAP in late 1950 until its untimely demise in a take-off crash at Calcutta on 20 November. LAC lost one of its last aircraft, G-AJZY, in a crash near Great Missenden on 8 March 1951. This was the former G-AHWM which had been converted by Short Brothers in 1947.

An era in civil charter operations had passed and with it the Halifax and its true civilianised cousin the Halton.

Above: **One of the relatively small number of A Mk IXs to find their way on to the civil register and in to use; the silver and black G-ALON of Bond Air Services Ltd. The large, floor positioned dropping hatch is open.**
/ A. J. Jackson

19 Development of the A Mk IX

With the cessation of hostilities the Halifax disappeared rapidly from the main bomber force, most squadrons being disbanded, or transferred to transport duties and re-equipped with Dakotas, Yorks or Liberators. Most of the Halifaxes from Nos 4 and 6 Groups ended up at Rawcliffe or No 29 MU, High Ercall, where they languished until broken up for scrap. This began at No 29 MU in January 1946 and by July contractors began breaking up some 300 non-effective Halifaxes. These were mainly Mk II and V airframes, the types having been declared obsolete from 14 March 1946. The next to go to the breakers were the B Mk III, GR Mk III and Met Mk III airframes, these being declared obsolete from 15 August. The engines were, however, retained and placed in storage.

However, the Halifax was by no means a spent force and in No 38 Group its potential remained high. The end of the war in Europe brought little change in tempo for the four Halifax squadrons concerned and when not engaged in repatriating ex-POWs from the Continent they were employed on training exercises or freighting duties.

No 190 Squadron began converting to Halifaxes on 4 May and had completed the task by the 26th. During June it undertook the task of converting crews for No 620 Squadron which had also begun to re-equip with Halifaxes. This was accompanied by an exchange of crews, a high percentage of No 620 Squadron's flying personnel being drawn from No 190 Squadron and the remainder being posted in from Nos 295 and 296 Squadrons plus some from odd OTUs.

On 19 June No 190 Squadron carried out Exercise Renaissance, the object being to combine the usual glider towing training with the removal of gliders from Great Dunmow to Thruxton for storage. The exercise was very successful and a second, Exercise Residue, was carried out on 30 June. On this occasion the remaining seven Horsa gliders were towed to Thruxton although one broke its tow but landed safely.

At the beginning of July this squadron was short of aircraft due to the general reshuffle with its sister unit No 620 Squadron which had finally been brought up to a strength of 20 crews. No 620 began operating its A Mk VII Halifaxes on 3 July, five aircraft transporting freight from Brussels to Copenhagen. It was joined by five of No 190 Squadron's Halifaxes who carried out a similar commitment the following day. These types of duty were fairly common during the next few months, Nos 296 and 297 Squadrons joining in the task of ferrying

Czechoslovakian repatriates and diplomatic mail to Prague during late July and August. Seven Halifaxes of No 190 Squadron performed a similar task to Athens with Greek repatriates.

During October a mobile OTU visited Earles Colne to train Nos 296 and 297 Squadrons' crews up to the standard required to fit them for operations over the Indian Trunk Route. Two Halifaxes from No 296 Squadron commenced duties on this run on 27 October. No 297 Squadron joined the scheduled mail run to Dum Dum and Alipore as of November, two routes being flown. The flight to Dum Dum went out via Istres - Luqua - Almaza - Shaibah - Mauripur - Dum Dum and returned via Jodhpur - Mauripur - Shaibah - Almaza - Luqua. The Alipore route was via Luqua - Almaza - Shaibah - Mauripur to Alipore, returning the same way.

When No 298 Squadron was sent to the Far East in July it had been suggested that No 644 Squadron might eventually join it in India. However, this was not to be and instead it was ordered to prepare for transfer to the Middle East along with No 620 Squadron. Between August and October both squadrons gradually re-equipped with tropicalised A Mk VII Halifaxes, complete with freight panniers, their original Halifaxes being ferried to Hawarden and Kinloss. No 644 Squadron departed first sending its 27 Halifaxes, two of which were non-tropicalised A Mk VIIs for cannibalisation, out to Quastina in six waves between 26 November and 1 December. The first element of the 30 Halifaxes of No 620 Squadron left for Aqir in Palestine on 30 December, going via El Aloine as had No 644 Squadron. Bad weather delayed the remainder of the squadron but the move was completed by 4 January 1946.

Both squadrons had barely settled in when they took part in Exercise Kickoff II on 16 January, transporting troops of the 6th Airborne Division. This particular exercise was carried out in several phases over the next month with both squadrons participating. In between there were a variety of duties to be carried out such as transporting freight and personnel to various points of the globe like Almaza, Kabrit, Nicosia, Kasafareet, Habbaniya etc, plus setting up and operating a regular mail run to the UK. The first two aircraft on the mail run were drawn from No 644 Squadron and arrived at Earles Colne on 27 and 28 January respectively. On 5 February both squadrons took part in Exercise Snatch, transporting troops to Ramat David and then retrieving them 24 hours later.

Spoiler control system (see p201)

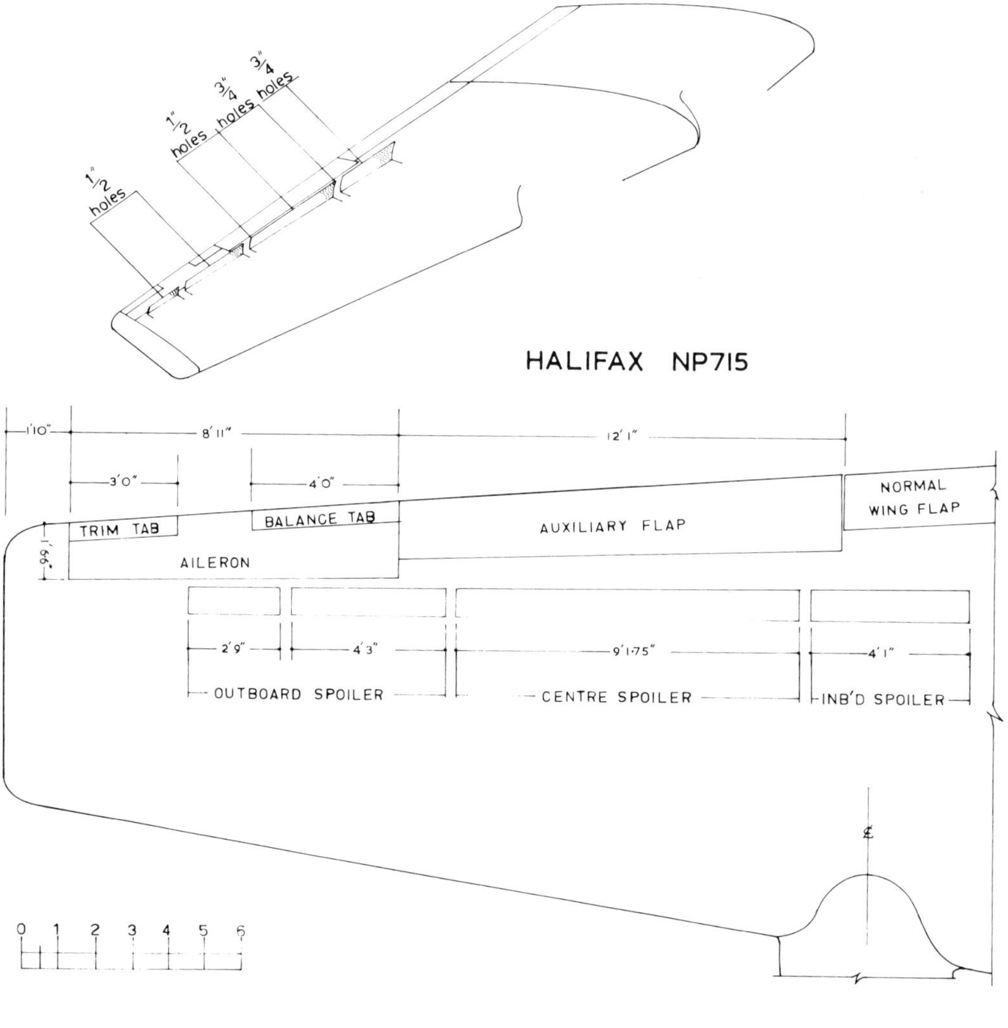

Top left: A Mk VII Halifaxes, unlike their bomber counterpart, enjoyed a postwar career in the RAF. Photographed in April 1945, NA366 awaits delivery from an MU to which it had been allotted on 23 March 1945. / *IWM*

Above: NA640:S-L5, an A Mk III of No 297 Squadron, drops a tight cluster of containers during a postwar airborne exercise. / Flight International

Below: No 620 Squadron took its tropicalised A Mk VIIs to the Middle East, beginning its first air exercise in January 1946. In the foreground is PP375:D4–X with PP345/D4–T, minus pannier, behind. Note the D Mk I tail turret. The mainwheel tyre nearest to the camera has Cairo West marked on it. The flight call sign letters in this instance denote B Flight. / *B. Robertson*

RT760 the second production A Mk IX which was delivered to the RAF on 9 November 1945 along with RT759. The former was sold for scrap on 24 August 1951. / *Handley Page*

Above: **Looking aft in the A Mk IX. The centre section rest bay seats remain and metal seats for 16 paratroopers are fitted aft of the rear spar. The paratrooping hatch in the rear floor opens upwards and inwards providing a 33in×59in opening.** / The Aeroplane

Below: **An A Mk IX, RT796, which was delivered to the RAF on 9 February 1946. It went to No 47 Squadron at Fairford on 4 November 1946.**

There was still an element of danger for these were times of great tension in the Middle East with Jewish nationalists fighting a guerilla war to establish their right to Palestine. At 2045hrs on 25 February a small group attacked the airfield at Quastina causing considerable damage with explosive charges. Two Halifaxes were completely destroyed by fire and eight others damaged beyond repair. While there were no injuries amongst the squadron personnel one of the guerillas paid with his life.

On 26 February No 644 Squadron flew up to the Elephant Ski Club near Beirut where they dropped containers of supplies to relieve the shortages caused by the club being cut off for several days by heavy falls of snow. As one member of the squadron remarked 'Just like the old SOE days, shades of Norway!'

Both squadrons had a wide variety of duties thrust upon them and to No 644 Squadron fell the responsibility for meteorological flights each morning and evening, two routes being flown, one east and one west, as from 20 January. No 620 Squadron took over the duties temporarily from 14 February but they were resumed by No 644 Squadron on 1 March. However, the westerly route was now the only one flown which reduced the number of aircraft required each day to two, one at 0400hrs and the other at 1600hrs local time.

On 3 March No 644 Squadron moved all its serviceable aircraft from Quastina to a temporary base in Egypt, Bilbeis. Two of the Halifaxes towed a Horsa each containing the necessary supplies. This move also marked the termination of the squadron's scheduled mail runs to the UK. On the 19th the squadron moved back to Quastina for Exercise Larney, picking up troops and transporting them to Nicosia in Cyprus.

In May both squadrons were involved in a major exercise, Exercise Gordon. In conjunction with eight Dakotas of No 78 Squadron they transported paratroops from Quastina to Khartoum in the Sudan, three of No 644 Squadron's Halifaxes towing gliders while the rest carried paratroops. A similar exercise took the Halifaxes to Castel Benito a few days later.

For his Majesty's birthday fly past over Jerusalem in June, No 644 Squadron provided 12 Halifaxes, Wg Cdr W. H. Ingle, the squadron CO leading the formation. The two squadrons continued their diversified duties, a No 644 Squadron Halifax flying a photo-recce mission to Cyprus on 21 July. The next day four crews from No 620 Squadron ferried the first four of No 644 Squadron's A Mk VII Halifaxes back to the UK carrying as passengers two more No 620 Squadron crews. All six crews were to return with the latest version of the Halifax, the A Mk IX.

Handley Page's last production order had been for 200 Halifaxes but with the close of hostilities this was reduced to 150 aircraft, the first five of which were built and delivered as A Mk VIIs. The success of the Halifax in the role of paratrooper and glider tug had prompted Handley Page to explore the possibilities of improving the A Mk VII. RT758 was selected for the redesign work and a new rear fuselage was fitted which contained a large inward opening paratroop hatch, some 33in by 59in, in the floor. Immediately above this was the normal panel with its twin signalling lights operated by the bomb aimer to alert the dispatcher. Two rails for static lines ran either side of the roof, a winch mounted on the rear spar being used to retrieve the lines after deployment. Hand rails along both sides of the fuselage leading to the dropping hatch were provided to steady the paratroopers as they moved from the four long bench seats, two either side, which were fitted just aft of the rest bay station. These accommodated 16 fully equipped paratroops.

As with all A versions of the Halifax there was no mid-upper turret, an extra escape hatch occupying the position instead. The rear turret was a Boulton Paul D Mk I type fitted with two Browning 0.5in machine guns, this version already being in use on late production Mk VIs. Late production A Mk IX Halifaxes were scheduled to be fitted with the Mk II version of this turret which was fitted with automatic gun laying.

Trials with a mock up of the automatic gun laying radar scanner housing had been initiated in May 1943 when a B Mk II Halifax, W1008, had had this device installed on its standard E Mk I tail turret. It proved to have very little effect upon the general handling qualities of the aircraft causing only a very mild pitching motion when the turret was rotated. The experiment progressed to an installation of a D-type turret, complete with AGLT as it was called, on one of the B Mk III Halifaxes which had been retained for experimental work, HX238. The turret balance flaps were fixed open at an angle of 40° and a $5\frac{3}{4}$in chord deflector plate, also set as 40°, was fitted to the lower circumference of the fuselage immediately in front of the turret.

Flight testing took place in April 1944 and results showed that while the problem had been partly solved, level flight characteristics being satisfactory, some problems still existed when the aircraft was dived. Unless properly trimmed, the foot loads on the rudder bar became excessive when the turret was rotated. At the end of these tests the brackets supporting the scanner housing were modified and the turret flap angle reduced to 20°. A further period of flight testing was undertaken during July but again the results were not entirely satisfactory and comparative speed measurements with HX226 showed that the deflector plates reduced the top speed of HX238 by 3mph, which corresponded to a reduction in the cruising ceiling of 250ft.

Some difficulties were also experienced with the turret itself due to severe vibration which made accurate radar assisted gun laying impossible. Another B Mk III, LV999/G (the G suffix denoted guard) was fitted with a D turret and AGLT and an extensive series of trials were carried out from 9 September 1944, to 10 April 1945. The turret itself was modified during this period and the metal stiffening ribs replaced by perspex ones, which, due to their translucency, helped reduce eye fatigue.

The oil damping device was replaced on this particular turret by a series of small diameter friction rings taken from the mounting units of an MG131 machine gun fitted to an Me410 being examined by the experts at Boscombe Down. This new mounting affected a considerable reduction in turret vibration when the guns were fired. Meantime, a B Mk VI, NP834, had also been fitted with a D turret and Village Inn as AGLT was code-named. This Halifax carried out a series of trials during December and January

Left and below: A mystery machine, which appears to be a hybrid Mk VII/Mk VIII. It is fitted with Hercules XVI engines of the Mk VIII and in addition to the nose mounted gun the upper fuselage shows evidence of the removal of a mid-upper turret and the fitting of a fairing panel. The tailcone is a Mk VIII feature which could have been retrospectively fitted but the number of port holes along the fuselage clearly show it to be a Mk VIII or Mk IX airframe. The side entrance hatch eliminates the Mk IX. The night bomber camouflage and armament is alien to the Mk VIII. Even the pannier is unusual, all hinge and lock fittings have been removed, the doors sealed and over painted. The metal rails usually fitted to the bottom surface are missing and a single large camera port is fitted. The damaged paintwork on the wing leading edge shows that the aircraft has done a reasonable amount of flying. / Flight International

Right: B Mk II W1008 photographed in May 1943, fitted with the mock up of the AGLT scanner housing.

AM.I1449.

Above: **HX238 one of the B Mk III aircraft retained for experimental work and thus marked with the regulation prototype sign. It is seen here as the test bed for the first functional AGLT installation.**
/ *B. Robertson*

Right: **The clear housing on HX238 showing the scanner dish and aerial assembly, and the modified supporting yoke.**

Above: **LV999/G, fitted with AGLT and the revised turret flap settings determined during trials with HX238.**

Left: **The interior of the AGLT equipped D turret fitted to the B MK III LV999/G. Trials continued between September 1944 and April 1945 with this aircraft.**

1945 to test the effects of the turret rotation on the auto-pilot. Although the effects were not entirely overcome the results were acceptable.

The fitting of the D Mk I turret to the A Mk IX Halifax produced some internal revisions, the rear turret ammunition ducts being shortened and the boxes themselves fitted further aft. The radio equipment of this version was also slightly more extensive than that fitted to the A Mk VIIs and additional radar navigation aids were also provided. The wing bomb cell fuel tanks were reduced in capacity from 150gal to 96gal which, in turn, reduced total fuel tankage to 2,772gal. Normal bomb facilities were fitted but the bomb doors could be removed and an 8,000lb freight pannier fitted to the bomb bay. Maximum all up weight remained the same as for the A Mk VII at 65,000lb and performance was identical.

Completed in mid-October 1945, RT758 was delivered to the AFEE on the 23rd, the first two production A Mk IXs, RT759 and RT760, being delivered on 9 November. While production continued steadily and the A Mk IX was tested, a drastic revision of home based squadrons was undertaken.

On 1 November No 190 Squadron began its move to Tarrant Rushton from Great Dunrow, all 28 Halifaxes arriving by the 5th. A fortnight later the squadron began towing training with Hamilcars but its activities were to be short lived and on 28 December it was disbanded. However, a change of policy resurrected it on 21 January 1946, albeit under the identity of No 295 Squadron this squadron also having been recently disbanded.

Two other squadrons were also marked for disbandment, Nos 296 and 297 Squadrons both being currently based at Earles Colne. Withdrawn from the Indian Mail Service in January, three of No 297 Squadron's Halifaxes were given the task of each taking seven tons of educational books to Vienna. Two left on 23 January but the third was delayed by the non arrival of its quota of freight. The first two reached Vienna but became unserviceable and had to languish there until spares could reach them.

No 644 Squadron's Middle East Supplementary Mail Service, which normally terminated at Earles Colne, had to be redirected to Tarrant Rushton from 21 February owing to the disbandment of the two resident squadrons. No 296 Squadron was officially disbanded on 23 January and No 297 Squadron crews were kept busy ferrying the other squadron's Halifaxes away for disposal. This did not prevent them from continuing their other duties and on 5 February two of their Halifaxes left Earles Colne for Athens, via Bari, carrying 10,700lb of Greek currency in 50 packages.

Several stragglers returned during the first week of March, the two Halifaxes from Vienna and NA117 from Bordeaux. The latter had been stranded, awaiting spares, since 24 November. They were only just in time for the squadron was officially disbanded that same month. However, the squadron number had barely been removed from the list of current units when the original No 295 Squadron was reformed at Tarrant Rushton on 1 April and renumbered No 297 Squadron.

Nearly three quarters of the A Mk IX production batch had been delivered by the time the first of the type was issued for squadron service. The first two to be issued were RT845 and RT846 both of which went to No 1 Parachute Training School on 11 and 15 April respectively. Apart from these two the main batch were directed to the Middle East based squadrons, RT880, RT881 and RT882 arriving on 10 August. Throughout the remainder of the month the A Mk VIIs were ferried back to the UK and replaced with A Mk IXs.

The squadrons wasted no time in putting them to work and No 620 Squadron had two on a paratroop dropping and glider towing exercise on 29 August. A change of identity occurred on 1 September, both Nos 620 and 644 Squadrons being renumbered, respectively, Nos 113 and 47 Squadrons. This had no effect on the training programme and No 47 Squadron made its first lift under its new guise on 12 September. Both units changed their bases, No 113 Squadron moving to Kabrit but No 47 Squadron went a little further afield, returning to Fairford in the UK on the 30th. No 113 Squadron continued its multiple tasks in the Middle East until reduced to a number plate basis on 5 April 1947, the squadron's Halifaxes and personnel, including HQ 283 Wing, returning to Fairford. By the end of April the move was complete with the exception of one Halifax.

No 47 Squadron, still resident at Fairford, had been very active since its return to the UK but in May 1947 there was a considerable increase in the number of hours flown, 351 being recorded which was well in excess of the normal post war reduced schedule laid down. During an exercise at Netheravon they had dropped 1,078 paratroops and later took part in a large demonstration of airborne support work at Fairford. This was in addition to the normal glider towing and navigation training exercises. Ground crews were also extra busy that month stripping excess items from No 113 Squadron's Halifaxes before they were ferried away for disposal.

In October a drastic cut in numbers took place and a reorganisation was issued embracing the four Halifax squadrons, Nos 47, 113, 295 and 297. Each was reduced to six aircraft and together they formed the Flying Wing of RAF Fairford. Although reduced in numbers they managed a collective total of 616 hours, flying time during November. This figure was to drop slightly later but remained fairly consistent at about 550 hours per month.

Losses through accidents were extremely rare although the occasional close call still occurred. Shortly after take off on Operation Demon 51 the pilot of RT852 reported that the cockpit was filling with smoke and ordered the glider to cast off. The Hamilcar force landed safely off the aerodrome while the Halifax was put down safely on the main runway. The cause of the smoke was a fault in some electrical wiring. Such faults were few and in July the normal Halifax servicing cycle of 50 and 100 hourly inspections and maintenance was extended to 75 and 150 hours.

In August a further reduction in numbers took place, the Halifax strength being reduced to 12 aircraft which were held against Nos 295 and 297 Squadrons. No 113 Squadron was finally disbanded and No 47 Squadron prepared to move to Dishforth where it was to surrender its Halifaxes for a new type, the Hastings C Mk I. It was

Above: Seven B Mk VI Halifaxes were purchased by the Royal Pakistan Air Force and allocated serial numbers in the M1100 range. Roundels and fin flashes are green and white. Precise identification is not possible but the D Mk I tail turret indicates a late production B Mk VI; the pannier was an optional fitting for all late model Halifaxes.

Above: One of the six A Mk IX Halifaxes that reached the Royal Egyptian Air Force. Standard Bomber Command night camouflage was retained but REAF serial numbers and green and white national markings were applied. Temporary civil registrations were granted: G-ALVK/1160 was formerly RT901.
/ *A. J. Jackson*

Above right: G-ALVL/1162 with its Royal Egyptian Air Force markings not yet completed. It was formerly RT907 and had served with No 47 Squadron from 22 November 1946. It passed to No 295 Squadron and then Aviation Traders on 18 August 1949. / *A. J. Jackson*

Right: G-ALVH/1163 was originally RT788, and had seen service in the Middle East from September 1946. It passed to Aviation Traders on 18 August 1949.
/ *A. J. Jackson*

Above: PP389, an A Mk VII used by de Havilland's for towing trials with a specially modified Horsa glider TL349. A mock-up of the Comet airliner's nose was fitted to determine the degree of visibility, particularly in rain. John Cunningham carried out the tests in January 1947. PP389 was delivered from No 29 MU on 17 December 1946 and went to No 48 MU on 4 November 1947. / *de Havilland*

Below: Originally delivered to de Havilland's on 30 May 1946, RG820, a B Mk VI, was returned to Handley Page on 5 May 1947 and then back to de Havilland's on 20 January 1948 for engine de-icing trials. It is seen here with the original single spray bar installation and fuselage reinforcing to withstand the impact of the ice.

The aircraft was eventually dismantled and removed by the RAF in October 1951, becoming instructional airframe 6903M on 29 September 1951 and allotted to No 4 Group. Two other Halifaxes, both B Mk IIIs, were used by de Havilland's; NA683 arrived from Farnborough on 2 April 1946 and went to No 45 MU on 9 May 1946 due to poor condition. MZ956 was used for propeller governor tests and went to No 45 MU on 7 April 1956. / *de Havilland*

Right: The multiple spray bar attachment fitted to RG820 during the engine icing trials. The reinforcing to the fuselage can be seen immediately behind the cockpit. / *de Havilland*

Above: The sad remains of PN323, a Mk VII retained by Handley Page for radio installation aerial tests and fitted with a false single fin. The front section of this fuselage was, until recently, the only tangible evidence of a Halifax preserved. Had it not been for the successful recovery of W1048 from Norway one might well have asked — what price glory! / *Handley Page*

fitting that the Halifaxes should be superseded by their lineal descendant. Dishforth became the Hastings OTU and in October No 297 Squadron moved in to begin its conversion to the new type. Its Halifaxes, along with the remaining Hamilcars and Horsas, had been ferried to No 29 MU along with No 295 Squadron's aircraft the latter having disbanded that same month.

Postwar the Halifax was also active in experimental research relating to a wide variety of aeronautical subjects. In January 1945 the Experimental Section and RAF Farnborough were merged into one establishment and it was there that the Halifaxes served for several years. Various marks were attached to the different sections ie the Structural and Mechanical Engineering Flight, the Armament Flight, the Gas Dynamics Flight, the Wireless and Electrical Flight, the Instrument Flight, the Aerodynamics Supersonic Flight and the Meteorological Research Flight.

Tasks ranged from multi disc brake trials to high altitude parachuting but it was the Armament and Meteorological Flights that provided the Halifaxes with their most sustained employment. This unit moved to Farnborough on 18 August 1946 and spent the next four months re-equipping with personnel and aircraft the latter comprising two Mk VI Halifaxes, ST796 and ST817, and two PR34 Mosquitos. In August 1947 a camera was fitted in the bomb bay of ST796, focused on a point 14in below the aircraft which was brilliantly illuminated from both sides. With this equipment the Halifax was used to photograph rain drops which appeared, in turn, as measurable streaks on the negatives. It was then possible to work out the size of the rain drops. ST817 was equipped to investigate the homogeneity of humidity in the lower troposphere, a task that was completed by November 1947. The following month ST796 began a lengthy programme investigating the sublimation of nuclei at various altitudes, Mr K. D. Palmer of Clarendon Laboratory, Oxford, flying with the crew to operate the special instrumentation.

In April 1947 the Universal Freight Container was ready for its first handling trials and the following month drop tests were begun using an A Mk VII Halifax, PP350, as the trials aircraft. The UFC enclosed a jeep and 10cwt trailer giving a loaded weight of 8,000lb. Of approximately the same shape and dimensions as the standard 8,000lb capacity freight pannier it proved to have no adverse effects upon the general handling characteristics of the Halifax. It was dropped near Odstone, cameras under each wing tip of PP350 recording its initial descent. The crash gear on one side collapsed on initial impact due to a faulty forging but no damage was done to the contents and the UFC was easily righted.

During September the UFC was modified to carry two observers internally with an automatic observation device fitted to the vents underneath it. This involved a considerable amount of work as intercom, seats, safety harnesses and emergency exits had to be fitted and checked by the stress department. The flight was completed without incident, both the human observers, Messrs Morely and Saville, and the automatic one functioned correctly. A considerable amount of useful data was obtained particularly that concerning suction on the undersurface of the container. The modified crash gear to be fitted incorporated air bags which inflated during the descent and projected from the undersurface of the container hence suction problems were very pertinent. The modified crash gear was tested in a live drop in December, the UFC being supported during the descent by eight 42ft canopies.

A most unusual Halifax arrived at Farnborough in December 1947. NP715 was a B Mk VI which had been extensively modified by Handley Page and it was attached to the Aerodynamic Supersonic Flight. Its most pronounced feature was its short span wings of the same dimensions as those fitted to the original model Halifaxes. The normal ailerons had been removed and replaced by a very small type fitted with a trim tab and a separate balance tab. Between the aileron and the normal flaps was an auxiliary flap. Immediately in front of these new control surfaces was a line of four spoilers of semi-circular cross section which were linked to the ailerons. The spoilers were very similar to those fitted to the Northrop Black Widow night fighter. The purpose of the experiment was to gain experience with this type of control system on heavy aircraft with a view to its adoption on future designs.

The tests commenced on 1 December and continued to 22 December, about nine hours actual flying time being logged. Results showed that for normal operations at speeds above 140mph (IAS) the characteristics of the linked aileron-spoilers were very similar to the conventional ailerons fitted to Halifaxes. Good turns could be made in either direction using only the aileron-spoilers. However, at lower speeds there was an appreciable increase in the lag in response to control movements and this increased as the stall was approached, the rate of roll being noticeably affected. It was considered that deterioration was sufficiently bad enough to render the control inadequate for bad weather landings even when allowing for the slight improvement brought about by lowering the auxiliary flaps.

In a stall, with all flaps down, the Halifax's normal mild handling characteristics were altered considerably with a tendency for the aircraft to roll. This could not be controlled even with coarse use of the aileron-spoilers at speeds below about 140mph (IAS) with flaps up and at about 100-110mph (IAS) with the auxiliary flaps lowered. In view of these results the experiments were discontinued.

With the disbanding of the Airborne Forces squadrons a considerable number of A Mk IX Halifaxes became available and most were put up for sale. Pak-Air, the Pakistan airline had bought three C Mk VIIIs and the Pakistan Air Force now decided to try the Halifax also, purchasing seven B Mk VIs, RG736, RG779, RG781, RG783, RG784, RG785 and RG813 during 1948. The French Air Force was still operating Halifaxes with Groupe 1/25, Tunisie, and Groupe 2/23, Guyenne, and had received an additional 26 B Mk VIs during 1946-47.

Not unnaturally further overseas military sales were sought and Aviation Traders Ltd sold 22 A Mk IX Halifaxes to the then Royal Egyptian Air Force. The Halifaxes were granted temporary civil status for the purpose of ferrying them. However, the heightening tension in the Middle East precipitated the 1950 arms embargo and only six reached their destination, the last to leave being

Left: The dangers of the solitary long distance ocean patrol did not cease at war's end. A Met Mk III:M-X9 of No 517 Squadron, afloat seven hours after it ditched. The crew was rescued by a ship freighting bananas. / IWM

Below: W1048:TL-S of No 35 Squadron sees the light of day for the first time in over 30 years. The object on the fuselage amidships is the lower, internal, section of the mid-upper turret. *P. Cornish & S. Usher*

Right: The paintwork on W1048 began to peel off rapidly once the aircraft had been exposed to the air. The diver is preparing to place a floatation bag beneath the wing. / *P. Cornish & S. Usher*

Below right: A survivor returns; W1048 lies glistening in the sunlight. A final, physical tribute to the countless people who were an integral part of the Halifax's career. / *Royal Norwegian Air Force*

RT938 the last A Mk IX to be built. Their ultimate fate is not known but during the Suez Crisis combat reports on Egyptian aircraft destroyed by strafing included what were possibly some if not all the remaining Halifaxes.

One other Halifax should be mentioned here since it was also a military 'export' to a foreign government. Stolen by an unknown aircrew PP263, registered G-AJPJ, was flown to the Middle East but crashed at Lydda on 20 July 1948, thus failing to become a clandestine bomber.

At the conclusion of the war the anti-shipping squadrons of Coastal Command equipped with the Halifax had disbanded. However, the squadrons engaged on meteorological duties remained active and were supplemented by a further Halifax squadron, No 519, which had begun to re-equip in August. The four Halifax meteorological squadrons continued their routine patrols until early in 1946 when a general re-organisation took place and they were disbanded along with the newly formed No 521 Squadron. When it disbanded in April, No 520 Squadron had transferred its Gibraltar detachment of five Halifaxes and six crews to No 518 Squadron. This detachment was then, in turn, transferred to the new meteorological squadron, No 202, which had formed on 1 October from the old No 518 Squadron.

This new squadron was equipped with the Met Mk 6 version of the Halifax. This was the definitive Coastal Command version and was produced in a basic form compatible with both meteorological and general reconnaissance/anti-shipping duties, most being fully tropicalised. Issued to No 1361 Meteorological Flight for acceptance trials in February 1946 the main production batch began to reach No 517 Squadron the following month.

No 202 Squadron was joined at Aldergrove by a second Halifax squadron when No 224 Squadron reformed on 1 March 1948. Once more the Gibraltar based detachment changed hands, No 224 Squadron absorbing it. The practice of flying virtually every day of the year, regardless of weather conditions, remained unchanged and each morning between 0730 and 0830hrs a lone Halifax would leave Aldergrove; following a 1,600-mile triangular course over the Atlantic, climbing and descending at the prescribed intervals to take readings, and finally returning to base 10-12 hours later.

The loneliness and danger of these long distance patrols never diminished and during the course of No 202 Squadron's career three of its Met Mk 6 Halifaxes failed to return. No 224 Squadron was more fortunate, apart from ST803 being burnt out only one Halifax ever failed to return, RG837 being listed as missing on 16 January 1951.

The re-equipping of Transport Command with Hastings produced a surplus of A Mk IX Halifaxes and three of this type found their way on to meteorological duties, RT786:A RT798 and RT923 being taken on charge by No 202 Squadron between August and October 1949.

It was with Coastal Command that the Halifax performed its last operational duties, the honours going jointly to No 224 Squadron and RG841. On 17 March 1952, Flt Lt Finch left Gibraltar in RG841 for No 48 MU at Hawarden.

Thus the operational, training and civil career of the Halifax drew to a close within a relatively close space of time. It had commenced its operational career at a time when four engined bombers were virtually an unknown quantity and both crews and aircraft had had to learn their measure by experience, sometimes at great cost to both. The Halifax, like its contemporaries, was far from perfect initially and it had taken a lot of work and thought before it reached the point where it became an efficient weapon. That it did reach this standard, in spite of its inauspicious beginning, speaks clearly enough for the soundness of the original design. It served in every British theatre of operations and in virtually every type of role from bombing, glider towing, agent dropping, transport, anti-shipping, meteorological reconnaissance and training; no role was too difficult nor too insignificant. In addition it also pioneered the use of equipment and techniques which were later put to good effect by others.

Fortunately for posterity there remains a single B Mk II Series I Halifax, W1048:S of No 35 Squadron; significantly the first unit to operate the type. Recovered from the dark icy waters of Lake Hoklingen, it emerged into the sunlight shortly after 1400hrs on Saturday, 30 June 1973. It had force landed on the frozen surface of the lake on 27 April 1942 and sank into 90 feet of water while the crew watched from the shore, never, they presumed, to be seen again. Fortunately the mud of the lake bed virtually embalmed the Halifax and its contents. Skilful work by a team of RAF sub-aqua enthusiasts, combined with the resources of the RAF, brought the veteran home for restoration and eventual display by the RAF Museum.

Fortunate indeed for posterity for the only other physical remains of this aircraft type are a single nose section and a small collection of panels bearing individual crew crests. Poor reward indeed for an aircraft which numbered in its thousands and which won a commendable list of battle honours.

Appendices
1 Unit Briefs

No 10(B) Squadron Codes: ZA

Based at Leeming, Yorkshire (4 Group). Converted from Whitleys to Halifax B Mk IIs in December 1941. Moved to Melbourne, Yorkshire, in August 1942. Converted to B Mk IIIs in March 1944. Last operational mission 25/4/45, target Wangerooge. Transferred to Transport Command 8/5/45, converted to Dakotas.

No 35(B) Squadron Codes: TL

Reformed 5/11/40 at Boscombe Down, Wiltshire (1 Group). Received first Halifax 13/11/40. Moved to Leeming (4 Group) 20/11/40. Moved to Linton-on-Ouse (4 Group) 5/12/40. Converted to B Mk IIs October 1941. Moved to Gravely (3 Group) as part of PFF in August 1942. (Became 8 Group on 8/1/43.) Converted to B Mk IIIs in December 1943. Converted to Lancasters in March 1944, the last Halifax operation occurring on 1/3/44 against Stuttgart.

No 47(GT) Squadron Codes: MOHD

No 644(GT) Squadron was renumbered No 47(GT) Squadron wef 1/9/46 at its base Quastina, Palestine. Equipped with A Mk IX Halifaxes it moved to Fairford, Gloucestershire, September 1946. Squadron strength reduced to six aircraft in October 1947 and with Nos 113, 295 and 297 Squadrons, formed the flying wing of RAF Fairford. Last Halifax relinquished on 1/9/48 and squadron moved to Dishforth to convert to Hastings.

No 51(B) Squadron Codes: MH (C Flight coded LK, changed to C6 January 1944)

Based at Snaith, Yorkshire (4 Group) and converted from Whitleys to B Mk II Halifaxes in November 1942. Converted to B Mk IIIs January 1944 and No 578 (B) Squadron formed from C Flight. Last operational mission 25/4/45, target Wangerooge. Reduced to two flights wef 7/2/45. Transferred to Transport Command 8/5/45. Converted to Stirlings June 1945 and last Halifax departed July.

No 58(GR) Squadron Codes: BY

Based at St Eval, Cornwall (19 Group) and converted from Whitleys to GR Mk II Halifaxes in December 1942. Moved to Holmsley South in July 1943 and then to St Davids in December. Transferred to control of 18 Group and moved to Stornoway, Outer Hebrides, in September 1944. Converted to GR Mk IIIs and began operations with them in April 1945. Squadron disbanded 25/5/45.

No 76(B) Squadron Codes: MP

Formed from C Flight of No 35(B) Squadron 1/5/41 and equipped with B Mk I and II Halifaxes; based at Linton-on-Ouse. Moved to Middleton St George, County Durham (4 Group), June 1941. Moved back to Linton-on-Ouse in September 1942. Converted to B Mk Vs in April 1943. Moved to Holme-on-Spalding Moor, Yorkshire, June 1943. Converted to B Mk IIIs in February 1944. Began conversion to B Mk VIs in April 1945 and both marks used on final operational mission, against Wangerooge, on 25/4/45. Transferred to Transport Command 8/5/45 and converted to Dakotas.

No 77(B) Squadron Codes: KN, C Flight TB

Based at Elvington, Yorkshire (4 Group). Converted from Whitleys to B Mk II Halifaxes in October 1942 but these were recalled and B Mk Vs issued. On 30/11/42 the latter were recalled pending issue of modified B Mk IIs. Between 9 and 11 November 1943 the B Mk IIs were again exchanged for B Mk Vs. Moved to Full Sutton, Yorkshire in May 1944 and converted to B Mk IIIs. Began converting to B Mk VIs in March 1945 and used both types for last operational mission, against Wangerooge on 25/4/45. Transferred to Transport Command 8/5/45 and converted to Dakotas. Last Halifax departed in August.

No 78(B) Squadron Codes: EY

Based at Croft, County Durham (4 Group). Converted from Whitleys to B Mk II Halifaxes in March 1942. Moved to Middleton St George in June 1942 and then to Linton-on-Ouse in September. Moved to Breighton, Yorkshire (4 Group) in June 1943. Converted to B Mk IIIs in January 1944. Began converting to B Mk VIs in May 1945 and used both types for last operational mission, against Wangerooge, on 25/4/45. Squadron had been reduced to two flights 10/4/45, surplus B Mk IIIs going to Nos 171(BS) and 199(BS) Squadrons. Squadron transferred to Transport Command 8/5/45 and converted to Dakotas.

No 96(T) Squadron Codes: 6H

Formed at Leconfield 30/12/44 under authority TCSD 155

No 2976/44. Establishment to be 25 C Mk III Halifaxes. On 9/2/45 authority received for squadron to be transferred to MAAF to replace No 267(T) Squadron. Notification received 16/3/45 to re-equip with Dakotas which were to be supplied from MAAF sources. Halifaxes disposed of to MU and No 10(T) Squadron.

No 102(B) Squadron Codes: DY

Based at Dalton, Yorkshire (4 Group). Converted from Whitleys to B Mk II Halifaxes in December 1941. Moved to Topcliffe, Yorkshire, in June 1942 and again to Pocklington, Yorkshire (4 Group) 7 August. Converted to B Mk IIIs in May 1944. Reduced to two flights 25/1/45 and began converting to B Mk VIs in February. Used both types for last operational mission, against Wangerooge, on 25/4/45. Squadron transferred to Transport Command 8/5/45 and converted to Liberators.

No 103(B) Squadron Codes: PM

Based at Elsham Wolds, Lincolnshire (1 Group). Converted from Wellingtons to B Mk II Halifaxes in July 1942. Began conversion to Lancasters in October 1942: last Halifax operation, against Milan on 24/10/42.

No 113(GT) Squadron Codes: MOHC

No 620(GT) Squadron was renumbered No 113(GT) Squadron 1/9/46 at its base Aqir, Palestine. Equipped with A Mk IX Halifaxes it moved to Kabrit. Squadron transferred to Fairford in April 1947 along with HQ 238 Wing. Squadron reduced to six aircraft in October and with Nos 47, 295 and 297 Squadrons, formed the flying wing of RAF Fairford. Squadron disbanded in September 1948.

No 138(SD) Squadron Codes: NF

Reformed from the nucleus of No 1419 Flight at Newmarket, Cambridgeshire, in August 1941; Lysanders equipped A Flight and Whitleys B Flight, B Mk II Halifaxes supplementing the latter in October. The squadron was under the control of the Directorate of Plans, but its parent station was Stradishall, Suffolk (4 Group)). Moved to Tempsford, March 1942, where, with No 161(SD) Squadron it came under control of ACAS(I). When not engaged on SOE operations it carried out bombing missions with 3 Group. Last Halifax operation carried out on 11/8/44 and began converting to Stirlings the following month.

No 148(SD) Squadron Codes: FS

No 148(B) Squadron was disbanded in December 1942 but leaving X Flight, its Special Liberator Flight, still active. The first of several B Mk II Halifaxes was received on 18/2/43 and on 13/3/43 the Flight moved from Shandur to Gambut. The following day the Flight was officially redesignated No 148(SD) Squadron. Moved to Derna on 3/4/43 and then to Tocra on 1/9/43 with detachments to Protville and Cairo West at various times. Moved to Brindisi, Italy, as part of 334 Wing in January 1944. Began conversion to Stirlings in November 1944 but ceased when notified in December that it was to receive Liberators instead. Conversion delayed until 23/5/45.

No 158(B) Squadron Codes: NP

Based at Driffield, Yorkshire (4 Group). Converted from Wellingtons to B Mk II Halifaxes in May 1942. Moved to East Moor, Yorkshire, in June 1942. Moved to Rufforth, Yorkshire, in November and again, to Lisset, Yorkshire, in February 1943. Converted to B Mk IIIs in December 1943. No 640(B) Squadron formed from C Flight in January 1944, and squadron strength expanded to three flights once more in March. Began conversion to B Mk VIs in April 1945 and both types used for final operational mission, against Wangerooge, on 25/4/45. Squadron reduced to two flights on 1/5/45 and transferred to Transport Command 8/5/45 and converted to Stirlings.

No 161(SD) Squadron Codes: MA

Formed at Newmarket on 14/2/42 for SOE operations and moved to Tempsford in March. Lysanders equipped A Flight, and Whitleys B Flight the latter receiving its first B Mk V Halifax on 18/10/42. In August 1944 B Flight began converting to Stirlings and the last Halifax operation was flown on 1/9/44.

No 171(BS) Squadron Codes: 6Y and EX

Formed at North Creake, Norfolk (100 Group), on 8/9/44 from third flight of No 199(BS) Squadron under authority of SD155 No 2033/44. Allocated a UE of 20 B Mk III Halifaxes but initially equipped with mixture of these and Stirlings, the first Halifax arriving on 16/10/44. Last Stirling operation took place on 21/11/44. Last wartime operation occurred on 2/5/45 and squadron disbanded on 27/7/45.

No 178(B) Squadron Codes: Unknown

Formed at Shandur, Egypt (240 Wing), on 15/1/43 and equipped with Liberators. Moved to Hosc Raui, Libya, in February 1943. Began converting to B Mk II Halifaxes in May 1943 but decision taken to keep Liberators and Halifax strength reduced in September. Last Halifax operation, against Manduria, on 7/8/43.

No 187(T) Squadron Codes: Unknown

Formed at Merryfield (47 Group), 1/2/45. Unit to have an establishment of 25 C Mk III Halifaxes under Establishment No LWE/AT/2235A of 30/12/44. Halifax Development Flight attached to squadron for servicing facilities on 1/3/45. Squadron notified on 14/3/45 of policy change, UE to be 25 Dakotas. Halifax Development Flight disbanded 3/4/45.

No 190(GT) Squadron Codes: G5, L9 and 6S

Based at Great Dunmow, Essex (38 Group). Squadron began converting from Stirlings to A Mk VII Halifaxes on 4/5/45. Used to convert No 620(GT) Squadron crews to Halifaxes and did not reach full strength until July 1945. Moved to Tarrant Rushton in November 1945. Squadron disbanded on 28/12/45 but reactivated as No 295(GT) Squadron on 21/1/46.

No 192(BS) Squadron Codes: DT

Formed from 1474 Flight at Gransden Lodge (8 Group) on

4/1/43. Squadron equipped with a mixture of Wellingtons and Mosquitos. First B Mk II Halifax received on 9/1/43. Moved to Feltwell (2 Group) in April and then to Foulsham on 25/11/43. Began operating B Mk IIIs in March 1944. Last wartime operation, using mixed force of Halifaxes and Mosquitos, on 2/5/45. Squadron disbanded on 22/8/45.

No 199(BS) Squadron Codes: EX

Based at North Creake and equipped with Stirlings. Began conversion to B Mk IIIs in February 1945 and last Stirling operation on 14/2/45. Last operational mission 2/5/45. Squadron disbanded on 24/7/45.

No 202(Met) Squadron Codes: Y3

No 518(Met) Squadron disbanded at Aldergrove on 1/10/46 and renumbered No 202(Met) Squadron. Squadron continued to maintain permanent detachment at Gibraltar, Met Mk VI Halifaxes being used in both cases. At least three A Mk IXs were used (RT786, '798, '923) by the squadron between August 1949 and January 1951. Crew conversion began in July 1950 and the squadron converted to Hastings in January 1951.

No 224(Met) Squadron Codes: XB then B

Squadron reformed at Aldergrove on 1/3/48 with initial strength of two Met Mk VI Halifaxes plus, in 1951, the five Met Mk VIs of the former No 202(Met) Squadron detachment at Gibraltar. This detachment was maintained. Squadron converted to Shackletons in 1952. The last Halifax to leave was RG841 from the Gibraltar detachment, the last Halifax to operate with a front line unit.

No 251(Met) Squadron Codes: AD

Reformed August 1944 and equipped with Hudsons, Fortresses and Halifaxes. No other details.

No 295(GT) Squadron Codes: 8E and 8Z

Based at Netherhaven (38 Wing) A Mk V Halifaxes began to replace the Whitleys of A Flight in February 1943; completed by 22/4/43. Halifaxes used for bombing missions between duties. Squadron moved to Holmsley South on 1/5/43 for Operation Beggar. Began converting to Albemarles in September and last Halifax operation was on 10/10/43. Postwar squadron disbanded but was reformed at Tarrant Rushton on 1/4/46 and renumbered No 297(GT) Squadron.

No 296(GT) Squadron Codes: 7C and 9W

Based at Earles Colne (38 Group) it began converting from Albemarles to A Mk V Halifaxes in September 1944, crew conversion being at 1665 HCU. Converted to A Mk IIIs in February 1945 and in October began transport work on the Indian Trunk Route. Began conversion to A Mk VIIs in December but disbanded on 23/1/46.

No 297(GT) Squadron Codes: L5 and P5 (Postwar MOHA)

Based at Earles Colne it began converting from Albemarles to A Mk V Halifaxes from 1/10/44. Converted to A Mk IIIs in February 1945 and in October began transport work on the Indian Trunk Route. Began conversion to A Mk VII in December but disbanded in March 1946. On 1/4/46 the original No 295(GT) Squadron was reformed at Tarrant Rushton and renumbered No 297(GT) Squadron. Moved to Brize Norton in August. In January 1947 began partial re-equipping with A Mk IX (six only). In October unit strength cut and with Nos 47, 113 and 295(GT) Squadrons it formed the flying wing of RAF Fairford. In August 1948 further reductions and 12 Halifaxes held against Nos 295 and 297(GT) Squadrons. Squadron moved to Dishforth in October and began conversion to Hastings.

No 298(GT) Squadron Codes: 8A and 8T (as from 20/5/44)

Initially activated on paper as a mixed Halifax/Whitley unit on 24/8/42 but formation suspended until 19/10/43. Physically formed at Tarrant Rushton on 4/11/43 with A Mk V Halifaxes in two flights; C Flight formed 5/2/44 but transferred as nucleus of No 644(GT) Squadron, on 18/3/44. In October began converting to A Mk IIIs. Began converting to A Mk VIIs in February 1945. Squadron transferred to Raipur, India (238 Wing) in July taking with them tropicalised A Mk VIIs. In September role changed to transport work but changed again in July 1946 under title of Bomber, Airborne Support and Heavy Equipment Dropping Squadron. Disbanded in December 1946.

No 301(SD) Squadron Codes: GR *Polish*

Reformed from 1586(SD) Flight at Brindisi, Italy, on 7/11/44; equipped with Liberators and B Mk V Halifaxes. Last operational mission 25/2/45. Squadron transferred to Transport Command and returned to UK, stationed at Blackbushe. Began re-equipping with Warwicks in May, Moved to North Weald on 3/7/45 and again, to Chedburgh, on 5/9/45. Began conversion to C Mk VIII Halifaxes in January 1946. Overseas flights cancelled as from 9/4/46 and squadron disbanded 10/12/46.

No 304(T) Squadron Codes: QD *Polish*

Based at Chedburgh when notified on 2/11/45 to convert from Wellingtons to Warwicks. Order amended on 11/1/46 in favour of C Mk VIII Halifaxes but due to embargo on overseas flights from 9/4/46 squadron did not become operational with Halifaxes. Disbanded 10/12/46.

No 346(B) Squadron Codes H7 *French*

Formed at Elvington (4 Group) on 16/5/44 with B Mk V Halifaxes. Began converting to B Mk IIIs in June. Converted to B Mk VIs in March 1945. Squadron ceased flying 6/10/45 and personnel, plus portion of squadron aircraft, transferred to French Air Force.

No 347(B) Squadron Codes: L8 *French*

Formed at Elvington on 20/6/44 with B Mk V Halifaxes. Began converting to B Mk IIIs in July. Converted to B Mk VIs in March 1945. Squadron ceased flying 6/10/45 and personnel, plus portion of squadron aircraft, transferred to French Air Force.

No 405(B) Squadron Codes: LQ *Canadian*

Based at Topcliffe (4 Group) and converted from Wellingtons to B Mk II Halifaxes in April 1942. Squadron transferred to 6 Group 1/1/43. Moved to Leeming 13/14 March 1943 and again to Gransden Lodge on 17/20 April 1943. Transferred to 8 Group 19/4/43; began converting to Lancasters in August. Last Halifax operation, against Modane, 16/9/43.

No 408(B) Squadron Codes: EQ *Canadian*

Based at Leeming and converted from Hampdens to B Mk V Halifaxes in September 1942; first Halifaxes did not arrive until 11/10/42. Advised on 30/11/42 of impending conversion to B Mk IIs the first of which arrived 7/12/42. Advised on 14/7/43 of impending move to Linton-on-Ouse for conversion to Lancasters. Last Halifax operation 2/8/43. Moved to Linton-on-Ouse 10/8/43. Began to re-convert to Halifaxes (mainly B Mk VIIs but some B Mk IIIs) July 1944. Began converting to Lancasters May 1945, completed by 21/5/45.

No 415(B) Squadron Codes: 6U *Canadian*

Based at East Moore (6 Group) and converted from Wellingtons and Albacores to B Mk III Halifaxes in July 1944. A few B Mk VIIs taken on charge in February 1945. Last operational mission, against Wangerooge, 25/4/45. Squadron disbanded 15/5/45.

No 419(B) Squadron Codes: VR *Canadian*

Based at Middleton St George and converted from Wellingtons to B Mk II Halifaxes in November 1942. Transferred to 6 Group 1/4/43. Began converting to Lancasters in April 1944 and last Halifax operation against Montzen, 27/4/44.

No 420(B) Squadron Codes: PT *Canadian*

Based at Tholthorpe (6 Group) and converted from Wellingtons to B Mk III Halifaxes in January 1944. Began conversion to Lancasters in April 1945; last Halifax operation, against Heligoland, 18/4/45.

No 424(B) Squadron Codes: QB *Canadian*

Based at Skipton-on-Swale (6 Group) and converted from Wellingtons to B Mk III Halifaxes in December 1943. Began conversion to Lancasters in January 1945; last Halifax operation 28/1/45.

No 425(B) Squadron Codes: KW *Canadian*

Based at Tholthorpe and converted from Wellingtons to B Mk III Halifaxes in January 1944. Last operational mission, against Wangerooge, 25/4/45. Converted to Lancasters in May 1945.

No 426(B) Squadron Codes: OW *Canadian*

Based at Linton-on-Ouse and converted from Lancasters to B Mk III Halifaxes in April 1944. Converted to B Mk VIIs in June 1944. Last operational mission, against Wangerooge, 25/4/45. Moved to Driffield on 26/5/45 and transferred to Transport Command. Moved to Tempsford on 26/6/45 and converted to Liberators.

No 427(B) Squadron Codes: ZL *Canadian*

Based at Leeming and converted from Wellingtons to B Mk V Halifaxes in May 1943. Converted to B Mk IIIs January 1944, but began conversion to Lancasters in February. Last Halifax operational mission, mining in Norwegian waters, 3/3/44.

No 428(B) Squadron Codes: NA *Canadian*

Based at Leeming and converted from Wellingtons to B Mk V Halifaxes in June 1943; these being supplemented by B Mk IIs in November. Began conversion to B Mk IIIs in January 1944 but suspended due impending conversion to Lancasters. Last Halifax operational mission in March.

No 429(B) Squadron Codes: AL *Canadian*

Based at Leeming and converted from Wellingtons to B Mk II Halifaxes in September 1943. Began a gradual conversion to B Mk Vs in November but ceased due impending conversion to B Mk IIIs which began in January 1944. Began conversion to Lancasters in March 1945; last Halifax operational mission, against Castrop-Rauxel oil refinery, 15/3/45.

No 431(B) Squadron Codes: SE *Canadian*

Based at Tholthorpe and converted from Wellingtons to B Mk V Halifaxes in July 1943. Moved to Croft in December and began converting to B Mk IIIs in March 1944. Began converting to Lancasters in October; last Halifax operational mission occurred 25/10/44.

No 432(B) Squadron Codes: QO *Canadian*

Based at East Moor and converted from Lancasters to B Mk III Halifaxes in February 1944. Began conversion to B Mk VIIs in June. Last operational mission, against Wangerooge, 25/4/45. Squadron disbanded 15/5/45.

No 433(B) Squadron Codes: BM *Canadian*

Formed at Skipton-on-Swale on 25/9/43 and equipped with B Mk III Halifaxes, the first of which arrived 3/11/43. Began converting to Lancasters in January 1945. Last Halifax operational mission, against Magdeburg, 16/1/45.

No 434(B) Squadron Codes: IP *Canadian*

Based at Tholthorpe and converted from Wellingtons to B Mk V Halifaxes in June 1943. Moved to Croft on 11/12/43. Began converting to B Mk IIIs in May 1944. Converted to Lancasters in December; last Halifax operational mission, against Köln, 21/12/44.

No 460(B) Squadron Codes: UV *Australian*

Based at Breighton the squadron was notified in June 1942 to prepare for conversion from Wellingtons to B Mk II Halifaxes. Conversion flight formed but notification received on 25/9/42 for Halifaxes to be withdrawn and replaced by Lancasters. Halifaxes did not become operational; first Lancaster operation 22/11/42.

No 462(B) Squadron Codes: Unknown *Australian*

Formed at Fayid, Egypt, 7/9/42, from amalgamation of

No 10(B) Squadron and No 76(B) Squadron detachments and placed under control of No 425 Wing, No 205 Group; equipped with B Mk II Halifaxes. Transferred to operational control of No 236 Wing on 27/11/42. Moved to LG 237, Egypt, 17/12/42; to LG 167 then to LG 237 and back to LG 167, Libya the same month. Moved to Solluch No 1, Libya in December and then to Gardabià Main in February 1943; to Hosc Raui in May; to Terria in October with a detachment to El Adem in December. The whole squadron moved to El Adem in January 1944 and then to Celone, Italy, in March where it was renumbered No 614(B) Squadron on 3/3/44.

No 462(B) Squadron Codes: Z5 *Australian*

Reformed at Driffield on 12/8/44 and equipped with B Mk III Halifaxes. On 22/12/44 screened from operations and transferred to Foulsham (100 Group) with a subsequent change of designation to No 462(BS) Squadron. Last operational mission 2/5/45. Disbanded on 24/9/45.

No 466(B) Squadron Codes: HD *Australian*

Based at Leconfield and equipped with Wellingtons. On 1/9/43 screened from operations and commenced training with B Mk II Halifaxes on 19/9/43. On 26/10/43 first batch of B Mk IIIs arrived and squadron operational with this mark by 1/12/43. Moved to Driffield in June 1944. Last operational mission, against Wangerooge, 25/4/45. On 5/5/45 ordered to dispose of B Mk IIIs and re-equip with B Mk VIs ex-640(B) Squadron. Transferred to Transport Command 8/5/45. On 20/6/45 renumbered No 10(B) Squadron RAAF. Moved to Bassingbourne in September and commenced converting to Liberators. Disbanded 26/10/45.

No 502(GR) Squadron Codes: YG and V9

Based at St Eval signal received on 9/1/43 notifying re-equipment from Whitleys to GR Mk II Halifaxes. Moved to Holmsley South on 30/6/43, then to St Davids on 10/12/43. In September 1944 squadron transferred to control of No 18 Group and moved to Stornoway. Began conversion to GR Mk IIIs in late January 1945. Disbanded in May 1945.

No 517(Met) Squadron Codes: X9

Based at St Eval No 1404(Met) Flight was renumbered No 517(Met) Squadron on 11/8/43 and allotted an establishment of 18+6 Met Mk V Halifaxes, other equipment Hampdens, Hudsons and Fortresses. On 5/12/43 ordered to move to Brawdy, a satellite of St Davids via the main station. Moved to Brawdy on 1/2/44. Squadron allocated Epicure patrols. In March 1945 began converting to Met Mk IIIs and operated them until March 1946 when it began converting to Met Mk VIs. Disbanded in April, the Met Mk VIs going to No 518(Met) Squadron.

No 518(Met) Squadron Codes: Y3

Formed at Stornoway on 9/7/43 and equipped with Met Mk V Halifaxes. Moved to Tiree on 25/9/43 and

allocated Mercer patrols. On 14/10/43 squadron screened from operations and used to train 58 Halifax crews for met duties. Squadron reduced to 12 Halifaxes but surplus crews retained for specific operations as detailed by HQ Coastal Command. On 10/11/43 strength increased to 14 Halifaxes. Trial flight of new flight plan coded Bismuth carried out on 24/2/44 and thereafter both Mercer and Bismuth routes used by squadron. Converted to Met Mk IIIs in March 1944 and moved to Aldergrove. Gibraltar detachment of No 520(Met) Squadron taken over 25/4/46 and squadron converted to Met Mk VIs. Disbanded 1/10/46 and renumbered No 202(Met) Squadron.

No 519(Met) Squadron Codes: Z9

Based at Wick and equipped with Fortresses and Spitfires, moved to Tain where it received some Met Mk III Halifaxes in August 1945. Moved to Leuchars in November 1945 and commenced Recipe patrols. On 11/11/45 commenced converting to Met Mk VIs but action not completed. Last flight made by squadron, using Met Mk IIIs, 30/5/46.

No 520(Met) Squadron Codes: 2M

Based at Gibraltar using Gladiators, Hurricanes, Spitfires and Hudsons the squadron received its first Met Mk V Halifax on 6/2/44 and flew first operation the same day. Squadron allocated Nocturnal patrols. A few Met Mk IIIs received in July 1945. Squadron disbanded on 25/4/46 having converted to Met Mk VIs five of which were left at Gibraltar and renumbered No 518(Met) Squadron detachment.

No 521(Met) Squadron Codes: 50

Based at Chivenor using Fortresses and Hurricanes. Began converting to Met Mk VI Halifaxes in February 1946 and used them only briefly before disbanding the next month.

No 578(B) Squadron Codes: LK

Formed at Snaith on 14/1/44 from C Flight of No 51(B) Squadron and equipped with B Mk III Halifaxes. Moved to Burn on 6/2/44 and on 30/3/44 Plt Off C. J. Barton earned the only 'Halifax' VC of the war. Last operational mission, against Wuppertal, 13/3/45. Squadron disbanded 16/3/45.

No 614(B) Squadron Codes: Unknown

Based at Celone, Italy, No 462(B) Squadron was renumbered No 614(B) Squadron on 3/3/44; equipped with B Mk II Halifaxes. Squadron role changed to that of target marking force for No 205 Group. Moved to Stornara in May and then to Amendola in July. Began converting to Liberators in August but process slow. Last Halifax operation, against Porto Marhamo, 3/3/45.

No 620(GT) Squadron Codes: D4 and QS (Postwar MOHC)

Based at Great Dunmow converted from Stirlings to A Mk VII Halifaxes in May 1945. Squadron posted to Aqir, Palestine; commenced move on 30/12/45 and completed by 14/1/46. In July began converting to

A Mk IXs and squadron renumbered No 113(GT) Squadron 1/9/46.

No 624(SD) Squadron Unknown

Formed at Blida, North Africa, 7/9/43. Establishment of 14+4 Halifaxes and 2+0 Venturas these coming from the disbanded No 1575(SD) Flight. Halifaxes mixture of B Mk IIs and Vs. In October detachment sent to squadron's advanced operational base at Protville; also small detachment sent to Malta for operations over Czechoslovakia. 16/10/43 Protville detachment moved to Sidi Amor. In December squadron moved to Brindisi, Italy, via Tocra, and placed under control of 334 Wing. Moved back to Blida in February 1944 and operated exclusively over France. Signal received 12/6/44 ordering conversion to Stirlings. Last Halifax operational mission 13/8/44.

No 640(B) Squadron Codes: C8

Formed from C Flight of No 158(B) Squadron at Lissett on 7/1/44; equipped with B Mk III Halifaxes. Moved to Leconfield in January. Five times squadron won the No 4 Group Bombing Cup trophy, a record for the Group. Began converting to B Mk VIs in March 1945. Last operational mission, against Wangerooge, 25/4/45. Disbanded 7/5/45.

No 644(GT) Squadron Codes: 2P and 9U (Postwar MOHD)

Formed from C Flight of No 298(GT) Squadron at Tarrant Rushton on 16/3/44; equipped with A Mk V Halifaxes. Began re-equipping with A Mk VIIs in August. Squadron posted to ME: move commenced 26/11/45 and completed by December. Based at Quastina. Began converting to A Mk IXs on 10/8/46 and squadron renumbered No 47(GT) Squadron 1/9/46.

No 301 (SD) Flight Unknown *Polish*

In July 1943 the Polish Flight of No 138(SD) Squadron was redesignated No 301(SD) Flight at Tempsford; equipped with B Mk V Halifaxes. In November Flight moved to Tunis, North Africa, and placed under control of No 334 Wing. On the 15th it moved once more to Brindisi, Italy. On 1/10/44 its identification was changed, for security reasons, to No 1586(SD) Flight.

No 1341(BS) Flight Unknown

Formed at West Kirby on 21/12/44 and personnel shipped to Digri, India, arriving 14/2/45. First two B Mk IIIs departed for India in March, and five on charge by 31/5/45. Authority received to amalgamate with C Flight of No 159(B) Squadron (equipped with Liberators for radar investigation work) 15/5/45. Last operational mission by Halifaxes, to Port Blair, 1/9/45. Disbanded wef 30/10/45.

No 1575(SD) Flight Unknown

Formed at Tempsford on 21/5/43 with an establishment of 3+1 B Mk V Halifaxes and 2+0 Venturas. Crews drawn from No 161(SD) Squadron. Moved to Maison Blanche, North Africa in June. On 25/6/43 moved to Blida;

operating mainly over Corsica, Sardinia and Italy. Authority for disbandment received 16/8/43, physically disbanded on 22/9/43 all personnel, aircraft and equipment being transferred to No 624(SD) Squadron.

No 1577 (Trials) Flight Unknown

Formed under HQ No 221 Group, India on 9/8/43 for trials work with Halifax and Lancaster aircraft. Equipment drawn from No 313 MU (No 184 Wing). Two B Mk V Halifaxes, two Lancaster IIIs and personnel departed Portreath on 29/9/43. Established in India by 7/10/43. On 5/12/43 Flight notified that it will engage in transport duties only. On 5/3/44 moved to Chakeri and then to Mauripur on 7/5/44 where aircraft modified for towing. Lancasters removed on 9/11/44 and following day two B Mk III Halifaxes received. Moved to Dhamal in December and then to Chaklala in January 1946. Disbanded May 1946.

No 1586(SD) Flight Unknown *Polish*

Formed at Brindisi on 1/10/44 from No 301(SD) Flight using Halifaxes and Liberators. Both Grottaglie and Rosignano used as alternative landing grounds. Flight renumbered No 301(SD) Squadron on 7/11/44.

No 28 Halifax Conversion Flight Unknown

Formed at Leconfield in October 1941, it received its first five B Mk Is Halifaxes on 28/10/41. Subsequently it was decided to equip each heavy bomber group with one conversion unit plus one small conversion flight per squadron. Moved to Marston Moor on 30/12/41. On 3/1/42 No 28 CF and No 107 CF disbanded and combined to form No 1652 Conversion Unit at Marston Moor. All CUs were renamed HCUs in October 1942.

No 10(B) Squadron (Conversion Flight) Codes: ZA

Formed February 1942 at Leeming, moved to Melbourne in August. Disbanded and absorbed by No 1658 Heavy Conversion Unit at Riccall 22/11/42.

No 35(B) Squadron (CF) Codes: TL

Formed February 1942 at Linton-on-Ouse, moved to Rufforth in September. Amalgamated with No 158(B) Squadron (CF) to form No 1663 HCU.

No 76(B) Squadron (CF) Codes: MP

Formed 5/2/42 at Middleton St George. Moved to Riccall Common 12/9/42. Amalgamated with No 78(B) Squadron (CF) to form No 1658 HCU.

No 78(B) Squadron (CF) Codes: EY

Formed 26/3/42 at Croft. Moved to Dalton 11/6/42 then to Middleton St George by 9/7/42, then to Riccall Common by 15/9/42. Amalgamated with No 76(B) Squadron (CF) to form No 1658 HCU.

No 102(B) Squadron (CF) Codes: DY

Formed 6/1/42 at Dalton. Moved to Pocklington 8/8/42.

Absorbed by No 1652 HCU on 23/11/42 but remained detached at Pocklington.

No 103(B) Squadron (CF) Codes: PM
Formed July 1942 at Elsham Wolds. Moved to Breighton in October and amalgamated with No 460(B) Squadron (CF) to form No 1656 HCU. Became B Flight.

No 107 Halifax Conversion Flight Codes: Unknown
Authority to form this unit at Leconfield was issued by December 1941, equipment to be B Mk I Halifaxes. None believed delivered before unit disbanded on 3/1/42 and combined with No 28 CF to form No 1652 CU.

No 158(B) Squadron (CF) Codes: NP
Formed 7/6/42 at East Moor. Moved to Rufforth 25/9/42. Amalgamated with No 35(B) Squadron (CF) to form No 1663 HCU.

No 405(B) Squadron (CF) Codes: LQ
Formed 29/4/42 at Pocklington with B Mk II Halifaxes. Moved to Topcliffe 7/8/42. Disbanded 7/10/42 and absorbed into 1659 HCU.

No 408(B) Squadron (CF) Codes: EQ
Formed 16/5/42 at Syerston with Manchesters but cancelled 19/6/42. Reformed 20/9/42 at Leeming with Halifax B Mk I, II and V aircraft. Disbanded 7/10/42 and absorbed into 1659 HCU.

No 460(B) Squadron (CF) Codes: UV
Formed June 1942 at Breighton. Moved to Holme-on Spalding Moor where UE increased from standard 4+0 to 8+0 B Mk II Halifaxes. Returned to Breighton 24/9/42. Next day ordered to dispose of Halifaxes and replace them with a UE of 4+0 Lancasters and 4+0 Manchesters. On 29/9/42 absorbed by No 1656 HCU as A Flight and four Halifaxes transferred to No 460(B) Squadron followed by two on 1/10/42 and final two the next day.

No 1652 HCU Codes: JA and GV
Formed 2/1/42 at Marston Moor from No 28 and No 107 Halifax Conversion Flights equipped with B Mk Is. Absorbed No 102(B) Squadron CF on 23/11/42. Received first B Mk IIIs 3/12/44 and completed conversion by 17/12/44. Disbanded 25/6/45.

No 1654 HCU Codes: UG and JR (Lancasters JF)
Based at Wigsley and equipped with Lancasters and Manchesters. Manchesters phased out and replaced with Halifaxes to a UE of 32+0 in September 1943. Replaced by Stirlings 1/1/44.

No 1656 HCU Codes: BL and EK
Formed 10/10/42 at Breighton with Halifaxes from Nos 103(B) Squadron (CF) and 460(B) Squadron (CF). HQ moved to Lindholme 26/10/42 followed by B Flight from Elsham Wolds 3/11/42 and A Flight, partly equipped with Lancasters, 11/11/42. Allocated full Lancaster flight and both types operated until November 1943 when Halifaxes began to be phased out.

No 1658 HCU Codes: TT and ZB
Formed 1/10/42 at Riccall Common with Halifaxes from Nos 76(B) Squadron (CF) and No 78 Squadron (CF) Absorbed No 10(B) Squadron (CF) 22/11/42. Received first batch of B Mk IIIs 28/10/44. Disbanded 13/4/45 and amalgamated with No 1332 HTCU.

No 1659 HCU Codes: FD, FV and RV
Formed 6/10/42 at Leeming and absorbed Nos 405(B) and 408(B) Squadrons (CF). Equipped with a UE of 32+0 B Mk II and V Halifaxes. Moved to Waterbeach 1/5/43, to Woolfox Lodge 5/6/43 and then to Tilstock 23/1/44. Began converting to B Mk IIIs from October. Moved to Saltby 26/3/45, changing its designation to No 1659 HTCU, then to Linton-on-Ouse 4/11/45. Moved to Dishforth and disbanded 13/7/46 and amalgamated with No 1332 HTCU.

No 1660 HCU Codes: TV and YW
Based at Swinderbury and equipped with Lancasters and Manchesters. Manchesters phased out and replaced with Halifaxes to a UE of 32+0 in September 1943. Replaced with Stirlings 1/1/44.

No 1661 HCU Codes: GP and KB
Based at Winthorpe and equipped with Lancasters and Manchesters. Manchesters phased out and replaced with Halifaxes to a UE of 32+0 in September 1943. Replaced with Stirlings 1/1/44.

No 1662 HCU Codes: PE, KF and N2
Formed 1/2/43 at Blyton with a UE of 16+0 Halifaxes and 16+0 Lancasters. On 12/2/44 Lancaster flight moved to Hemswell (Lancaster Finishing School). Began converting to Lancasters in November 1944 and last Halifax left January 1945.

No 1663 HCU Codes: OO and SV
Formed 2/3/43 at Rufforth with Halifaxes from Nos 35(B) Squadron (CF) and 158(B) Squadron (CF) a UE of 24 B Mk Vs was authorised but later increased to a UE of 32+0. Began converting to B Mk III Halifaxes in late 1944. Disbanded 28/5/45.

No 1664 HCU Codes: DH and ZU
Formed 10/5/43 at Croft, five B Mk V Halifaxes having already been received on the 7th. Moved to Dishforth 7/12/43. Began conversion to B Mk IIIs in December 1944. Disbanded 6/4/45.

No 1665 HCU Codes: OG (Stirlings FO, MN and NY)
Based at Woolfox Lodge and equipped with Stirlings, it received A Mk V Halifaxes in late September 1943. Unit trained crews for 38 Group. Moved to Tilstock 29/1/44 then to Saltby on 26/3/45, then to Marston Moor on 1/8/45. With transfer of 4 Group to Transport Command, unit used to train crews for four engined transports and designation changed to No 1665 HTCU. Equipped with A Mk III and C Mk VI Halifaxes. Moved to Linton-on-

Ouse 7/11/45. Disbanded at Dishforth 15/7/46 and amalgamated with 1332 HTCU.

No 1666 HCU Codes: QY and ND

Formed 6/6/43 at Dalton with 32+0 B Mk II and V Halifaxes. Reduced to a UE of 16+0 B Mk IIs. Moved to Wombleton 21/10/43, sharing it with No 1679 HCU (Lancasters) which disbanded 28/1/44; its remaining Lancaster conversion commitments being taken over by No 1666 HCU. Remaining Lancasters transferred to No 408(B) Squadron in April. UE increased to 40+0 B Mk II and V Halifaxes and three flight system used. Received first B Mk IIIs 3/11/44 but allocation cancelled and Lancasters issued, first course begun 27/12/44 and last B Mk V and III Halifax courses completed by the end of January 1945. Last Halifax left in March.

No 1667 HCU Codes: GG and KR (Lancasters LR)

Formed 2/6/43 at Lindholme with one B Mk V Halifax flight and one Lancaster flight. Moved to Faldingworth 8/10/43 and then to Sandtoft wef 14/2/44. A, B and C Flights formed 1/5/44 and D (Instructors) Flights formed 26/6/44. Commenced re-equipping with Lancasters in November and remaining two Halifax flights ceased operations in December.

No 1668 HCU Codes: IG (Lancasters 2K and J9)

Formed 15/8/43 at Balderton and equipped with a UE of 16+0 B Mk II and V Halifaxes and 16+0 Lancasters but re-equipped with Stirlings in November and moved to Syerston.

No 1669 HCU Codes: L6 and 6F

Formed 1/3/43 at Topcliffe with 32+0 B Mk II and V Halifaxes. Began converting to B Mk IIIs in late 1944 but allocation cancelled and Lancasters issued December 1944.

No 1674 HCU Codes: AK (No 111 OTU Codes H3, X3 and 3G)

Formed 10/10/43 at Aldergrove and equipped with Halifaxes and Fortresses. Unit trained crews for Met and VLR duties. On 31/10/44 unit became No 1674 Training Wing and organised as an OTU. Moved to Milltown, on 14/8/45 as well as converting to Met Mk IIIs. Unit renamed No 111 OTU 21/3/46.

No 1(C) OTU Codes: Unknown

Based at Thornaby in 1943 and equipped with GR Mk II Halifaxes for training Coastal Command crews. In view of No 518 Squadron's training commitment to met crews during 1943/44 it is thought that No 1(C) OTU trained crews exclusively for anti-shipping operations.

Coastal Command Development Unit Codes: Unknown

Formed November 1940. Moved to Angle, satellite of Pembroke Dock on 5/9/43, then to Thorney Island January 1945. UE one B Mk II Halifax, one Liberator, two Beauforts, two Wellingtons and one Proctor. Administered by No 19 Group, it was responsible for trials and development work with all new Coastal equipment. No other details.

No 1361(Met) Flight Codes: Unknown

Began converting to Met Mk VI Halifaxes in February 1946 but disbanded and absorbed by No 521(Met) Squadron at Chivenor.

Central Landing Establishment Codes: Unknown

The Experimental Flight was formed at Ringway 1/10/40 and equipped with Hotspurs, Hectors and Lysanders. Renamed No 1 Glider Training Squadron and moved to Side Hill, near Newmarket, 21/11/40 and then to Haddenham (Thame) in January 1941 where it received the first of its Halifaxes in October. Removed from AFE control and placed under No 70 Group 28/11/41. Moved to Upper Heyford 28/3/46 and renamed No 1 Parachute and Glider Training School 1/1/47. Believed to have operated the last Halifax in service on second line duties; RT936 which was issued 1/9/50 and soc 21/4/53. The Development Unit formed at Ringway 22/10/40, and equipped with Wellingtons, Whitleys, Hectors, Lysanders and various miscellaneous types. Shared use of the modified B Mk II Halifaxes with the Experimental Flight. Undertook technical research into glider towing and paratrooping. Renamed Airborne Forces Establishment late 1941 and initially controlled by No 1 GTS. Renamed Airborne Forces Experimental Establishment and moved to Sherburn-in-Elmet 1/7/42. Placed under control of FTC and No 21 Group with detachments at Snaith and Ringway. Conducted heavy glider towing trials. Moved to Beaulieu 11/12/44 and believed to have ceased Halifax operations in 1946.

Airborne Forces Tactical Development Unit Codes: Unknown

Formed 1/12/43 at Tarrant Rushton with a mixed establishment of Halifaxes, Whitleys, Wellingtons, Albemarles, Dakotas, Horsas and Hamilcars. Moved to Netheravon 1/9/44 and five days later renamed Air Transport Tactical Development Unit and transferred from No 38 Group to Transport Command. First B Mk III received in October. On 9/6/45 PP217, a C Mk VIII arrived for service trials. In September moved to Harwell and trials work continued until Halifaxes disposed of in late 1946.

Transport Command Development Unit Codes: Unknown

Based at Brize Norton it received its first two A Mk III Halifaxes in August 1945. Initially using a mixed establishment of Halifaxes, Stirlings and Albemarles but Halifaxes selected as superior and other types disposed of. In May 1946 the Army Airborne Transport Development Centre moved in from Amesbury and the TCDU Halifaxes undertook their development work in addition to normal test duties. The A Mk IX Halifax tactical handling trials were also undertaken by TCDU. The first Halifax replacement arrived June 1948 and thereafter the Halifax establishment was reduced over the next 12 months. On 28/6/49 moved to Abingdon along with the remaining two Halifaxes. No further details.

Operational Refresher Training Unit Codes: OX

Formed at Thruxton it moved to Matching being initially equipped with Halifaxes and Stirlings; first three A Mk VIIs being received 1/3/45. By 30/3/45 all Stirlings put up for disposal, to be replaced with 12 A Mk III Halifaxes. Disrupted by Operation Varsity and 29 Stirlings received instead; but on 2/4/45 first two A Mk IIIs received and unit gradually re-equipped. In June 1946 A Mk VIIs replaced the A Mk IIIs. Moved to Weathersfield 15/10/45 and presumed to have disbanded on, or about, 15/1/46.

No 1331 HTCU Codes: Unknown

Reformed at Syerston on 14/12/46 from the Halifax Training Unit at Dishforth. Equipped with A Mk VII Halifaxes. Disbanded and absorbed by 241 OCU on 5/1/48.

No 1332 HTCU Codes: YY

Based at Riccall Common with Yorks and used as a finishing school for 38 Group crews. Moved to Dishforth 7/11/45. In July 1946 absorbed the Halifaxes of No 1659 and No 1665 HTCUs. Redesignated No 241 OCU on 5/1/48 and received A Mk IX Halifaxes the same day. It continued to operate these until they were withdrawn early in 1949.

No 1333 Transport Support Training Unit Codes: ODY

Based at Syerston and equipped with A Mk VII Halifaxes it received its first batch of A Mk IXs in November 1946. Moved to North Luffenham in July 1947. Designation changed to No 1333 HTSTU, its function being similar to that of No 1332 TSCU. Unit disbanded on 5/1/48 and Halifaxes transferred to No 241 OCU.

No 1385 Heavy Transport Support Conversion Unit
Codes: Unknown

Formed at Weathersfield April 1946 having already begun receiving A Mk III Halifaxes from 21/3/46 along with No 1 Course personnel. This was a finishing school for crews from normal HCU courses, providing a concentrated six week course in glider towing, heavy equipment and stores dropping. Duration reduced to four weeks shortly after No 1 Course commenced. A Mk IIIs disposed of in May and replaced by A Mk VIIs. Only four courses completed before unit transferred to Syerston to become a flight of No 1333 HTSTU on 1/7/46.

Halifax Development Flight Codes: Unknown

No 246(T) Squadron reformed at Lyneham 11/10/44, with a UE of 25 Dakotas, Liberators and Yorks. Moved to Holmsley South with four B Mk III Halifaxes from No 41 Group to form the HDF whose task it was to study conditions under which passengers could be carried. On 1/3/45 attached to No 187(T) Squadron for servicing facilities and transferred to Merryfield 12/3/45. Disbanded under authority dated 3/4/45.

No 21 Heavy Glider Conversion Unit Codes: FEP, FEQ, FER, FES and FET

Formed February 1945 at Brize Norton as a Horsa glider training unit and moved to Elsham Wolds. Received 12 A Mk III Halifaxes, ex-No 296(GT) Squadron, in February 1946, followed by A Mk VIIs later in the year. Moved to North Luffenham and disbanded 3/12/47.

No 22 HGCU Codes: Unknown

Equipped with A Mk III Halifaxes in March 1946, its function being the same as that of No 21 HGCU to which unit its Halifaxes were transferred in October. No other details.

No 301 Ferry Training Unit Codes: Unknown

Formed 1/11/40 at Kemble as HQSFP and No 7 FPP. Moved to Honeybourne and renamed No 301 FTU on 11/11/41. Moved to Lyneham 20/3/42 and received two Halifaxes in September. Moved to Pershore 16/3/44 and absorbed, along with the servicing wing from Lyneham, into new unit entitled No 1 Ferry Unit. Halifaxes retained to complete commitment.

No 16 FU Codes: Unknown

Moved to Dunkeswell from Talbenny 6/8/45. UE three Halifaxes, two Dakotas, three Warwicks, three Oxfords and eight Ansons. Station closed 26/4/46. No other details.

No 13 Maintenance Unit Codes: 3J

Based at Henlow this MU carried out all major instrument, airframe and engine modifications for Halifaxes. Using mobile working parties it visited units in all groups, except Coastal Command, and including Halifaxes held at No 29 MU (High Ercall), No 45 MU (Kinloss) and No 48 MU (Hawarden). At least one B Mk VI still on unit charge in 1946 (RG872 3J E).

Telecommunication Flying Unit Codes: Unknown

Formed at Hurn with four Wellingtons. Moved to Defford May 1942 where it received its first B Mk II Halifax. Unit worked in conjunction with No 1 BDU. A succession of B Mk II, III, VI and VII Halifaxes were used between 1942 and 1945.

TR 1335(Gee) Development Unit Codes: OT (As No 1 BDU)

Formed at Boscombe Down 14/12/41. Renamed No 1418 Bomber Development Flight 5/1/42. Moved to Feltwell 8/4/42 where it was renamed No 1 Bombing Development Unit; carried out service trials of experimental equipment. Moved to Gransden Lodge in August 1942 equipped with Wellingtons, Blenheims, Mosquitos and five Halifaxes (B Mk IIs and IIIs). Moved to Newmarket in August 1944 and believed to have disbanded in 1947.

Bomb Ballistics Development Unit Codes: OR

Moved from Martlesham Heath to Woodbridge in late 1943. Engaged on trials work and known to have had the HR756 the B Mk II Series II Halifax on active strength in 1944. No further details.

Radio Warfare Establishment Codes: V7 and U3
(Fortresses also U3, Mosquitos 4S)

Flying Wing and Servicing Wing formed September 1945 at Foulsham from disbanded No 192(BS) Squadron. HQ Tactical Wing and Y Wing forming at Swanton Morley. On 6-7/10/45 23 Halifaxes, 10 Mosquitos, seven Fortresses, one Oxford and one Ju88 were ferried to Watton (No 60 Group), the unit's new base from 9/10/45. Unit engaged in specialist radio warfare trials. Renamed Central Signals Establishment. No further details.

Farnborough Research Flight Codes: Unknown

The Experimental Section and RAF Station Farnborough were merged into one establishment on 22/1/45. The following specialist sections used Halifaxes for trials/research work from April 1946; Engineering Flight, Armament Flight, Instrument Flight, Wireless and Electrical Flight, Aerodynamics Supersonic Flight. On 18/8/46 the Meteorological Research Flight moved to Farnborough and re-equipped with two Met Mk VI Halifaxes, two Mosquitos and personnel, reaching full strength on 17/12/46. No further details available after 31/3/48 but believed that some Halifaxes were still on charge as late as March 1951.

Bomber Command Instructors School Codes: IK and IP

Formed at Finningley 5/12/44 under control of No 7 Group (station belonged to No 91 Group); 22 Wellingtons, 10 Lancasters and five B Mk III Halifaxes. The latter began operating 28/12/44 and ceased 7/5/45, being replaced by Lancasters.

PFF Navigation Training Unit Codes: Unknown

Formed 10/4/43 at Gransden Lodge with a UE of 24 Halifaxes and Stirlings. First B Mk II Halifax received 12/4/43. Moved to Upwood and Warboys 11/6/43. Halifaxes replaced by Lancasters September 1944.

Empire Air Navigation School Codes: FGE

The Central Navigation School was renamed EANS at Shawbury in January 1945 and received 18 B Mk III Halifaxes and two Lancasters, a Mosquito and either a P-47 or a P-51, these being additional to its holdings. Unit divided into flights; No 1 Halifaxes, No 2 Wellingtons, No 3 (Special Liaison) two Halifaxes, two Lancasters, one Mosquito, two Ansons and a Proctor. A single B Mk VI was taken on charge November 1946, the bulk of the B Mk IIIs being disposed of over the next three months and replaced by Lancasters. The B Mk VI was finally sent to No 45 MU in January 1948.

Empire Radio School Codes: FGF

Based at Debden it received one B Mk VI Halifax and one Lancaster in June 1946, a B Mk II being added in July but disposed of the next month. The Halifax was equipped as a flying classroom for long distance flights. Three more B Mk VIs were added over the next two years but all were disposed of by the end of September 1948.

No 1 Radio School Codes: TCA and TCR

No details known other than unit equipped with modified B Mk VIs in 1946. eg PP214:TCA-B. Aircraft fitted with C Mk VIII tail cone and front of fuselage faired in.

2 Civil Halifax Register

Serial No	Mark No	C of A Issued	Civil Reg	Details of Ownership
PP287	VIII		G-AGPC	Anglo French Distributors; TAI Paris F-BCJS 1947; Aero Cargo; crashed 1/12/48
PP274	VIII		G-AGTK	Anglo French Distributors; TAI Paris F-BCJX 1947
NR169	III	16/5/46	G-AGXA	G. N. Wickner; Air Carriers Ltd VH-BDT 1946; derelict 1947
PP336	VIII	20/3/46	G-AGZP	Maharajah Gaekwar; British American A/S; Alpha Airways ZS-BTA
PP224	VIII	18/9/46	G-AHDL	Halton *Fitzroy* BOAC; Aviation Traders; Westminster Airways; crashed 1/4/49
PP228	VIII	20/7/46	G-AHDM	Halton *Falmouth* BOAC; Aviation Traders; Westminster Airways; converted as *Reindeer* G-AFOH for film *No Highway*
PP234	VIII	24/3/47	G-AHDN	Halton *Flamborough* BOAC; Aviation Traders
PP236	VIII	13/8/47	G-AHDO	Halton *Forfar* BOAC; Alpha Airways; Aviation Traders; Bond Air Services
PP268	VIII	24/3/47	G-AHDP	Halton *Fleetwood* BOAC; Aviation Traders; Alpha Airways
PP269	VIII	7/7/47	G-AHDR	Halton *Foreland* BOAC; Alpha Airways; Aviation Traders; E. Sutton F-BECK
PP277	VIII	24/8/46	G-AHDS	Halton *Freemantle* BOAC; Bond Air Services; Aviation Traders
PP308	VIII	4/6/47	G-AHDT	Halton *Fife* BOAC; Bond Air Services; Aviation Traders
PP310	VIII	10/7/46	G-AHDU	Halton *Falkirk* BOAC; Bond Air Services; Aviation Traders
PP314	VIII	19/8/46	G-AHDV	Halton *Finnesterre* BOAC; Bond Air Services; Aviation Traders; Westminster Airways; LAC
PP315	VIII	29/7/46	G-AHDW	Halton *Falaise* BOAC; Bond Air Services; Aviation Traders
PP316	VIII	4/6/47	G-AHDX	Halton *Folkestone* BOAC; Aviation Traders; World Air Carriers; crashed 16/4/50
PP309	VIII		G-AHKK	Anglo French Distributors; F-BCJV
PP287	VIII		G-AHVT	Anglo French Distributors; TAI Paris F-BCJR 1947
PP331	VIII		G-AHWL	Anglo French Distributors; TAI Paris F-BCJT 1947
PP238	VIII		G-AHWM	Handley Page Ltd 4/7/47; RAF; became G-AJZY
PP230	VIII	1/10/48	G-AHWN	Handley Page Ltd; RAF; Lancashire Aircraft Corporation *Air Viceroy*
PP261	VIII	29/10/48	G-AHYH	BOAC; RAF; Lancashire Aircraft Corporation *Air Merchant*
PP311	VIII		G-AHYI	BOAC; RAF; Anglo French Distributors; G-AIID
PP247	VIII	18/9/46	G-AHZJ	London Aero & Motor Service Ltd *Port of Marsailles*; crashed 19/8/47
PP246	VIII	15/11/46	G-AHZK	LAMS *Port of Naples*; Skyflight
PP242	VIII	26/10/46	G-AHZL	LAMS *Port of Oslo*
PP260	VIII		G-AHZM	LAMS
PP244	VIII	28/8/46	G-AHZN	LAMS
PP239	VIII	24/12/46	G-AHZO	LAMS *Port of London*; Skyflight
PP271	VIII		G-AIAN	BOAC; RAF (Used for training only by BOAC)
PP272	VIII		G-AIAO	BOAC; RAF (Used for training only by BOAC)
PP281	VIII	15/2/49	G-AIAP	BOAC; RAF; Airtech; Eagle Aviation Ltd; crashed 20/11/50
PP326	VIII	9/2/49	G-AIAR	BOAC; RAF; Airtech; British American Air Services; Chartair Ltd
PP327	VIII		G-AIAS	BOAC used for spares
RG790	VI		G-AIBG	LAMS
PP222	VIII	25/9/47	G-AIHU	LAC *Air Adventurer*; crashed 5/12/47
PP262	VIII	10/4/47	G-AIHV	LAC *Air Trader*
PP284	VIII		G-AIHW	LAC; crashed 8/5/48
PP294	VIII	7/6/47	G-AIHX	LAC *Air Merchant*; crashed 1948
PP241	VIII	19/6/47	G-AIHY	LAC *Air Explorer*
PP317	VIII		G-AIID	See G-AHYI

PP280	VIII	27/10/47	G-AILO	College of Aeronautics; LAC
PP240	VIII	15/5/47	G-AIOH	CL Air Surveys; Bond Air Services; crashed Barcelona
PP243	VIII	16/1/47	G-AIOI	CL Air Surveys; Bond Air Services; crashed
PP320	VIII	2/12/47	G-AITC	College of Aeronautics; World Air Freight Ltd; crashed 20/1/50
PP218	VIII	13/5/48	G-AIWI	LAMS
PP286	VIII	15/5/47	G-AIWJ	LAMS *Port of Athens*
PP295	VIII	21/7/47	G-AIWK	LAMS *Port of Sydney*; derelict Mascot airport, Australia
PP291	VIII		G-AIWL	LAMS
PP266	VIII	5/12/47	G-AIWM	LAC *Merchant Venturer*
PP235	VIII	23/5/47	G-AIWN	LAMS *Port of Darwin*; Payloads Ltd; R. Sanderson
PP290	VIII		G-AIWO	
PP288	VIII	26/1/48	G-AIWP	LAMS
PP245	VIII		G-AIWR	LAMS *Port of Durban*; LAMS (Africa) Ltd ZS-BUL; crashed November 1947
PP265	VIII	3/4/47	G-AIWT	LAMS *Port of Sydney*; Payloads Ltd
PP293	VIII	18/8/47	G-AIZO	Southern Air Carriers (Gatwick) Ltd; Union Air Services; Bond Air Services; crashed 23/5/48
RG785	VI		G-AJBE	LAMS; to Pakistan 21/10/49
PP264	VIII	11/7/47	G-AJBK	Air Freight Ltd; TAI Paris F-BCJZ 18/10/47
PP276	VIII	15/9/47	G-AJBL	Air Freight Ltd
PP328	VIII	20/8/47	G-AJCG	Peteair Ltd *Sky Tramp*; Vingtor Luftveier LN-OAS
PP259	VIII		G-AJNT	Payloads Ltd; to France
PP279	VIII		G-AJNU	Payloads Ltd; Pak-Air Ltd AP-ACH 1948
PP292	VIII		G-AJNV	Payloads Ltd; Air Globe Ltd HB-AIV 1947
PP296	VIII	27/4/49	G-AJNW	Payloads Ltd; Westminster Airways Ltd
PP312	VIII	30/1/48	G-AJNX	Payloads Ltd; R. Sanderson; Pak-Air Ltd AP-ABZ 1948; crashed 6/5/48
PP322	VIII	2/4/48	G-AJNY	Payloads Ltd; Bowmaker Ltd; Pak-Air Ltd AP-ACG 1948
PP323	VIII	26/11/47	G-AJNZ	Payloads Ltd; World Air Freight Ltd; crashed 28/9/48
NA684	III		G-AJPG	College of Aeronautics. Dismantled
PP263	VIII	15/10/47	G-AJPJ	Chartair Ltd; BAAS; Mayfair Air Services; stolen 20/7/48 crashed
PP313	VIII	20/8/47	G-AJPK	LAMS; Payloads Ltd; R. Hoyes
RG722	VI		G-AJSZ	LAC
RG720	VI		G-AJTX	LAC
RG756	VI		G-AJTY	LAC
RG757	VI		G-AJTZ	LAC
RG824	VI		G-AJUA	LAC
RG825	VI		G-AJUB	LAC
PP330	VIII		G-AJXD	Anglo French Distributors Ltd; SANA F-BCJQ
PP238	VIII	18/3/48	G-AJZY	Handley Page Ltd; LAC *Air Monarch*; crashed 8/3/51
PP334	VIII	8/7/48	G-AJZZ	Handley Page Ltd; LAC; destroyed 22/3/49
PP267	VIII	2/11/48	G-AKAC	Payloads Ltd; World Air Freight Ltd; destroyed 29/4/49
PP283	VIII	1/3/48	G-AKAD	Payloads Ltd; BAAS; crashed 17/5/48
RG763	VI		G-AKAP	Airtech Ltd
RG784	VI		G-AKAW	LAMS; Pakistan
PP219	VIII	8/3/48	G-AKBA	Airtech Ltd; Alpha Airways; crashed 25/5/48
PP237	VIII	16/4/48	G-AKBB	Airtech Ltd; BAAS; crashed 11/2/49
RG716	VI		G-AKBI	LAC
PP233	VIII	8/12/48	G-AKBJ	LAC *Air Ambassador*; crashed 1/6/49
PP231	VIII	17/1/49	G-AKBK	LAC
PP289	VIII		G-AKBP	Payloads Ltd; Air Globe Ltd HB-AIL 1947
PP239	VIII	9/9/48	G-AKBR	Payloads Ltd; Anglo French Distributors; Skyflight Ltd; Eagle Aviation Ltd
PP273	VIII		G-AKCT	Payloads Ltd; Air Globe Ltd HB-AIK 1947
PP282	VIII	4/2/48	G-AKEC	Henniker Smith & Co; LAC *Air Voyager*
PP333	VIII	25/8/48	G-AKGN	BAAS; Chartair Ltd
PP324	VIII		G-AKGO	Airtech Ltd
PP223	VIII		G-AKGP	Airtech Ltd; SANA F-BESE *Ker Goaler* 1948
PP338	VIII	28/1/48	G-AKGZ	World Air Freight Ltd *North Wind*; crashed 8/10/48
PP329	VIII		G-AKIE	LAMS as G-AKBR
PP217	VIII		G-AKJF	LAMS
RG695	VI		G-AKJI	Air Freight Ltd
RG698	VI		G-AKJJ	Air Freight Ltd
RT885	IX		G-AKKP	Aviation Traders

RT928	IX		G-AKKU	Aviation Traders
RG783	VI		G-AKLI	LAMS; Pakistan
RG781	VI		G-AKLJ	LAMS; Pakistan
RG779	VI		G-AKLK	LAMS; Pakistan
RG658	VI		G-AKNG	LAC
RG700	VI		G-AKNH	LAC
RG717	VI		G-AKNI	LAC
RG759	VI		G-AKNJ	LAC
RG712	VI		G-AKNK	LAC
PP171	VI		G-AKNL	LAC
RG736	VI		G-AKUT	LAMS; Pakistan
RG813	VI		G-AKUU	LAMS; Airtech Ltd
PP220	VIII	29/12/48	G-AKXT	LAC *Air Rover*
PP229	VIII		G-ALBS	Hyland Automobiles Ltd; Hylands Ltd
PP270	VIII		G-ALBT	Hyland Automobiles Ltd; Hylands Ltd
PP319	VIII		G-ALBU	Hyland Automobiles Ltd; Hylands Ltd
PP321	VIII		G-ALBV	Hyland Automobiles Ltd; Hylands Ltd
PP275	VIII	2/2/49	G-ALBZ	LAC; ground accident 10/5/49
PP335	VIII	18/11/48	G-ALCX	LAC *Air Regent*
RG719	VI		G-ALCY	LAC
RG774	VI		G-ALCZ	LAC
RG822	VI		G-ALDZ	LAC
RG826	VI		G-ALEA	LAC
RG827	VI		G-ALEB	LAC
RG847	VI		G-ALEC	LAC
RG853	VI		G-ALED	LAC
RG877	VI		G-ALEE	LAC
PP337	VIII	11/10/48	G-ALEF	Handley Page Ltd; Vingtor Luftreir LN-OAT 1948; Eagle Aviation Ltd *Red Eagle*
RT791	IX		G-ALIR	Aviation Traders Ltd
ST801	VI		G-ALOM	Aviation Traders Ltd
RT763	IX	1/6/49	G-ALON	Aviation Traders Ltd; Bond Air Services Ltd
RT787	IX		G-ALOO	Aviation Traders Ltd; Egyptian Air Force 1158
RT846	IX		G-ALOP	Aviation Traders Ltd; Egyptian Air Force 1155
RT888	IX		G-ALOR	Aviation Traders Ltd; Egyptian Air Force 1157
RT937	IX	15/6/49	G-ALOS	Aviation Traders Ltd; Bond Air Services Ltd
RT832	IX		G-ALSK	Aviation Traders Ltd
RT924	IX		G-ALUT	Aviation Traders Ltd
RT879	IX		G-ALSL	Aviation Traders Ltd
RT848	IX		G-ALUU	Aviation Traders Ltd
RT873	IX		G-ALUV	Aviation Traders Ltd
RT788	IX		G-ALVH	Aviation Traders Ltd; Egyptian Air Force 1163
RT793	IX		G-ALVI	Aviation Traders Ltd; Egyptian Air Force 1156
RT852	IX		G-ALVJ	Aviation Traders Ltd; Egyptian Air Force 1159
RT901	IX		G-ALVK	Aviation Traders Ltd; Egyptian Air Force 1160
RT907	IX		G-ALVL	Aviation Traders Ltd; Egyptian Air Force 1162
RT938	IX		G-ALVM	Aviation Traders Ltd; Egyptian Air Force 1161
RT884	IX		G-ALYI	Aviation Traders Ltd
RT776	IX		G-ALYJ	Aviation Traders Ltd
RT785	IX		G-ALYK	Aviation Traders Ltd
RT837	IX		G-ALYL	Aviation Traders Ltd
RT772	IX		G-ALYM	Aviation Traders Ltd
RT762	IX		G-ALYN	Aviation Traders Ltd
ST808	VI		G-ALCD	LAC
RT935	IX		G-AMCF	Aviation Traders Ltd
RT816	IX		G-AMCG	Aviation Traders Ltd
RT759	IX		G-AMBX	R. A. Short
RT895	IX		G-AMCB	Aviation Traders Ltd
RT836	IX		G-AMCC	Aviation Traders Ltd
RT893	IX		G-AMCD	Aviation Traders Ltd
RT890	IX		G-AMCE	Aviation Traders Ltd

3 Contracts and Serial Numbers

Handley Page Ltd (199 aircraft)
Contract No 69649/37, requisition 102/E11/37 issued for 100 aircraft but increased under contract No 73328/40, requisition 24/E11/39 to 199 aircraft. Deliveries commenced 6/8/40 (L9485) and 11/10/41 (L9610).
B Mk I   L9485-9534, L9560-9584, L9600-9608.
B Mk II   L9609-9624, R9363-9392, R9418-9457, R9482-9498, R9528-9540.
Note: These aircraft supplied for pattern purposes to contractors; these to be completed to appropriate Halifax standards and delivered in addition to those aircraft ordered by contract: R9538 to English Electric Co Ltd, R9539 and R9540 to London Passenger Transport Board (LAPG).

English Electric Co Ltd (200 aircraft)
Contract No B982938/39, requisition 116/E11/39. Deliveries commenced 5/9/41 (V9976).
B Mk II   V9976-9994, W1002-1021, W1035-1067, W1090-1117, W1141-1190, W1211-1253, W1270-1276.

Handley Page Ltd (200 aircraft)
Contract No B73328/40, requisition 24/E11/39. Deliveries commenced 24/3/42 (W7650).
B Mk II   W7650-7679, W7695-7720, W7745-7784, W7801-7826, W7844-7887, W7906-7939.

London Passenger Transport Board (London Aircraft Production Group) (200 aircraft)
Contract No B124357/40, requisition HA1/E11/39. Deliveries commenced 10/1/42 (BB189).
B Mk II   BB189-223, BB236-285, BB300-344, BB357-391, BB412-446.

Rootes Securities Ltd (150 aircraft)
Contract No ACFT/637, requisition HA3/E11/40. Deliveries commenced 1/4/42 (DG219), 12/8/42 (DG231).
B Mk II   DG219-230.
B/Met Mk V   DG231-253, DG270-317, DG338-363, DG384-424.
Note: DG223 crashed on factory test flight, not delivered; DG399 sent to Canada as a production model.

Fairey Aviation Co Ltd (150 aircraft)
Contract No ACFT/891/SAS C4, requisition HA1/E11/41. Deliveries commenced 27/10/42 (DJ980).

B/Met Mk V   DJ980-999, DK114-151, DK165-207, DK223-271.

English Electric Co Ltd (250 aircraft)
Contract No B982938/39, requisition 116/E11/39. Deliveries commenced August 1942 (DT481).
B/GR Mk II   DT481-526, DT539-588, DT612-649, DT665-705, DT720-752, DT767-808.

Rootes Securities Ltd (100 aircraft)
Contract No ACFT/637, requisition HA3/E11/40. Deliveries commenced April 1943 (EB127).
B Mk V   EB127-160, EB178-220, EB239-258, EB274-276.

Handley Page Ltd (200 aircraft)
Contract No ACFT/1688, requisition HA4/E11/41. Deliveries commenced 21/12/42 (HR654)
B/GR Mk II   HR654-699, HR711-758, HR773-819, HR832-880, HR905-952, HR977-988.

Handley Page Ltd (150 aircraft)
Contract No ACFT/1688, requisition HA4/E11/41. Deliveries commenced July 1943 (HX147) and 7/9/43 (HX226).
B/GR Mk II   HX147-191, HX222-225.
B/GR Mk III   HX226-247, HX265-296, HX311-357.

English Electric Co Ltd (350 aircraft)
Contract No ACFT/1808, requisition 116/E11/39. Deliveries commenced 21/2/43 (JB781).
B/GR Mk II   JB781-806, JB834-875, JB892-931, JB956-974, JD105-128, JD143-180, JD198-218, JD244-278, JD296-333, JD361-386, JD405-421, JD453-476.

LPTB (LAPG) (250 aircraft)
Contract No 124357/40, requisition HA1/E11/39. Deliveries commenced July 1943 (JN882).
B/GR Mk II   JN882-296, JN941-978, JP107-137, JP159-207, JP220-259, JP275-301, JP319-338.

Fairey Aviation Co Ltd (200 aircraft)
Contract No ACFT/891, requisition HA1/E11/41. Deliveries commenced July 1943 (LK626) and 20/1/44 (LK747).

B/Met Mk V   LK626-667, LK680-711, LK725-746.
B Mk III   LK747-766, LK779-812, LK826-850,
LK863-887.

Rootes Securities Ltd (480 aircraft)
Contract No ACFT/637, requisition HA3/E11/40.
Deliveries commenced (LK890) and 13/5/44 (LL543).
B/A/Met Mk V   LK890-932, LK945-976, LK988-999,
LL112-153, LL167-198, LL213-258, LL270-312,
LL167-198, LL213-258, LL270-312, LL325-367,
LL380-423, LL437-469, LL481-521, LL534-542.
B/A Mk III   LL543-559, LL573-615.

Handley Page Ltd (240 aircraft)
Contract No ACFT/1688, requisition HA4/E11/41.
Deliveries commenced December 1943 (LV771) and
31/5/44 (LW196).
B Mk III   LV771-799, LV813-842, LV857-883,
LV898-923, LV935-973, LV985-999, LW113-143,
LW157-179, LW191-195.
B Mk VII   LW196-210.
Note: LV776 was a B Mk VI (28/2/44); LV838 converted
to B then C Mk VI.

English Electric Co Ltd (360 aircraft)
Contract No ACFT/1808, requisition HA1/E11/42.
Deliveries commenced 25/8/43 (LW223) and 19/10/43
(LW346).
B Mk II   LW223-246, LW259-301, LW313-345.
B/A Mk III   LW346-348, LW361-397, LW412-446,
LW459-481, LW495-522, LW537-559, LW572-598,
LW613-658, LW671-696, LW713-724.

LPTB (LAPG) (180 aircraft)
Contract No ACFT/2595, requisition HA10/E11/42.
Deliveries commenced 31/3/44 (MZ282).
B Mk III   MZ282-321, MZ334-378, MZ390-435,
MZ447-495.

English Electric Co Ltd (360 aircraft)
Contract No ACFT/2553, requisition HA9/E11/42.
Deliveries commenced 11/3/44 (MZ500).
B Mk III   MZ500-544, MZ556-604, MZ617-660,
MZ672-717, MZ730-775, MZ787-831, MZ844-883,
MZ895-939.

Rootes Securities Ltd (340 aircraft)
Contract No ACFT/637, requisition HA3/E11/40.
Deliveries commenced August 1944 (MZ945) and 4/2/45
(NA311)
B/A/Met Mk III   MZ945-989, NA102-150, NA162-205,
NA218-263, NA275-310.
A Mk VII   NA311-320, NA336-380, NA392-431.
Note: Two A Mk IIIs NA428 and NA452 in A Mk VII
batch. Last Rootes built Halifax, NA468, completed
12/7/45.

Fairey Aviation Co Ltd (180 aircraft)
Contract No ACFT/891, requisition HA1/E11/41.
Deliveries commenced April 1944 (NA492).
B/A Mk III   NA492-531, NA543-587, NA599-644,
NA656-704.

Handley Page Ltd (200 aircraft)
Contract No ACFT/1688, requisition HA16/E11/42.
Deliveries commenced June 1944 (NP681) and 28/9/44
(NP821).
B/Met Mk VI/B Mk VII   NP681-723, NP736-781,
NP793-820.
B Mk VI   NP821-836, NP849-895, NP908-927.

English Electric Co Ltd (200 aircraft)
Contract No ACFT/2553, requisition HA15/E11/43.
Deliveries commenced August 1944 (NP930).
B Mk III   NP930-976, NP988-999, NR113-156,
NR169-211, NR225-258, NR271-290.

Fairey Aviation Co Ltd (150 aircraft)
Contract No ACFT/891, requisition HA1/E11/41.
Deliveries commenced October 1944 (PN167) and
February 1945 (PN208).
B Mk III   PN167-207.
B/A Mk VII   PN 208, PN223-267, PN285-327, PN343.
Note: Only 131 aircraft built as shown, remainder of order
cancelled.

LPTB (LAPG) (200 aircraft)
Contract No ACFT/2595, requisition HA10/E11/42.
Deliveries commenced November 1944 (PN365).
B Mk III   PN365-406, PN423-461.
Note: Only 70 aircraft built as shown (PN461 not built,
PN460 was last to be constructed; delivered 16/4/45).
Remainder of order cancelled.

Handley Page Ltd (200 aircraft)
Contract No ACFT/3294, requisition HA16/E11/42.
Deliveries commenced 19/1/45 (TW774), 23/3/45
(PP217), 23/8/45 (PP339).
B Mk VI   TW774-796, PP165-187, PP203-216.
C Mk VIII   PP217-247, PP259-296, PP308-338.
A Mk VII   PP339-350, PP362-389.
Note: C Mk VIII block included one A Mk VII (PP277)
and one B Mk VI (PP225).

English Electric Co Ltd (400 aircraft)
Contract No ACFT/3362, requisition HA5/E11/43.
Deliveries commenced 2/12/44 (RG345), 12/1/45
(RG447), 13/2/45 (RG480).
B/Met Mk III   RG345-390, RG413-446.
B Mk VII   RG447-458, RG472-479.
B Mk VI   RG480-513, RG527-568, RG583-625,
RG639-679, RG693-736, RG749-776.
B/Met Mk VI   RG777-790, RG813-853, RG867-879.

Handley Page Ltd (200 aircraft)
Contract No ACFT/3645, requisition HA16/E11/42.

Deliveries commenced 1/11/45 (RT753) and 23/10/45 (RT758).
A Mk VII   RT753-757.
A Mk IX   RT758-799, RT814-856, RT868-908, RT920-938.
Note: RT937 and RT938 last Halifaxes built, both delivered 26/11/46. Only 150 aircraft built as shown, remainder of order cancelled.

English Electric Co Ltd (350 aircraft)
Contract No ACFT/3860, requisition HA9/E11/43. Deliveries commenced 27/9/45 (ST795)
B/Met Mk VI   ST794-818.
Note: Order reduced to 175 in July 1945 and then to 25 shortly after. Only nine B Mk VIs ST795, 797, 799, 800, 805, 806, 808, 814, 817.

Two other contracts issued but cancelled due to reduced requirements:

Handley Page Ltd (200 aircraft)
Contract No ACFT/2403, requisition HA6/E11/44.

English Electric Co Ltd (200 aircraft)
Contract No ACFT/4418, requisition HA7/E11/44

Total Halifax production was 6,116 aircraft plus the first two prototypes. Breakdown of production: English Electric Co Ltd 2,145; Handley Page Ltd 1,539; Rootes Securities Ltd 1,070; LPTB (LAPG) 700; and Fairey Aviation Co Ltd 661.

4 Design Data

Design data and specifications common to all marks except where noted.

Wing Span: 98ft 8in (late Mk III, VI, VII, VIII and IXs 103ft 8in)

Height (tail down): 21ft 4in over W/T mast or 20ft 9in over D/F loop

Length: 69ft 9in (Series IA and all later marks 71ft 7in except C Mk VIII: 73ft 7in)

Fuselage: maximum width 5ft 6in, maximum depth 9ft 6in

Aspect Ratio: short span 7:8, long span 8:4

Aerofoil: centre and inner mainplane NACA 23021, outer NACA 23009

Wing Incidence: at wing root $+3° \pm 15'$ (late model aircraft $+2° 45' \pm 15'$)

Dihedral: inner mainplane $0° \pm 15'$, outer $2° 25' \pm 15'$

Chord: root 16ft 0in, tip 6ft $11\frac{1}{2}$in

Sweep Back: inner mainplane $0°$, outer $9° 31'$

Tailplane Span: 30ft 4in

Dihedral: $0° \pm 15'$

Incidence: $+\frac{1}{2}° \pm 15'$ (C Mk VIII $0° \pm 15'$

Undercarriage Track: 24ft 8in

Areas: (gross):
Ailerons   85sq ft
Flaps   inner 55sq ft; outer 52.4sq ft
Tailplane   223.4sq ft
Elevators   98.3sq ft
Fin (each)   triangular 59.3sq ft, oblong 88.1sq ft
Rudder (each)   57.3sq ft
Wings   1,250sq ft (nett 1,162) short span
1,275sq ft (nett 1,190) long span

Note: A Mk X data not included as this did not progress beyond the proposal stage. It was basically an A Mk IX with Hercules 100 engines.

Company Type No	Mark	Weights				Propellers	Engines	Rated bhp	Altitude	Gear
		Maximum	Mean	Light	Tare					
HP57	B Mk I	55,000	46,300	37,590	33,720	Rotol	Merlin X	1,130	5,250	M
	Series I					R6/35/1		1,010	17,750	S
	Series II	60,000	49,000	38,000	34,130					
	Series III	60,000	40,500	38,240	34,500		Merlin XX	1,220	11,250	M
								1,120	19,250	S
HP59	B Mk II Series I	60,000	51,500	39,200	35,800	R7/35/54 R7/35/55	Merlin XX			
	Series IA	60,000	50,000	39,820	35,577		Merlin 22			
HP61	B Mk III	65,000	54,600	42,860	38,322	de Havilland 55/18	Hercules XVI	1,675	4,500	M
								1,455	12,000	S
	A Mk III	65,000	N/A	41,210	37,630					
	C Mk III	65,000	N/A	39,970	37,700					
HP63	B Mk V Series I	61,500	51,800	39,500	36,400	R7/35/54 R7/35/55	Merlin XX			
	Series IA	61,500	51,800	40,420	36,177	R7/4B5/4	Merlin 22	1,480	6,000	M
								1,480	12,250	S
HP61	B Mk VI	65,000	54,600	42,900	38,300	55/18 55/19	Hercules 100	1,680	9,500	M
								1,465	21,000	S
	*	68,000	56,400	43,540	39,000			1,800	9,000	M
								1,625	19,500	S
HP61	B Mk VII	65,000	54,700	43,130	38,500	55/18 55/19	Hercules XVI	1,675	4,500	M
								1,455	12,000	S
	A Mk VII	65,000	N/A	41,590	38,010					
	C Mk VII	65,000	N/A	40,390	38,036					
HP70	C Mk VIII	65,000	N/A	40,110	37,760	55/18 55/19	Hercules 100	1,800	9,000	M
								1,625	19,500	S
HP71	A Mk IX	65,000	N/A	41,960	37,800	55/18	Hercules XVI	1,675	4,500	M
								1,455	12,000	S

* Postwar figures

Mark	Take-off (yd)	Landing (yd)	Speeds 1 & 2 Maximum 3 Economic crsg 4 Weak mxtr crsg (mph/ft)	Time to Height (at max wt) (min/ft)	Service Ceiling at Maximum weight (ft)	Stalling Speeds Clean (mph)	Full flap u/c down (mph)
B Mk I	1,400	850	(1) 255/7,000 (2) 262/18,000 (3) 195/15,000 (4) 233/15,000	29.5/15,000	18,000	110	86
B Mk II/V Series I	1,250	850	(1) 254/12,750 (2) 261/19,500 (3) 190/15,000 (4) 228/15,000	23/15,000	22,000	95	80
B Mk II/V Series IA	1,200	850	(1) 250/13,000 (2) 253/19,000 (3) 205/20,000 (4) 210/20,000	43.5/20,000	21,000	98	82
B Mk III	1,150	1,100	(1) 277/6,000 (2) 281/13,500 (3) 225/20,000 (4) 227/20,000	45/20,000	20,000	104	90
A Mk III	1,150	1,200	(1) 285/6,000 (2) 289/13,500 (3) 195/10,000 (4) 242/10,000	12/10,000	20,000	118	102
C Mk III	1,200	1,100	(2) 290/9,000 (2) 309/19,500 (3) 230/20,000 (4) 256/20,000	31/20,000	23,000	118	102

Mark	Take-off (yd)	Landing (yd)	Speeds 1 & 2 Maximum 3 Economic crsg 4 Weak mxtr crsg (mph/ft)	Time to Height (at max wt) (min/ft)	Service Ceiling at Maximum Weight (ft)	Stalling Speeds Clean (mph)	Full flap u/c down (mph)
B Mk VI	1,200	1,100	(1) 290/9,000 (2) 309/19,500 (3) 230/20,000 (4) 256/20,000	31/20,000	22,000	118	102
B Mk VII	1,150	1,100	(1) 277/6,000 (2) 281/13,500 (3) 225/20,000 (4) 227/20,000	45/20,000	20,000	118	102
A Mk VII	1,150	1,200	(1) 285/6,000 (2) 289/13,500 (3) 195/10,000 (4) 242/10,000	12/10,000	20,000	118	102
C Mk VII	1,150	1,200	(1) 288/6,000 (2) 293/13,500 (3) 195/10,000 (4) 245/10,000	11.5/10,000	20,000	115	102
C Mk VIII	1,100	1,200	(1) 304/9,000 (2) 322/19,500 (3) 200/10,000 (4) 258/10,000	10/10,000	25,000	115	101
A Mk IX	1,150	1,200	(1) 285/6,000 (2) 289/13,500 (3) 195/10,000 (4) 242/10,000	12/10,000	20,000	118	102

Note: These are official figures averaged for each mark type and considerable variation occurred between individual aircraft, even from the same production run.

Fixed Armament

Mark	Nose	Midships	Tail
B Mk I	Boulton Paul C Mk II turret 2×0.303in Brownings with 1,000rpg Azimuth: 100° port & starboard Elevation: 60° Depression: 45°	Pillar mounted Vickers GOs 2×0.303in each side with 500rpg Azimuth 27° forward, 21° aft Elevation 45° Depression 26°	Boulton Paul E Mk I turret 4×0.303in Brownings with 1,700rpg, 4,000 reserve Azimuth: 90° port & starboard Elevation: 60° (later turrets 56.5) Depression: 50°
B Mk II Series I	As for B Mk I	Beam guns deleted Boulton Paul C Mk II turret 2×0.303in Brownings with 1,000rpg Azimuth: 360° Elevation: 60° Depression: 45°	As for B Mk I
Series I (Special)	Turret deleted	Turret deleted initially Boulton Paul A Mk VIII turret 4×0.303in Brownings with 1,160rpg Azimuth: 360° Elevation: 74° Depression: 2.5°	As for B Mk I
Series IA	Gimbal mounted Vickers GO 1×0.303in with 300 rounds	As above	As above but 4,800 reserve
GR Mk II/IA	As above	As above	As above
Met Mk II/IA	As above	As above	As above
B Mk III	As above	As above	As above
GR Mk III	As above	As above	As above

Mark			
Met Mk III	As above	As above	As above
A Mk III	Nil	Nil	As above
C Mk III	Nil	Nil	Nil
B Mk V	As for B Mk II series	As for B Mk II series	As for B Mk II series
A Mk V Srs I(Sp)	Turret deleted	Turret deleted	As above
A Mk V/IA	As above	As above	As above
GR Mk V/IA	As for GR Mk II Series IA	As for GR Mk II Series IA	As for GR Mk II Series IA
Met Mk V/IA	As above	As above	As above
B Mk VI	As for B Mk III	As for B Mk III	As for B Mk III
Met Mk VI	Nil	As above	As above
C Mk VI	Nil	Nil	Nil
B Mk VII	As for B Mk III	As for B Mk III	As for B Mk III initially. Late model aircraft fitted with Boulton Paul D Mk I turret 2×0.5in Brownings with 1,00rpg Azimuth: 90° port & starboard Elevation: 45° Depression: 45°
A Mk VII	Nil	Nil	As above
C Mk VII	Nil	Nil	Nil
C Mk VIII	Nil	Nil	Nil
A Mk IX	Nil	Nil	Boulton Paul D Mk II turret with radar gun laying. Details as for D Mk I turret

Disposable Loads

Mark	Fuselage	Wings	Total
B Mk I	2×2,000lb		
	6×1,000lb	6×500lb	13,000lb
	4×2,000lb	6×500lb	11,000lb
	2×1,500lb mine		
	6×500lb	6×500lb	9,000lb
	9×500lb	6×500lb	7,500lb
B Mk II/V Series IA	As for B Mk I plus		
	1×8,000lb	6×500lb	11,000lb
	2×4,000lb	6×500lb	11,000lb
GR Mk II/V Series IA	8×250lb depth charge	Nil	2,000lb
	4×600lb	Nil	2,400lb
	5×500lb	Nil	2,500lb
*at auw 63,000lb	10×250lb	Nil	2,500lb
	6×500lb*	Nil	3,000lb

Mark	Fuselage	Wings	Total
B Mk III	As for B Mk II Series IA	As for B Mk II Series IA	
GR Mk III	9×500lb	Nil	4,500lb
B Mk VI	2×2,000lb		
	6×1,000lb	4×500lb	12,000lb
	4×2,000lb	4×500lb	10,000lb
	2×1,500lb mine		
	6×500lb	4×500lb	8,000lb
	9×500lb	4×500lb	6,500lb
	1×8,000lb	4×500lb	10,000lb
	2×4,000lb	4×500lb	10,000lb
B Mk VII	As above	As above	As above

Range with associated load at most economical speed

	With max bomb load	With perm't tanks full	With auxiliary tanks full		Remarks
Fuel carried (gal)	955	*1,552 †1,640	2,330		B Mk I *With 160gal Hampden tanks in fuselage
Fuel allowance (gal)	220	220	220		†With additional tanks in wing bomb cells
Range (miles)	1,000	*1,740 †1,840	2,720		
Bomb load (lb)	13,000	*8,500 †7,750	1,500		
Fuel carried (gal)	985 *830	1,886 *1,882	2,576 *2,342	†2,572	B Mk II Series I *Series IA
Fuel allowance (gal)	210 *290	210 *290	210 *290	†290	†With three auxiliary tanks
Range (miles)	920 *650	1,900 *1,660	2,650 *2,100	†2,320	

	With max bomb load	With perm't tanks full	With auxiliary tanks full		
Bomb load (lb)	13,000	6,500	———		
	*13,000	*5,250	*1,500		
Fuel carried (gal)	900	1,886	2,576		B Mk V Series I
	*760	*1,882	*2,342	†2,572	*Series IA
Fuel allowance (gal)	210	210	210		†With three auxiliary tanks
	*290	*290	*290	†290	
Range (miles)	830	1,900	2,650		
	*580	*1,660	*2,100	†2,320	
Bomb load (lb)	13,000	6,000	———		
	*13,000	*4,750	*1,000		
Fuel carried (gal)	1,020	1,802	2,492		B Mk III
	*1,077	*1,998	*2,688		*Postwar figures
Fuel allowance (gal)	220	220	220		
	*350	*350	*350		
Range (miles)	930	1,770	2,430		
	*980	*2,005	*2,785		
Bomb load (lb)	13,000	7,250	———		
	*13,000	*6,250	*500		
Fuel carried (gal)	1,029	1,998	2,688		A Mk III
	*1,200	*1,998	*2,228		*C Mk III
Fuel allowance (gal)	145	145	145		
	*145	*145	*145		
Range (miles)	1,020	2,190	3,080		
	*1,240	*2,230	*2,520		
Load (lb)	15,000	7,900	2,100		
	*15,000	*9,200	*7,100		
Fuel carried (gal)	1,090	1,982	2,442	†2,672	B Mk VI
	*1,530	*2,190	*2,880		*Post war figures
Fuel allowance (gal)	320	320	320	†320	†With three auxiliary tanks
	*300	*300	*300		
Range (miles)	970	1,965	2,490	†2,745	
	*1,450	*2,280	*2,920		
Bomb load (lb)	13,000	6,500	2,500	†500	
	*12,000	*7,000	*1,500		
Fuel carried (gal)	1,177	2,190	2,650		B Mk VII
	*1,140	*2,190	*2,420		*C Mk VII
	†977	†1,890	†2,760	†2,070**	†A Mk VII
Fuel allowance (gal)	350	350	350		**With two 90gal auxiliary tanks
	*145	*145	*145		
	†145	†145	†145	†145**	
Range (miles)	1,075	2,225	2,630		
	*1,165	*2,470	*2,780		
	†960	†2,050	†3,170	†2,270**	
Bomb load (lb)	12,000	4,500	500		
	*15,000	*7,300	*5,400		
	†15,000	†8,300	*1,000	†6,800**	
Fuel carried (gal)	1,180	2,190	2,420		C Mk VIII
Fuel allowance (gal)	140	140	140		
Range (miles)	1,190	2,420	2,710		
Load (lb)	15,000	7,600	5,700		
Fuel carried (gal)	927	1,890	2,760	†2,070	A Mk IX
Fuel allowance (gal)	145	145	145	†145	†With two 90gal auxiliary tanks
Range (miles)	910	2,050	3,170	†2,270	
Load (lb)	15,000	7,900	600	†6,400	

THE HANDLEY PAGE

(Four Rolls-Royce Merlin

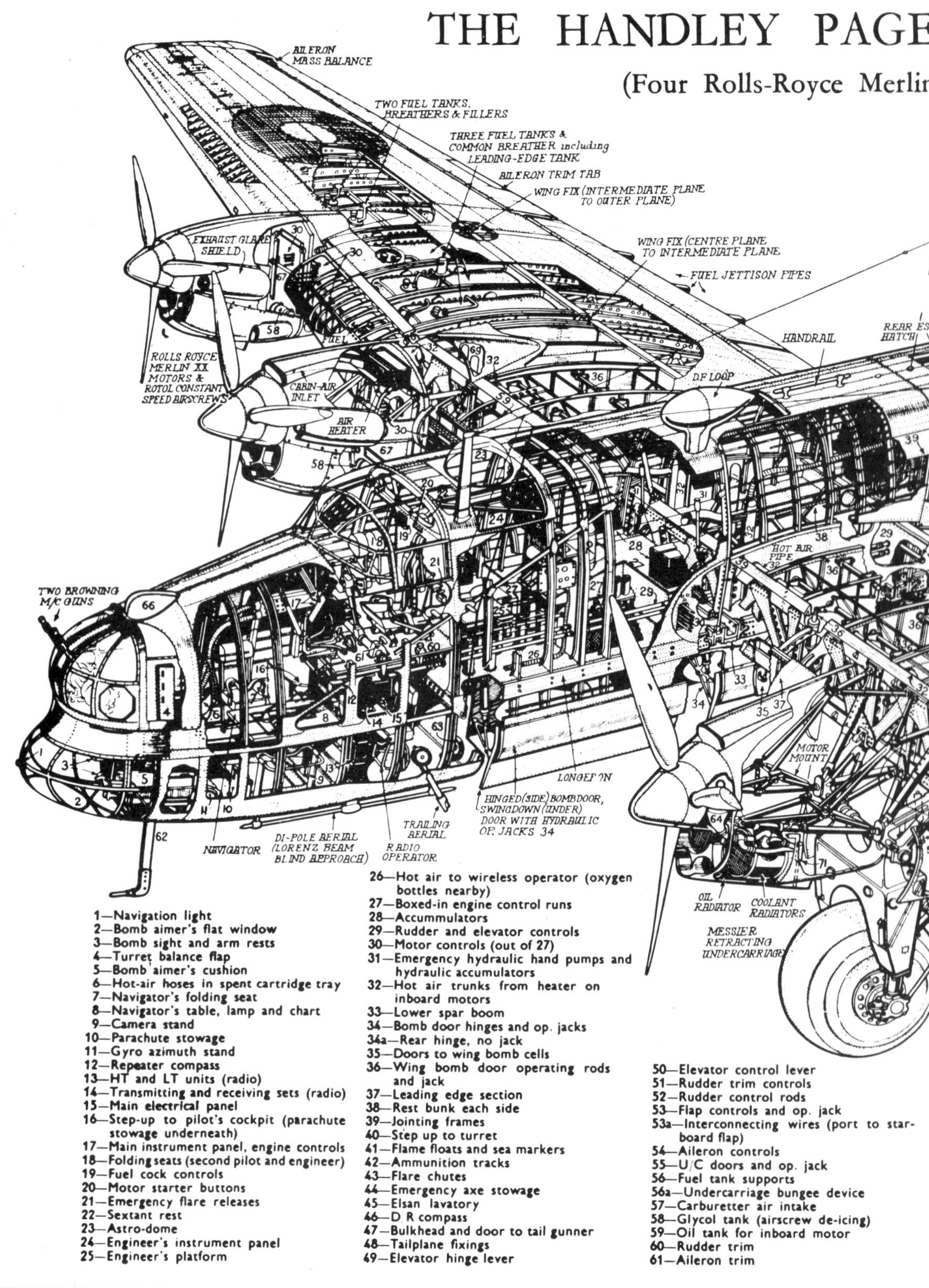

1—Navigation light
2—Bomb aimer's flat window
3—Bomb sight and arm rests
4—Turret balance flap
5—Bomb aimer's cushion
6—Hot-air hoses in spent cartridge tray
7—Navigator's folding seat
8—Navigator's table, lamp and chart
9—Camera stand
10—Parachute stowage
11—Gyro azimuth stand
12—Repeater compass
13—HT and LT units (radio)
14—Transmitting and receiving sets (radio)
15—Main electrical panel
16—Step-up to pilot's cockpit (parachute stowage underneath)
17—Main instrument panel, engine controls
18—Folding seats (second pilot and engineer)
19—Fuel cock controls
20—Motor starter buttons
21—Emergency flare releases
22—Sextant rest
23—Astro-dome
24—Engineer's instrument panel
25—Engineer's platform

26—Hot air to wireless operator (oxygen bottles nearby)
27—Boxed-in engine control runs
28—Accummulators
29—Rudder and elevator controls
30—Motor controls (out of 27)
31—Emergency hydraulic hand pumps and hydraulic accumulators
32—Hot air trunks from heater on inboard motors
33—Lower spar boom
34—Bomb door hinges and op. jacks
34a—Rear hinge, no jack
35—Doors to wing bomb cells
36—Wing bomb door operating rods and jack
37—Leading edge section
38—Rest bunk each side
39—Jointing frames
40—Step up to turret
41—Flame floats and sea markers
42—Ammunition tracks
43—Flare chutes
44—Emergency axe stowage
45—Elsan lavatory
46—D R compass
47—Bulkhead and door to tail gunner
48—Tailplane fixings
49—Elevator hinge lever

50—Elevator control lever
51—Rudder trim controls
52—Rudder control rods
53—Flap controls and op. jack
53a—Interconnecting wires (port to starboard flap)
54—Aileron controls
55—U/C doors and op. jack
56—Fuel tank supports
56a—Undercarriage bungee device
57—Carburetter air intake
58—Glycol tank (airscrew de-icing)
59—Oil tank for inboard motor
60—Rudder trim
61—Aileron trim